The Psychology of Menu Selection:

**Designing Cognitive Control
of the Human/Computer Interface**

HUMAN/COMPUTER INTERACTION
A Series of Monographs, Edited Volumes, and Texts

Series Editor
Ben Shneiderman

The Psychology of Menu Selection:

Designing Cognitive Control of the Human/Computer Interface

Kent L. Norman

Department of Psychology
University of Maryland

ABLEX PUBLISHING CORPORATION
NORWOOD, NEW JERSEY

Cover designed by Thomas Phon Graphics

Library of Congress Cataloging-in-Publication Data

Norman, Kent L.
    The psychology of menu selection : designing cognitive control at
the human/computer interface / Kent L. Norman.
        p.   cm.—(Human/computer interaction)
    Includes bibliographical references (p.   ) and index.
    ISBN 0-89391-553-X
    1. Human-computer interaction.   2. System design—Psychological
aspects.   I. Title.   II. Series: Human/computer interaction
(Norwood, N.J.)
QA76.9.H85N67   1990
005.1—dc20   90-1198
                                                       CIP

Ablex Publishing Corporation
355 Chestnut Street
Norwood, New Jersey 07648

Table of Contents

Preface

One of the most pressing problems in the development of computer systems is the design of the human/computer interface. How can it be implemented so to maximize the work efficiency of the user? Many new and innovative approaches are being tried. New workstations with sophisticated displays and powerful software are being designed. Most of this development is being guided by the good and common sense of the designers. Often they are on the mark, but at times they totally miss it because they simply don't have the time or resources to prototype the system on real users. Designers often commit the error of thinking that others think and approach tasks in the same ways that they do. Consequently, there is a mismatch between what the majority of users want or expect the system to do, and what it actually does.

This book was primarily written to aid researchers and designers of human/computer systems. The book presents in an organized fashion the application of menu selection as a mode of human/computer interaction. Menu selection is emphasized as a technique of communication which allows the user to control program branching in conjunction with other modes of interaction. Much of the theoretical and applied research on menu selection systems is summarized in an attempt to distill guidelines that can be used in human/computer interface design.

The book is divided into three parts. The first part is conceptual and theoretical in nature. Chapter 1 introduces the issues of design and flow of control at the human/computer interface. In the next three chapters, taxonomic frameworks are proposed concerning (a) the type of menu selection system being used, (b) the nature of the task being performed by the user, and (c) the cognitive elements involved in performing the task.

In the second part of the book, experimental research on menu selection is discussed. Experimental research in the area of human/computer interaction stems from paradigms developed in experimental psychology and more recently in human factors and cognitive psychology. This orientation to research is presented in Chapter 5, and then research conducted at the Human/Computer Interaction Lab at the University of Maryland as well as a number of other labs is presented in Chapters 6 through 10.

The third and last part of the book deals with the topic of implementation and evaluation. Chapter 11 discusses principles of when and how to use menus, and Chapters 12 and 13 discuss the topics of prototyping and evaluation. Finally, Chapter 14 attempts to plot some of the future directions of menu selection.

Research on menu selection is one of those applied areas that has the double benefit of reaping results that not only have practical value in their application to a developing technology, but also helps to feed the theoretical developments of cognitive psychology. Much can be learned about memory, problem solving, and decision making from tasks involving software that makes use of menu selection. The theoretical contribution of this literature to cognitive control is more lasting; for, as we all know, the design of the human/computer interface is rapidly changing. In 10 years, the applied questions will no doubt be different. Issues concerning response time, display rate, and screen size will change, and new sets of issues will arise. Menu selection will become more complex and varied. Although the computer interface may undergo vast change, the human mind will be much the same and issues surrounding its limitations and abilities will remain. Consequently, this book was written to the wider audience of those interested in the psychology of cognitive control.

Acknowledgments

The goal of this book is to summarize as much of the thinking and research on computer menu selection as possible. The many researchers in the area of human/computer interaction are to be commended for their painstaking work. Their names are acknowledged throughout the text and in the reference list. Certainly there are many others who have conducted research that should have been included if space, time, and author's awareness had only permitted.

In addition, the encouragement, viewpoints, and feedback from colleagues, students, and designers have been invaluable in the course of writing and rewriting. It has been a challenge to appeal to all of the different directions and dichotomous viewpoints. Special appreciation must be expressed to my colleagues Ben Shneiderman for his help, his knowledge, and his enthusiasm; Nancy S. Anderson for her help, her counsel, and her friendship; and Ed W. Israelski for his careful critique of the manuscript.

Then appreciation must go to our graduate students and former graduate students at the University of Maryland associated with the Human/Computer Interaction Laboratory: John P. Chin, Jeffrey P. Schwartz, Andrew Sears, Daniel F. Wallace, and Scott A. Butler who have all contributed to the work reported here.

Professional support is necessary but not sufficient. It is the love, the prayers, and the down-to-earth support of family and friends that make it all happen. In this light, I thank my wife, Karen, who has the gift of encouragement and our two children, Kirk and Katryn, who have the gift of joy. Ultimate thanks for all goes to the Lord God.

Kent L. Norman
University of Maryland
College Park, MD

I

THE THEORY AND IMPLEMENTATION OF MENU SELECTION SYSTEMS

Menu selection is often considered the easiest form of interaction with the computer. At first glance it appears to be straightforward to both user and programmer. It is easy to implement and easy to use. Such is the thinking of the naive designer. Over the past few years, the complexity of menu selection systems has grown to keep pace with the increasing functionality of interactive systems. Designers are faced with more and more difficult questions about how to set up menus. Researchers are asking more probing questions about the relationship between design and performance. Finally, users are demanding more power, control, and access to a wide variety of applications that are more consistent, intuitive, and require less training.

The first part of this book is concerned with the implementation and theory of menu selection. The central focus of Chapter 1 is the nature of the human/computer interface—the medium through which the user exercises control over computer processes. In the recent past, the heart of a computer program was its set of algorithms and data structures. Today, it is becoming the human/computer interface. A general model of the interface is proposed as a means of delineating the type of information flowing between the user and the computer and the characteristics of each. Chapter 1 serves as a background for understanding the issues involved in the implementation and theory of menu selection.

Menus come in many different shapes and forms and require different things of the user. Chapter 2 presents a detailed taxonomy of the types of information structures used in constructing menus. These structures are related to the way in which the user organizes and understands things cognitively. Types of information contained in the single menu frame are discussed as well as types of user responses required by the menus.

Menu selection is not an end in itself, but rather is a means to an end. Chapter 3 considers the types of tasks performed using menu selection and expands on the theory of cognitive control. The specific functions performed by menu selection are discussed. Finally, menu selection is presented as a mode of human/computer interaction for (a) control of computer operations, (b) making complex decisions, (c) information retrieval, and (d) classifying information.

Menu selection engages most aspects of human information processing. It involves visual scan and search, reading and comprehension, judgment and decision making, response selection and production, and over all that, thinking and problem solving. Chapter 4 expands on the cognitive elements involved in making menu selections. The user must read and comprehend the alternatives, decide on the appropriate selection, implement the choice by making a response, and finally evaluate the outcome of the choice. However, over all of the component processes there must be a driving strategy or plan. Such a plan operates within the context of the user's mental model for how menu selection works. The metaphor of the restaurant menu serves as a useful vehicle for understanding the user's strategy.

1

Introduction to the Theory of Control at the Human/ Computer Interface

In the development of any new technology, the last frontier always seems to be the encounter with the end user of the product. The challenge is to develop a product that can be easily and efficiently used to accomplish its intended purpose. The key element is to design an interface between the user and the machine that allows for the proper flow of control between human and machine processes. This is particularly true of computer-based systems. The development cycle of computers is now well past the point where computers are used exclusively by computer scientists. The general work force and the public-at-large are already using or beginning to use the computer in one form or another. It is at this point that careful consideration must be made in how to lay out the architecture and the building code in each new community of users. Without such forethought, users are likely to become prematurely locked into an arbitrary and archaic structure.

Among the new architectures of the human/computer interface that specifically deal with the flow of control is the design of menu selection systems. Figure 1.1 illustrates several such systems. Users are presented with a list of options from which they can choose and some mechanism by which to indicate their choice. The characteristics of menu selection are that (a) the interaction is, in part, guided by the computer; (b) the user does not have to recall commands from memory; and (c) user response input is generally straightforward. The four examples shown in Figure 1.1 highlight the variety of such menu systems.

In the early days of interactive systems, menu selection seemed to be an intuitively simple solution to the problem of user control. The unfortunate result was that without additional thought, poorly designed systems proliferated. A number of basic questions about menu selection were overlooked. For example, when is menu selection preferable over other forms of interaction, such as a command language? How should the menu selection systems be designed? How does the structure of menu selection change the process of control in the mind of the user?

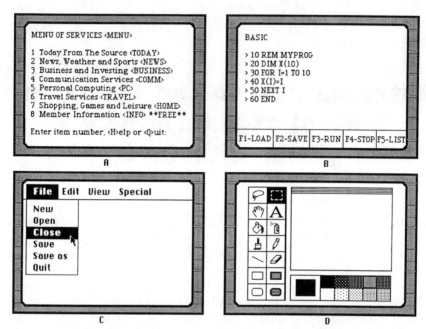

Figure 1.1. Examples of the current variety of menu selection types. Portions of menus from (a) The Source™ time-sharing network, (b) a Basic interpreter on the IBM-PC, (c) the Macintosh™ Finder menu, and (d) the MacPaint® tool palette.

How should menu selection systems differ in use by novice and expert users? The answers to these questions and many others are crucial in helping to determine how to design a usable and efficient human/computer interface.

Menu selection is emphasized in this book as a principle mode of control used in conjunction with other modes, such as form fill-in, command languages, natural language, and direct manipulation. It is felt that in terms of flow of control, menu selection is emerging as the mode of choice. Other modes come into play to handle different demands on the human/computer interface. Switching from one mode to another is often necessary and must be done gracefully with clear expectation on the part of the user. Specialized modes, their integration with menu selection, and the problems of switching between modes will be discussed as it is appropriate.

In this chapter we will consider the human/computer interface in terms of the flow of control. The user has certain tasks to accomplish and, consequently, wants to direct the computer to perform a subset of those tasks. The problem from the user's perspective is knowing what the computer can do and knowing how to direct it to do those tasks. The problem from the system designer's point of view is knowing what functions to implement and how the computer should inform the user about the availability and invocation of these functions. In doing so, the computer must be assigned a certain measure of control over the flow of operations; but ultimately, control rests with the user.

In the next section the process of designing the human/computer interface and its importance will be discussed. Following this a cognitive model of the human/computer interface is proposed that helps to define and specify the issues of how humans work with machines and how machines must be designed so that they are usable by humans. Finally, the use of experimental methods in the design process will be discussed. Empirical research is the mainstay of human factors and ergonomics, and it is important to understand how and why experiments are conducted.

1.1 RESEARCH AND DESIGN OF THE HUMAN/COMPUTER INTERFACE

One of the major steps in the software development life cycle is the translation of system requirements into an integrated set of task specifications that define the functional capabilities of the software and hardware (Jensen & Tonis, 1979). The problem is that such requirements are often dictated by analysts with little thought about the end user. Consequently, user's needs and limitations are often not factored into the equation. No matter how well implemented other parts of the system may be, if the human/computer interface is intractable, the system will falter and ultimately fail. Ledgard, Singer, and Whiteside (1981) pointed out the incredible cost of poor human engineering in the design of interactive systems. They identified four costs:

1.   The direct costs of poor design are observed in wasted time and excessive errors. The system itself may have been designed for maximum efficiency in terms of memory management, input/output, and computation, but it may sit idly by as the user ponders an error message or thumbs through documentation looking for the correct command. Menu selection systems may alleviate such wasted time by self-documenting the system, and they may reduce errors by limiting user input to only the set of legal options.
2.   Indirect costs are incurred in the time it takes to learn a system. A novice user often has a lot to learn about a system. This typically involves reading manuals, working through tutorials, memorization of commands, and development of performance skills. The time to learn

such systems can be a great cost that must be born by either the employee or the employer or both. For the employer, cost of training employees is particularly important when employee turnover is high, often an indirect result of poor human engineering due to a third cost.
3. A cost that is paid when users are frustrated and irritated by a poorly designed system. The psychological cost can be great and can result in a number of spin-off problems, such as low morale, decreased productivity, and high employee turnover rate. It has been said that systems should be fun to use rather than frustrating. They should encourage exploration rather than intimidate users and inhibit use.
4. Finally, this leads to the cost of limited or lack of use. Poorly designed systems, no matter how powerful, will simply not be used. Users will tend to employ only those components that are of use to them. It is typically the case that for systems with 40 plus commands, only about 7 commands show any frequency of use. Limited use is one of the greatest costs because it negates the benefit side of the equation.

Since the turn of the century psychologists and engineers have been interested in studying the generic man/machine problem in order to reduce costs such as these. Research has been conducted under a number of different names conveying the varied intent of the researchers. The term *human engineering*, for example, conveys the idea that the user's or operator's limitations and capabilities may be engineered into the system. The human is a part of the mechanism. The early time and motion analysts realized that both man and machine could be retrained or redesigned for greater efficiency and compatibility. The term *human factors* arose during World War II when it was realized that equipment was not performing at its rated levels. There was a human factor that introduced error into the system. Other terms, such as *biomechanics, ergonomics,* and *psychotechnology*, emphasize the physiological and psychological aspects. The more generic term, *applied experimental psychology*, indicates the importance of systematic practical research methodology but, unfortunately, de-emphasizes theoretical development. For the present discussion, the term *ergonomics* will be used to convey the importance of both theory and research, as well as the idea that we are dealing with systems.

Today a multidisciplinary approach to the human/computer problem is being taken. Research teams include cognitive psychologists, computer scientists, specialists in subject domains, such as management, library and information science, medicine, and so on, as well as a new breed of specialists in the emerging discipline of human/computer interaction. The multidisciplinary approach is extremely important insofar as menu selection is concerned in that designs generally attempt to implement a task domain on a computer system while satisfying the cognitive constraints of the users. The team approach allows each set of concerns to be represented and voiced.

1.1.1 Issues in Design

In this book we are interested in the issue of user control over automatic processes. The control mechanism that we will consider is that of menu selection. Users select one or several options, levels, or settings on the computer. Communication between the user and the computer takes place via a finite, well-defined set of tokens, rather than via an open-ended command language. In the evaluation of the human/computer interface as a means of communication and control, a number of global factors may be generated. Some of these are listed in Table 1.1. The acceptable levels of such ergonomic factors and the tradeoffs between them depend, of course, on the particular task and the user community.

From a managerial perspective, productivity is the bottom line. The software must first and foremost be applicable to the task at hand. When

Table 1.1. Factors to be Considered in the Design of Human/Computer Systems.

- System Productivity
    - Applicability of system to task
    - Number of tasks completed
    - Quality of output

- Human Performance
    - Speed of performance
    - Rate and type of errors
    - Quality of solutions to problems

- Training time and effectiveness
    - Time to learn how to use the system
    - Frequency of reference to documentation
    - Human retention of commands over time
    - Transfer of training

- Cognitive Processes
    - Appropriateness of the mental model
    - Degree of mental effort

- Subjective satisfaction
    - Satisfaction with self
    - Satisfaction with system
    - Satisfaction with performance

this is the case, one may assess the factors of quantity and quality of work performed. Much has been written about productivity and its measurement in the business and management literature; however, in this book we are not primarily interested in productivity at the global level, but in the factors that ultimately contribute to that end.

Human performance is an observable factor that is most often used in assessing the ergonomics of a system. Performance is a function of three basic variables: speed, accuracy, and quality. Well-designed systems reduce the time that it takes for the user to perform a task. At the same time, error rate should be kept at a minimum. The severity of errors depends on their type. Some are easily correctable, others are devastating. Finally, a well-designed system should promote optimal solutions to problems. This is the ultimate goal of many systems that involve planning, decision making, design, and information retrieval.

Training time and effectiveness are also an extremely important factor. How long does it take for the user to come up to speed? This involves both the acquisition of knowledge about the system, skill in using it, and the ability to accommodate changes. Rumelhart and Norman (1978) referred to these three components as accretion (the acquisition of knowledge or accumulation of information), tuning (the modification of categories or adjustment), and restructuring (reinterpreting, reorganizing, or gaining a new understanding of information). Training may emphasize one of these to the exclusion of the others so that users may learn rote tasks but may not be able to figure out how to perform other functions. Furthermore, systems may be designed so as to minimize the need for training. Designers may want a system that brings the novice on very rapidly by reducing the need for accretion, even though it may limit the speed of asymptotic performance. Menu selection systems have often served this purpose by using menus that list and explain all of the options. Speed is reduced due to transmission and display time of text as well as reading time. Alternatively, one may want to maximize the speed of performance of experienced users, even though training time is greatly lengthened. Command languages, as well as highly abbreviated menus, have accomplished this purpose. However, to make use of command languages, users must spend a considerable amount of time learning the commands and options.

The amount of documentation for the user varies greatly from system to system and depends on the level of user. More documentation is not necessarily better, and certainly a high frequency of reference to the documentation during use is detrimental to performance. Menu systems have been used to drastically reduce the need to refer to documentation, although in older systems with slow response time it has not been without cost in terms of speed of performance. This may not be a factor in newer systems allowing near instantaneous access to pull-down or pop-up menu displays.

An often overlooked factor in the use of computers is the human retention of commands over time. Once a user has learned a command or a function to a specified level, is it retained over time? A command that has been learned, but infrequently used, may not be remembered. Each time the user desires to use it, he or she must consult the documentation. On the other hand, in a menu selection system, an infrequently selected option is not lost. However, another retention problem often occurs. The user may forget where an item is located in a complex menu tree and spend an inordinate amount of time searching for it.

Transfer of training has always been an important factor in ergonomics. The question is whether training on one system will reduce the amount of training necessary to learn another system. If it does, there is positive transfer. If it doesn't, there is no transfer. Positive transfer depends on the degree to which one system shares common elements with another system, and the degree to which the user is able to restructure the knowledge gained about one system to knowledge about the new system. Negative transfer depends on the degree to which one system has elements that conflict with another. "Integrated" software packages for office automation share many concepts and commands across specific applications. Incompatible packages may include similar commands or menu options that perform different functions, or similar functions that are evoked by different commands or options. Observing the user learning a new system, coming back to a system after time, and switching between systems tell us a lot about the design of the software.

The effectiveness of human/computer interface design may also be assessed on the grounds of cognitive processes on the part of the user. It has been suggested that well-designed systems promote an effective mental model for the user on how the system operates. The user possessing this model gains a high-level understanding of how things work, and is able to perform tasks and solve problems faster and more effectively than without such a model.

Another cognitive factor has to do with the mental effort expended by the user in performing a task. The designer's goal should be to allow the user to concentrate on higher-level processing rather than on mundane, low-level tasks. For example, a word processor should reduce the mental effort required for scrolling, cutting and pasting, and other mundane functions, so that the writer may concentrate on composing the text.

A factor that is increasing in importance is user satisfaction. Satisfaction takes on a number of dimensions (Norman & Anderson, 1981). Users are able to assess their own performance and mastery of the system. User's satisfaction with one self is often independent of satisfaction with the system. Many user's take pride in the fact that they have mastered a very poorly human-factored system and implemented work arounds. Users may also assess satisfaction with the system attributes that are independent of productivity. Users are often impressed with bells, whistles, and brand names that have nothing to do with usability and performance.

These first two factors aside, a user's ratings of subjective satisfaction can be directed to assess human/computer performance and productivity as a whole. Often such ratings are directly related to objective measures of performance. In addition, measures of satisfaction tap factors that cannot be objectively measured. The user may be viewed as a sensitive monitoring instrument of the system. Much care must be taken in assessing user satisfaction and many problems surround such measurements. Nevertheless, user satisfaction is being seen as a key in unlocking the complex interactions at the human/computer interface.

1.1.2 Three Paradigms of Design

It has been pointed out by Anderson and Olson (1985), Sterling (1974), and Holt and Steveson (1977) that human factors considerations must be integrated into the design process from the beginning and as it progresses. Unfortunately, very few systems have been designed with human factors as a high priority item. The reason for this may be traced to the historical development of machines, and it will prove instructive to review this design process.

Historically, the design of man/machine systems proceeded first with the power unit, the drive mechanism, the mill, and finally the control, as shown in the top panel of Figure 1.2. The early automobile with its internal combustion engine had a very unfriendly requirement. The driver or an assistant had to get out of the car to crank the engine to get it going. Only later was the starter motor added to give the driver a simple control to start the thing. Consideration of the characteristics and the convenience of operator came in only as an afterthought. The problem with this method is that fixes are often expensive or impossible. Consequently, the user must often contend with an intractable control interface. This same paradigm unfortunately continues in many areas of hardware and software development today.

A somewhat better paradigm is to establish ergonomic guidelines, first as shown in the middle panel of Figure 1.2. They become a set of standard specifications. Software development must then proceed from the guidelines inward to the machine through the control interface. This can also lead to some problems. It is not truly possible to codify er-

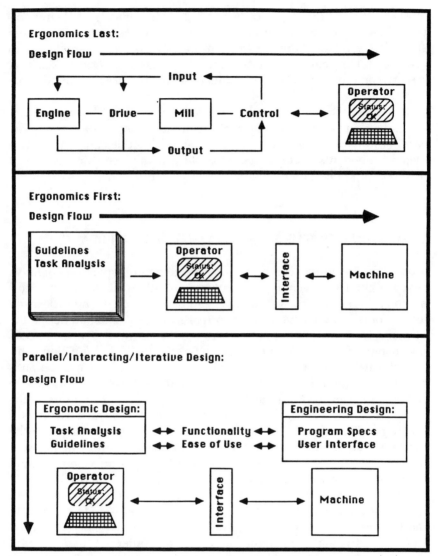

Figure 1.2.   Three paradigms of design for human/computer interaction.

gonomics in a dynamic environment, nor can software development afford to wait for the publication of such handbooks. Consequently, this approach generally leads to standardization on the obsolete and suboptimal.

The paradigm that is advocated here is to develop the ergonomics and the engineering together in a parallel-interacting process as illus-

trated in the bottom panel of Figure 1.2. This paradigm is being employed by more and more of the industry. Teams of human factors
specialists are being linked up with software development teams to
provide initial analysis of tasks and user characteristics, to conduct
research on prototypes, and to conduct user acceptance tests on the final
product.

This approach is particularly important for systems that are heavily
dependent on the flow of control at the human/computer interface. The
work of human/computer interaction specialists in design rests on two
major components: theoretical models of the man/machine interface and
methods of applied experimental research. These are discussed in the
next two sections.

1.2 A MODEL OF THE HUMAN/COMPUTER INTERFACE

Models of the human/computer interface depend heavily on cognitive
psychology. The psychological processes of attention, memory, information processing, decision making, and problem solving must be taken
into account. One of the most important features in such models is the
flow and feedback of information through the interface. The user needs
information from the computer, and the computer cannot function without information from the user. A major component of this interaction is
the flow of control information. The computer gives information to
prompt the user for input, and the user supplies input that directs the
subsequent operations. Smooth operation of the system requires a
timely flow of information that is relatively free of error states in the
machine and in the user. Error states in the machine can be well-
defined. Generally machine errors at the interface occur when (a) input
values fall outside an allowable range or disagree with required type, (b)
required resources are not available, or (c) a call is made to a nonexistent
function or location. Error states also occur in the user. In contrast to
machine errors, user error states are not well-defined since they arise
from subjective states when for some given computer output or prompt,
the user does not know what to do. User error states are characterized
by confusion, lack of understanding, and lack of knowledge of what to
do next.

Figure 1.3 shows a schematic model of the flow of information and
control at the human/computer interface that has been adapted from
Norman et al. (1980). The model first emphasizes that the system is
embedded within a task situation. The user, for example, may be monitoring an industrial process, or he or she may be engaged in information retrieval. The task determines a number of overriding factors, such
as the cost of errors, importance of speed, and considerations that define

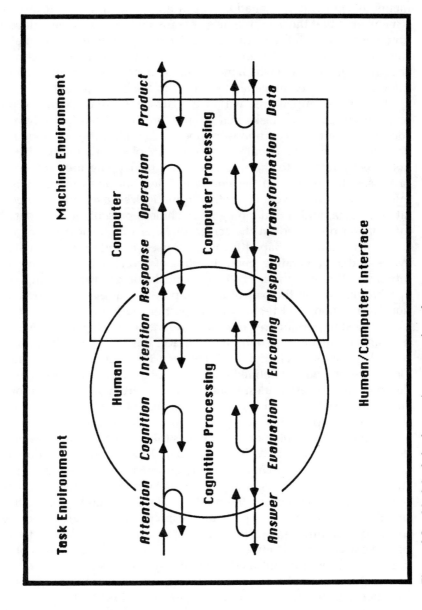

Figure I.3.   Model of the human/computer interface.

the successful completion of the task. Both the human (represented by a circle) and the machine (represented by a rectangle) reside in environments that provide information, constraints, and contexts. It must be remembered that the user interacts not only with the machine, but more fundamentally with the environment. He or she attends to information coming in and generates information going out. A similar picture is shown for the machine which may monitor an environment and retrieve information, as well as generate output to the environment.

The nonoverlapped area within the circle represents cognitive processes involved in the tasks that are not directly related to the human/computer interface. The nonoverlapped area within the rectangle similarly represents the computer procedures involved in the tasks that are not directly related to the interface. The overlapping area represents processes that pertain to the interface. These include the mapping of information through keying or other input devices to machine representation of data, and the mapping of machine representations of data to information presented on the screen or other output device.

At each point, U-shaped arrows are used to indicate the feedback cycles and reverberating characteristics of information flow through interfaces. We may think of this as handshaking, error checking, and synchronization on the part of the computer, or as eye-hand coordination, verification, and timing on the part of the human.

The most important area from the present perspective is the overlapping area of the human/computer interface. It is in this area that flow of control is passed back and forth between the user and the machine. Flow of control will be defined as a sequence of steps in a process that is determined by a set of rules. Control is passed from one step to another such that the next step in the sequence is determined by the outcome of the current step and the rules of control. Within the computer, the program residing in memory determines the flow of control in conjunction with the processor. Within the human, flow of control is thought of as a sequence of mental operations determined by cognitive processes. Although we are only beginning to understand the processes of mental operations, we can observe the products of thought and generate theories about the likelihood of particular responses on the part of the user. In human/computer interaction, flow of control is shared and at times passed back and forth between the user and the machine. In light of our limited knowledge about user thought processes and the added complexity incurred by shared control, it is no wonder that the design of the human/computer interface is no easy matter, and that it remains as a major area of concern in computer science, cognitive psychology, and ergonomics.

Although the model in its present form is largely conceptual in nature, it helps to delineate the concerns that an ergonomics specialist should have when helping to design the interface. These include the four areas shown in Figure 1.3: (a) the characteristics of the task and the environment, (b) the characteristics of the human cognitive processing, (c) the specifications for the computer processing, and (d) the implementation of the human/computer interface.

1.2.1 Characteristics of Tasks and Environments

It is obvious that different tasks and different environments impose different needs and constraints on human/computer interaction. What is not so obvious is how to meet these requirements. An analysis of the task and environment is the first step. Take, for example, the task of balancing one's checkbook. The task requires data input to the computer, verification of records, and a series of computational steps. The environment includes information about current balance, cancelled checks, and so on, as well as time and resource constraints that affect the motivation and/or frustration level of the user.

Tasks may be characterized along the following dimensions:

- *Simple–Complex.* Simple tasks involve few steps with little demand on the user or on the computer. Complex tasks involve many steps and impose high demands on the user and possibly the computer as well. Of course, the task as implemented may allocate simple or complex parts to the human or computer. Writing a novel on a word processor is a complex task for the human and a comparatively straightforward one for the computer. On the other hand, an information retrieval problem may be rather straightforward to the user, but comparatively complex for the system.
- *Structured–Unstructured.* Structured tasks have a preplanned course; whereas, unstructured tasks may involve creative planning and redirection. In structured tasks, such as checkbook balancing, the flow of control may be relegated to the computer. On the other hand, for unstructured tasks, such as writing a novel, the user maintains control over most aspects of the task except the mundane operations of computer housekeeping.

Tasks may be characterized by many other dimensions, such as the degree to which input versus output predominates, or the extent to which the user is an active versus passive participant. Chapter 3 discusses task analysis in greater detail; however, at this point it is sufficient to be aware of the fact that task characteristics impose certain demands on the user and on the system.

Environments are often linked to tasks, but we may also define two characteristics of environments as follows:

- *Time Critical–Resource Limited.* In many situations the environment imposes a time constraint. For example, the information must be retrieved before the Senate Subcommittee hearing at 10:00 a.m.; the decision to deploy the torpedo must be made in 30 seconds. Such environments have a psychological impact on the user and require thought as to how to implement the human/computer interface to achieve acceptable levels of performance.
- *Controllable–Immutable.* The user and the system may be able to alter the environment. This may be an inherent part of the task in industrial control. Control of resources adds an additional level of concern to the user and needs to be considered in terms of the cognitive demands on the user. On the other hand, the environment may be immutable in the sense that neither the user nor the computer can have an effect on it.

Environments may also be characterized by a number of other dimensions, such as whether they are information rich versus information scarce, or safe versus hazardous. These characteristics will prove to be important when it comes to the design and evaluation of the user interface, particularly as it relates to the flow of control.

1.2.2 Characteristics of the Human User

Two views of the user exist. The user is either an extension of the system, or the system is an extension of the user. In the first case, the user may, unfortunately, be viewed merely as an input device, not unlike an optical scanner or an analog-to-digital input channel. In the second case, the system is seen as providing enhanced memory, processing, and communication abilities to the user. The particular view adopted has strong implications concerning the flow of control between the user and the system and the particular mental operations involved in the cognitive processing of the user.

Eight components of cognitive processing are specified in the model and are indicated by the arrows into and within the circle shown in Figure 1.3. The first arrow at the top left indicates the user's *attention* to certain input from the task environment, such as instructions, data, documentation, and so on. The second arrow moving to the right represents *problem solving*, which may involve planning and information processing that occurs before the user inputs information into the computer. The third arrow across the top represents the user's *intention* for input to the computer. It may involve the formulation of a command or a plan for menu search. The fourth arrow represents the actual *response* production that transfers information to the computer. The user may type a command, select an option, or point to a screen location.

Take a situation in which the user directs his or her attention to a memo requesting that John Smith's telephone number be changed to 454-6333. The user conceives of the solution to the problem as follows: Find John Smith's file, locate the telephone number in his file, and then change the number. The intended solution must then be implemented in terms of the human/computer interface. The user may find John Smith's file by selecting an option, "find by name," and then by typing in the name. To accomplish this the user must generate the response productions to select this option and to type the name. Given that the file is located, the user may select the options "update" and "telephone number" and finally type the new number.

The bottom chain of arrows in Figure 1.3, starting from the rightmost arrow into the circle, indicates the reverse processing of information originating from the computer and ultimately altering the task environment. The first arrow at the right represents the *display* of information. Typically, this is information displayed on the screen, but may also include displays in other modalities. The next arrow indicates the user's *encoding* and interpretation of that information. The next arrow moving left represents internal *evaluation* and cognitive processing of the computer output, and the last arrow shows the final result of the process in supplying an *answer* to the task environment.

At each stage of interaction a different display is generally shown. In the example above, the first display may list a set of functions. The user interprets this display by encoding the information as meaningful options or messages. The option "find by name" is encoded and then evaluated as the desired function. Feedback is also encoded and evaluated. For example, if the message is "John Smoth not found," the evaluation is that a typographical error was made. Finally, when the change of number is acknowledged, the user may produce an overt answer to the memo indicating that the task was completed.

User characteristics affect the processing at each of these points as they depend on perceptual skills, attention, memory, and motor skills. User characteristics may be grouped into three types:

• *Knowledge Characteristics.* Users vary in terms of their knowledge about the system. In general, we can no longer say that novice users have little or no knowledge of system operation and that expert users do. Amount of knowledge cannot be considered as a unidimensional attribute. Instead, we must consider more carefully what the user knows about (a) the task domain in terms of semantic and procedural knowledge, (b) the representation of the task domain on the computer, and (c) the computer in terms of semantic and syntactic knowledge.

- *Cognitive Characteristics.* Users vary in their ability to solve problems, make decisions, and perform mental tasks. The assessment of information-processing capacities and their relationship to performance have been the subject of much work in cognitive psychology (e.g., Hunt, 1978; Sternberg, 1977). An analysis of the particular cognitive components involved in a task should prove useful in system design.
- *Skill Characteristics.* Users vary in their ability to read and type text, draw graphic images, point at objects, and track moving targets. These skills may be of varying importance in using a system, and in many cases require considerable training and practice. It should also be mentioned that new skills are developed by users through extensive practice.

1.2.3 Computer Processing

An analogous set of arrows is shown in the box in Figure 1.3 representing the computer. These pertain to input/output to the environment that is not necessarily a part of the human/computer interface and to internal processing. The arrows that point into and out of the intersection between the human and the computer will be discussed in the next section. In terms of the characteristics of the computer, designers must take into consideration its speed and memory and processing capacities. However, in the present context we are only interested in how these characteristics manifest themselves at the human/computer interface.

1.2.4 The Human/Computer Interface

The intersection of the circle denoting the human and the box denoting the computer in Figure 1.3 represents the human/computer interface. In the present conceptualization, the interface is an area. The reason for this is to capture the idea that the interface is not merely a surface through which information travels, but rather it is a shared area that includes the user's cognitive model of the system and the system's model of the user. The idea of a shared area is particularly important when it comes to modeling the flow of control.

Interactive systems have been designed to provide users with different types of control over the operating system. We can characterize these types in terms of the amount and complexity of information transmitted by the computer in prompting the user for input, and the amount and complexity of information transmitted to the computer by the user in directing the next action.

Menu selection provides a highly interactive style of control by listing available options. Menus can convey much information to the user and aid novice users as well as more experienced users. In general, little or no training may be required at the onset, depending on how self-explanatory the menus are. However, as the user works with the system, he or she gains knowledge about the alternatives, the structure, and the capability of the program. Menus require some type of selection process that may or may not involve the keyboard. Interaction is structured so that there are rarely points at which the user is functionally locked out of the system. Unfortunately, menus can appear, and in fact, be restrictive in the capabilities offered to the user.

Command languages have always been seen as offering the user the most powerful and flexible control over the system. They allow for complex input on the part of the user but provide little in the way of prompting the user. The two problems with command languages are that substantial training is required and that it is difficult to provide user aids. Attempts have been made to take into consideration the wealth of natural language knowledge of the user and provide natural language command and query systems. These tend to reduce but do not eliminate the need for extensive training.

Software designers working with human/computer interface designers need to determine the optimal level of complexity and flow of control that will best serve the needs of the user. Furthermore, it is often the case that one needs to change the levels of complexity and the amount of information flow at different points in the interaction and with different levels of experience. A number of guidelines have been generated as to when one mode or another is appropriate and how to implement a particular mode. Some are based on research and others are often speculative, sometimes based on extant theory in cognitive psychology and otherwise based on the opinion of the writer, In this book, we emphasize empirical research as directed by cognitive theory.

1.3 RESEARCH METHODS

No matter how reasonable and intuitive a guideline may be, if it is not supported by data, it is mere conjecture. The rational approach to design suffers from two fallacies. First, what's rational to the designer may be idiotic to the user. The designer views the system from a different perspective. A certain feature or attribute may make sense in light of the whole system, but to the user that feature (or lack thereof) makes no sense for the specific task at hand. The second fallacy is that designers are rarely objective about their design. Having spent a number of man-years developing a system, there may be no end to ego-involvement in the system. Empirical studies provide the objective proving ground for claims between competing systems and design features. Fortunately, empirical research does more than settle arguments, it also reveals the importance of design issues. Some aspects of design may have a critical impact on performance, while others may be irrelevant.

Three basic paradigms exist for research on ergonomic issues. These are discussed briefly in the next sections and in greater detail in a subsequent chapter.

1.3.1 Observational Studies

Observational studies are the easiest to conduct. Unfortunately, they are also the most unreliable and open to interpretation. In an observational study, one or several systems may be selected, and researchers observe users interacting with the system. Verbal protocols may be elicited in which the user explains what and why he is doing something. Time, productivity, and error data may be collected. Analysis may be at a purely verbal descriptive level or based on quantitative measures. Conclusions are tentative at best since researchers have little or no control over conditions. For example, one may conclude that users took longer to perform tasks on System A than on System B; but the tasks may not be comparable, system response time may be different, the groups of users may not be equated, and so forth. Investigators must thoroughly weigh and rule out alternative explanations.

The major strength of observational studies is the ability to generate hypotheses about design features that can be studied in more controlled environments not open to multiple interpretation.

1.3.2 Survey Studies

Questionnaires provide a structured approach in which the user assesses factors related to the human/computer interface. Users may record objective events or subjective evaluations. Objective events include the number of times they have used a particular system, the number of times a system crash occurred while using the system, and number of tasks completed. In each case, since the events are objective, the researcher could also record these events and compare that record with the user assessments. Although user assessments bear a strong correlational relationship to the actual measure, they are not perfect. User assessments are introspective and, therefore, are subject to the properties of human memory and to biases in reporting. Because of this, one cannot assume that user assessments reflect the true values of the measures. On the other hand, it is quite possible to establish, through empirical verification, the reliability and validity of user responses. Furthermore, when comparisons are between different groups of subjects, rather than with an absolute criterion, it may not matter that responses are biased as long as the sources of the biases are constant among the groups.

Users may also be asked to make subjective evaluations of system attributes. For example, they may be asked to check statements that apply to the system (e.g., "Documentation is adequate" or "I do not understand program operation"), or rate system attributes on a 10-point scale (e.g., ease of use, speed, tendency to make errors). When users make subjective evaluations, there is generally no way to compare their responses with objective measures of those attributes. However, evaluations, such as overall satisfaction with the system, may be statistically related to objective system attributes, such as system response time or screen resolution.

The key to measuring subjective evaluations is to ensure reliability and internal consistency of the ratings. By reliability we mean that users display little error in making ratings, and that if they rated the same attributes a second time, there would be a relatively strong relationship between the two ratings. By internal consistency we mean that the ratings follow a logical relationship. For example, if subjects are asked to compare three systems, A, B, and C, and they rate A superior to B, B superior to C, then they must rate A superior to C in order to be internally consistent. Without internal consistency, the meaningfulness of the results are in question.

Survey data are useful in describing systems, for detecting strong and weak points, and for suggesting improvements. For example, in a study by Norman (1986), students rated the overall ease of use of hypothetical systems described by lists of positive and negative attributes. The impact of each attribute was scaled relative to all others. Figure 1.4 lists the descriptions of the attributes, and graphs the impact of each attribute on the ratings. One of the most important positive attributes, at least for this group of students, was the ability of the system to adapt to different types of users. The most telling negative attribute was having a display described as confusing and difficult to read. Such ratings help to set design priorities.

Survey questionnaires should include demographic data on the user. Typically we want to know the age, sex, work experience, and training of the user. We may also want to include psychometric measures to assess intellectual skills, cognitive functions, and knowledge. Analysis of the data may look for interrelationships among the variables. For example, we may be interested in whether there is a relationship between memory ability and preference for a particular type of software, or between the rated number of errors and rated overall satisfaction with the system. Questionnaires may also be effectually used in conjunction with controlled experimental studies.

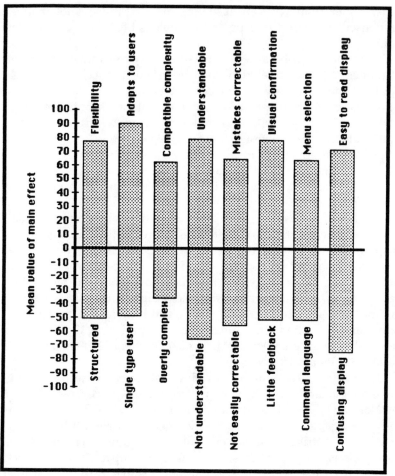

Figure 1.4.   Mean effect on ratings of "user friendliness" of positive and negative attributes of systems (Norman, 1986).

1.3.3 Experimental Studies

The major strength of the experimental study is its ability to localize unambiguously an effect in a particular design factor. Experimental design is used to control all variables except those that are being tested. The steps are as follows:

First, sample participants for the study are selected from the population of interest. To the extent that users are a diverse group, it is important to assess the individual differences of the users. For example, one might need to know (a) the level of experience with computers, terminals, and so on; (b) familiarity with the generic task such as accounting, information retrieval, or programming; (c) demographic variables of age and sex; or (d) cognitive measures of analytical skills, verbal and visual memory, reaction time, and so on.

Second, one or several design features are selected for study. These are systematically varied in such a way that their impact on performance can be unambiguously assessed. For example, we may be interested in comparing alphabetic versus random ordering of options in a menu, as well as the number of options (e.g., 4, 8, 16, 32). Software must be written or altered so that the features are implemented at each level.

Finally, we must select one or several variables to measure. Table 1.1 lists some of the types of variables that may be of interest. The variables must be defined in such a way as to allow valid and reliable measurements to be taken. Typically, additional software must be written to capture these measurements.

The experiment must be carefully monitored as it progresses in order to detect flaws in the design and methodology. Once it is completed, statistical analysis is used to sort out the results and give evidence as to the reliability of the findings.

The experimental approach is not without its drawbacks. Experiments are costly and often overly restrictive. The results may not generalize beyond the artificial conditions set in the lab. However, to the extent that the investigator establishes realistic conditions and assesses appropriate dependent measures, the results gain validity.

1.4 SUMMARY

The architecture of the human/computer interface is of concern to designers of computer-based systems. Menu selection as a mode of communication and control is playing an increasing role as part of that architecture. The relationship between ergonomic research and the design process is fundamental in developing guidelines in the use of menu selection. The type of ergonomic research advocated here for design involves a parallel interaction of system designers and researchers as development progresses. A number of ergonomic issues were discussed relating to tradeoffs between factors, such as speed of performance and error rate, amount of training necessary, and asymptotic performance.

A conceptual model of the human/computer interface was advanced that helps to delineate the ergonomic factors into (a) the task environment, (b) the cognitive processing characteristics of the user, (c) the characteristics of the computer, and (d) the flow of information through the human/computer interface. Menu selection as a mode of control involves planning and decision processes on the part of the user. These processes may be facilitated or restricted, depending on whether the implementation matches the needs and expectations of the user and the task environment.

In the next chapter we take an analytic look at the various types of menu selection systems. A number of features and design characteristics will be outlined. Many of these are factors that have been the subject of empirical research and are discussed in subsequent chapters.

2
Types of Menus and Cognitive Structures

A few years ago the idea of menu selection simply meant that at some point in the program a list of options would be presented and the user would select a number or letter corresponding to the option desired. Today, menus take on a much wider range of form and diversity of application. Although the concept is much the same, the appearance and the power of menu selection has changed as exemplified by systems such as SmallTalk (Tesler, 1981), ZOG (McCraken & Akscyn, 1984; Robertson, McCraken, & Newell, 1981), and a host of commercially available software that spans the whole gamut of applications and user audience.

In this chapter, menu structure, physical format, and response requirements will be discussed. Menu structure refers to the branching capabilities of the menu. Menu structure determines the extent to which the current selection affects subsequent options. We will see that some highly constrained menus serve a purpose in determining the proper sequence of transactions between the user and the system. On the other hand, users often wish to or need to jump to another activity. Menu selection systems in the past have been criticized because they have not allowed the user to escape from a particular menu path in order to complete some other task and then return to the previous point in the menu. More and more systems are beginning to allow the user to perform tasks according to the user's plan of action rather than a constrained path of options. These menus allow the user nearly unlimited control over program flow to jump to any location desired.

The physical format of the menu may either facilitate the user or retard performance, depending on how well it conveys information. The format should highlight the options and organize them in a meaningful way to help in visual search; it should help to set the context of where the user is in the flow of control through the menu structure; and it should aid the user in the decision process.

Finally, the user must have some means of indicating his or her choice. Menu selection systems vary widely in this respect. The response may be a number, a letter, a string of characters, a special function key, the positioning of a cursor using a sequence of arrow keys, a mouse, a trackball, or a joystick, or via a touch screen or light pen. The system must clearly indicate how the user is to make a selection. Responding to menu items may be disassociated from the main task (e.g., using a mouse to make selections in a word processing application where the main task is keyboard entry) or it may be integrated with the task (e.g., using a touch screen to indicate moves in a chess playing program).

In the following sections various attributes and aspects of different types of menu systems will be discussed. The intent of this chapter is to lay out all of the possibilities for designing a menu selection system before considering the cognitive processes by which users navigate through these systems.

2.1 MENU STRUCTURES

The user's cognitive structure of a task embodies a set of expectations about what happens when and what leads to what. We will see that menu structure should be consonant with the user's cognitive structure. There should be a graceful guidance of activities that meshes with the user's expectations. For example, in a financial transaction, if the system asks "Would you like to (1) deposit funds or (2) withdraw funds?" and the customer chooses the first option, he then expects to be asked something like, "Would you like to deposit in your (1) checking account or (2) savings account?" Program flow conforms to the user's schema of the task. On the other hand, it would unnerve the customer to be asked at this particular point, "Would you like to rent a safety deposit box (yes or no)?"

Menu structures embody the flow of the control given to the user in a task. The formal structure of a menu system can be defined using the concepts of set theory, abstract algebra, or state-action graphs as has been done by Arthur (1986) and others. However, from the perspective of the user, it is more important to identify the general types of menu structures and the sense in which they control program flow. These are the single, sequential linear, simultaneous, hierarchical, cyclical/acyclical, and event menus.

2.1.1 Single Menus

Menu selection in its simplest form is a single menu frame that is presented to the user in order to elicit input. Single menus conceptually involve a one-shot choice rather than a series of choices. The user views this selection in isolation from other aspects of the task. For example, in a game program a menu might be presented as follows: "Select level of difficulty: (1) easy, (2) moderate, (3) hard." The user need only consider the immediate consequences of his choice and need not factor in other choices. Although a program may include a number of other single menu choice points (such as "Play another game (Y/N)?"), the user does not perceive these menus as forming a series of choices.

Even in its simplicity, the single menu involves an iterative cycle in which (a) the menu frame is presented; (b) a procedure is executed to get the user's selection; (c) an error-checking routine is called to determine if the input is valid; and (d) if it is valid, a parameter is set or a procedure is executed as specified by the input or (e) if it is not valid, an error message is generated and program control returns to b. The cycle for the single menu is shown in the shaded box in Figure 2.1.

When one menu frame naturally leads to another, or when a set of menus are clustered together, the user begins to perceive a series of choices. This series defines a path going from one menu frame to another.

2.1.2 Sequential Linear Menus

Linear menus have only one path. Menu frames are presented in a preset order for parameter specification or for data entry. In essence all flow of control is determined by the system. The path of a linear menu system may extend from 2 to n levels and incorporates an iteration of single menu frames as shown in the whole diagram of Figure 2.1. The system is initialized to the first menu frame in the series; it presents a single menu, and advances to succeeding menu frames until it reaches the terminal node. Figure 2.2 shows such a menu applied to a questionnaire.

Two main problems with linear menus are that (a) the user may need to go back and change an answer in a previous menu, and (b) the user may want to answer the questions in a different order than preset by the system. Solutions to the first problem can be handled using an undo command that jumps back to a specified frame; but, in general, it is rather awkward and confusing for the novice user to control movement along an extended linear path.

2.1.3 Simultaneous Menus

Simultaneous menus solve the problems caused by preset orders of menu frames. All menu options are available simultaneously. The user can enter the responses in any order as one could in filling out a form.

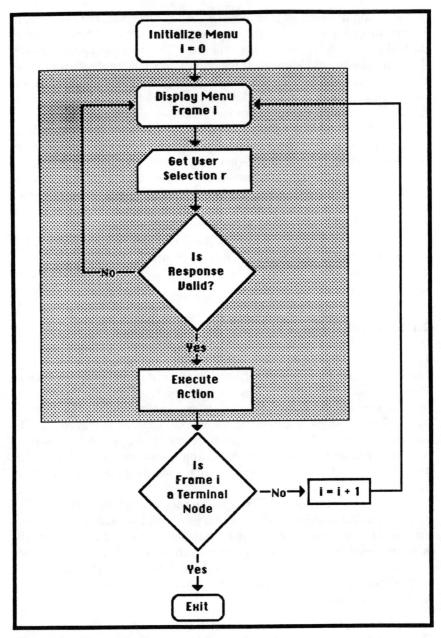

Figure 2.1.   Menu selection processing cycle.

These menus are, in fact, a form fill-in method with the restriction that items are selected rather than typed into fields. Questions may be skipped and returned to later or simply left blank. Figure 2.3 gives an

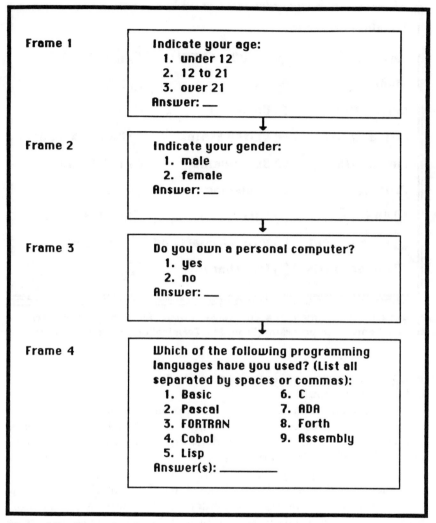

| Frame 1 | Indicate your age:
  1. under 12
  2. 12 to 21
  3. over 21
Answer: __ |

| Frame 2 | Indicate your gender:
  1. male
  2. female
Answer: __ |

| Frame 3 | Do you own a personal computer?
  1. yes
  2. no
Answer: __ |

| Frame 4 | Which of the following programming languages have you used? (List all separated by spaces or commas):
  1. Basic   6. C
  2. Pascal   7. ADA
  3. FORTRAN 8. Forth
  4. Cobol   9. Assembly
  5. Lisp
Answer(s): _____ |

Figure 2.2.   Example of a linear menu used for administering a questionnaire.

example of the simultaneous menu in setting parameters of a terminal communications program.

The problem with the simultaneous menu is that for a large number of options, it may not be possible to display all of the choice sets on one screen, and some mechanism must be used to scroll or page to other parts. An additional technical problem is that response input must define both the menu number and option number. When keyboard input is required, it is rather tedious to enter both, such as "12A" for option A of menu 12. On the other hand, using direct selection with a

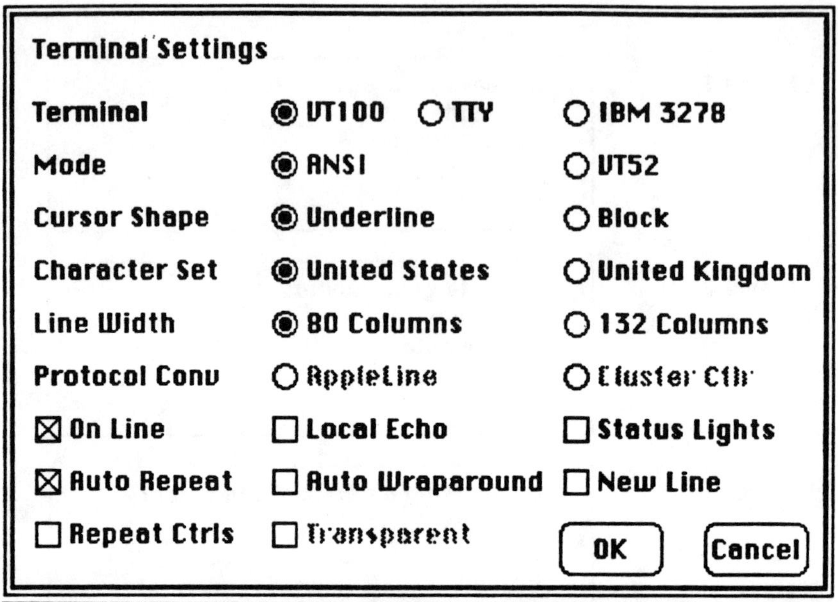

Terminal Settings

Terminal	◉ UT100 ○ TTY	○ IBM 3278
Mode	◉ ANSI	○ UT52
Cursor Shape	◉ Underline	○ Block
Character Set	◉ United States	○ United Kingdom
Line Width	◉ 80 Columns	○ 132 Columns
Protocol Conu	○ AppleLine	○ Cluster Ctlr
☒ On Line	☐ Local Echo	☐ Status Lights
☒ Auto Repeat	☐ Auto Wraparound	☐ New Line
☐ Repeat Ctrls	☐ Transparent	⬭ OK ⬭ Cancel

Figure 2.3.   An example of a simultaneous menu for setting parameters of a terminal emulation program. (From MacTerminal on the Apple Macintosh™)

mouse or light pen, the curser location identifies both the menu and the option simultaneously.

Although simultaneous menus are appealing in many applications, sometimes the preset order of the linear menu is preferred. This is particularly true when there are underlying relationships or interactions among the options. When the interactions are strong, in that they make other options inappropriate, the menu system should have a hierarchical structure that reflects these relationships. For example, if one frame asks, "Do you own a personal computer?" and the user indicates, "no," then it is not appropriate to ask, "Which of the following computers do you own?" More complex menu structures allow branching to maintain a natural series of questions.

2.1.4 Hierarchical Menus

The hierarchical structure of a menu results in the increasing stepwise refinement of choice. In database search, it may be the specification of categories, subcategories, and so on. In parameter specification and data entry, it may be the selection of options, suboptions, and so on.

The hierarchical menu can be presented as an inverted tree structure leading to more and more branches. Hierarchical menus may be either symmetric or asymmetric as shown in Figure 2.4. Symmetric menus vary only in depth and breadth. Depth is defined as the number of levels that one must traverse to reach the terminal node. Breadth is defined as the number of alternatives at each level. The structure of symmetric menus can be defined by a series of numbers indicating the number of

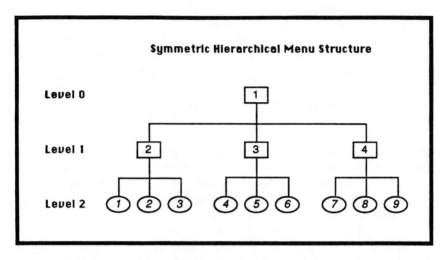

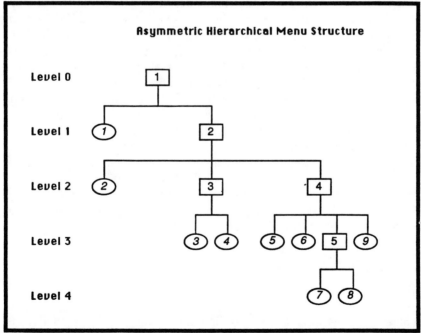

Figure 2.4.   Examples of symmetric and asymmetric menus. (Boxes indicate choice nodes and circles indicate terminal nodes.)

alternatives at each level. For example, the menu structure shown in the top panel of Figure 2.4 is indicated by 3 × 3. On the other hand, a 4 × 2 × 8 menu would have 4 alternatives at the first level, 2 at the next level, and 8 at the last level, resulting in 64 terminal nodes. In general, symmetric menus with a constant breadth of k alternatives at n levels will have k^n terminal nodes.

Symmetric menu structures are rare in a real-world system owing to the asymmetric nature of categories and subcategories. However, they are used quite often in empirical research on menu selection because the number of alternatives at each level and the length of all possible paths are constant across the tree. When this is the case, it is easy to vary depth and breadth and evaluate their effect on performance. Furthermore, symmetric menus have the advantage in that users can expect the same number of alternatives at each level and the same number of levels. Sometimes this constancy is important in routine tasks. It sets a simple pattern of response on the part of the user who is often anticipating the next transaction with the system.

Asymmetric menus, however, are the rule in most practical applications. The number of alternatives varies throughout the structure and the length of paths to terminal nodes is not necessarily constant. Although menus do not have a constant depth and breadth, they may be described statistically by their average depth and breadth. The amount of variability in the structure may be assessed by the standard deviations of depth and breadth. The definitions of the average and standard deviation for depth and breadth, however, are not straightforward. One could look at the average path length for all possible paths and the average number of alternatives across all frames; however, this does not take into account the actual utilization of the menu. If a user visits all terminal nodes with equal frequency, he experiences a different average depth than if he makes all choices with equal probability. Consequently, a weighting scheme needs to be applied in assessing average depth and breadth. For average depth, we may use (a) equal weighting of all possible paths, (b) weighting by probability of a path given equal choice probability, and (c) weighting by probability of a path given observed choice probabilities. The equations for the weighted average and weighted standard deviation for depth are:

$$\text{Avg. } D = \Sigma w_i n_i / \Sigma w_i \tag{1}$$

$$\text{Sd. } D = \sqrt{(\Sigma w_i (n_i - \text{Avg. } D)^2 / \Sigma w_i)}, \tag{2}$$

where n_i is the number of nodes visited for path i, and w_i is the weight for path i. Table 2.1 gives an example of the weights and computations for the asymmetric menu shown in Figure 2.5.

Table 2.1.   Measures of Depth in Asymmetric Menus.

Path	Depth	Probability Weights		
		Equal Path	Equal Choice	Observed Choice*
I	I	1/11	1/2	.8000
2	2	1/11	1/6	.1200
3	3	1/11	1/12	.0100
4	3	1/11	1/12	.0100
5	3	1/11	1/24	.0120
6	3	1/11	1/24	.0180
7	3	1/11	1/24	.0240
8	4	1/11	1/96	.0015
9	4	1/11	1/96	.0015
10	4	1/11	1/96	.0015
11	4	1/11	1/96	.0015
Average		3.09	1.87	1.29
Standard Deviation		.90	.97	.62

*Calculated from the hypothetical choice probabilities shown in Figure 2.5.

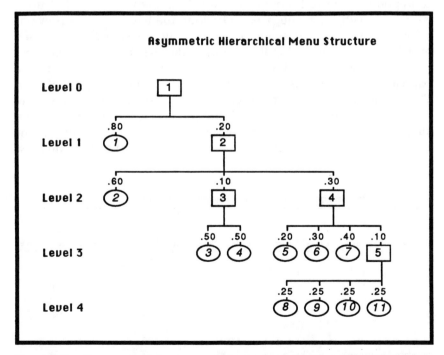

Figure 2.5.   An asymmetric menu varying in depth and breadth. (Number on the lines indicate hypothetical choice probabilities. Numbers in the boxes are frame numbers and numbers in the circles are path numbers.)

For breadth, one may use either (a) an equal weighting of the number of alternatives across all nodes, or (b) a weighting by the frequency of times the node is visited. In the second case, these frequencies may be determined by (a) equal path frequency, (b) equal choice probability, or (c) observed choice probabilities. The equations for weighted average and weighted standard deviation of breadth are:

$$\text{Avg. B} = \Sigma w_j k_j / \Sigma w_j; \tag{3}$$

$$\text{Sd. B} = \sqrt{(\Sigma w_j (k_j - \text{Avg. B})^2 / \Sigma w_j)}, \tag{4}$$

where k_j is the number of alternatives at node j, and w_j is the weight for node j. Table 2.2 gives an example of these weights and computations for the asymmetric menu in Figure 2.5.

Hierarchical menus have the virtue of allowing the user to branch as a part of the flow of control. No such branching is allowed in linear menus. However, the order of branching and structure of the branching in the hierarchy are preset. The flow of control is one-way, top-down. The disadvantage is that the hierarchical order may not fit the user's conception of the task flow of control. It is often the case that users unfamiliar with the menu need to back up the tree, change a previous selection, or start over again. The user may not consider answering questions in the order that the hierarchy dictates, or the user may not know what suboptions the system will offer given the selection of a particular choice. The first problem is that of cognitive representation. The second is the problem of uncertainty. It will be shown in subsequent chapters that menus should be designed so that (a) their hierarchical structure is consistent with user expectations, and (b) they reduce the uncertainty of choice as much as possible. In an effort to alleviate these

Table 2.2.   Measures of Breadth in Asymmetric Menus.

Frame	Breadth	Weighting			
		Equal Frame	Equal Path	Equal Choice	Observed Choice*
1	2	1	11	1	1.000
2	3	1	10	1/2	.200
3	2	1	2	1/6	.020
4	4	1	7	1/6	.060
5	4	1	4	1/24	.006
Average		3.00	2.94	2.49	2.26
Standard Deviation		1.00	.85	.69	.54

*Calculated from the hypothetical choice probabilities shown in Figure 2.5.

problems, most hierarchical menu systems provide options or commands that allow the user to move to the previous frame or to return to the main menu. Although these are considered solutions to the problem, they are often cumbersome to the user.

2.1.5 Connected Graph Menu Structures

The most general of the sequential menus is the connected graph network. A connected graph is a set of nodes connected by arches such that all nodes are directly or indirectly linked. Movement through the structure of menu frames need not be restricted to a hierarchical tree, but may include links from any node to another in the network. Technically, hierarchical trees that allow the user to move to the previous node or to jump to the top of the tree are also connected graphs. However, in the present discussion, we will use the term *connected graph* to denote a menu system that does not embody the central idea of a hierarchy, but rather that of a network of connected nodes. Consequently, from the user's perspective there is no sense of top-down traversal of the menu. Instead, it is a question of determining the path from Node A to Node B that accomplishes the task at hand. Network menus convey the idea of a geographical map of a road system. One may want to find the fastest (or shortest) route from Point A to Point B, or one may want to select the route between the two points that passes through Points C, D, and E as well.

Figure 2.6 shows several examples of connected graphs. These structures may be cyclical if they either allow or require multiple passes along the same path to accomplish a function or acyclical if they do not. For example, Graphs A and B are cyclical; Graph C is acyclical; and Graph D is for the most part acyclical but contains a cyclical part. Connected graphs may also be characterized as symmetric or asymmetric. For example, Graphs A, B, and C are symmetric, and Graph D is asymmetric.

Connected graphs like the hierarchical graphs vary in terms of the number of menu frames, average number of alternatives, and length of path. Estimates depend on how the values are weighted. As before, they may be given equal weights or weights that depend on menu use and probability of paths. A major difference between connect graphs and hierarchical menus is that in connected graphs there may be multiple paths between two nodes. Menus vary in terms of connectivity, that is, the extent to which nodes are linked by multiple paths.

The connected graph is generally used to provide the user with a full sense of control over the flow of actions. These systems are found most

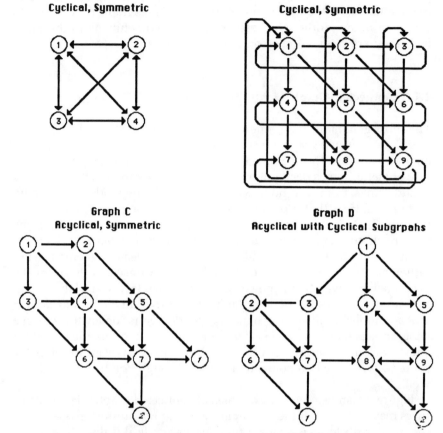

Figure 2.6. Examples of connected graph menu structures. Graph A is cyclical, symmetric, and completely connected. Graph B is cyclical and symmetric. Graph C is symmetric and acyclical. Graph D is asymmetric, acyclical with cyclical subgraphs.

often as menu replacements of command languages for operating systems and application programs. For the control of program flow, the connected graph is typically sequential. The options open to the user are limited to the number of paths leading from the current node. While this limitation is helpful in providing focus for the user, it may also prove frustrating when there is a need to perform a concurrent task unrelated to the current location in the graph, or a need to break the current flow of control and jump out of the graph to select some new entry point. Event trapping menus which allow for this level of control are described in the next section.

2.1.6 Event Trapping Menus

Event trapping menus provide, in essence, a set of simultaneous menus superimposed on a sequential hierarchical or connected graph menu system and may be activated at any point in a task. Typically, these menus appear as special function keys or as pull-down or pop-up lists of options. In the case of special function keys, the user selects a menu or item in a menu by pressing a specially denoted key. In the case of pull-down or pop-up menus a cursor is placed on the menu label and the items are revealed. Figure 2.7 shows such a system with a menu bar at the top of the screen and one of the lists pulled down.

Event trapping menus may be characterized by the number of special function keys or the number of items in pull-down menus. Furthermore, the selection of an item generally serves one of three functions:

1. It may immediately change a parameter in the current environment or perform some function without leaving the current environment. For example, in a word-processing program one may select the option to left and right justify the text. Once the selection has been made, the user continues where he or she left off.
2. It may call a subroutine that momentarily takes the user out of the current environment to perform some function and then returns to the previous environment. For example, in a file management application, the user may be scrolling through file entries and may want to change the format. The user would select from the menu bar the

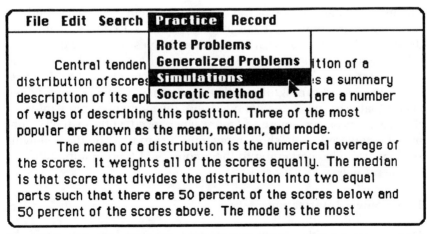

Figure 2.7. An example of the use of a pull-down menu in a computer-assisted instruction application.

option to format and then enter an environment that allows re-definition of the format. Upon completion, the user would automatically return to the previous environment.

3. Finally, it may exit the current environment and move to a totally new environment. For example, the user may select "quit" to return to the operating system, or select among other application programs.

Event trapping menu systems vary in terms of the number and mix of these three types of items. The greater the flexibility and complexity of a system, the greater the number of event trapping options.

Event trapping menus provide an ever present background of control over the system state and parameters while the user is working on a foreground tasks. The menus are constantly available and help to establish a sense of context while things are changing in the foreground. The menu bar may change from one application program to another, but typically there is some degree of communality between the event trapping menus and some degree of distinctiveness that helps to remind the user where he is. However, if the meaning of special function keys and the particular items in pull-down menus vary greatly or change without warning, the user may experience a loss of position or disorientation and make habitual errors. We will see in the next section how the user must be kept informed of the current state of the system in terms of information conveyed to the user by the menu frame.

2.2 MENU FRAMES

The menu frame consists of the context, the stem, the leaves, and the response instructions. Needless to say, menu selection systems vary drastically in terms of what information is presented, the amount of information, and the format of the frame. The design of a particular system must take into consideration how much information the user needs to work meaningfully with the system. In general, one would expect that users who are unfamiliar with the menu need more information. As users become more and more experienced, verbose descriptions may be replaced with short mnemonic reminders. In the following sections variables pertaining to the amount and type of information in the menu will be discussed.

2.2.1 Context Information

The context provides feedback that tells the user where he is in the process, what the past choices and outcomes were, and possibly how much further it is to the terminal node. Context information is extremely important in complex menus where the user may experience a subjective loss of position and associated disorientation. The user may not recall how far down the tree he or she has come, or how successful past choices have been in getting closer to the goal, or how many more choices must be made before reaching the goal. It is too often the case that halfway through a search, the user asks, "Now what was it that I was looking for?" Human memory, being what it is, needs assistance.

At a minimum, the frame should provide information that the user is accessing the right function. In a bank transaction, if the customer has selected his checking account, then all further choices (balance, withdraw, deposit) should be clearly in the context of the checking account. This feedback provides the user constant assurance that he is on the right track. On the other side, context information should not be overly verbose. If it is, it obscures the current choice and may add to the confusion.

Context may be established by various methods of linkage between successive menu frames as illustrated in Figure 2.8. The most fundamental linkage is merely the temporal sequence of one frame following the selection of an option in a previous frame. Temporal sequence implies a cause-effect relationship; however, it does not indicate the nature of the relationship between one frame and the next. The context established by temporal linkage decays with time and may need to be maintained by other methods of linkage.

Verbal linkage may be accomplished by using the previously selected option as the title for the next menu frame. The title may be cumulative as one goes further along a path. For example, in a videotext service the title of a menu frame may be, "News: New York Times: World News: India: Today," indicating the path to the current set of options which may be a list of stories.

Spatial linkage may be accomplished by graphic methods that preserve temporal linkage and enhance verbal linkage. In the bottom panel of Figure 2.8, the user selected the second option. A link is shown by displaying the next menu frame in a window overlapping the previous frame. The complete path down a menu tree may be shown as a series of overlapping frames in a single view. Linking information such as this can provide the user with a sense of progress and distance from the start to the goal.

2.2.2 Stem Information

The stem provides the label for the current set of choices. It may be merely the beginning of a question—"Would you like to . . .?"—or it may be the label of the alternative selected in the previous frame. For example, if the user was asked what communication parameter he

Verbal Linkage:

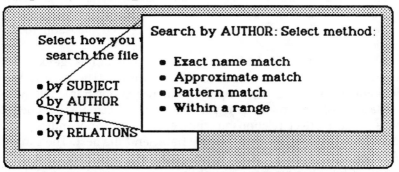

Spatial Linkage:

Figure 2.8. Two types of linking information: Verbal linkage by titles of menu frames, and spatial linkage by interposition and occlusion.

wished to change and he selected "baud rate," the stem might be "Select baud rate." The stem may be merely the current choice or it may include a record of all choices in the path up to the present choice. In nested hierarchical menus, the stem information may increase with each choice. Selections may include a trace of the whole path down to the current point. For example, along the lines of the Dewey Decimal System a stem in an information retrieval system might be: History-U.S.-Civil War-Economic-Impact on?-.

However, in generating stem information, there is a tradeoff between specificity and clutter. When one could easily get lost in the maze of choices, cumulative stem information is essential. In other cases, however, the user may not need to see all of the stem information. Only that which is likely to be lost from short-term memory and that which is crucial to specifying the current choice must be displayed.

Stem information should provide the novice user with a rationale for why this choice is being made and what it's impact will be on subsequent processes. For the set of choices, "Gothic, Roman, Modern," a stem such as "Select one of the following:" is devoid of information. The novice user does not know what they refer to or what the choice will affect. On the other hand, a stem such as "Set the type font to one of following for printing document:" provides that information. Research in cognitive psychology shows an enormous impact by providing a meaningful title on a person's interpretation and understanding of subsequent information (Bransford & Johnson, 1972).

2.2.3 Leaf Information

The leaves are the alternatives available to the user. Leaf information can vary from a brief listing of response options (e.g., "/A/T/S/Q/H/") to single words or phrases (e.g., "A—Author; T—Title; S—Subject; Q—Quit; H—Help"), or to a complete description (e.g., "A—Search for a book by author's name; T—Search for a book by it's title; S—Search for a book by the subject; Q—Quit searching and return to beginning; H—Request detailed help on searching for a book"). Leaf information is rarely complete in the sense of telling the user precisely what will happen if a particular selection is made. This is generally the case in nested hierarchical menus where the user would like to know what options will be available following a particular choice. For example, some systems allow the user to move a scroll bar over an alternative and at the same time the next level of choices are displayed.

A number of guidelines have been suggested for the wording of leaf information. Alternatives should be unambiguous, mutually exclusive, exhaustive, and nonoverlapping. The wording of alternatives should emphasize the critical features of their differences rather than the similarity. Furthermore, it has been suggested that alternatives should be brief noun phrases (Shneiderman, 1987). Most of these guidelines have yet to be validated by empirical research.

The list of alternatives appearing in the menu frame may not necessarily be exhaustive. Many systems include constant alternatives that are not explicitly listed. Constant alternatives may be commands such as "move to the previous menu," "jump to the top," "help," or "quit." Generally, systems that include unlisted options include an option to display the full set of choices. This may be a question mark or "help." Generally, however, the command to list unlisted alternatives is also unlisted. One would expect that hidden alternatives are less likely to be used by novices.

2.2.4 Response Information

Finally, response instructions tell the user how to indicate the choice. For example, it may say "Enter the number of your selection and press the return key," or simply "Press key" when special function keys are labeled. Explicit instructions are often needed for first time users of the system. With experience, users gain a sense of what is expected of them by the system. Overly verbose instructions generally confuse the user or are simply not read. Instructions for response procedures which are different from the usual mode of interaction need to highlight those differences. For example, a response may be recognized and processed by the system (a) immediately after a single key is pressed, (b) only when terminated by pressing the return key, or (c) only when terminated by pressing a special "send" key. If users habitually terminate lines with a return key, errors and confusion may occur if a different type of response is required.

Response information may also include feedback or verification that a particular alternative was activated or is about to be activated. Systems vary from providing no feedback, to a single auditory beep that some response was recorded, to confirmation of the response in an input field or by highlighting the selected alternative.

2.2.5 Information Format

In early alphanumeric applications of menus, information was presented sequentially in the following order: context, stem, leaf, response. The three panels of Figure 2.9 show variations of this format. Systems have varied the degree to which the menu is organized on separate lines. Some systems have run all of the menu together in prose form (top panel on Figure 2.9); others have grouped information on one line (middle panel of Figure 2.9); and others have used multiple lines to list the options in an outline form (bottom panel of Figure 2.9). The number of possible layouts is unlimited; however, it is obvious that some layouts are to be preferred over others. The prose layout, for example, is particularly bad because the user cannot easily scan the list of items.

With the advent of graphics and screen based systems, other methods of displaying information have been used. Context is often given by the background on which the menu appears. A pop-up window or pull-down menu appears over the work at hand, thereby retaining a sense of position. The stem and leaf information in these systems remains much the same except that options may be graphically displayed using icons. Often the stem information may be implicit rather than expressly stated. It is expected that the layout of such information will greatly affect the user's ability to comprehend the functioning of the system.

Prose Format

You are searching for an article. You may select to search by
by the author's name, keywords in the title, or by subject.
Press A for author's name search, K for keyword search, or
S for subject search. If you need help press H.

Enter choice: ___

One Line Brief Format

Article search by /A-author/K-keyword/S-subject/ : ___

Outline Format

Article search by:
    A-author's name
    K-keyword in title
    S-subject

Enter choice: ___

Figure 2.9.   Examples of formats of alphanumeric menu frames.

2.3 RESPONSE MODE

The method of response selection is an important one and varies substantially among systems. We will see later that there are a number of
cognitive implications regarding the response mode. Some response
modes require a mapping of the alternative to a code and the manual
entry of that code. Other systems require a manual pointing to the
alternative. Some allow for verification of the response before activating
it and others do not. The sections that follow discuss these and other
variables as they pertain to the major forms of response input.

2.3.1 Standard Keyboard Input

Keyboard input requires the user to identify the alternative he wishes to select and then determine the appropriate keystrokes to make that selection. Menus may use (a) sequentially numbered alternatives, (b) nonsequentially numbered alternatives, (c) alphabetically labeled alternatives, (d) randomly labeled alternatives, or (e) mnemonically labeled alternatives.

The keyboard response may or may not require a terminating character such as the return key or send key. If it does, it provides the user with the opportunity to verify that he has entered the correct label. If it does not, the response requires one less keystroke. The tradeoff is between speed of operation and cost of errors. If errors can easily and quickly be corrected without confusing the user, and if speed is of the essence, then self-terminating responses are called for. For novice users, response verification is important; however, confusion and frustration can arise when the user does not know that he must press the return key to continue.

Standard keyboard input requires some familiarity with the layout of the keys. Performance is facilitated if the user knows how to type and does not have to search for the keys. Number keys have the advantage of being sequentially placed along the top row of keys or on a separate numeric keypad. Multiple character abbreviations are the most difficult for the nontypist.

2.3.2 Special Function Keys

Special function keys are used in many systems instead of standard keyboard input. The keys may only be labeled sequentially (e.g., "F1", "F2", "F3", . . .), or they may be meaningfully labeled with words or phrases (e.g., "NEXT PAGE," "FORMAT," "QUIT," . . .). If the keys are not meaningfully labeled, then the user must identify the item to be selected on the screen, note the number of the function key, and then locate the function key on the keyboard. With practice the user will remember the function of the keys and not have to refer to the information key on the screen. When the keys are meaningfully labeled, the user needs only to locate the key on the keyboard.

The problem with special function keys is that for complex systems hundreds of such keys may be required. In some CAD/CAM systems, large keyboards are used for selection of items. Similarly, a number of fast food restaurants use registers with the entire menu on a special keyboard for fast input. Large keyboards require a great deal of familiarity with the location of items to reduce search time. In other cases, where one does not have the luxury of a large keyboard, special function keys are used repeatedly for different functions or for only high frequency or event trapping alternatives. For example, a system may have a "HELP" key available for online information, and a "RESTART" key to start the search over again. Alternatives that are not listed on the screen but that are constantly available to the user can be wisely implemented with the use of special function keys.

2.3.3 Virtual Keypads

A number of menu selection systems have attempted to circumvent the problem of keyboard input and large response keypads by the use of screen pointing devices or by the use of automatic labeling of keys. One solution focuses on the screen as a direct input device, the other focuses on the keypad as an indicator of options.

When the options are listed on the screen, it seems natural to be able to point at or touch the desired item. The screen becomes in essence the keypad. Direct selection may be accomplished using a light pen or a touch screen. The use of a light pen requires that the user pick up the pen and direct its sensor at the desired item and press a select button. The touch screen is less encumbering and merely requires that the user physically touch the item on the screen. The advantage of a touch screen is the simplicity of selection. Among the disadvantages are the problems that the finger can obscure the item, the accuracy of pointing may be low, and the user may experience arm fatigue after long periods of interaction.

Indirect pointing methods may be used to select items on virtual keypads as well. Indirect pointing is done by the movement of a cursor across the items in the menu. The cursor may be directed by a continuous analog input device, such as a mouse, a trackball, or a joystick. Alternatively, the cursor may be placed by discrete presses of arrow keys or a space bar. With continuous movement of the cursor, the user must be able to select the target item by placing the cursor into a spatial field and pressing a select button. Generally, visual feedback is required so that the item turns reverse video when the cursor is on that item. When the cursor is not on an item and the select button is pressed, generally no action is taken. The advantage of continuous input devices is that users can rapidly move the cursor to the target in a continuous move. The disadvantage is that good eye-hand coordination and hand steadiness is required and the user may miss the target. The user must grab the input device, find the current location of the cursor, locate the target, plot a trajectory from Point A to Point B, verify when the cursor is on target, and then press the select button.

With discrete input devices, a number of keystrokes may be required to move the cursor to the desired item. The advantage, however, is that most systems jump the cursor from item to item so that the cursor is always on a target and never on an undefined choice. Arrow keys can be used to move up or down a vertical list or move to the left or right in a horizontal list. Arrow key selection requires the user to locate the arrow keys, find the current position of the cursor (or highlighted alternative), locate the target, press direction keys until the cursor is on target, and then press the select button.

A disadvantage in many cases in using the screen as the input device is that the menu options obscure or disrupt the process of work. A virtual keypad that automatically labels keys depending on the current set of options solves this problem. The keypad in essence becomes an output device listing the current menu frame. The active alternatives are indicated by LCD or LED displays on or next to the keys. This solution is analogous to having a separate window or second screen for menu selection.

2.4 SUMMARY

A survey of menu systems indicates that they differ along a number of factors and characteristics. In this chapter, menus were characterized by (a) the structure of the menu tree, (b) the type and amount of information presented in the menu frame, and (c) the mode of response selection. The many factors that go into designing a menu system define a space of all possible systems. The ideal system must blend the right levels of factors and attributes to maximize user performance and satisfaction. The solution, however, is highly dependent on the particular task and the need for control. In the next chapter we will consider the types of tasks and the control functions of menu selection.

3
Tasks and Flow of Control

Menu selection systems are used to perform a variety of types of work from word processing to information retrieval, from computer-aided instruction to computer-aided design, and from teleconferencing to file management. In each case, a task analysis would indicate that work is performed by executing a number of component tasks and subtasks. Furthermore, such analyses would reveal a plan of attack that specifies the order in which the tasks and subtasks must be executed. Experienced workers have a fairly clear idea about what the component tasks are and have learned a number of protocols, rules, and strategies for applying the component tasks. When computers are used to automate part of the task, there should be a close match between user-defined component tasks and system-defined functions. Few things can be more frustrating than wanting to perform some function that seems necessary and logical to the user but that is not available on the system. Furthermore, there must be an agreement between the order in which the user would like to perform the tasks and the order allowed by the system. Users should be allowed to perform tasks in an order that makes sense to them, even though it may not be optimal in terms of computer processing. The overriding principle is that computers should be designed to increase human control rather than optimizing computer processing at the expense of human control.

This chapter extends the theory of cognitive control and discusses general types of tasks accomplished by menu selection. These tasks include the specific functions of selecting items frame by frame and the global task of traversing a menu structure for specific applications. The theory developed and the distinctions drawn in this chapter serve to set the foundation for understanding the empirical research conducted on menu selection.

3.1 TAXONOMIES OF TASKS AND INFORMATION STRUCTURES

In designing a menu selection system, it is necessary to develop a taxonomy of the tasks and subtasks that the user desires in performing the work. Tasks need to be considered at the cognitive level; that is, they need to be defined in terms of the components that the user thinks about when he or she is formulating a plan of action. They must not be too elemental nor too global in nature. Instead, they must be gauged to the level of action as defined by the user. If actions are too elemental, the menu structure will be more complex than it needs to be. If actions are too global, the menu structure will be simple but it will overshoot the user's goal.

For any task, the designer must create a list of all the actions implemented by the system. In formal programming languages, this list constitutes the set of allowable program statements and functions. In menu selection systems, this list becomes the set of menu items that evoke actions or changes. An analysis of the task is necessary for the designer to determine what functions need to be implemented. In developing a taxonomy, one may take either a *top-down* or a *bottom-up* approach (Chin, 1986). In a top-down approach, the designer lists major top-level functions which are then refined in greater and greater detail. In a bottom-up approach, the whole list of specific functions is analyzed and organized into groups. Which approach is used depends on the particular task and functions. For example, in text editing one may start with a top-down approach as shown in Figure 3.1. The major task components are (a) file functions, (b) printing, (c) text modification, (d) formatting, and (e) browsing. Each of these may then be refined to more specific functions. The top-down approach has the advantage in that as functions are added they are incorporated in a hierarchical structure.

On the other hand, when a list of specific functions already exists, the bottom-up approach may be used. Tasks that have been manually performed in the past may be analyzed into subtasks. The subtasks are then clustered into groups. Figure 3.2 gives an illustration of a task analysis of a message handling system.

3.2 HUMAN VS. COMPUTER CONTROL OF FLOW

Once the list of tasks has been determined, designers must consider the order in which tasks are performed. The order may be either user-directed or computer-directed. In user-directed tasks, the user starts from a plan of action and directs the computer to perform those tasks in that order. Although command language has traditionally been the mode of interaction for user-directed tasks, menu selection is playing an increasingly important role. The two major problems with command language are that the user must remember the command (both its semantic function and syntactic structure) and correctly enter the command via the keyboard. Menu selection can often be used more effec-

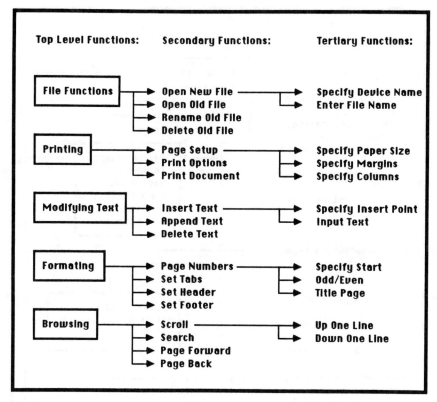

Figure 3.1. Example of a top-down analysis of functions in a text editor.

tively without burdening the user with the added memory and time required to type commands.

In computer-directed tasks, the designer formulates the plan of action and software elicits input from the user in a prescribed order. Computer-directed tasks lead the user through a series of queries in structured tasks that must be carried out in a specific order. Prompts and form fill-in screens are often used to guide users in computer-directed tasks; however, structured menus which follow a prescribed order are also becoming popular.

The distinction between user-directed and computer-directed tasks is partly one of program branching, but also one of user attitude. Just who or what is directing the course of events may be a matter of opinion. Users may feel that they are in command, or they may get the impression of being passively led down the garden path. Whichever impression dominates will be a function of the user's level of experience and the complexity of the system. Menu systems may increase the complex-

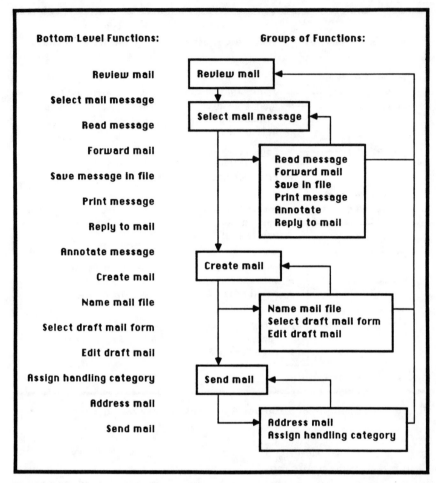

Figure 3.2.   Example of a bottom-up analysis of functions in an electronic mail system.

ity of the system by providing breadth of choice at any particular level and by providing successive levels of options. The user's impression may be one of great choice latitude, flexibility, and power. On the other hand, a limited number of menu items may result in a feeling of constraint, inflexibility, and powerlessness. The user's impression, however, is relative and depends on the match between the degree of latitude desired and that provided. It will be argued in the next section that systems may err in providing too little or too much flexibility. A system with scores of superficial options may appear very powerful on the surface but lack true usability. Alternatively, a system that appears very simple may prove to be efficient. But a system that is too limited may require added work on the part of users.

Another issue related to user- versus computer-directed tasks is that of switching control between the user and the computer. Typically, human/computer interaction is a dialog in which control is passed back and forth between the user and the computer. The user issues a command, the computer executes a procedure and informs the user, who in turn evaluates the result and responds with another command. For users to interact effectively in such an environment, they must know three things: (a) who's turn it is; (b) given that it is the user's turn, what the currently valid set of commands or appropriate input is; and (c) given that it is the computer's turn, what the computer is currently doing or what the result will be. Techniques used in menu selection help to provide some of this information. Menu prompts indicate when the user has control to select options. Menus display the currently available set of options, reducing the probability of selecting an invalid command. Additional feedback is required to inform the user of computer operations and results once a menu selection has been made. To the extent that this information is available and meaningful, the user will be able to operate efficiently. When it is lacking, users will experience confusion and loss of control while performance will be slow and error prone.

3.3 A THEORY OF COGNITIVE CONTROL

The primary function of the human/computer interface is to provide users with an efficient means of controlling a complex process. In the same way that one would exercise control of an automobile, the user controls a computer. The operator of an automobile monitors displays (from instruments on the dashboard to the scene outside the windshield) and manually adjusts controls (from the steering wheel, accelerator, and brake to the light switches, turn signals, and radio). Control of computer processes, of course, differ in a number of ways. Computer processes are generally more autonomous in the sense that they are started and left to run on their own; whereas, automobiles require continuous close control (Wickens, 1984). Control of computer processes is primarily digital rather than analog although increasingly analog input devices are being used. Finally, computer processes vary extensively in their level of complexity (Card, Moran, & Newell, 1983). Control of the process may be as simple as turning on or off a switch or as complex as controlling a simulation of the universe.

Control theory deals with the interrelationships among ongoing processes, informative feedback, and control mechanisms. In general, one is interested in using control theory to optimize efficiency, productivity, and/or quality. Similarly, in human/computer interaction, the designer is interested in optimizing some aspect of performance. The challenge is considerably greater than optimization of a purely mechanical process since the human is a prime source of control in the process. The user is not only a part of the control loop, but he or she typically maintains a higher strategic level of control. This *metacontrol* may be thought of as control of the control process and may involve such functions as (a) initialization, (b) parameter specification, and (c) programming of the control process itself.

Menu selection is an attractive mode of human/computer interaction in that it explicates interrelationships of the control process in terms of a menu structure. The list of menu items and succession of menu frames help to reveal the underlying states and transitions of a program to the user. Menu selection is a particularly attractive mode of control when it allows users to exercise metacontrol over computer processes. Such systems may allow users to design their own menus, program macro-menu actions via direct manipulation, and organize files into menus using hierarchical file servers. These types of metacontrol will be discussed in a later chapter.

In Chapter 1, a model of human/computer interaction was presented in Figure 1.5. The central part of the figure is the overlap of the circle (cognitive processes) and the square (computer processes). Control involves information output from the computer (top left-going line) and commands from the user (bottom right-going line). A theory of cognitive control, however, must entail more than directions of information flow. In this section the issue of a system function will be addressed. Listed below are the main tenets of a theory of cognitive control dealing with system functionality.

The Apparent System Complexity/Functionality Should Match User/ Task Need. To maximize user efficiency, the complexity of the system functionality should match user need. Dehning, Essig, and Maass (1981) assert that for optimal performance and the human/computer interface, the system must provide maximal flexibility while at the same time minimize subjective operating complexity. In addition to the consideration of complexity, the present theory emphasizes a match in functionality between the system and user needs.

To express this more formally, let F_S be the set of active system functions, and let F_U be the set of functions required by the user to perform a set of tasks—T. In general, system functions do not directly perform all the possible tasks. If they did, one would need as many functions as there are tasks. A statistical package, for example, would not have a function to calculate the mean of 2 numbers and another to calculate the mean of 3 numbers, 4 numbers, and so on. Rather, the package would include another function to let the user set the sample size. At the other extreme, a system may be developed with a minimum number of functions capable of performing all of the desired tasks. A six-function calculator could be used to perform all of the statistical calculations needed. However, to do so would require a lengthy application of functions on the part of the user. Cognitive control is facilitated when the user's conceptualization of functions required to perform a set of tasks matches the set of system functions—$F_S = F_U$.

To the extent that $F_S < F_U$, performance will decrease because the user will have to work around the system's lack of functionality by repeated application of existing functions. To the extent that $F_S > F_U$, performance will also decrease because the user will have to sort through a number of superfluous functions to locate needed functions. With experience, users may learn to overcome these problems. However, the learning time and ongoing cognitive overhead may be too much of a burden to bear.

A second problem in matching functionality has to do with the structure of the menu. The menu which implements system functions may be overly complex or impoverished. Menus are overly complex when scores of infrequently used items are constantly displayed. Well-designed hierarchical menus may direct the user to frequently required items, while at the same time allowing access to highly specialized items. Menus may be impoverished even though they contain all of the necessary items if they allow only a limited set of paths to those items. Impoverished menus require the user to spend an inordinate amount of time traversing the menu to get to the needed items.

Functional complexity and menu complexity may be thought of as two somewhat related dimensions of a system. As shown in Figure 3.3, the ideal system exists when the complexity along both dimensions matches that of user need and proficiency. To the extent that the system is off center, performance will decrease. When menus are inadequate, users must contend with inefficient paths; whereas, when they are overly complex, users must contend with more menu items per frame. Moreover, when functional complexity is inadequate, users must select more functions to accomplish a task; whereas, when it is overly complex, users must search through more functions to find the appropriate one. Proper positioning on these two dimensions is the key to matching software to tasks.

The System State Transition Diagram Should Optimize the User Subtask Transition Matrix. A state transition diagram specifies a set of states (indicated by circles), the possible transitions from one state to another (indicated by arrows), and the conditions under which a transition occurs. In menu selection systems, the allowable transitions are determined by the menu structure and the conditions for transitions are

Functional Complexity

Menu Complexity	Inadequate	Adequate	Overly Complex
Inadequate	Users must select more functions and traverse less efficient paths		Users must search through more functions using less efficient paths
Adequate		Ideal	
Overly Complex	Users must select more functions in menus with more items		Users must search through more functions in menus with more items

Figure 3.3.   Two dimensions of complexity in cognitive control.

determined by user selection. To perform a task, users call upon a number of subtasks. Given the set of subtasks, a transition matrix specifies the probability that one subtask follows another.

The upper panel of Figure 3.4 gives an example of a probability transition matrix for a set of subtasks for playing a computer game. For each subtask implemented at state n (shown in the rows), there is a set of probabilities that the user needs to go to for particular subtasks at state $n+1$ (shown in the columns). For example, if the user is at subtask A, there is a .5 probability of going to subtask B and a .5 probability of

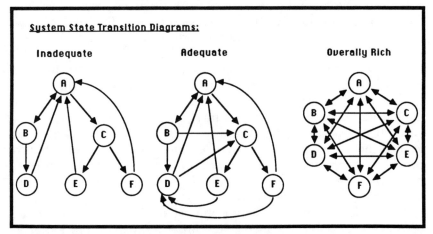

Transition Matrix   **State n + 1**

	A	B	C	D	E	F
A-Start/Quit	.0	.5	.5	.0	.0	.0
B-Load History	.1	.1	.6	.2	.0	.0
C-Set Values	.0	.0	.0	.0	.5	.5
D-Replay	.5	.0	.5	.0	.0	.0
E-Play White	.1	.0	.0	.8	.1	.0
F-Play Black	.1	.0	.0	.8	.0	.1

(rows labeled "State n")

System State Transition Diagrams:

Inadequate   Adequate   Overally Rich

Figure 3.4. User subtask transition matrix and system state transition diagrams representing inadequate, adequate, and overly complex menu structures.

going to subtask C. Given this probability matrix, one may evaluate the graph structure of a menu system which implements these states. A good menu should allow direct paths for high-probability transitions. On the other hand, low-probability transitions need not be direct, but may require successive selections.

Menus that control such state transitions may be either impoverished in the paths that they provide, or they may be too rich by including a number of seldom used paths. Impoverished menus are inefficient because they require the user to make longer traversals of the menu system. In doing so, the user must make more decisions, selections, and planning. The graph in the bottom left of Figure 3.4 illustrates a hierarchical menu from the root node A to terminal nodes D, E, and F with transitions back to the root node. Although it contains 13 transitions, including transitions to previous nodes indicated by double arrows, it does not implement several important high-probability transitions as seen in the matrix: $B \rightarrow C$, $D \rightarrow C$, $E \rightarrow D$, and $F \rightarrow D$. Lateral transitions are not implemented; hence, the user must return to the root node and proceed down to the next node in the sequence. The menu graph at the bottom middle of Figure 3.4 provides a better match with the same number of transitions. A number of unnecessary paths up the tree are eliminated and the high-probability lateral transitions are incorporated in the structure.

The degree to which a menu structure is impoverished can be estimated from the probability transition matrix. For a given number of subtasks that have to be performed, one can estimate the percent of the expected number of transitions required by an impoverished menu relative to a menu that implements a path for all non-zero transitions. For example, the percent of extra traversals for the "inadequate" menu in Figure 3.4 is 60% over that of the "adequate" menu.

On the other hand, menus may be overly rich when they include a number of superfluous or underutilized paths in the structure. An overly rich menu is shown at the bottom right of Figure 3.4 which allows a transition from any node to any other node. Although a rich menu minimizes the number of frames traversed, the increased number of alternatives may retard choice and response times of the user. Impoverished menus will evidence faster response times per frame, but the overall time to perform a task may be longer since more responses are required. Designers must tradeoff the costs between rich and lean menus to optimize performance.

The efficiency of menus can be compared by estimating expected user response time across the menu. Response times are a function of the number of alternatives in each frame. For the present, assume that the response time is given by a power law—$R = n^p + 1$—where n is the number of items per frame and let $p = .7$. Table 3.1 gives the response times at each node of the three menu graphs shown in Figure 3.4. Using the transition probabilities also in Figure 3.4 and the graphs, the expected response times were calculated and are shown at the bottom of Table 3.1. The expected response time for the "inadequate" menu is much longer, due to the fact that 60% more responses are required for the desired state transition. The "overly rich" menu also shows a higher response time due to slower responses at each frame. It can be seen that changes in the menu structure can result in rather large changes in performance. Similarly, designers should compare alternative implementations of menus or iteratively vary menu structures to find one that optimizes performance.

3.4 FUNCTIONS OF MENU SELECTION

In this section the specific functions of a menu selection will be discussed. Each selection made by the user in a menu performs one or more functions. The function may be merely to branch to another menu or it may be to do something else. This section will define the four functions of (a) pointing, (b) command control, (c) output, and (d) input. Other taxonomies of menu function could be specified based on program operation; however, the present one will prove useful from the perspective of understanding cognitive control by the user.

3.4.1 Pointing: Moving to a New Node

Each selection by the user branches to a successive node in the menu tree. Although this is an inherent function of all menus, the importance of this function varies among systems. In some cases, it is the sole purpose of the selection to traverse the menu tree. Selections serve in a stepwise specification of an object or command. The overriding purpose

Table 3.1. Expected User Response Times for Three Menu Types.

	Inadequate	Adequate	Overly Rich
A	2.62	2.62	4.09
B	2.62	3.16	4.09
C	3.16	2.62	4.09
D	2.62	2.62	4.09
E	2.62	2.62	4.09
F	2.62	2.62	4.09
Expected Response Time	4.24	2.64	4.09

is one of pointing to something. From the perspective of the user, menu selection is like navigation. The sole purpose of each selection is to steer the system toward a destination. In this way the process is goal-oriented. Although selection errors take the user off track and lead to a loss of time, they are not destructive and are in general undoable.

The pointing function is essential in hierarchical menu systems. An example would be a menu system for a timesharing utility. A number of services are available to the user; but in order to access one, the user must specify its name. Rather than having to type in the name of the service, the user is given a series of choices. The services are typically clustered by type into a hierarchy. Each selection by the user does nothing except move to the next level of specification. Once the user comes to a particular service on the system, the function of the menu changes from traversal to implementation.

3.4.2 Command Control: Executing a Procedure

The second function of selection is to direct the computer to execute a procedure or to implement some action. In this case, the choice evokes a procedure that performs some function. It may open or close a file, write or read to a file, transform data, and so forth. As noted, this may only occur after the user has traversed the menu tree and is at some terminal node. On the other hand, every selection made by users may initiate a program procedure as they traverse a menu network. In this case, successive selections evoke a sequence of procedures. The users determine the selection and order of procedures. From the user's perspective, selections are "go-ahead" commands for the system to execute a function. It should be clear to users that selections are not merely pointing to items, but that they are activating changes. Errors in command control may not be so inconsequential as in pointing to the wrong node. Consequently, the user needs to be informed if selections are undoable before they are selected.

An example of command control would be a telecommunication program with menu selection. If the user selects the option PHONE, the system executes a procedure to dial and connect to a remote system. The user may then select RECORD to open a file and save the text of the interaction. Later the user may select STOP RECORDING to close the file and HANG UP to disconnect from the system.

3.4.3 Output: Displaying Information

The main function of menu selection may be to display information. The user may be searching for a specific piece of information in a database, or merely browsing through information contained in a menu hierarchy.

The output function is very similar to the pointing function of menu selection except that from the perspective of the user, attention is focused on the content of the output information rather than on the pointer to it. Like the pointing function, the output function is non-destructive. If the user gets off track, he or she may loose time but should be able to recover from selection errors. Information search may be either goal-directed or casual browsing, but the path taken will be determined by the content material and the user's interests. Consequently, users will spend considerable effort processing output information in order to evaluate subsequent menu items.

Online technical manuals provide a good example of the output function. A particularly good example is the interactive encyclopedia system (HyperTies) developed by Shneiderman and his associates (Shneiderman & Kearsley, 1989) which displays articles containing highlighted words or phrases. If the user selects an item, the system displays a definition and/or a related article. The user may then browse through a set of interrelated articles.

3.4.4 Input: Data or Parameter Specification

The last function is one of input. Each selection by the user specifies a piece of data to be input into the system or the desired value of some parameter. Input values may be indicated by single menu selections or by traversing a menu hierarchy. In the latter case, traversing the menu specifies an input value incrementally. Although this type of input function is again similar to the pointing function, the emphasis from the perspective of the user is on input of information to the system. Menu selection adds structure to data input by limiting input to allowable values and reduces errors due to incorrect syntax and typing. In general, selection errors can be easily corrected if detected. Nevertheless, undetected errors remain a problem, as usual, in data entry.

3.4.5 Four Menu Functions in Perspective

It should be emphasized that this fourfold taxonomy of menu selection should be interpreted from the perspective of the user. In terms of the code driving the system, it is no doubt meaningless. In actuality the code may be written so that for every selection (a) a new frame is pointed to, (b) a procedure is evoked, (c) information is displayed, and (d) data is input. The main distinction among these functions is not so much in what the software does but in what the user thinks it is doing.

Furthermore, these functions apply most directly to individual menus or sequences of menus in a system; whereas, most menu systems are mixtures of these functions. Parts of the menu tree may exist merely to branch to some procedure; other parts of the system may exist for the purpose of displaying information; and still other parts may provide menus of executable procedures.

Having said this, it is also true that systems may emphasize only one function. Menus for timesharing systems, file management, and document retrieval systems lean more toward traversal of a database via the pointing function. Menus for operating systems and application programs, such as word processors and spread sheets, lean more toward executing procedures via the command control function. Menus for help systems, tutorials, and information retrieval systems lean more toward displaying information via the display function. Finally, menus for online questionnaires and data entry systems lean more toward data and parameter specification via the input function.

The way in which a menu is designed should be commensurated with the perceived task and the way in which the system is used to accomplish the task. MacGregor, Lee, and Lam (1986) distinguished between "command" menus and "videotext" menus, and noted that command menus are designed to select a relatively limited set of items (30 to 100). Experienced users have learned the positions of menu items. On the other hand, videotext menus are likely to access relatively large databases with thousands of documents requiring a large number of menu frames. In command menus the user generally does not read all of the items but merely scans to the desired one and selects it. In videotext menus the user may need to read each item carefully in order to determine the next selection. While command menus may be designed with a relatively large number of options, videotext menus, according to Paap and Roske-Hofstrand (1986), should focus the user down a narrower path by presenting a smaller number of items distributed across more menu frames.

Menus that merely serve to point successively to other frames should be designed to facilitate traversal, possibly by jump-ahead commands, and they should provide the user with a sense of position, possibly by displaying a path or a global map of the menu tree.

3.5 OPERATION BY MENU SELECTION: COMMAND MENUS

Many applications use menu selection as a replacement for command languages. Rather than specifying a command by entering it via the keyboard, the command is selected along with its operand via menu selection. Command menus have the advantage of overcoming two inherent problems of command languages. First, menus help to disambiguate terms that can have multiple meanings. A term such as *list* may be a command to display a list of items, or it may be the name of an object. The particular meaning of a term can be determined by the context. The second problem is that a function could have a number of equally likely names. Menus help to resolve which of a number of synonyms is recognized by the system as a command. For example, the function of terminating a process may be labeled: stop, halt, quit, end, fin, bye, kill, term, and so on. With a command language, one must remember which term is appropriate. Natural language systems may recognize a number of synonyms; however, users must still go through the cognitive process of generating a term and wondering if it was correctly recognized. Further difficulty arises if two or more synonyms result in different actions by the system. For example, "quit" may exit a program and return to the operating system, "halt" may stop the processor until a continue command is used, "kill" may terminate a process without storing the results, and "end" may gracefully terminate a process and store the results. By listing all four commands as menu items the user is alerted to the fact that each has a different effect.

Menus for control of operations usually involve a sequence of selections from (a) a set of commands, (b) a set of operands, and (c) a set of options or parameter values. Commands are essentially synonymous with verbs, operands with names of objects, and options with qualifiers, such as adjectives and adverbs. The sequence of selections to perform a task constitutes a sentence which must conform to the grammatical order required by the system. For example, the command to open a specific file could be implemented by first selecting the option "Open" from a list of operations and then selecting a file from a list of names of files. Depending on the application, a different order of selections for the command, the operands, and the options may be required. A document (operand) may be selected first, then the command (print), and finally the print options (e.g., draft, letter quality). On the other hand, the application may require that the print options and the document be specified prior to the print command. For command languages, research suggests that the command precede the operand (Barnard, Hammond, MacLean, & Morton, 1982; Barnard, Hammond, Morton, Long, & Clark, 1981).

On the other hand, with menu selection and particularly with direct manipulation, the preferred order may offer operand first. In this order, a file would first be selected from a list, then a command (copy, delete, duplicate, etc.) would be selected. The order in which selections are made may have a number of implications. When commands, operands, and options are considered, there are six possible orders to consider. Table 3.2 lists these orders and some considerations for each.

All possible orders can be implemented with menu selection. The system may impose a fixed order or allow the user to select commands,

Table 3.2. Possible Orders of Selection of Commands, Operands, and Options and Their Implications.

Order	Implications
Commands-Operands-Options	Actions are planned first. Operands are thought of as objects of commands. Options refine commands as applied to selected operands.
Commands-Options-Operands	Actions are planned first. Options refine commands irrespective of operands or preconditionalize operands. Operands are thought of as objects of commands.
Operands-Commands-Options	Targets are planned first and are thought of as the subjects of commands. Options refine commands as applied to selected operands.
Operands-Options-Commands	Targets are planned first. Options refine operands or preconditionalize commands. Commands are thought of as action verbs applied to the targets.
Options-Commands-Operands	Options preconditionalize commands and operands before they are selected. Operands are thought of as objects of selected actions.
Options-Operands-Commands	Options preconditionalize commands and operands before they are selected. Operands are thought of as subjects of commands.

operands, and options in any order. The particular order used has implications about the way in which the user is thinking about the task and forming a plan to be executed. In many cases the selection of commands, operands, and options may be left at a default or preset value. The prior specification of options requires that the user plan ahead, but has the advantage in that he does not have to process the option menu each time a command is made. However, if it is likely that the values change or that incorrect options could lead to serious problems, it is advisable that the option menu be presented following command selection. Prior specification of operands allows the user to apply a series of operations to the same set without repeatedly specifying its members. A user may select several files (operands) and the command to print and then the command to delete. Both operations apply to the same set of files.

When the number of commands is large, they are often presented in a hierarchical structure. Commands may be grouped by type. For example, commands may be grouped that have to do with file operations, resource allocation, account management, and so forth. When commands must be selected by a series of menu choices, two problems arise. First, the top menu does not list commands, but only labels standing for the sets of commands. Sometimes these labels are not very informative about the commands they represent. For example, the label "Goodies," which has been used in some packages to represent a mixed set of commands that do interesting things, is provocative but less than informative. The second problem is that it takes more than one selection to locate and execute a command. Experienced users may be able to type the command name faster than making a series of choices. However, if the menu hierarchy is broad and system response time is fast, menu selection has the potential of resulting in faster execution of commands rather than typing command names on the keyboard.

System operations are generally much more complicated than just making selections. One command may change the state of the system such that subsequent commands have different effects or such that the system enters a different mode that implements different commands. For example, users face one set of commands when they are working with the operating system and a different set when running a particular application program. The availability and effects of commands change drastically depending on the environment. One of the major advantages of menus over command language is that the menus serve to provide information about the current program state. Since users frequently have to move from one mode to another, explicit lists of commands in the form of menus have the additional advantage in such situations by restricting the allowable set of commands to those that are currently active. Menus may display only the allowable commands, or they may display the full set with inactive items grayed out as shown in Figure 3.5. The advantage of retaining the grayed-out items in the list is that the

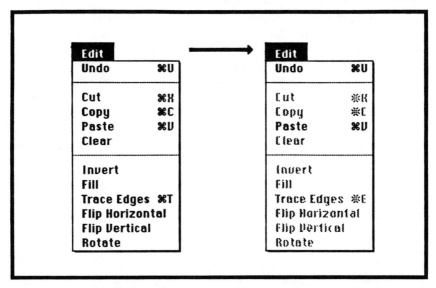

Figure 3.5.   An example of graying-out menu options when they become inactive (MacPaint®).

presence and location of items are fixed. Users are exposed to all the items and are informed as to which are current. What they may not know, however, is how to switch modes so as to activate desired items.

Items may also be switched or rephrased depending on the current state. In one state the menu may display the item "Open File." In another state, it may change the item to "Close File." Or it may display both "Open File" and "Close File" with one or the other grayed out. The first form allows for shorter lists, but may confuse even the experienced user who must carefully check the current state of the menu before selecting items. When menus switch options depending on context, it can be frustrating to the user who is perplexed about the cause-effect relationships between program state and menu lists. An interesting example is provided by MicroSoft-File™ in which the pull-down file menu has three states, depending on whether the user has opened a file, a report, or a form (see Figure 3.6). The spreadsheet program Excel™ handles this problem in a different way by providing a generic open command with a subsequent menu for specifying a spreadsheet, chart, or form (see Figure 3.7).

3.6 DECISION BY MENU SELECTION: DECISION MENUS

Menu systems can effectively be used to assist users in making decisions. Decision making is a complex task when the number of competing alternatives is fairly large and/or when the alternatives are composed of many positive and negative consequences. When the decision can be structured as a series of sequential choices, menu selection provides an appealing method of simplifying the task. Such systems present a series of choices that help formulate the decision. The decision may be as simple as which help file to access, or as complex and critical as deciding among alternative courses of action to rescue a stranded vehicle in outer space.

Decision systems may be implemented using menu selection in several different ways, depending on the formal properties of the decision and the method of handling decision trees and matrices of alternatives.

3.6.1 Decision Trees

One way of handling complex decisions is to use decision analysis to decompose a complex decision into a hierarchical decision tree. The decision tree represents each sequential choice as a node in a graph. Alternative actions on the part of the human are represented as arcs pointing to other choice nodes or to states of the world. Alternative

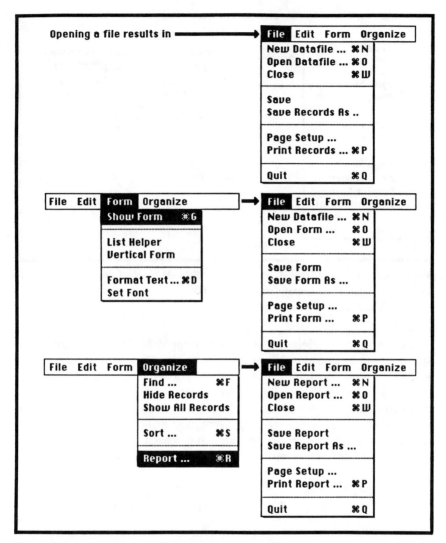

Figure 3.6. Changes in pull-down menus caused by other menu selections in MicroSoft™ File. The File menu has three states depending on whether one has opened a file, a form, or a report.

consequences in the environment are also represented by arcs leading to subsequent choice nodes or states of the world. In a sense, decision making then entails traversing the decision tree by making a selection at each choice point. The advantage of implementing the decision on a menu system is that choices are laid out at each level and the user can

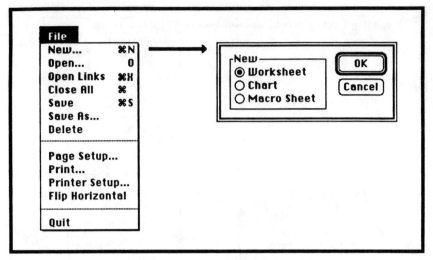

Figure 3.7. An example of adding an additional level of menu selections in MicroSoft™ Excel to specify the type of file.

easily traverse the decision tree by making selections. However, the shortcoming is that the decision maker may focus on only one choice node at a time and ignore more remote consequences. In general, the goal of decision analysis is to provide a more comprehensive analysis in order to locate an optimal terminal node. To some extent menu systems may avoid this problem by displaying one or several plies down the decision tree. However, when extensive search through the decision tree is required, other approaches are called for, such as Bayesian analysis or tree-searching techniques.

When menu selection attempts to implement a decision tree, it should be evaluated on how well it captures the decision process and whether it has hidden consequences. It is easy to misrepresent the decision space in the menu tree and lead the user down a "garden path." Figure 3.8 gives an example that is not atypical of many such applications. The extremely complicated decision of career choice is laid out in terms of interests and abilities. Such systems may be provocative and even instructive in the way they elucidate a number of decision factors. But they are often misleading in that early choices have unanticipated consequences on subsequent options. Although users may be ambivalent about early choices, they are nevertheless forced to commit themselves to one path, thereby eliminating other paths that would have led to more desirable options. Such systems have the potential of actually degrading decision-making ability. However, properly used,

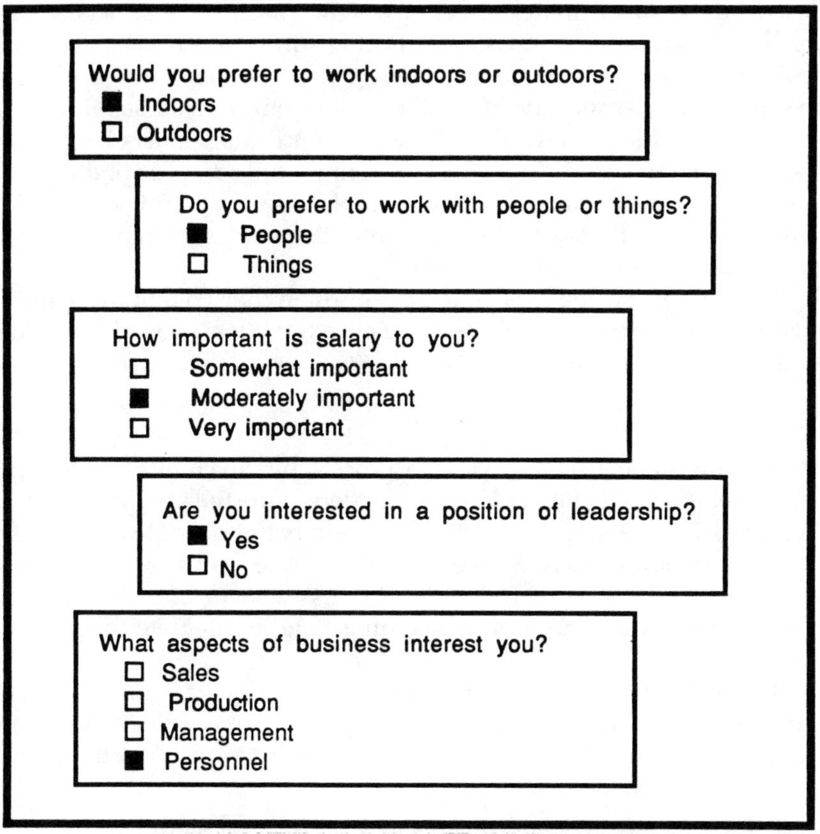

Would you prefer to work indoors or outdoors?
■ Indoors
☐ Outdoors

Do you prefer to work with people or things?
■   People
☐   Things

How important is salary to you?
☐   Somewhat important
■   Moderately important
☐   Very important

Are you interested in a position of leadership?
■ Yes
☐ No

What aspects of business interest you?
☐   Sales
☐   Production
☐   Management
■   Personnel

Figure 3.8.   An example of using menu selection in the decision-making task of career choice. (Note that the order of selections, choice structure, and completeness of the tree can lead to substantial differences in choice.)

menu selection may capture the decision sequence in a way that explicates a complex decision process in a straightforward and complete manner in order to facilitate the decision process. In general, one would expect menu selection to be most applicable when the structure of the decision tree is well-known or clearly determined by a prescribed rule.

3.6.2 Decision Matrices

Many decisions involve a selection among a complex set of alternatives. Decision theory provides a formal method of representing alternatives as sets of attributes. Alternatives can be thought of as multidimensional vectors of attributes. Consider running shoes, for example. They may be described by the attributes of price, weight, midsole construction, outsole construction, type of last, and heel lift. In turn, physical attributes result in subjective preferences along the attributes, such as overall comfort, shock absorption, flexibility, toe room, overall stability, heel counter, sweat loss, and so on. Table 3.3, for example, lists 15 running shoes with their price, and judge's ratings on seven attributes. The decision task is difficult even in this simple case of deciding on running shoes. Decision theory in conjunction with menu selection, however, can simplify the task considerably.

Decision theory operates on the assumption that a quantifiable utility measure exists for each attribute. Each alternative i can then be described by an array of numbers:

$$A_i = \{u_{i1}, u_{i2}, u_{i3}, \ldots u_{ik}, \ldots u_{iK}\}.$$

Decision making then involves a process by which attribute utilities are compared and combined in order to determine the preferred alternative. Decision theory has investigated a number of possible methods for doing this (Montgomery & Swenson, 1976). A few of these are outlined below. Each requires a different level of assessment of preference and makes different assumptions concerning how to integrate the relevant attributes.

Ordinal Dominance Rule. An alternative is selected if for every relevant attribute the decision maker prefers that alternative, or at least does not prefer another alternative over that one. To implement the prefer-

Table 3.3. Object-Attribute-Utility Matrix for Running Shoes

Brand and Model	Price	A	B	C	D	E	F	G
New Balance 470	$53	5	4	5	5	3	3	2
Asics Tiger Epirus	$80	5	5	5	4	4	4	5
Turntec Quantum Plus	$60	4	4	5	5	4	4	4
Saucony Shadow	$59	5	5	5	4	2	4	5
Asics Tiger Ultra 1000	$57	5	4	5	4	3	4	5
Saucony America	$48	4	4	4	4	3	4	5
Brooks Trilogy	$70	5	4	4	4	3	3	3
New Balance 1300	$130	4	5	4	4	4	4	3
Adidas ZX500	$75	4	4	3	3	5	4	2
Brooks Chariot	$62	3	3	3	4	5	5	3
Reebok DL5600	$56	4	4	5	4	3	3	4
Nike Venue	$60	3	3	3	4	4	4	4
Nike Vortex	$60	3	3	4	3	3	4	3
New Balance 575	$66	3	4	3	4	4	4	4
Etonic Mirage	$45	3	3	4	4	2	2	4

Note: 5 = better, 1 = worse, A = overall comfort, B = shock absorption, C = flexibility, D = toe room, E = overall stability, F = heel counter, G = sweat loss.
From "Running Shoes," *Consumer Reports*, October 1986, pp. 654–655. Reprinted by permission.

ence rule in menu selection, the system would present a menu for each attribute listing the available levels. Decision makers would select the preferred level for each and the system would identify the alternative(s) possessing those attributes. Unfortunately, it is usually the case that such ideal combinations do not exist and no alternative completely dominates the rest. In Table 3.3 for example, there are no running shoes that are the least expensive and have the highest ratings on all the attributes. Consequently, one must in some way relax the requirements.

Minimum Criteria Rule. An alternative is selected if it meets or surpasses a minimum criteria on each attribute set by the decision maker. This rule would again be implemented by presenting menus to the decision maker for each attribute listing the available levels. But instead of selecting only the preferred level, the decision maker selects all acceptable levels (e.g., price less than $60, overall comfort > 3, etc.). If no alternatives are located, the decision maker may iteratively relax the criteria until an alternative is selected. If a number of alternatives meet the criteria, the decision maker may raise the criteria.

The minimum criteria rule is similar to the "satisficing" rule discussed by Simon (1976) in which the decision maker selects the first alternative that meets a set of minimum criteria. The difference is that the satisficing rule is self-terminating; whereas, the minimum criteria rule requires that the system perform an exhaustive search through the entire set of alternatives.

It is usually the case that some attributes are more important than others. Neither of these two rules takes this into consideration. An alternative may be dropped because it does not meet a criterion on a relatively unimportant attribute. The remainder of the rules below take into consideration attribute importance.

Lexicographic Rule. An alternative is selected if it tends to be preferred over other alternatives on attributes judged to be of greater importance than others. To implement this rule the system would first present a menu of all of the attributes and the decision maker would select the most important. Then the levels on that attribute would be presented and the decision maker would select the preferred level. The system would then list the remaining attributes and the decision maker would select the next most important attribute. The levels on that attribute would be listed and the decision maker would select the preferred level, and so on. For example in Table 3.3, overall comfort might be selected first, and a rating of 5 preferred. Price might be next in importance, and among those having a rating of 5 on overall comfort, the price of $57 is preferred. The decision process would stop there since there is only one pair at that price.

Elimination by Aspects. An alternative is selected if it remains after the decision maker has sequentially eliminated alternatives not possessing desired attributes. A series of studies by Tverski (1972) suggested that in many situations people make decisions through a process of elimination. The decision maker considers one attribute at a time. Alternatives that do not possess a desired aspect are dropped from consideration. Those that possess the aspect are retained. The process continues until all but one alternative remains. The elimination by aspects rule corresponds closely to the process of menu selection. The rule may be implemented in a way similar to the lexicographic rule. The difference is that the rule is to eliminate alternatives not possessing an aspect as opposed to retaining alternatives having preferred levels of attributes.

There are several disadvantages with the elimination-by-aspects rule. Strict adherence to cut-offs can lead to less than desirable outcomes. For example, the first attribute may be price and the decision maker selects the aspect "less than $60." In this case Turntec Quantum Plus is eliminated although it is only one dollar more than Saucony Shadow. A second problem occurs with the desirability of one attribute that is contingent on the level of another. Only through backtracking and extensive exploration of the menu can the user consider tradeoffs between attributes.

Menu selection can be a very effective method of decision making when the order of the aspects reflects their importance and there are no important interactions between attributes (the presence or absence of one attribute negates the value of another). Unfortunately, menu-aided decision making can be misleading (a) if the order of aspects is ill-chosen, (b) if a weak preference eliminates alternatives that have desirable aspects on other attributes, or (c) if strong interactions exist between the values of attributes. When sales and promotion techniques are embedded in menus (e.g., menu selection for online catalog shopping services), the order of aspects may not be in the decision maker's best interest. For example, the shopper may wish to spend no more than $60 on running shoes. However, the menu may commit the decision maker to certain brand names or features first, and present price only near the end of the choice process. At that point, the decision maker may be lured to spend much more than $60.

Several algebraic rules have been proposed to optimize the outcome of the decision process. These rules make full use of the utility values and are used in computer-aided decision systems.

Weighted Utility Rule. Select the alternative that has the maximum sum of weighted utilities. Multiattribute utility theory (Keeny & Raifa, 1976) makes full use of the utilities of the attributes. For each alternative one may calculate an overall utility:

$$U_i = w_1 u_{i1} + w_2 u_{i2} + w_3 u_{i3} \ldots + w_k u_{ik} \ldots + w_K u_{iK},$$

where U_i is the overall utility for alternative i; u_{ik} is the subjective utility of attribute k on alternative i; and w_k is the weight of attribute k. For example, assume that the weights are 15, 30, 20, 10, 10, 5, 5, and 5 for price and the subjective attributes A through G. Furthermore, let the ratings in Table 3.3 represent the subjective utilities for the attributes, and let the utility for price equal 10/(log price). Then the running shoe with the highest evaluation is the Asics Tiger Epirus.

Cognitive Algebra Rules. Select the alternative that has the maximum value resulting from an algebraic rule that simulates the decision maker's judgment rule. Information integration theory has demonstrated that for different types of judgments people apply different cognitive rules in order to combine attribute values to make an overall assessment (Anderson, 1980; Norman, 1981).

$$U_i = f(u_{i1}, u_{i2}, u_{i3}, \ldots u_{ik}, \ldots u_{iK}).$$

It could be that consumers average the utilities of the attributes A through G and multiply by the subjective utility of price. If this is the case, then the running shoe with the highest evaluation would be the Asics Tiger Ultra 1000.

The weighted utility and cognitive algebra rules require considerable quantitative information from the user in order to make decisions. Functionally, they are much more complex than the other rules and as such are not particularly condusive to menu selection as a mode of interaction. What is important in decision making by menu selection is that the level of menu interaction be appropriate for the level of decision rule. Menu selection is beginning to be used in conjunction with decision support systems, computer-aided decision systems, and expert knowledge systems. In each case, menu selection may used to input information, to set criteria, and to query the system. In some cases, menu selection replaces command language interaction, but often it is used to structure the decision task according to a prescriptive model of decision making. Decision by menu selection represents one of the most challenging applications of menu selection.

3.7 INFORMATION RETRIEVAL BY MENU SELECTION: INFORMATION MENUS

Large databases may be (a) organized as hierarchically nested records of information, (b) indexed by a number of attributes called facets, or (c) linked as a relational database. For example, retail goods in a department store may be organized in a hierarchy from department (e.g., men's clothing, electronics, etc.) to category (e.g., men's suits, televisions, etc.) to subdivisions (e.g., size 38, 21 inch color) down to particular brands and models. An example of a faced database would be a file of photographs indexed by date, photographer, location, and subject. Some attributes might be collections of other attributes. If the subject is *people*, then they might also be indexed by number, group composition, activity, mood, and so forth. Finally, an example of a relational database would be hypertext documents. The original concept of hypertext was to link all written text together in a network such that a reader could travel from one article to another at will. In actual practice, the reader might start with a general introductory article on some subject that mentions more detailed ideas. The reader would then select one of these ideas and access other articles relating to it.

The structure of the database generally dictates the way in which users may search for information. Menu selection provides a particularly good interface for information retrieval since the user is often unfamiliar with the specific organization and content of the database. The user needs extensive prompting as to existing categories, available attributes, and permissible keywords. Because of the size and complexity of typical databases, even experienced users cannot be expected to be sufficiently knowledgeable about their structure. For that matter, one major reason for searching a database is to find information that was previously unknown to the user. Actually there are two different cases. Users may be searching for an unknown goal object that satisfies some preset conditions (e.g., a book on whale song). On the other hand, they may be locating a known goal object in order to access information about it (e.g., the call number of *Whale Song* by Tony Johnston). As users become more familiar with the system, they learn top-level menus and acquire knowledge about the inherent structure of the data base. But unlike command menus, users will rarely, if ever, become familiar with the extensive lower-level menu information except in well-searched local areas.

In general, menu familiarity is a function of the frequency of access and the user's prior knowledge about objects in the database. In turn, frequency of access is a function of user experience and level of menu. Figure 3.9 shows this relationship in terms of familiarity profiles for a selected set of inexperienced and experienced users and for known and unknown target objects as a function of menu information level. These profiles help to predict the amount of time, difficulty, and effort required on the part of users for accessing information. Designers should realize that the greatest difficulty will be at the intermediate levels of menu search for all but highly experienced users of relatively small databases. Consequently, great care needs to be taken at this point in providing help to users.

In many cases users may have less than a goal-directed approach to database retrieval. Indeed, they may be browsing the database to gain

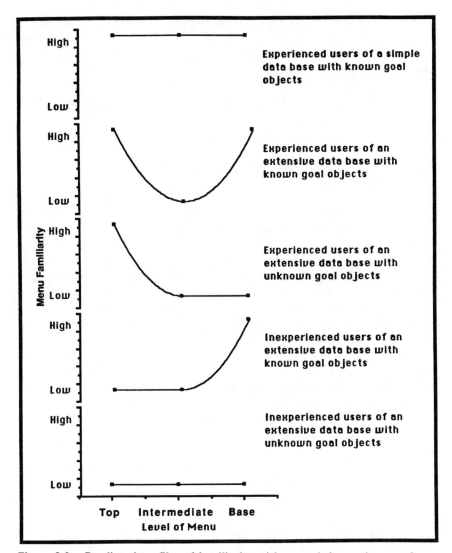

Figure 3.9. Predicted profiles of familiarity with menu information as a function of level in the search for experienced and inexperienced users with known and unknown goals.

an idea of what's there. Menus which list the sets of categories and/or facets quickly reveal the scope of the database. On the other hand, users may be pursuing a serendipitous walk through the pathways of a database. Menus allows for a relatively effortless selection of paths through the system.

Unlike command menus or decision menus, users of information menus are driven by the information displayed rather than commands required or alternatives desired. This is to say that users are concentrating on the output function of menu selection rather than on the pointing, execution, or input functions. To be sure many information retrieval systems use command menus and decision menus; however, for the actual process of the direct user search of a database, the output function is the most important.

3.8 CLASSIFICATION BY MENU SELECTION: CATEGORY MENUS

Classification is in a sense the inverse of information retrieval. The user has a known object and seeks to place it in a structure or the user specifies the parameters of the object by selecting settings. Menu selection is a natural technique for implementing classification. In particular, classification makes extensive use of the output function of menu selection. At a simple level, a menu may be used to classify cases by gender, income, age, and so on. At a more complex level instances may be classified by the presence or absence of a series of attributes or classified in a hierarchical structure of categories.

The problem of categorization has been the subject of much research in cognitive psychology (e.g., Rosch & Lloyd, 1978; Smith, Shoben, & Rips, 1974). Two different approaches can be taken in classifying instances. One method is to assign instances to categories on the basis of their similarity to a prototype. The prototype is the most typical example of the category. For example a robin is a good prototype of the category *bird*; whereas, an ostrich is not. For a large number of categories, prototypes may be hierarchically arranged in a menu system. The selection of prototypes (labels) and the organization of categories in the database can greatly affect the resulting classification.

The second method of categorization is to assign instances to categories on the basis of defining attributes. For example, an animal is classified as a bird if it has wings, lays eggs, and is warm blooded. The particular attributes used to define categories have a great effect on the resulting classification. Designers may inadvertently bias the user by the types of dimensions used or by the order of attributes in the menu. Early attributes have a tendency to be more salient to the user, setting the context of subsequent choices, and being ascribed as of higher importance than other attributes. The classification scheme used to generate the hierarchical structure sets an agenda for the user. This agenda may not be in the best interest of the user. Instead it may be designed to lead the user to commit to choices that he or she would not have selected under other situations.

The ordering of prototype categories or defining attributes may be set according to a number of concepts.

Scope. Higher levels in the hierarchy may pertain to divisions that are more global in nature. Lower levels move toward a stepwise refinement. Nested classifications must by necessity follow this plan. One must first specify the phylum before specifying the class in the animal kingdom. One must specify the country before specifying the city. Some hierarchies are completely nested. Other hierarchies may be crossed in the sense that lower levels share a number of alternatives in common. Linear menus are completely crossed since all levels have the same set of alternatives. Linear menus may be arranged in an arbitrary order but they may be effectively organized by scope. A news service may ask for region at the first level (e.g., world, national, and local); type of news at the second level (e.g., politics, business, science, arts, and society, etc.); and date at the third level. Since the attributes are crossed, the service could have date at the first level, type of news at the second, and region at the third.

Refinement. Objects may be classified as members of a linear sequence by successively subdividing the linear order. For example, the name Smith may be classified in an alphabetic list by first selecting Quigley-Sutton, then Silverman-Sutton, then Sloane-Smithers, and so on until single names are listed. In some cases this approach may be more efficient than typing in the name, depending upon the ratio of letters to type versus menus to select.

Subjective Importance to the User. The order of attributes may be programmed to agree with the order of importance to the user. Attributes along which objects seem to vary the most are presented first. For example, in classifying documents on one's disk, the user may first make a distinction between personal and business. Within personal, they may then be classified by addressee, and finally by date.

Formal Order. It is often the case in formal data collection that information is received in a prescribed temporal order and form. For example, in classifying claims for health insurance, the prescribed order corresponds to the printed claim form and takes advantage of the interaction mode of form file.

Natural Script. Finally, the order of attributes may follow a natural course of events or the process of some mental activity. In this way input follows the temporal progression of events and fits the expected protocol of interaction. For example, classification of automobile accidents may first specify location, direction, and speed of the moving vehicles; second, the point of impact; third, the amount of damage done; and finally, the determination of whose fault it was. By following an expected order of input the user anticipates each choice point and interprets it in light of a well-understood sequence.

3.9 SUMMARY

A variety of tasks may be performed using menu selection. In this chapter it was proposed that a task analysis be used to determine the functions to be implemented via menu selection. A theory of cognitive control was set forth in which system complexity/functionality was related to user/task need. It was shown how the system state diagram matrices should optimize user performance. A fourfold taxonomy of specific functions of menu selection was proposed listing pointing, command control, output, and input. Finally, four major types of systems were discussed which make use of menu selection, command menus, decision menus, information menus, and classification menus.

4
Cognitive Elements of Menu Selection

In order to understand the principles of designing for cognitive control, one must have a model of user behavior. Such a model for menu selection must incorporate the basic cognitive elements involved in the menu selection. These components include the processes of visual information search, judgment and decision processes, choice and response production, and evaluation of feedback. To an extent these processes follow the temporal sequence of menu selection at the level of the frame.

At a higher level, the model of the user must concern itself with the user's strategies of search and problem solving. If an item is not found on the first path through a database, how does the user redirect the path of search? In a command menu system how does the user minimize the number of steps to complete a task by changing the order in which subcomponents of the task are performed? The answers to these questions depend on the user's model of the system and strategies for navigation throughout that model. Mental models have been represented in several ways in cognitive psychology. Scripts have been used to lay out the expected series of events. Metaphors have been used to map the elements and relations from a familiar system to a less familiar one. Production rules have been used to capture the knowledge that the user may have about the workings of the system. In each case, the idea of a cognitive layout may be used to describe the way in which users may engage a particular model and cast a visual representation or layout of the model. Such a layout defines the way in which the user thinks about using the system and serves as a vehicle for formulating plans.

It will be seen that a number of models of user behavior can be formulated depending on the level of analysis and the processes of interest. There is no single unified model, but rather a collection of modeling techniques that can be applied to particular situations and performance variables. This chapter will cover a number of these models and techniques as they apply to menu selection.

4.1 THE MENU SELECTION PROCESS

The previous chapter dealt with the menu frame as a stimulus. This section will consider the cognitive processing of that stimulus frame. The menu selection process involves a number of cognitive elements. Within a particular menu frame, the user must read the alternatives, choose the desired option, effect the choice, and finally ascertain the consequences. Across menu frames, the user must maintain a sense of direction, evaluate proximity to the goal, and effect a plan of search or problem-solving strategy. This section will examine the process within the frame. A theoretical model of these processes will help to evaluate the design of menu frames.

Menu processing is both a time-relevant and information-relevant task. For the most part, theories have been more concerned with user response time than with information received or information transmitted. While time is an important variable, its overall impact on performance may not be great when it only accounts for a second here and there. However, the time that it takes to respond to a menu frame can be used to test models of how the user processes information received via menu labels and options. "Information transmitted" refers to the choices made by the user. Each time the user makes a selection, information is transmitted to the computer. Choice behavior is subject to user preferences, goals, and expectations. An adequate theory must involve both response time and information transmission.

4.1.1 Information Acquisition and Search

Figures 4.1 and 4.2 show several information processing models. The way in which a user scans a menu frame for information depends on the task and the user's prior knowledge about the frame. Typically the user starts with either an explicitly known target or a partially specified target. If the target is explicitly known (Figure 4.1), the user engages in a visual matching process. For each alternative scanned, the process detects either a match or a mismatch. Since errors can occur, the classic two-way table of possibilities from signal detection theory (Green & Swets, 1966) obtains what is shown in the bottom panel of Figure 4.1. It is generally the case that the processing time is faster for a match than for a mismatch. Second, to the extent that any transformation on the stimulus is required to process a comparison, response time will be increased. Third, to the extent that alternatives are similar and confusing, there will be an increase in the number of errors (e.g., Kinney, Marsetta, & Showman, 1966). Menus which use visually and semantically distinct alternatives will result in faster response times and fewer

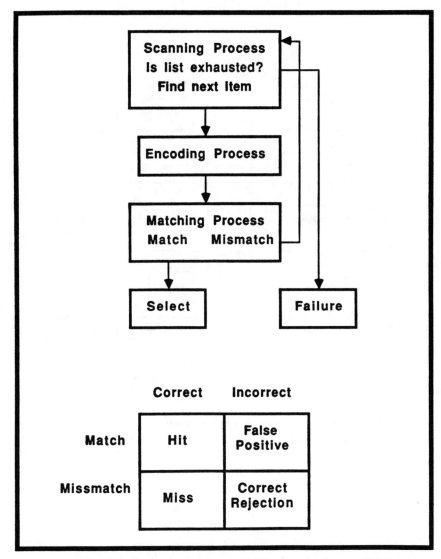

Figure 4.1. An information processing model for search of an explicitly known target. Bottom panel shows the signal detection matrix that results from selecting an alternative.

errors. In practice, however, labels are not always distinct and may lead to increased processing time and selection errors.

If the target is partially specified, the user engages an encoding and evaluation process as shown in Figure 4.2. The user must read each alternative, understand its meaning, and generate an assessment. If the

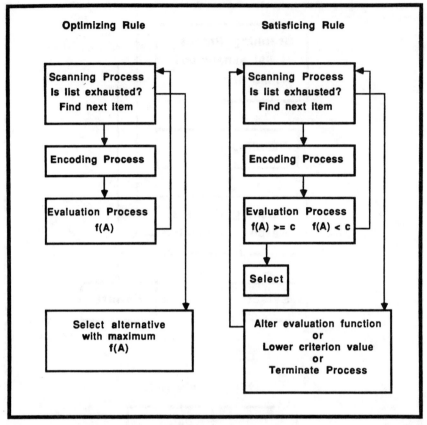

Figure 4.2. Information processing models for search of a partially specified target. The left panel shows the process given an optimizing rule. The right panel shows the process given a satisficing rule.

selection is construed as having a correct response, the user generates a subjective likelihood that the alternative satisfies the requirements of the partial specification. If the selection is construed as a preference on the part of the user with no correct answer, he or she generates a subjective utility for the alternative as a function of its worth relative to prior goals or requirements in the specification. For example, in information retrieval, if the user is looking for the population of India, alternatives such as "History," "Demographics," "Politics," "Religion," and "Facts at a Glance" may be evaluated for their subjective likelihood of supplying the answer. On the other hand, if the user is looking for something interesting about India, the alternatives would be evaluated on the basis of user preferences. In either case, an evaluation is made and the user makes a selection on the basis of its value.

In the case of partially specified goals, users may either evaluate all of the alternatives and select the alternative having the highest evaluation (left panel of Figure 4.2), or they may select the first alternative that exceeds a predetermined criterion value (right panel of Figure 4.2). This strategy is called *satisficing* (Simon, 1976). When the cost of an error or the negative consequences of selection of a less than optimal alternative is great, users will tend to engage in a careful and complete processing of alternatives. On the other hand, when time is of the essence, users will curtail their processing and select the first alternative that exceeds a preset criterion value (Beach & Mitchell, 1978).

One might initially suppose that novice users would search a menu by reading each item one by one from the top of the list down and stop when the desired item is reached. While this may be at times the case, the evidence is that things are not so simple (Card, 1982). Users often scan menus in an idiosyncratic manner, glancing across the list of alternatives, hoping to light upon the desired alternative.

Three alternative search models are shown in Figure 4.3. Search may be (a) a serial inspection of items, (b) a random inspection without repetition, or (c) a random inspection with replacement. A serial search requires that the user inspects each item one by one without skipping around. Random inspection without repetition allows the user to skip around, but requires the user to keep track of items already inspected. Finally, random search with replacement allows the user to skip around; but because an item may be randomly inspected over again, the search lacks efficiency.

Search strategies are also characterized by their stopping rule. In a self-terminating search, the user stops when the desired item is encountered. An exhaustive search requires the user to inspect all of the items prior to making a choice. Finally, in a redundant search after all the items have been inspected, the user still cannot make a choice and must reinspect some items. Menus and tasks that promote self-terminating search are expected to be faster than when users must examine all items exhaustively and redundantly. Typically, self-terminating search occurs when the user has an explicitly known target in mind and need only recognize a match between the target and an item. Self-terminating search may also occur if the subject uses the strategy of satisficing. If none of the alternatives meet the criteria before the list is exhausted, no decision has been achieved, and the user must adopt a different strategy. If the user kept track of an evaluation of each alternative, he or she may pick the alternative having the highest score. But more likely than not, the user may have to go back and reevaluate alternatives in order to weigh the pros and cons associated with items still in the running.

Even after assessing all of the alternatives, it is possible that none of them proves satisfactory. The user has exhausted the list of options and

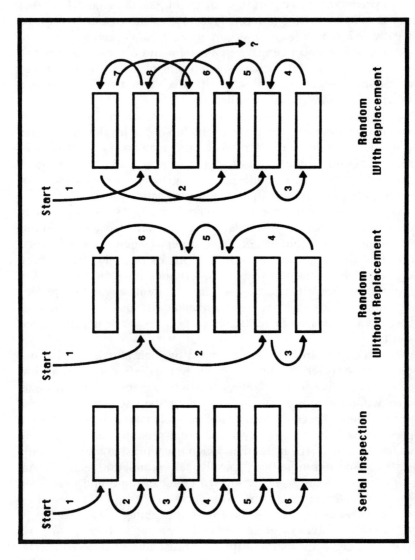

Figure 4.3. Three models of visual search of menu lists.

not found any that meet his or her needs. Since menu selection provides only a finite set of alternatives, the user may feel limited and frustrated. In traditional decision making, the decision maker at this point would attempt to generate new alternatives. Within the confines of menu selection, the user may need to move to some other area of the menu tree. But more often than not, the menu simply does not provide the particular alternative needed. And the user must abandon the search and try to solve the problem or find the information in a totally different manner. More will be said about this in a later section on strategies and problem solving.

The amount of time that it takes to process a menu and select an alternative depends on the processing model and the number of alternatives per menu frame. Menu processing time as a function of the number of items has become an important issue in designing efficient hierarchical menus. If broad menus require an inordinate amount of time to search, then designers are advised to limit the number of items per frame and increase the depth of the menu hierarchy. On the other hand, if each decision requires a certain amount of overhead time, then depth will add to the total time, and designers are advised to increase the breadth. Consequently, the type of search process within each frame is extremely important.

Response time for menu scanning is a function of the number of items scanned and the time required to scan each item. Lee and MacGregor (1985) presented a model in which search time within a frame is a linear function of the number of alternatives. For any search there will be an expected number of alternatives that will be inspected—E(A). For an exhaustive search, $E(A) = a$, is the total number of items in the frame. With a self-terminating search, if the correct alternative is at a random position, then $E(A) = (a + 1)/2$. Furthermore, E(A) may be greater than a if users need to re-evaluate alternatives in order to make a choice. Lee and MacGregor assume that the total time for each choice is

$$S = E(A)t + k + c,$$

where t is the time required to read one alternative, k is the key-press time, and c is the computer response time. The type of processing model operating determines the value of E(A).

Lee and MacGregor's model assume that users scan in a systematic fashion as if they were reading text. However, when alternatives are graphic or the alternatives can be recognized on the basis of graphic characteristics, the locus of search may jump around considerably. Card (1982) has proposed that users sample from a portion of the display randomly with replacement (rightmost panel of Figure 4.2). Each sample is dependent on a saccadic movement of the eyes. The assumption of random replacement means that the user may re-examine items. This model also assumes that the search is self-terminating. Card drew upon a model originally developed by Kendall and Wodinsky (1961) for searching for airplanes in the sky or for blips on a radar screen.

If p is the probability of finding the target on a single saccade, and k is the number of saccades required to find the target, then the cummulative probability of finding a target in k saccades under the assumption of sampling with replacement conforms to the geometric probability distribution:

$$P(k) = 1 - (1 - p)^k.$$

Assuming that each saccade takes about the same amount of time t, the average time to detect a target will be $S = t/p$.

If there is one correct alternative in a list of n, the probability of finding the target on a particular saccade will be $p = 1/n$ and $S = nt$.

Consequently, search time is again a linear function of the number of items. And the geometric model predicts the same average time as the Lee and MacGregor model for an exhaustive search. The major difference is that the predicted variability will be much greater in the Card model than in the Lee and MacGregor model. Lee and MacGregor emphasize reading time because they are primarily addressing videotext systems. Card emphasizes saccade and visual search time for command menus. Unfortunately, both models ignore the decision process and assume that choice time (distinct from reading or visual scanning time) does not vary with the number of alternatives. (A later section will address this issue.)

It is often the case that users have more than one possible target for which they are searching. Several different items may satisfy the requirements of the search. For example, the user may be looking for either "stop" or "quit." An extensive series of studies on visual and memory scanning (Neisser, 1963; Schneider & Shriffin, 1977; Shiffrin & Schneider, 1977) show the relationship between the number of possible targets and the total response time. The experimental task is analogous to menu selection. A subject is asked to search for a target in a display of characters. For example, one might be asked to search the array shown in the upper panel of Figure 4.4 and report when the target has been found. The target may be simply defined as "the letter L," or the "letters L, M, or Y." In general, the greater the number of possible targets, the longer it takes to detect the one that is actually there. The upper panel of Figure 4.5 shows the idealized results of such experiments using from one to six possible targets. The results indicate that there is a linear increase in search time as the number of possible targets increases. Presumably subjects scanned each item and then compared each of the

X	I	O	I	S
E	D	P	E	R
U	D	O	R	D
S	E	N	A	T
Q	U	P	Z	W
X	B	F	D	G
K	J	H	L	V
U	V	W	B	T

Figure 4.4. Visual display of target letters. Subject is to find a target simply defined as "the letter L" or the "letters L, M, or Y."

possible targets in the target set with the item. Each comparison added a constant amount of time.

The intriguing result of these studies occurs when subjects practice the same set of targets over an extended period of practice week after week and month after month. The results of these studies indicate that differences due to both the number of targets and the number of items scanned decrease greatly. The lower panel of Figure 4.5 shows the idealized results after practice. Schneider and Shiffrin (1977) found that subjects looking for the same targets eventually could search for four targets about as quickly as they could for one. They could also search through four characters about as quickly as they could through one.

These results indicate that scanning and recognition processes may become automatic with extensive practice. Detection becomes a rapid, effortless, and almost unconscious process. Users of menu selection systems that routinely proceed through the same processes of scanning and selection develop to a point where their response times are no longer affected by the number of items or number of targets. Furthermore, the selection process becomes so engrained that they do not think about it. The user of a word processor or spreadsheet package over many months of use no longer operates at the level of linear scanning for items. Recognition and selection becomes automatic, allowing the user to think about the task at hand rather than the control of the human/ computer interface.

4.1.2 Choice Process and Time

The choice process may either occur after the user has scanned and evaluated all of the alternatives or it may occur in conjunction with the scanning and recognition process. In an exhaustive search, the choice

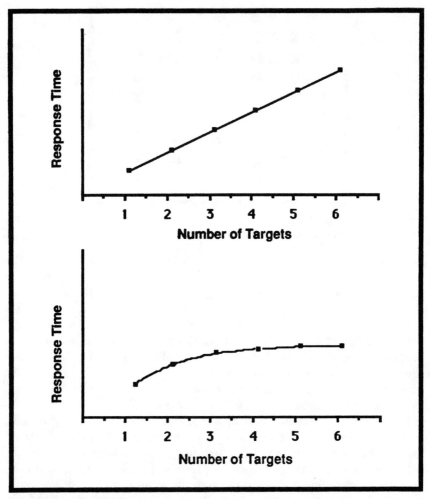

Figure 4.5. Idealized response times of unpracticed subjects (top panel) and highly practiced subjects (bottom panel) in a visual scan task as a function of the number of targets.

process occurs only after all of the alternatives have been scanned. In a self-terminating search, the choice process is engaged following the evaluation of each alternative.

When the choice is separated from the linear scanning of alternatives, it is governed by the same process as in choice reaction time experiments. In these experiments, the subject is presented with a linear array of potential stimuli and a corresponding array of response buttons. When a stimulus is presented, the subject must press the response button corresponding to the stimulus. For example, the stimulus may be a number 1, 2, 3, or 4, and the buttons may be listed as 1, 2, 3, and 4. The results of such an experiment are summarized in Figure 4.6. Response time is a linear function of the uncertainty as to which stimulus will be presented. For equally likely stimuli, uncertainty is given by the number of bits of information or $\log_2 n$. This relationship is known as the Hick–Hyman law (Hick, 1952; Hyman, 1953).

A log model has been proposed for menu selection by Landauer and Nachbar (1985), based on the Hick–Hyman law for choice reaction time and on Fitts' law for movement time (discussed in the next section). According to the Hick–Hyman law, the time that it takes to select one out of n items in a choice reaction time study is

$$S = a + b \log_2(n),$$

where a and b are constants. When applied to menu selection, the equation requires that the probability of selecting any item is equal (i.e.,

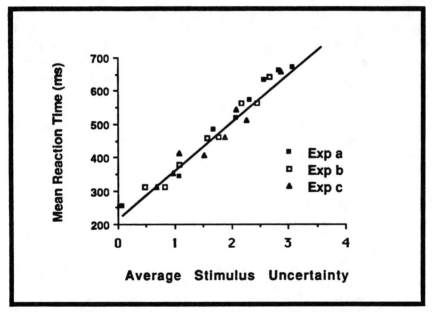

Figure 4.6. Mean reaction times for one subject. Hyman used small lights as stimuli and vocal responses. The three experiments varied stimulus uncertainty by (a) different numbers of equally frequent stimuli, (b) different relative frequencies of a fixed number of alternatives, and (c) different first-order conditional probabilities subject to equal relative frequencies.

(From "Stimulus information as a determinant of reaction time," by R. Hyman, 1953, *Journal of Experimental Psychology, 45*, 188–196. Copyright 1953 by the American Psychological Association. Reprinted by permission.)

1/n). This is generally not the case in real world menu systems. Menu items vary greatly in the probability of selection. When the probability is greater than 1/n, the choice time is even faster.

$$S = a - b \log_2(p_i),$$

where p_i is the probability that alternative i is the desired alternative.

The log law predicts that users can choose among a relatively large number of alternatives rapidly, since choice time is a linear function of the amount of information rather than n. However, it must be remembered that this is true only when reading time is negligible. Consequently, the log law pertains more to highly practiced command menus.

For complicated choice processes in which simple matching cannot be used as a basis for choice, response times will be subject to the difficulty of the choice as well as the number of alternatives. Menu selection becomes difficult when alternatives are complex bundles of attributes and no one alternative clearly dominates the rest. The evaluation process can be time-consuming and mentally taxing. It has been shown, however, that when the choice difficulty exceeds the maximum cognitive load of an individual, response time decreases. The decision maker may resolve the choice on an ad hoc basis and circumvent the evaluation process. Hogarth (1975) presented a model for response time of complex decision processes.

As noted earlier, the selection may be based on either a target match or based on (a) the subjective likelihood of an alternative being correct, or (b) the subjective utility of an alternative to the user. Subjective likelihoods and utilities can be scaled on the basis of choice probabilities with Luce's (1959) choice axiom. Suppose that the user is faced with a menu of n alternatives. Let p_i be the probability that alternative i is chosen out of the whole set, and let p_{ij} be the probability that alternative i is preferred over alternative j when only the alternatives i and j are available for selection. The choice axiom has two parts which are summarized below as they might apply to menu selection:

Axiom 1. If all pairwise preferences between alternatives are imperfect (e.g., $0 < p_{ij} < 1$ for all i and j) then a Constant Ratio Rule holds that the probabilities of choice from any subset of all the alternatives are naturally induced from p_i according to the rules of conditional probability. For example,

$$p(a_1|a_1, a_2)/p(a_2|a_1, a_2) = p(a_1|a_1, a_2, ..., a_n)/p(a_2|a_1, a_2, ..., a_n).$$

Consequently, in selection among four alternatives, if the probabilities are .10 and .40 for alternatives 1 and 2, then the ratio of probabilities in a binary choice would also be .25 (.10/.40) and the respective probabilities would be .20 and .80.

Axiom 2. If for any alternative a_i in the total set of alternatives there is an a_j such that $p_{ij} = 0$ (i.e., such that a_i is never preferred over a_j), then a_i may be deleted from the set of possible choices (i.e., a_i is never chosen from the total set). In other words, alternatives that are never chosen may be effectively considered as not existing.

These two axioms result in a ratio scale of measurement for the alternatives. A positive real number v_i can be assigned to each member a_i such that for $i = 1 ..., n$,

$$p_i = v_i / \sum_{j=1}^{n} v_j.$$

One possibility is to let $v_i = p_i$ since the sum of the probabilities equals one. Alternatively, $v_i = kp_i$.

Luce's choice axiom is particularly useful in predicting choice probabilities when the menu set is restricted. This occurs when menu items are not appropriate and are dropped from the list or grayed out. Restricted sets also occur when the user has already selected one or several items and found out that they are not correct or do not lead to the desired goal. The effect of Luce's choice axiom is that the probabilities are essentially normalized to the number of effective alternatives in the set. Table 4.1 shows what happens, for example, when there are initially six menu items and the set is restricted.

The probabilities change in the restricted sets so that there is a constant ratio between any pairs of alternatives. These probabilities can be used to predict the user choices in restricted sets.

Table 4.1. Example Choice Probabilities in Restricted Menus According to Luce's Choice Axiom.

Total Set		Restricted Set A		Restricted Set B	
Option	Probability	Option	Probability	Option	Probability
1	.10	1	.18	1	.14
2	.15	2	.27	2	.21
3	.20	3	.37	3	.29
4	.10	4	.18	4	.14
5	.30	—		—	
6	.15	—		6	.22

4.1.3 Response Process

In order for the user to effect a selection, he or she must produce an overt response that can be detected by the computer. Two basic types of response production are used. The user may be required to enter a code for the alternative (e.g., "press 1 for Account") or to point to the alternative using some sort of pointing device, such as cursor keys, a mouse, or a touch screen. Selection by code is complicated by the fact that it requires encoding and production processes. The user must read the instructions from the screen, encode their meaning, plan an intended action, and produce the overt response on the keyboard. Selection by pointing takes advantage of the fact that the pointing response has been highly practiced since infancy. Pointing requires the user to locate the current position of the pointing device (cursor or hand), locate the position of the desired alternative, and plan a trajectory from the current position of the pointing device to the desired alternative. To the extent, however, that any transformation or translation is required, time will be increased. The touch screen requires the least translation since it is a direct eye-hand response. The use of a mouse, drawing tablet, joy stick, or trackball requires a degree of transformation since the pointing device is generally on a horizontal plane, whereas the menu items are on a vertical plane. Furthermore, the user must translate the extent of hand movement to movement of the cursor. With practice, these times are reduced and the use of the pointing device seems quite natural.

Pointing by cursor keys requires the greatest amount of response transformation and translation since the trajectory must be translated into a discrete sequence of moves. For simple list menus, the cursor may be positioned with only the up and down arrows. For array menus and pull-down menus, all four arrow keys may be required. To change direction, the user must change keys. This requires additional response time and could produce errors. While cursor key positioning is rather simple with list menus, it becomes excessively difficult with large array menus requiring the user to traverse long distances.

Studies on stimulus–response compatibility strongly suggest that the layout of the alternatives on the screen match the physical layout of the response buttons (Fitts & Seeger, 1953; Fitts & Switzer, 1962). Without such compatibility, the user must engage a translation process to remap the location of items. The worst cases are when the layouts are reversed and when directional indicators are reversed as in mirror writing (i.e., physical movement to the right moves the cursor to the left on the screen).

Motor response time depends on the distance from the current position of the pointing device to the location of the desired target as well as the difficulty of hitting the target. For analog pointing devices the time depends on the distance to the target and the size of the target. According to Fitts' law (Fitts, 1954), the time that it takes to move a target is a logarithmic function of the ratio of its distance and width:

$$R = a \log (d/w) + b,$$

where, d is the distance to the target, w is the width of the target, and a and b are constants. For analog movements motor time is inversely related to the log of the width of the target. Consequently, it would behoove designers of analog input devices to display large menu targets rather than small buttons.

Motor response time for discrete pointing using arrow keys is governed by a different process. One would expect that the time to select an alternative using arrow keys would be a linear function of the $x + y$ distance of the cursor from the alternative.

$$R = a(d_x + d_y) + b,$$

where d_x and d_y are the x and y displacements of the cursor position from the target location, and a and b are constants. Although this model is intuitive and simple, it is not entirely correct. In general, with such motor movements, there is a large initial startup time or acceleration and a slow-down time or deceleration upon approaching the target. Nevertheless, the equation serves as a good first approximation for motor time.

For short list menus, cursor arrow keys may be faster than analog pointing devices. However, when there are a large number of alternatives, the analog device has the distinct advantage.

In both discrete and analog situations, the constant b is the time to plan and move to the response device. If the user's hand is already on the device, the time to move to the device is eliminated. However, a common complaint is that to use a pointing device one has to take one's hands off home position on the keyboard and locate either the arrow keypad or the analog device. If the majority of time is spent navigating through menus, then the home position may in practice be on the pointing device. The problem is critical only when the user must frequently alternative between devices.

4.1.4 Evaluation and Error Detection

Once the user has made a selection, the system generally provides feedback of some type. The feedback may be the receipt of some information, the location of a target item, the execution of a function, or the presentation of a subsequent menu frame. The feedback may immediately indicate to the user that the selected alternative was correct or incorrect. If it is correct, the user is reinforced and the processes leading to that selection are strengthened. For example, prior to the selection, the user may have assessed only a .5 probability that the alternative would lead to the goal. Following the feedback, that probability can be updated.

On the other hand, feedback may not directly indicate whether the selection was correct. The user may have only partial knowledge about the success of the prior selection. This is particularly true in hierarchical menus. The next frame may give some indication about whether the user is on the right path; but since it is not the target item itself, the user cannot be sure if he or she is on the right path. If the feedback is positive, the user is likely to continue. If it is negative, the user may turn back depending on how unlikely the path now appears. Consequently, feedback engages another decision-making process in a hierarchical menu search. How this affects the search strategy will be discussed in the next section.

4.2 PROBLEM SOLVING AND SEARCH STRATEGIES

Although much goes on at the frame level of menu processing, the cognitive control of the interface is more properly positioned at a global level. How does the user plan a task that requires a series of menu selections? What is the user's strategy for effecting a search through a complex database? These questions strike at the very essence of thinking and problem solving as they apply to cognitive control of the human/computer interface.

The menu interface provides the user with options that if applied in the right order may achieve the goal state. For example, the goal may be to align the left edges of cubes in a three-dimensional drawing program. The user must use the menu interface to select the cubes, select their left edges, and finally select the command to align. The exact order of operation is determined by the rules of the system. Each menu selection constitutes a move which may or may not get closer to the desired state. The steps to solving such problems include planning the solution, carrying it out, and finally checking the results. The difficulty and length of each step depend on the complexity of the problem. The drawing program above is relatively easy and the length of each stage is short. The problem of generating a three-dimensional image of a space station using a drawing program is much more difficult yet involves the same idea.

Menu interfaces often do more than just provide options. Problems or tasks that are repetitively solved or performed in the same way can be gracefully directed by the menu. For example, in an electronic mail system there is a natural order of steps that may be incorporated in the order of menus—check if there are new messages, read the first message, respond, read the next message, respond, and so on. The menu system can incorporate this order and bypass a number of redundant steps by initially listing new messages. The user may immediately select a message to read and then select options to reply, forward, or delete. One system that explicitly attempts to incorporate the user's plan of work gives the user an "inbox" menu in which the user may either select messages to view or select other program functions. The concept is to position the user at the most likely point of entry rather than at the beginning of a hierarchical command path.

4.2.1 Heuristics

A number of heuristics, strategies, and problem-solving styles have been discussed in the literature that are relevant to search in menu selection. Heuristics are plans for attacking problems. They are usually simple sequences of steps that generally work but are not guaranteed to result in a solution in the same way that an algorithm would. The advantage of heuristics is that they require a minimum of time and effort.

Generate-Test. The generate-test heuristic is one of the simplest heuristic strategies with only two steps (Newell & Simon, 1972): (a) generate a candidate for a solution, and (b) test to see if it is actually a solution. If the candidate fails the test, the problem solver keeps generating candidates until the goal is attained. The generate-test heuristic is, however, only as effective as the heuristic is at generating potential responses. The advantage of menu selection is that the user generates responses by selecting options. Newell and Simon (1972) note four difficulties in the generate-test strategy. First, it may be difficult to generate candidates. Menu selection reduces this problem by explicitly listing a set of potential candidates. Second, it may be hard to test to see if the candidate is actually a solution. For explicit targets a simple matching test is all that is required. For partially specified goals, the test may be more complex. And for complex problems requiring a number of steps, it may be extremely difficult to evaluate if the selection is on the right path. For example, it is easy to generate a chess move, but very difficult to know if it is the best of all possible moves. Third, if there are a large number of candidates with a low probability of any one achieving the goal, the generate-test heuristic is unlikely to work. A random trial-

and-error approach is doomed to failure in complex systems and large search spaces. On the other hand, in simple systems, the trial-and-error approach may work well. In fact, a number of systems advocate trial and error as a good way to start learning how to use functions. Fourth, it may be that the correct solution has a low probability of being selected by the problem solver. The user is likely to pick a number of other candidates before selecting the correct one. Menu selection as an interface to problem solving may help to direct the problem solver to the correct solution by the order in which alternatives are listed. Highly likely candidates should be listed first and unlikely candidates buried at the bottom of the menu.

One of the greatest problems with the generate-test heuristic is that often a candidate cannot be evaluated until it is completely generated. For many problems this is inefficient. The problem solver may be able to evaluate partial solutions. For example, in solving a crossword puzzle, one does not fill in all of the spaces and then check to see if it is the correct solution. Instead one looks for and evaluates partial solutions along the way. Furthermore, there is a great utility in breaking the problem into subgoals. The problem-reduction approach (Nilsson, 1971) reduces the overall size of the search space. Menu systems that organize search into a series of substeps can make effective use of the problem-reduction approach. Rather than searching an index of all newspaper articles, the system may break the search into the substeps: (a) select the year, (b) select the topic, and (c) finally search through the remaining articles. Similarly in a drawing program, problem-reduction may be implemented by allowing the user to construct elementary objects as subgoals. These objects may then be selected for use in achieving more complex goals.

Hill Climbing. A similar strategy takes as its metaphor the idea of hill climbing. One can climb to the top of a simple hill (monotonically increasing in height from any point) blindfolded by merely taking each step so that it results in a higher position than before. Similarly, in the formal strategy of hill climbing, the problem solver selects each move so that an evaluation function results in a higher value than the previous move. Ultimately, one assumes that the goal has been reached when no move can be found that increases the function. In a menu selection system, each menu selection constitutes a move. The resulting frame generally provides informative feedback indicating if the user is getting "hotter" or "colder."

More formally, assume that for each selection i the user has an expected value of the feedback that will be received—$e(F_i)$. When the user evaluates the feedback, it results in a subjective value, $s(F_i)$. These two values are compared. If $e(F_i) - s(F_i)$ is less than a criterion value c_i, then the user will proceed. If it is not, the user will terminate or redirect the search path. It is expected that the value of c_i will depend on the depth of search and on the ease of redirecting the path in a more profitable direction. Users will probably be more and more reluctant to shift off the path the further they have committed themselves to a particular course. Consequently, the further down the tree and closer to the terminal level, the greater c_i. Moreover, if there was another alternative in a previous menu judged to have a high likelihood of leading to the goal, the value of c_i will be reduced. Users will shift to another path if it requires little extra in the way of repositioning. The option to move back to the previous menu frame allows repositioning at a local level; whereas, the option to move back to the top of the menu allows repositioning at a distal but fixed level. Very few systems allow for user-set repositioning by way of markers. An innovative technique would be to allow the user to define markers to be placed at various points along the search as one might drop bread crumbs on a path through a maze to find one's way back. Search could be repositioned by selecting one of the markers and restarting from there.

Studies of hill climbing indicate that problem solvers tend to concentrate on only one attribute at a time in selecting their next move rather than selecting moves that change several attributes and achieve the goal in fewer moves (Norman, 1983). In a database search of a library catalog, this would be analogous to searching first on the basis of an author's name to reduce the set, and then switching to search on the basis of title. Ultimately, the user may need to switch back to a name search if the title search does not result in a find.

Hill climbing is an effective strategy only if the evaluation function is well behaved and there is only one global maximum. If this is not the case, the problem solver may only find the solution by taking a detour in which the evaluation function goes down for one or several moves before it raises again. Moreover, if local maxima exist, the problem solver may get trapped at what appears to be the solution, but is not really the optimal selection.

Test-Operate-Test-Exit. One of the basic ideas behind the generate-test heuristic is that of feedback. The problem solver monitors the current state and generates responses to change that state to satisfy some criterion. But many tasks require a more complicated strategy. Miller, Galanter, and Pribram (1960) discuss a strategy that not only incorporates the idea of feedback, but also the hierarchical structure of interlocking component processes. This plan is called *TOTE* for Test-Operate-Test-Exit. A simple plan for hammering nails is shown in the left panel of Figure 4.7. The object is to hammer a nail until it is flush with the surface. The first stage is to test the nail. If it sticks up, then one goes to the second stage; otherwise one stops. The second stage is to test the hammer. If it is down, one lifts it up, otherwise one goes the third

96

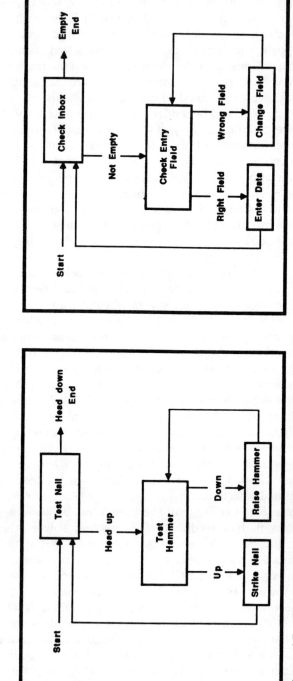

Figure 4.7. The Test-Operate-Test-Exit algorithm for hammering a nail (left panel) and for data entry (right panel).

stage. The third stage is to strike the nail after which one goes to the first stage.

Many tasks involve just this sort of combination of feedback and hierarchical structuring of components. The right panel of Figure 4.7, shows the same sort of TOTE for a data entry task. The first stage is to check the inbox for data. If there is data, then one goes to the second stage; otherwise one stops. The second stage is to test the entry field. If it is not the correct one, the correct field is selected; otherwise one goes to the third stage. The third stage is to enter the data after which one goes to the first stage again.

The value of hierarchical plans for solving problems has been emphasized by Simon (1969). To illustrate the advantage of hierarchical structure, Simon presented a parable about two watchmakers, Tempus and Hora. Both made watches consisting of 1,000 parts. Tempus built his watches in one assembly of 1,000 parts. However, if he was interrupted in the middle of the assembly by a customer, the partially assembled watch fell apart into its original pieces. Hora's watches were built in units of 10 pieces. Ten single parts make a unit, 10 units made a larger component, and the 10 components made the entire watch. If Hora was interrupted he lost only a small portion of the unfinished watch. Simon estimated that Tempus would lose an average of 20 times as much work per interruption as Hora. Although, problem solvers may not suffer from the problem of loosing prior work, hierarchical structure may prove beneficial in that the problem solver needs to think about only a limited number of elements at a time.

Menu interfaces are particularly germane to problem solving involving simple hierarchies. Menu systems can incorporate the hierarchical nature of the task into their own structure. The question is whether they do so in an effective and efficient manner that facilitates performance.

Means-Ends Analysis. Another important strategy in problem solving is the means-ends analysis. This heuristic involves a number of components already discussed. In the means-ends analysis the problem solver works on one goal at a time. If that goal cannot be achieved, the problem solver sets a subgoal of removing the obstacle that blocks that goal. The problem solver constantly monitors the difference between the current state and the goal state desired. If a difference exists, an attempt is made to generate a response that will reduce that difference. Simon (1969, p. 112) summarized the means-ends analysis as follows: "Given a desired state of affairs and an existing state of affairs, the task of an adaptive organism is to find the difference between these two states and then to find the correlating process that will erase the difference."

A typical problem for the computer user that would be addressed by the means-ends analysis might be the task of viewing File X. But this goal is blocked because the file is not loaded and the user doesn't know the path to that file. Consequently, the first subgoal is to find File X. This may be solved by getting a directory listing. But that can only be accomplished if the program listing the directory can be run. So the sub-subgoal is to run the directory program. Running the directory program may itself entail the solution of a number of sub-subgoals. Once File X is found, the second subgoal is to run a browsing program to view the file. Again, a number of sub-subgoals may have to be achieved to accomplish this.

The means-ends analysis can be mentally taxing when the user must keep track of a number of embedded subgoals. Although the computer may easily store such goals on a push-down-pop-up stack, it is not so easy for the user. However, solutions to problems requiring the means-ends analysis may be facilitated by the use of hierarchical menu selection and event trapping menus. The main advantage of the menu interface is the ability to traverse goal and subgoal states up and down the hierarchy of operations and to access menu options from numerous points during the interaction. The menu interface reduces the memory load of the user by keeping track of goal states (e.g., location in the hierarchical structure) and prompting the user for input appropriate to each subgoal. Furthermore, the hierarchical menu structure may allow the user to solve subgoals in an order more amenable to human thinking rather than in an order dictated by formal problem solving. For example, in order to view File X in the problem above, the user of a menu selection system might first select a browsing program from a menu before knowing the location of File X. The browsing program prompts the user for a file. A means-end analysis reveals that the user should have solved the problem of the location of File X first. The user would then have to back out of the browsing program in order to find the file. However, a menu interface that allows the user to select concurrent processes, frees the user from having to perform tasks in a predetermined order. While in the browsing program, the user could select the file directory program, find the file, and pass its location to the browsing program.

4.2.2 User Strategies and Styles

The types of strategies that users employ and their effectiveness depend not only on the tasks but on characteristics of the users. For example, users vary in their repertoire of generating solutions—an attribute important in the generate-test heuristic. Users differ greatly in their ability and willingness to plan ahead—an attribute important in the means-ends analysis. Finally, users differ in the degree with which they will pursue a particular course of action before they give up. This attribute is particularly important in menu selection since problem solving often involves a search through a hierarchical menu structure.

Search behavior by problem solvers have been characterized as either (a) shallow and broad, or (b) narrow and deep. A shallow problem solver is likely to survey a wide number of possible solutions but explore them only superficially. This type of problem solver considers a solution and if it is not immediately apparent that it will led to the solution, drops the alternative and turns to another one. This user is likely to look only one or two levels deep before going back to the top again. On the other hand, the narrow and deep problem solver is likely to limit his or her search to only a few alternatives and explore them in depth. In this style, the problem solver picks one path and follows it out until it either results in the solution or its potential is completely exhausted. Different types of problems are more conducive to a solution by different styles of problem solving. The shallow and broad strategy is more appropriate for placing pieces in a jigsaw puzzle; whereas, the deep and narrow strategy is more appropriate for solving the Tower of Hanoi puzzle or playing chess. In a similar way different types of menu systems are more conducive to different types of search strategies. The shallow and broad strategy seems appropriate for the broad range of easily scannable alternatives provided by pull-down menus. The deep and narrow strategy would be more appropriate for navigation in a complex database.

A mixture of these strategies is known as progressive deepening. In this strategy each alternative is explored to a certain level. If no solution is found, alternatives are pursued to a further level. Thus, a progressive deepening is conducted in search. This type of strategy is particularly useful when there are a fair number of possible solutions and it is not clear to what extent each alternative must be explored to determine its suitability. Unfortunately, it is hard to see how users of a hierarchical menu system could effectively use this strategy unless they could keep track of previous search depths and jump to those points quickly. However, menu interfaces that allow concurrent searches or that allow the users to place bookmarks for fast return can facilitate the progressive deepening strategy.

Search styles can be much more complex than merely varying on depth. A number of patterns and additional factors have been characterized by Canter, Rivers, and Storrs (1985) for navigation through complex data structures. Canter et al. defined six indices that could be used to quantify search patterns. The patterns were based on paths, rings, loops, and spikes in database traversal (see Figure 4.8).

Pathiness: A path is any route through the data that does not visit any node twice. It starts at one point and terminates at another. Menu traversal may be characterized by many short paths (high pathiness) or few long paths (low pathiness).

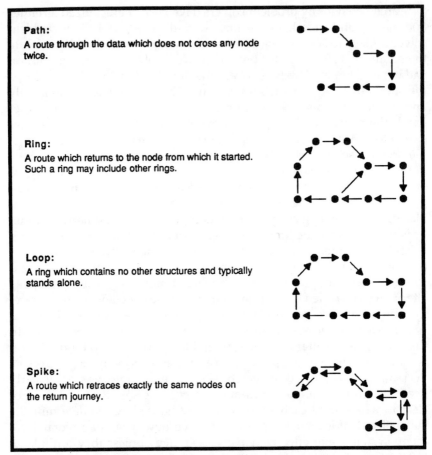

Path:
A route through the data which does not cross any node twice.

Ring:
A route which returns to the node from which it started. Such a ring may include other rings.

Loop:
A ring which contains no other structures and typically stands alone.

Spike:
A route which retraces exactly the same nodes on the return journey.

Figure 4.8. Four types of menu traversal. (Points indicate nodes in the database and lines indicate route and direction taken.)

From "Characterizing user navigation through complex data structures," by D. Canter, R. Rivers, and G. Storrs, 1985, *Behaviour and Information Technology, 4,* 93–102. Copyright 1985 by Taylor & Francis, Ltd. Reprinted by permission.

Ringiness: A ring is a route through the data which returns to the node from which it started. Since a ring has a home base, it may be thought of as an "outing." Such a ring may include other rings. Menu traversal may be characterized by many rings returning to home base (high ringiness) or a few rings (low ringiness).

Loopiness: A loop is a ring which contains no other rings. A loop is a simple ring and is distinguished by the fact that no node is visited twice except the home base.

Spikiness: A spike is a route through the data which goes out to a node and returns exactly the way it came. Hierarchical databases are likely to result in high spikiness since one could traverse the hierarchy down and retrace the path back out.

NV/NT: The ratio of the number of nodes visited (NV) to the total number of nodes available in the system (NT) gives the proportion of available nodes utilized by the user. A high NV/NT ratio indicates a more comprehensive coverage of the database.

NV/NS: The ratio of the number of different nodes visited (NV) to the total number of visits to nodes (NS) gives the proportion of first time visits. A low NV/NS ratio indicates a high degree of repetitive visits to nodes.

Canter et al. (1985) used these definitions to further characterize search strategies.

Scanning: When users are scanning, they tend to cover a large area of the menu system, but without going into great detail or depth. Scanning will result in a long spikes and short loops which traverse through the database but do not extend very far into it. It is characterized by a high proportion of nodes visited relative to the total number of nodes available.

Browsing: Users may be happy to go wherever the data leads them. Users will pursue a path as long as it sustains their interest. Browsing behavior may be characterized by many long loops and a few large rings.

Searching: When users are searching for a particular target, the pattern may include ever-increasing spikes with a few loops. It is also characterized by a high redundancy of nodes revisited relative to the total number of different nodes visited.

Exploring: Many different paths of medium or short length suggest that the users are trying to grasp the extent and nature of the database. They may be attempting to gain a global map of the menu system.

Wandering: Users may wander more or less randomly through the database. The unstructured journey will lead to many medium-sized rings.

These strategies give an idea of the different types of search patterns that may occur as a function of motivational factors. Although Canter et al. characterized them in terms of the indices defined earlier, it remains to be seen whether one can delineate the type of search strategy based on the six indices.

4.3 COGNITIVE LAYOUTS OF MENTAL MODELS

Problem solving is governed by the way in which the problem space is represented. One may represent a problem mathematically, another visually, and still another metaphorically. Studies of problem-solving behavior suggest that the key to problem solving is more often having the proper representation rather than the ideal strategy (Wickelgren, 1974).

When the user plans a task involving a menu selection system, both the menu and the task domain comprise the problem space. The menu representation and the task representation help to define the way in which the user thinks about a problem. The term *mental model* has been used loosely to refer to these representations in the sense that the user adopts a conceptual model of computer operations that may relate abstract ideas (e.g., storage registers, I/O drivers, etc.) to concrete things (e.g., mailboxes, TV channels, etc.). The user's mental model of the system has been defined and illustrated numerous ways in the literature (Norman & Draper, 1986). Representations may take the form of metaphors, schemata, scripts, or cognitive layouts. These representations are by no means exhaustive or nonoverlapping. However, they serve to characterize the way in which users think about cognitive control of the human/computer interface.

4.3.1 Menu Selection as a Metaphor

The purpose of a metaphor as a literary device is to transfer the reader's concrete knowledge about a familiar thing to an unfamiliar subject being written about. The author draws upon the wealth of existing knowledge to shed light on a novel topic. It has been suggested that the same process of transference be capitalized upon in human/computer interaction. Carroll and Mack (1985) discussed the issue of how interfaces can be designed to take advantage of the metaphors new users generate spontaneously as they apply their prior knowledge to novel learning situations. The extent to which the design suggests and actually conforms to the metaphor determines the amount of transference of knowledge. Part of the knowledge transferred is prior experience in problem-solving strategies. For example, if the metaphor for a telecommunication program is a scrolling teletype, then the user would infer that the text that scrolled off the top of the screen can be viewed again by scrolling backwards.

In most metaphors for computer operations, the base is more familiar but the novel area is more functionally rich. The typewriter is well understood, but it's functionality is considerably less than the word processor. Similarly, the card catalog is well understood, but it's functionality is considerably less than the online catalog. However, when it comes to metaphors for human/computer interaction the functionality of the base is often greater than that of the computer application. Natural language has greater familiarity *and* functionality than computer command languages. In a similar but more structured way, restaurant menu selection has a greater familiarity *and* functionality than computer menu selection.

Computer menu selection is, quintessentially, a metaphor. The original knowledge base is that of ordering items in a restaurant. However, the correspondence of elements between the two domains runs deeper than a superficial application of the metaphor. *Webster's New Universal Dictionary of the English Language* (1976) gives the following definition of menu:

menu n.   [Fr., small, detailed, from L. *minutus*, pp. of *minuere*, to lessen, from *minor*, less] **1.** a detailed list of the foods served at a meal; bill of fare. **2.** the foods served.

The menu represents a finite set of items available at the establishment. The customer then makes a selection and informs the server. The order is then prepared and served to the customer. In a similar vein the computer displays a detailed list of options available using that program. Current applications of computer menu selection bear a strong correspondence to restaurant menus and reinforce the metaphor. However, as with every metaphor, there are certain aspects that may either be deficient or enhanced in the target domain.

Table 4.2. A Comparison of Restaurant Menus (*n* = 56) and Computer Menus (*n* = 4)

Attribute	Restaurant		Computer Programs	
Total Number of Selectable Items	119.0	(83.1)	316.4	(158.5)
Number of Pages (Frames)	3.8	(3.5)	70.2	(65.7)
Number of 1st-Level Categories/Items	11.0	(6.3)	7.8	(3.6)
Average Items per 1st-Level Category	8.0	(4.7)	6.0	(3.2)
Average Items per 2nd-Level Category	3.4	(1.7)	5.4	(3.2)
Average Items per Bottom-Level Category	2.5	(3.0)	4.7	(3.0)

Note: The computer programs were Smartcom II™, Lotus 123™, Wordstar 3.31™, Procomm 2.4™, and Word Perfect 4.2™.
From "The menu metaphor," by K. L. Norman and J. P. Chin, 1989, *Behaviour and Information Technology, 8,* 125–134. Copyright 1989 by Taylor & Francis, Ltd. Reprinted by permission.

Noman and Chin (1989) provided a comparison between restaurant menus and computer menus used in common software packages such as Lotus 123™. Their sample of computer programs contained nearly three times as many selectable items as the restaurant menus. However, the ratio of pages in restaurant menus to frames in computer menus did not match that ratio. Restaurant menus contained considerably fewer pages with many more items per page. The organization of items also varied. The number of items per category level (i.e., per frame) was somewhat greater for restaurant menus for first-level categories but fewer for bottom level. At the top level, restaurant menus averaged 11 categories (e.g., appetizers, sandwiches, main courses, beverages, etc.); whereas, computer menus averaged only 7.8 (e.g., Print, Rename, Copy, Delete, Run, Exit, etc.). At the bottom choice level, restaurant menus averaged 2.5 items (generally several sizes such as large, medium, or small); whereas computer menus averaged 4.7 (e.g., a list of font sizes, or baud rates).

Furthermore, Norman and Chin identified a number of common aspects between restaurant and computer menus (see Table 4.3).

Both restaurant and computer menus often provide not only the names of items but also descriptions, definitions, and pictures or icons to help in making an informed choice. Both typically provide alternate response modes so that an item may be selected by name, number, or pointing. Both organize items along some line to help in the search process. Restaurant menus are customized for breakfast, lunch, and dinner, by day of the week, by type of customer (adult or child), by nationality, and by type of food. Similarly, computer menus are customized from one computer application to another; and one picks the package that will be the most functional for the task at hand. The selection of a restaurant serves to restrict the set of options available to the customer and thereby helps to focus the decision process. Similarly

Table 4.3. A Comparison of the Aspects of Restaurant Menus and Computer Menus

Aspect	Restaurant	Computer
Selection mode	name, number, pointing	letter, number, pointing
Information about options	name, description, price, picture	definition, explanation, icon
Organization	by course, type of food	hierarchical clustering alphabetic, etc.
Customization	by time, day of week, type of food	by application, experience of user
Complexity of selection	multiple items, combinations	pick lists, predefined configurations
Menu bypass	order when seated	jump ahead commands
Menu specials	chef's choice, seasonals	enhancements, premium options

the selection of a particular software package restricts the functionality, but provides a finite set of options that helps to simplify the interaction. The menu, consequently, conveys the speciality of the restaurant or software package.

Both restaurant and computer menus can allow for complex selection. The restaurant allows the customer to order (a) multiple items, (b) several of any one item, and (c) combination platters. In a similar manner, some computer applications provide pick lists, multiple selections, and preprogrammed selections. Both allow for a form of menu bypass. If the customer is familiar with the menu, there is no need to refer to it when ordering. Similarly, many computer menus incorporate this feature with jump ahead or menu bypass commands (Laverson, Norman, & Shneiderman, 1987).

Restaurant menus handle specials of the day by clipping them to the standard menu or displaying them on a chalk board. Such specials take advantage of seasonal variation, market fluctuations, or the whim of the chef. Some timeshare systems make use of this too. The variety of the menu adds interest to the menu for regular users that are looking for something new. In addition, computer systems may take advantage of prevailing system conditions, such as access to the LAN, the printer, or other system resources.

While there are many aspects in common, there are several aspects of the computer menu that do not correspond to the static menus of restaurants. These result primarily from the dynamic nature of the computer and its ability to update its display. Although restaurant menus typically organize and group items by course or food category, they are limited in terms of the number of levels that can be meaningfully displayed. Computer menus have the capability of organizing and displaying items in a hierarchical structure with unlimited depth.

Another aspect that computer menus have over most restaurant menus is the dynamic ability to add or delete items from the menu depending on the current state of the system. For example, pull-down menus can display grayed-out items if they are not currently available. In contrast, the restaurant customer may place an order only to be informed that the kitchen has run out of that item. In a sense this is equivalent to generating an error message. The computer menu has the capability of avoiding such errors.

Despite the power and versatility of the computer, restaurant menus still possess two major features not yet shared by computer menu systems. The first is the appeal and complexity of graphic layout. Visual inspection of the restaurant menu in comparison to the computer menu reveals that the typical computer menu is extremely information lean, displaying only alphanumeric lists of items. In contrast the restaurant menu may display tantalizing pictures, descriptions of entrees, and stylized type. The graphic layout of a menu not only helps to organize items but it also conveys additional information about the items. The intent of the restaurant menu, however, is not only to inform, but also to sell. Eye-catching graphics help to do this. Computer menus are only beginning to exploit this aspect of the metaphor. For example, Hyper-Card™ provides a menu system that allows designers full graphics capability.

Perhaps the greatest deficiency of computer menus is not in the menu itself but in the absence of a submetaphor; namely, the server. In the restaurant the server facilitates communication between the customer and the kitchen. The counterpart in a computer system might be a natural language parser in conjunction with a menu to provide the user with extensive online help concerning the choices on the menu. The server possesses a great deal of knowledge about the menu and the relationships between items and functions as an intelligent database. Customers may query about items by aspects such as cost and food type.

As computer menus become more and more complex, the user needs such an expert system analogous to the server to assist in navigating and pruning the menu tree. For example, a server could perform complex relational searches by specified conditions and generate a shortened menu, or narrow the user's search in a large menu. The server acts as a constantly available context-dependent help facility. The server is called upon for suggestions, definitions of terms, and even directions. Likewise, online help in computer menu selection is needed to provide context-dependent help.

Overall, the restaurant menu generates a powerful metaphor for human/computer interaction. The user's understanding of the interface and proficiency in using it is for the most part enhanced by the metaphor; however, at times it may also limit thinking. Norman and Draper (1986) caution that metaphors as mental models may fix the way in which a user thinks about the interface. If the concept of a computer menu is limited to restaurant menus, which are essentially single linear menus, it may be difficult to understand how the selection of one item eliminates the availability of other items.

4.3.2 Schemata and Scripts

Metaphors transfer knowledge from one base or media to another. Schemata attempt to capture the structural representation of knowledge. A *schema* is a diagrammatic outline of something that conveys its essential characteristics. One understands incoming information to the extent that it conforms to our schema or ways of knowing. If it fits a predefined pattern, it can be understood and incorporated into the knowledge base. If it doesn't, it is gibberish. Most information fits somewhere in between perfect conformity and total chaos. Consequently, information is filtered and modified by existing schema so that it fits with our understanding of things (Bartlett, 1932). Furthermore, missing information may be inferred as required by the schema. For example, a schema for a menu requires that there are options, a method of selection, and a result. When one encounters different types of menus, an attempt is made to understand them in terms of the overriding menu schema. Pull-down menus become meaningful when the user understands that options are displayed by selecting a pull-down from the menu bar and evoked by moving the cursor down to the desired item.

A special type of schema is the *script* (also called an *event schema*). A *script* is an expected or stereotypical sequence of actions and events. Schank and Abelson (1977) give an example of the restaurant script. They describe a normal pattern of actions as listed in Figure 4.9. The stereotypical script, however, may vary from one instance to another. For example, at a fast food restaurant, the script is changed so that one orders the food and pays before being seated and eating. This sequence allows the customer to leave with the food or right after finishing the meal, rather than having to wait for the check.

In the same way, computer users learn scripts for how one interacts with computers, application programs, and particularly menus. Menu selection provides a simple script for cognitive control: Read the options, decide on a selection, input the alternative, and evaluate the result. The script varies somewhat for different menu structures, but its simplicity makes for a powerful and compelling user interface.

Scripts also apply to the wider context of a session of interaction to perform a task, such as working with a spreadsheet or a word processor. The script may start with how the program opens files and initializes the environment; then how functions are performed; and finally, how files are closed before one exits the program. Scripts not only help users plan their actions, they also help to evaluate the course of action. The user has an expectation of the proper flow of events. When they do not conform to those expectations, the user knows that something is wrong, however, as with the restaurant, certain variations are tolerated. Some programs require specification of a file name prior to entering data rather than upon completion. Some programs also periodically save the contents into this file during the session to prevent accidental loss due to system failure while others require the user to explicitly save the file before exiting the program.

Experienced users acquire a number of scripts through their interaction with different programs. Cognitive control of the interface is facili-

```
┌─────────────────────────────────────────────────────┐
│                                                       │
│   Scene 1:  Entering                                  │
│                                                       │
│           Customer enters restaurant.                 │
│           Customer looks for table.                   │
│           Customer decides where to sit.              │
│           Customer goes to table.                     │
│           Customer sits down.                         │
│                                                       │
├─────────────────────────────────────────────────────┤
│                                                       │
│   Scene 2:  Ordering                                  │
│                                                       │
│           Customer picks up menu.                     │
│           Customer looks at menu.                     │
│           Customer decides on food.                   │
│           Customer signals waitress.                  │
│           Waitress comes to table.                    │
│           Customer orders food.                       │
│           Waitress goes to cook.                      │
│           Waitress gives food order to cook.          │
│           Cook prepares food.                         │
│                                                       │
├─────────────────────────────────────────────────────┤
│                                                       │
│   Scene 3:  Eating                                    │
│                                                       │
│           Cooks gives food to waitress.               │
│           Waitress brings food to customer.           │
│           Customer eats food.                         │
│                                                       │
├─────────────────────────────────────────────────────┤
│                                                       │
│   Scene 4:  Exiting                                   │
│                                                       │
│           Waitress writes bill.                       │
│           Waitress goes over to customer.             │
│           Waitress gives bill to customer.            │
│           Customer gives tip to waitress.             │
│           Customer goes to cashier.                   │
│           Customer gives money to cashier.            │
│           Customer leaves restaurant.                 │
│                                                       │
└─────────────────────────────────────────────────────┘
```

Figure 4.9.   Script of stereotypic sequence of actions involved in dining at a restaurant.

From *Scripts, Plans, Goals, and Understanding*, by R.C. Schank and R.P. Abelson, 1977, Hillsdale, NJ: Erlbaum. Copyright 1977 by Erlbaum. Reprinted by permission.

tated by well-worn paths that conform to these scripts. It is suggested that designers take advantage of prior expectations of users. New programs that violate accepted scripts for whatever good reasons may not be understood or accepted by users.

4.3.3 Cognitive Layouts of Menus

Mental models, whether metaphors, schemata, or scripts, are in the mind of the user. Often they remain there dormant as the user muddles along step-by-step or frame-by-frame without engaging any planning or problem-solving approach. Norman, Weldon, and Shneiderman (1986) have proposed that performance may be facilitated if such user models take on a visual form that engages the appropriate cognitive layout. Formally, a cognitive layout is defined as a mental representation of the elements and relationships in a system that conform to a cognitive model of operations and is tied to the surface layout of elements on the display. Norman et al. (1986) gave the example of the three-box human memory model as one of many possible cognitive layouts. Users may conceive of the system as having a short-term sensory store (a buffer), a short-term memory (working memory), and a long-term memory (file storage). When the surface layout of the system (its graphic representation) matches that of the user's cognitive layout, the user's involvement with and understanding of the system will be maximized. Norman et al. applied this idea to the operation of multiple windows and screens. Windows could promote the human memory model by displaying incoming information in one window, working contents or clipboard information in another window, and a directory of files in a third window.

In essence the graphic layout should engage the way in which the user conceptualizes the operation of the program. The problem is that too often menus hide the organization and structure of the tree rather than explicitly using it to the benefit of the interface. A number of cognitive layouts present themselves as possible models for how the user thinks of menu interaction. Each layout has its strengths and weaknesses. The particular surface layout used to drive the interface may be able to emphasize the strengths and make accommodations for the weaknesses.

A number of menu systems have used graphic layouts that have suggested different types of metaphors. Several of these are discussed below.

Road Map. The cognitive layout of a menu selection system may be a map. As such, the user views menu traversal as navigation. The road map layout associates menu frames with junctions in the road; alternatives are different locations or roads to those locations. The user is engaged in the process of determining routes between points. Initially, the user may search for possible routes by exploring alternatives branching out from the current location. But one may also work backwards from the destination. In general, search starts from highly familiar points and proceeds from there. Once a route has been found and repeatedly used it becomes habitual, even when shortcuts may be available. The value of the map is to display a graphic representation showing all of the major locations and connectors. When implemented on a computer, there is an additional advantage. The user may be able to select a point on the map and jump to that location in the system. The map is merely a large menu, but the cognitive model conveyed is much more powerful since the user is aware of both the location and the connections of items. Although the road map is appropriate for a number of systems, only a few actually present a surface layout that conveys that idea. HyperCard™ gives one instance of a road map layout in its help system (see Figure 4.10).

Tree. A related cognitive layout is that of a tree with branches or inversely a tree with roots. These layouts confine the user's cognitive layout to a hierarchical menu. The tree layout dictates directional menu traversal from a central node (the root) to increasing levels of specificity. The directional nature of the tree is pervasive and is reinforced by much of the terminology used in menu traversal. In many cases interaction may need to be guided by the hierarchical nature of the database and it

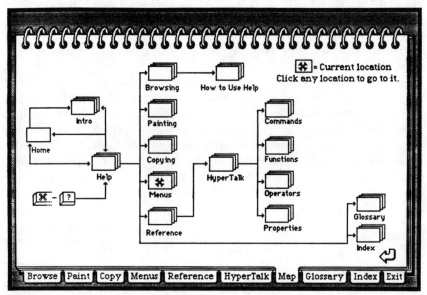

Figure 4.10. An example of a road map layout used in the help stack of HyperCards™.

does not make sense to go from one location to another without at least conceptually referring to the hierarchical location of a node. In other cases, the hierarchy may be a superficial or arbitrary clustering of items (e.g., a catalog of gift items). When this is the case, the hierarchy may prove to be more of a burden than a strength. The general layout of the hierarchical menu requires that the user back out of a branch and return to the root before traversing back out to another branch.

Smorgasbord. Another layout is that of the Swedish Smorgasbord. All of the options are spread out before the user. There is a clustering and organization of items, but anything may be sampled. While there may be a linear layout of items, there is no sense of rigid menu traversal, rather one of simultaneous availability. Other layouts make use of the artist's pallet and the worker's tool box. Parameter settings (hues, shades, fonts, lines, etc.) are laid out in a meaningful order and are simultaneously available. Functions (text, graphic objects, grabbers, etc.) are also laid out for direct selection. The major strength of the smorgasbord layout is that experienced users learn the locations of items and can make rapid selections despite the very large number of options that may be available.

These layouts are by no means exhaustive of the number of cognitive layouts that may be effectively used to engage the user. The challenge of good design is not so much to invent new interfaces but to borrow existing cognitive layouts from the world of common knowledge and thought.

4.4 SUMMARY

Although the cognitive processing of the user imposes a number of limiting factors on menu selection performance, that same ability to process and control is what drives the interaction. The user must search for information, encode the meaning of alternatives, assess the alternatives, make a choice and effect a response. All of these processes are governed by the laws of human information processing. Good menu design takes into consideration such human factors to increase speed and reduce errors.

At another level, however, the user enters not as a limiting force but as a driving force. The user is a problem solver with goals, strategies, and styles of attack. As such, the computer interface becomes a media for effecting solutions. Theories of human problem solving suggest that the problem solver's understanding and representation of the problem domain aids in solution. To this end good user interface design should convey a sense of meaning and engage schemata that lend themselves to solutions of the tasks being performed.

II
DESIGN GUIDELINES FROM EMPIRICAL RESEARCH

In the past few years a flurry of research has been conducted in human/computer interaction. Much of this work has been exploratory, testing the waters and establishing reliable experimental methods and designs in a new application. The result has been extremely productive and exciting. A number of firm conclusions have been reached; many interesting leads have been uncovered; and researchers have gained experience in how one does good research in human/computer interaction.

Part II presents the bulk of this work as it applies to menu selection. The first chapter in this part, Chapter 5, gives a brief overview of the research method used in experimental research involving human subjects. This chapter is not meant to be a primer in experimental methods. The serious student of research should be directed to a good text in experimental methods and applied experimental statistics (e.g., Hays, 1981; Kirk, 1982; Winer, 1971). Instead, Chapter 5 highlights special issues and problems involved in the research on menu selection.

Much of the research in human/computer interaction has been directed specifically at menu selection. Several literature reviews have already been published (Raymond, 1986; Shneiderman, 1987). The remainder of Part II extends these reviews, presents a number of new results, and most importantly, organizes the findings around major themes and theories that were discussed in Part I.

A number of aspects of the menu frame effect performance. Chapter 6 deals with the physical layout and the organization of the frame as well as the organization and meaningfulness of textual information. The physical layout directs attention and affects the order of processing information. The menu content and organization of items has been shown to have a dramatic effect on the time that it takes for the user to scan, encode, and respond to menu items.

Designers of menus attempt to create a powerful and efficient interface. Users of menus attempt to adapt their behavior to access menu items efficiently. Performance is the result of the joint function of design and use. No matter how we define performance, its value generally changes over time. Users learn many things about menus with practice and change their behavior accordingly. Chapter 7 reviews the findings on the acquisition of menu performance with practice. In general, human response time decreases with practice. Furthermore, different training methods are effective in helping users to learn menu relationships and structure.

5

Research Issues and Methods in Menu Selection

It is one thing to generate theory. It is another thing to prove it. When it comes to theory that involves human behavior, verification cannot rest on intuition, argument, or opinion. Instead verification must rest on the bench of empirical research. In the arena of human/computer interaction it is all too easy to generate theory, principles, and guidelines and to apply them without restraint. Although intuition aids in good design, there are many cases in which the best design is initially counterintuitive even to experts in the field. Research in the form of controlled laboratory experiments, observation in usability labs, and even field observations is needed to verify decisions about design options. Furthermore, research is needed to generate theory and to discover general principles in design.

This chapter emphasizes the importance of research based on systematic experiments involving human subjects. It is conceded that such research is difficult, costly, and time-consuming. However, it is argued that menu design in the absence of empirical research spells disaster. Two examples of a lack of verification will be discussed.

A number of issues central to empirical research will be discussed as they pertain to studies of menu selection. The first question is how to provide reliable, valid, and efficient results. The issues of statistical reliability and generality will be discussed. Second, the principles of experimental design will be presented along with the unique problems faced in human/computer interaction research. Finally, the issue of efficiency of design and statistical power will be examined.

The material in this chapter is not meant to be a review of statistical methods. A familiarity with statistics is assumed. Rather, it is meant to elucidate particular issues and to motivate researchers to conduct more and better experiments.

5.1 INTUITION AND DATA IN CONFLICT

Design with the absence of data results in arbitrary, capricious, and uninformed decisions. Of course, such decisions have to be made. Production deadlines force the designer to operate on intuition rather than data when established guidelines do not exist. The result is uncertain and the cost of design errors varies due to type and severity. Five different types of errors are defined below:

1. *Undetected Positive Feature.* The designer may not realize that some factor has an effect either positive or negative on performance. Since the factor is not viewed as relevant, an arbitrary level may be selected that has a positive effect. Since enumerable design decisions are made for any menu system, it stands to reason that designers must make some good decisions. The problem is that they may not realize when they have hit upon an important feature. It may well be that the positive nature of a feature may only be discovered when it is changed or omitted in subsequent versions of the software.
2. *Undetected Negative Feature.* Again, the designer may not realize that a factor has an effect, but in this case, may arbitrarily select a level that has a negative effect. It may only be after successive usability testing or field observation that the negative feature is detected and changed.
3. *False Relevance.* The designer may think that some factor has an effect when it is actually irrelevant. Although design decisions along such factors do not affect behavior, they may affect cost. Much time and effort may be expended to provide a feature that has little or no benefit.
4. *False Positive Feature.* The designer may think that a design option has a positive effect when in actuality it is negative. This is often the result of designers thinking that users think like they do. But what is good for the expert may be bad for the novice and vice versa.
5. *Missed Positive Feature.* Finally, the designer may totally miss a feature that could have a positive effect on performance.

All but the first of these errors result in negative outcomes and could be avoided by careful research. However, as noted, there is little time for empirical research at the point of design, although some have run studies on crucial design questions. Rather, the time for research is prior to design in an effort to establish literature that will answer design questions as they arise. Such literature may also be used to generate guidelines and design principles.

The central question is how to build such literature. In essence the answer lies in what research questions to ask. Basic research progresses from the question, "Does Factor X have an effect on Performance Y?" Such questions arise either from theories about human/computer interaction that postulate the effects of factors on behavior, or from lists of design features that could have an effect. In the first case research is theory driven, in the second it is design driven. In either case, the effect must be subjected to empirical testing or it remains in the realm of intuition.

5.2 REPLICABILITY

Empirical research demands replicability. If the same result cannot be replicated, the conclusion is not valid. Replicability adds inductive support to the conclusion. Anecdotal evidence and single case studies lack replicability. They constitute one instance without corroborating evidence. Empirical evidence must be provided that the results have predictive power and application beyond the one case at hand.

Consider a comparison between two systems A and B. Imagine that only two users 1 and 2 are randomly sampled and each assigned to one system. Now suppose that User 1 on System A performed better than User 2 on System B. The advantage could be due to the fact that (a) System A is superior to System B, (b) User 1 is more proficient than User 2, or (c) User 1 happens to work better on System A, and/or User 2 happens to work better on System B. The problem is that the difference cannot be unambiguously ascribed to a system advantage. The question is whether the same advantage would remain if two more users were randomly sampled and assigned to groups. When additional observations corroborate the result, one's confidence in the conclusion is increased. The question is - "How much?"

Statistical theory provides an estimate of replicability within a population. The significance level of a test indicates the probability that the result was due to a sampling variation rather than a true effect. For example, consider that the means of two groups are compared and a p value of .01 is reported for significance. One would be assured that a difference of this size or greater would occur only one time out of a hundred when no true (repeatable) difference exists. The power of a statistical test is defined as the probability that a result is significant when indeed there is a true difference in the population. Statistical power is gained by increasing the number of observations. In general, this means increasing the number of users tested in the experiment or by repeating observations on the same user.

Another form of replicability occurs across experiments. One researcher may find that condition A results in better performance than condition B. However, another researcher runs a similar study and does not replicate the finding. Such a result raises interesting questions. It could be that the first study was in error and that no true difference exists. Additional research is required to resolve the conflict. On the other hand, it could be that some difference existed between the two studies that resulted in the discrepancy (e.g., different levels of user experience, different equipment, different tasks, etc.). Subsequent research is required in which additional factors are varied to see when the effect occurs and when it does not. These studies investigate moderating factors and interactions of factors.

But to the extent that results are replicated in different experiments by different researchers, and under somewhat different conditions, the effect under investigation is said to be *robust*. Robust effects are extremely important because they are most likely to impact the performance of current design. In addition, procedures have been developed to combine results from a number of experiments to generate a *meta-analysis* of the effect (e.g., Hedges, 1985; Hunter, 1982). Meta-analyses are often useful in resolving discrepancies among studies when they categorize studies by factors that were not initially varied in any one experiment. One result may have occurred, for example, in studies using only novice users and a different result in studies using only experienced users. Thus, meta-analytic procedures may uncover issues not originally considered by the researchers.

5.3 IMPORTANCE OF THE RESULT

Just because a factor has a reliable effect it does not necessarily mean that it has a big effect on performance or should have great impact on design. It all depends on the size of the effect and its frequency of occurrence. Effect size may be measured in two ways. It may be measured in terms of absolute magnitude. For example, the difference in user response time between one menu layout and another may be only 100 ms. If the menu is accessed only a few times in a session, the effect is certainly not an important one. However, if the difference were one second and the menu was accessed hundreds of times, the impact would be more substantial. Effects which are measured in terms of time, number of transactions, or percent error can be easily translated into impact. Furthermore, one can gauge the importance of the effect by percent improvement. A menu organization which reduces selection error by 15% can be directly compared to others.

Effect size is also gauged against total variability in performance. Total variability is the sum of all effects due to differences among conditions *and* users. Effect size can be defined as the observed difference divided by the population standard deviation (Cohen, 1977). An effect of size .2 is said to be a small effect, .5 a medium effect, and .8 a large effect.

Small Effects. An effect may be small either because it truly has a minor effect on performance or because the experimental conditions tested only subtle variations (e.g., font size of 10 vs. 12 rather than 10 vs.

24). If small effects are the result of subtle variations in conditions, it suggests that a large effect may surface when conditions differ to a greater degree. Furthermore, it must be remembered that even though an effect may truly be small, its cumulative impact on system design can be substantial if there is a high frequency of occurrence. Finally, the fact that an effect exists, no matter what its size, is important from a theoretical standpoint in that it reveals something about the cognitive processing of the user.

Medium Effects. Most experimental results seem to produce effects in the moderate range. These are often the design features that must be carefully traded off against time and cost, aspects of productivity, and throughput of work. A number of medium effects can work together to gain an overall advantage.

Large Effects. Large effects must always be considered. To the extent that a new feature results in a substantial improvement in performance, it is worth the effort. These are the effects that will help to drive technology and design change. There are large effects, however, that the designer can do little about. It would be nice to design a system in which the users are immediately trained experts. In practice, one has to live with some large effects. Furthermore, some large effects are reported in the literature that do not bear on design. The experiment may have compared a reasonable design with a severely crippled version to illustrate a point. For example, a large effect in search time may be found using an alphabetic listing of names versus a randomly ordered listing. Hopefully, no designer would consider using the random order.

5.4 GENERALIZATION OF RESULTS

It has been noted in previous chapters that subject variables, task variables, and system variables all affect performance. Statistical theory stringently limits the generality of the results to the same subject population sampled, the same experimental conditions, and the same fixed levels of the independent variables. Strict adherence to this requirement would make all research futile. Instead, a principle of reasonable generalization must be adopted. Results from one class of users may be generalized to a *similar* class of users. Results from one type of task may be generalized to a *similar* set of conditions. But it should be clear that one cannot generalize results found using a group of novice users to a group of experienced users without empirical evidence that the same results will be obtained for both groups.

Table 5.1 lists a number of variables that should be considered when one attempts to generalize results. This list is by no means exhaustive. Any specific experiment can only manipulate a small number of these

Table 5.1.   Classes of User, Task, and System Variables that Should Be Considered in Generalization

User Classes
   Experience (knowledge, understanding, automaticity, etc.)
   Skills (typing, clerical, writing, drawing, motor, visual, etc.)
   Motivation (achievement, excitation level, etc.)
   Personality (style, temperament, etc.)

Task Conditions
   Knowledge domain (structure, concreteness, richness, etc.)
   Definition (problem definition, types of targets, restrictions on solution)
   Demands (time pressure, costs of errors, etc.)

System Conditions
   Input Devices (keyboard, mouse, etc.)
   Display Devices (monitor, audio, etc.)

Environmental Conditions
   Social/Organization (audience, status, role, etc.)
   Physical (lighting, sound, etc.)

variables. The rest are typically fixed at some arbitrary value. The question is whether the effect will be the same at different levels of other variables. If so, then the results are robust and can be generalized to other conditions. If not, additional experiments are needed to investigate the limits of generalizability.

The insightful researcher must ascertain the relative impact and importance of conditions and the way in which they may attenuate or mitigate the effects of other variables. First, the generalizability of results is increased if the experimenter arranges the experimental conditions so that they are as similar as possible to the conditions to which the results are to be applied. For example, standard equipment may be used, similar users, typical task demands, and so on. The experiment is said to be ecologically valid if the conditions in the laboratory simulate the real world conditions or ecology (Neisser, 1976).

In order to generalize the results from a specific experiment to a design situation, a number of steps must be considered. These steps are outlined in the following four questions:

- What are the specific conditions (Source Conditions) under which the empirical results were obtained?
- To what extent can these specific conditions be assumed to generalize to a wider set of conditions (Generalized Conditions) and how robust are the empirical results (Generalizability Factor)?
- What are the specific conditions (Target Conditions) to which the empirical results are to be applied?

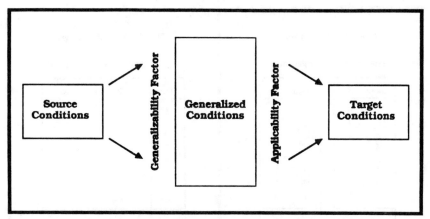

Figure 5.1.   Schematic of the process of generalization of results.

- To what extent are the specific conditions in the application subsumed by the wider set (Applicability Factor)?

Figure 5.1 shows a schematic of the generalization process. The box on the left-hand side symbolizes the specific conditions of the experiment. The box in the middle symbolizes equivalence classes for the original conditions. Finally, the box at the right-hand side symbolizes the set of conditions to which the results are applied.

5.5 EXPERIMENTAL DESIGNS

Experimental design is concerned with the assignment of cases to conditions. Assignment is made in such a way that confounding factors, called nuisance variables, are systematically controlled or cancelled out while allowing true effects to be clearly ascribed to the independent variables of interest. Experimental design is a very complex topic and beyond the scope of the present discussion. Nevertheless, a few key issues will be presented as they relate to experimental research on menu selection.

In a typical experiment on menu selection, one or more design features are selected and varied systematically to create treatment conditions. There are two basic ways of assigning treatments to subjects. In a *between subjects design* (also called a *completely randomized design*), treatment levels are assigned to independent groups of subjects (see the left panel of Figure 5.2). In a *within subjects design* (also called a *randomized block* or *repeated measures* design), the treatment levels are assigned to the same subjects, that is, each subject participates in multiple treatments

Between Subjects Design			Within Subjects Design		
System A	System B			System A	System B

User	X	User	X	User	X	X
1	6	9	4	1	5	5
2	7	10	7	2	6	8
3	4	11	6	3	3	7
4	6	12	8	4	5	9
5	2	13	4	5	1	5
6	5	14	7	6	4	8
7	4	15	6	7	3	7
8	3	16	5	8	2	6
$\overline{X}$ = 4		$\overline{X}$ = 6			$\overline{X}$ = 3	$\overline{X}$ = 7

Figure 5.2. Between subjects (left panel) and within subjects (right panel) designs.

(see the right panel of Figure 5.2). The advantage of the within subjects design is that the performance of individual subjects in one condition can be directly compared to their performance in another. In a sense, subjects serve as their own baseline or control. The between subjects design has less statistical power because comparisons are made between two independent groups of subjects.

Unfortunately, the within subject design is not without problems. Since each subject participates in several conditions, differences may be due to practice and/or sequence effects. Subjects may get better with practice so that the second treatment has an order advantage. The second panel of Figure 5.2 illustrates this case. One does not know if the four-point advantage for system B is due to the system or to being second. This problem can in general be controlled by counterbalancing treatments orders. Half of the subjects work with system A first and system B second. The other half work with system B first and system A second. Essentially, the order of treatment is added as a between subjects factor in the design. The left panel of Figure 5.3 shows how order is added to the design. In these data there is a two-point difference due to system and a two-point difference due to order.

Sequence effects occur if there is an advantage or disadvantage when participating in one condition before the other. Directional transfer of training and contrast effects can cause sequence effects. For example, in working with system A first, the user may gain a full understanding of

Example of Practice Effects

	First	Second
User	A X	B X
1	2	7
2	3	6
3	4	7
4	3	8
	$\overline{X}$ = 3	$\overline{X}$ = 7

User	B X	A X
5	5	5
6	4	5
7	5	6
8	6	4
	$\overline{X}$ = 5	$\overline{X}$ = 5

	First	Second
Order	$\overline{X}$ = 4	$\overline{X}$ = 6

	A	B
System	$\overline{X}$ = 4	$\overline{X}$ = 6

Example of Sequence Effects

	First	Second
User	A X	B X
1	5	6
2	6	5
3	6	7
4	7	6
	$\overline{X}$ = 6	$\overline{X}$ = 6

User	B X	A X
5	5	4
6	4	5
7	3	4
8	4	3
	$\overline{X}$ = 4	$\overline{X}$ = 4

	First	Second
Order	$\overline{X}$ = 5	$\overline{X}$ = 5

	A	B
System	$\overline{X}$ = 5	$\overline{X}$ = 5

Figure 5.3. Examples of practice effects (left panel) and sequence effects (right panel).

the task which subsequently results in a good performance on system B. However, in working with system B first, the user may become confused which subsequently results in a poor performance on system A. The right panel of Figure 5.3 illustrates the problem with such a system by order interaction. Overall, there is no difference in the means for the two systems and no difference due to order. However, there is a two-point difference between the sequence A-B and B-A. When this occurs the only clear indication that one system is superior to the other is in first session performance. The experimenter must fall back on a between subjects comparison using only first session performance. Thus, in the first session data, one can see the two-point difference due to the system.

Between subjects designs should be used when one wants to exclude any transfer of information or practice from one condition to another. It is often the case, that the same test material or database is used to assess performance on different systems. A between subjects design allows the experimenter to use that same database and test questions. A within subjects design requires difference databases and test materials for each system. Unless the databases and test materials are matched, they must also be counterbalanced for order effects. Figure 5.4 shows the layout for such a design. The analysis of such designs and the interpretation of the results become more and more complex due to the three-way interaction of order by system by material.

Within subject designs are particularly called for when one is interested in practice effects and effects due to time. Mixed designs are used

	First Test One	Second Test Two
User	A X	B X
1	2	7
2	1	8
3	2	9
4	3	8
	$\overline{X}$ = 2	$\overline{X}$ = 8

User	B X	A X
5	5	6
6	4	5
7	4	6
8	6	4
	$\overline{X}$ = 4	$\overline{X}$ = 6

	First Test Two	Second Test One
User	A X	B. X
9	5	6
10	4	5
11	4	7
12	3	6
	$\overline{X}$ = 4	$\overline{X}$ = 6

User	B X	A X
13	5	4
14	6	5
15	6	4
16	7	3
	$\overline{X}$ = 6	$\overline{X}$ = 4

	First	Second
Order	$\overline{X}$ = 4	$\overline{X}$ = 6
	One	Two
Test	$\overline{X}$ = 4	$\overline{X}$ = 6
	A	B
System	$\overline{X}$ = 4	$\overline{X}$ = 6

Figure 5.4.   A counterbalanced design with system varied within subjects, and order and test materials counterbalanced between subjects.

when learning curves are compared between two different systems. Successive practice is varied as a within subject factor and system is varied as a between subjects factor.

Within subject designs are also required when users are asked to make comparisons among different systems. In order to rate systems, users must be familiar with them prior to the ratings. Ratings made using between subjects designs are made in isolation and are often insensitive to true system characteristics and biased by prior expectations.

5.6 SUMMARY

There are many other issues to consider in the design of experiments. The serious researcher must have a background of statistics and experimental design courses to do good work. The issues are complex and the best design is not always intuitively obvious. Every experiment seems to have its unique set of problems and requires a well thought-out design.

The serious reader of empirical literature must also be knowledgeable of statistical issues and experimental design and be critical of the results. Rather than accepting the author's conclusions at face value, the reader should ask the questions: Are the results reliable? Are they valid or confounded by other variables? How far can they be generalized?

The research reported in the following chapters must be subjected to the same questions. Although reported in leading journals and conducted by respected researchers, one must nevertheless view all results with a healthy degree of scepticism. As noted earlier, it is all too easy to write guidelines on the basis of intuition. It may be even more dangerous to write them armed with only a little knowledge.

6

Formatting and Phrasing the Menu

Although it is often the last thing to be considered by the software designer, the appearance and intelligibility of the screen display is the first thing to be assessed by the user. "What is it telling me? What does it mean? What does it expect me to do?" are all questions that the user is likely to ask upon first encountering the system. One may brush off these questions and say that after the user has worked with the system long enough, everything will make sense. But this is not always true. Experienced users have even more telling questions: "Why is that phrase used when it's not performing that function at all? Why is the screen organized this way? Why do I keeping making the same error over and over again?" In general, users can adapt to a less than optimal human/computer interface, but it is always at the expense of training time and cognitive effort. When these are in short supply, interface design is critical.

Screen display and the formatting of a menu frame are an art. The phrasing of stems, leaves, and other information in the menu frame is a wordsmithing activity that without proper attention can lead to many problems. Fortunately, a growing body of literature in cognitive psychology and more directly in ergonomic research is helping to define the factors of menu design and to set guidelines for "do's and don'ts" in designing menus. Many of these guidelines and the research supporting them will be reviewed in this chapter.

6.1 FORMATTING THE MENU FRAME

The purpose of a well-designed menu frame is to convey information to the user in the most efficient manner possible. It must be remembered that users read and search for information with expectations. They do not necessarily read the menu frame word-by-word from the beginning. Rather they scan it and are highly influenced by its organization and layout. It follows that organization and layout should facilitate the search process rather than work against it.

Much has been written about screen display in computer systems (e.g., Galitz, 1981; Cropper & Evans, 1968; Engel & Granda, 1975; Foley, Wallace & Chan, 1984; Mitchell, 1983; Peterson, 1979; Shurtleff, 1980; Tullis, 1981, 1983). Many of these references serve as excellent guides for designing menus.

In terms of menu display, the designer must decide what information to display, in what form, and where. As seen in Chapter 2, menus include information about the context, the stem and leaves of the choice options, and response and feedback information.

6.1.1 Amount of Information per Screen

The first decision that must be made has to do with how much information should be displayed. Most guidelines in the literature suggest that only information essential to the user's needs should be displayed. Irrelevant information clutters up the screen and makes it more difficult and time-consuming for the user to locate the option that he desires. The problem is knowing what the user needs and determining what is irrelevant versus what is necessary.

The designer must contend with a set of tradeoffs.

Amount of Information vs. Scan/Reading Time. The more information, the more difficult and time-consuming it is to search for target information and to read the information. Research in human information processing indicates the obvious: It takes longer to search for a word as the amount of surrounding information increases. When time is a critical factor in performance, brevity of the menu is essential in reducing human processing time. Furthermore, readability is affected by the density of text on the screen. It is suggested that no more than 30% of the available character spaces on the screen should be used (Danchak, 1976; Poulton & Brown, 1968; Ramsey & Atwood, 1979).

Level of Experience vs. Need for Explanation. The less familiar the user is with the system, the more detailed the explanations need to be of menu options. Menus need to be information rich for novices. The implication is that performance will be slow, but this is generally not a major concern for novices and casual users. On the other hand, menus may be information lean for experienced users. The terms serve only as cues to jog the memory of the user and to indicate the allowable options at the current state. Furthermore, the speed of scanning and selection is a function of the training of the user. In terms of the theory of cognitive control, the experienced user has acquired sufficient knowledge about the system so that information flow from the computer to the user is no longer necessary.

Amount of Information per Screen vs. Number of Screens. The less information presented per screenful, the more screens that are necessary. One of the major concepts in menu systems is to subdivide information and user control into a network of screens. Typically, when all of the information and options do not fit on one screen, the designer divides the menu into two or more screens. Ultimately, this leads to the depth vs. breadth tradeoff which will be discussed in a later chapter. At this point it is sufficient to say that when screens must be subdivided, it adds to the cognitive complexity of the system. Performance of both novice users and experienced users is lowered due to the added steps necessary to access additional screens. This problem is alleviated in part by larger screens or multiple screens displaying longer menus, but then one must contend again with the first tradeoff having to do with scanning and reading time.

6.1.2 Focusing Attention on the Menu

Principles of good screen layout may be derived from theories of perception in Gestalt psychology and more recently cognitive psychology. One of the basic processes in perception is the segmentation of the field into figure and ground. The figure contains those objects that are the focus of attention; whereas, the background is amorphous and undifferentiated. Studies in visual perception indicate that the figure-ground distinction is the first and most fundamental aspect to be perceived in a display. However, the figure-ground distinction may vary with the stimulus. At one extreme, figure-ground may be a potent aspect of the display that forces the viewer to perceive one area as figure and the rest as ground. On the other hand, the distinction may be weak and driven primarily by the current need state of the viewer. For some displays, we are quite capable of totally reversing figure and ground or of refocusing attention to generate new segmentations of the field.

When a user is accessing a menu, the menu becomes the figure and the rest of the screen, which may be displaying previous output, becomes the background. Although the focus of attention is on the foreground, the background can either serve to enhance this focus or to distract from it. Figure 6.1 illustrates three levels of figure-ground distraction for a pull-down menu.

When a gray background is used, as in the top panel in Figure 6.1, figure-ground segmentation is maximized; when other information clutters the background, as in the middle panel, segmentation is reduced; and when the information in the background is similar to the figure, as in the bottom panel, segmentation is minimal. Systems supporting the cluttered desktop metaphor can suffer from figure-ground ambiguity.

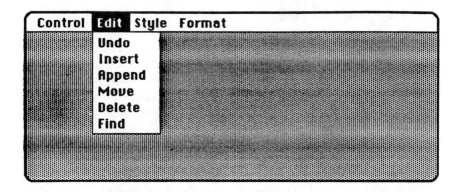

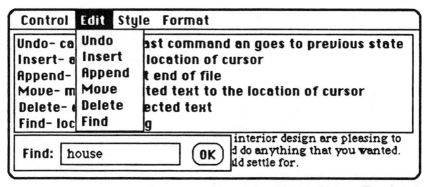

Figure 6.1. Figure-ground segmentation of the screen display. (Top panel: Good figure-ground distinction. Middle Panel: Moderate distinction with figure over figure. Bottom Panel: Poor distinction with figure over distracting figure.)

Fortunately, the figure-ground distinction can be enhanced by the proper use of graphic devices, such as borders, highlighting, overlapping, graying out, colors, and so forth.

6.1.3 Perceptual Grouping

Perceptual grouping is an important process that aids in interpreting what something is and its relationship to other objects in the field. Characteristics of the objects suggest an organization of the field of view. We perceive objects that are similar in appearance or close in proximity as belonging together. Such perceptual grouping affects subsequent processing of the information in terms of the meaningfulness and expectations regarding functions. These concepts may be effectively used in menu design; or if not attended to, perceptual effects can be quite detrimental.

Studies have found that spatial proximity of options in a menu affect the grouping of items in the long-term memory of the user. Items may be *chunked* together. *Chunking* is the cognitive process of storing/retrieving a set of items as a unit. For example, single letters may be chunked as a word, and words may be chunked as a sentence. Card (1982) used a recall test in order to assess the chunking process in menu selection. After a series of search trials using an 18-item menu with boxes containing two to four items, subjects were asked to write down all of the items that they could remember. When items are recalled from memory, items that are in the same chunk tend to be recalled together with a short time interval between recall. Items in different chunks tend to be separated by a longer time interval. Card found that items next to each other or in the same box in the list tended to be clustered together in recall.

Similarity of appearance also leads to perceptual grouping. Items may be similar in phrasing or in graphic shape. One menu uses the items "SAVE" and "SAVE AS. . ." The first option saves the current memory buffer by writing over a file that had been previously opened, thus destroying the old contents. The second option saves the current memory buffer by opening a new file and writing to it while doing nothing on the old file. The similar phrasing of the items helps the user to group them together as having a similar function with respect to writing the memory buffer to a file. It may be detrimental, however, by obscuring the effect on the old file. The user often has to learn such subtle distinctions the hard way.

Spacing of alternatives can lead to perceptual grouping and has a strong effect on visual search. In their study of menu selection using large menus of 64 items, Parkinson, Sisson, and Snowberry (1985) compared menus having either no spacing between category groups or having one additional space between groups. Menus with additional space were searched in 25% less time. It is interesting to note that this difference as not substantially reduced with practice. Perceptual grouping induced by spacing seems to have several beneficial effects. First, it

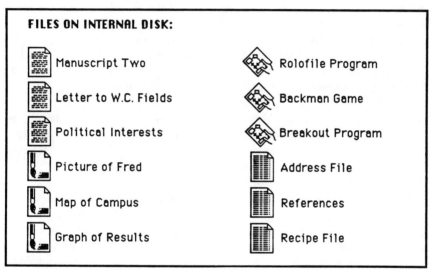

Figure 6.2. Illustration of the effect of icons on perceptual grouping of file names.

appears that grouping helps users to recognize the type of organization and structure of the list (e.g., organization by alphabetical or natural categories). Second, perceptual grouping allows the user to mark and locate the beginning and ending of groups when visually scanning for target items.

Menu systems that display icons can also make good use of perceptual grouping. Scanning and perceptual grouping is often enhanced by graphic images. Figure 6.2 shows the effect of adding icons. In the top panel the names of 12 files are displayed. The bottom panel adds icons indicating the type of file. It is expected that search time for selecting files with the icons will be faster than without the icons, even though files in both cases are clustered by type. Icons serve to add perceptual features that aid in grouping and search processes.

6.1.4 Menu Context

Screen design involves setting a context in which the items are perceived and interpreted. Two types of context must be considered. A *sensory* context is set by the background and explicit context information displayed. The recognition and meaning of items in the list are affected by this surrounding information. A *nonsensory* context is set by previous events remembered by the user and by his current task and goal states. In a bibliographic search, for example, sensory context may be established by displaying that the user has located a set of 10 bibliographic citations by a title search and that menu options refer to this set. The nonsensory context of the user may be that he is searching for a particular book and he has not been able to locate it by an author search.

The interpretation of menu items and their consequences are highly influenced by the context. Terms such as "list," "print," "kill," "find," "change," and "load" are highly context dependent. *List* may refer to a command to display a listing of a program or it may refer to a list of words. The problem is that words are often ambiguous outside of a clear context. For terms such as these, the user must disambiguate the meaning on the basis of their frequency of use and the recency with which a particular meaning was evoked (Anderson, 1988). The point is that menu systems must provide sufficient context for the users to easily disambiguate the meaning of the menu items.

Context that relies on nonsensory mechanisms is often unpredictable. Consequently, guidelines suggest that every screen explicitly display the user's last selection which led to the current screen or state of the system in order to aid in a step-wise refinement of the interpretation of items. For example, a search through a hierarchical database of employees in an organization may retain the context by adding to the title after each menu selection in the following manner:

West Coast
West Coast Sales Division
West Coast Sales Division Manager
West Coast Sales Division Manger of Government Services

Although theory would predict a beneficial effect of having menu titles, the empirical results are marginal. The effect of menu titles was investigated in a study by Gray (1986). Subjects searched a hierarchical menu of animals, machines, and plants for 20 target words. A symmetric 3^4 hierarchical menu was used. In one condition, titles were stacked following each choice. In the control condition submenus did not have titles. Overall the menu traversal times were not significantly different. Furthermore, the total number of errors (incorrect choices at each level) did not differ significantly between conditions. However, when looking at the number of incorrect choices at each level in the tree, Gray suggests that submenu titles may have helped to reduce errors at levels 3 and 4 of the hierarchy. The group with titles made 40% of their errors at levels 3 and 4 while the group without titles made 59% of their errors at levels 3 and 4. At levels 1 and 2 titles may have been only one more piece of information to process. However as depth increased, the menu title may have served to maintain context. While suggestive, these results are not reliable due to the small number of subjects per group (seven per group) and the level of significance used.

6.1.5 Ordering of Menu Items

What is the best order of the items in a menu? There are three major purposes behind the ordering of items. The first is to facilitate search for an item in a list. When items are organized along some characteristic or dimension, the user's search strategy can use that information to locate items faster. Alphabetic ordering helps the user know approximately where to look in a list for a word. The second is to convey additional information about the structure and relationships among the items. This information may aid in helping to make choices by knowing the similarities and dissimilarities among items. The third is merely to agree with the user's inferred ordering so as not to disrupt cognitive processing by creating dissonance between the user's knowledge base and the system's knowledge base. Items may be organized according to a number of characteristics.

Random Order. As a baseline, we will consider the case of no perceived organization. For all intents and purposes, the list appears to be random. There may be some underlying software rationale for the order depending on system constraints, but the reason for this order is not apparent to the user and has nothing to do directly with the human/computer interface. For example, the order of desk accessories on the Apple Macintosh is determined by tool priorities. The user can generate no algorithm to facilitate search other than a rote memorization of item position. However, it should be mentioned that frequent users of systems quickly acquire a knowledge of the spatial location of items in a randomly ordered (but constant) list. Card (1982) and others have shown that differences in performance due to the organization of the items are reduced or eliminated entirely with practice. Subjects apparently learn the organization, albeit random, and know where to look for items in the list. Consequently, the detrimental effects of random order are observed when the user has not yet gained extended familiarity with the items or when a different random order occurs every time the menu is viewed.

Alphabetic Ordering. An alphabetic ordering of alternatives may be used when there is a particular keyword, command name, or title that can be meaningfully alphabetized and scanned.

Numeric Ordering. Numeric ordering can be used for the selection of alternatives that are associated with numbers, such as type size, baud rate, and number of copies.

Chronological Ordering. Items that refer to dates and times may be ordered from oldest to newest. For example, articles in a news service, entries on an electronic bulletin board, and the list of months may be chronologically ordered.

Frequency of Use. Items may be ordered by frequency of use with often-used options listed first and infrequent options listed last. Frequency of use may be determined a priori by a logical analysis of the typical tasks or a posteriori from observed frequency of use.

Sequential Processing Order. Items may be listed according to their inferred order in a process or according to a cognitive ordering of items. The items "OPEN FILE," "ADD RECORD," "CHANGE RECORD," "DELETE RECORD," "CLOSE FILE," and "QUIT" imply a logical ordering of steps. The task analysis not only dictates the functions that are required but also dictates their usual order of operation. Cognitive order refers to the order that users would list items. For example, in a news network the items "WORLD," "NATIONAL," "STATE," and "LOCAL" are ordered in terms of an underlying dimension of scope.

Semantic Similarity Ordering. Items may be ordered in terms of some semantic dimension, such as impact, reversibility, potency, and so forth. Items that are most similar appear close to each other in the list. For example, a menu of style of type may be ordered in terms of emphasis: Plain, Underlined, Italicized, or Bold. Parkinson et al. (1985) gave an example of semantic ordering in which words sharing the most semantic features were presented adjacent to each other. For the category of topography, the order of the following names would be: Mojave, Sahara, Everest, Matterhorn, Atlantic, Pacific, Huron, Erie. The first four are land areas consisting of two deserts and two mountains. The last four are bodies of water consisting of two oceans and two lakes.

Categorical Grouping. Items may be categorized and then ordered within groups according to the characteristics listed above. Categorization operates on the similarities and dissimilarities of the items. Categorization allows for hierarchical search and decision processes on the part of the user as discussed in Chapter 3. Designers must also consider that categories and items within categories must be ordered.

The order of items in a menu should be consistent with the expectations and cognitive order held by the user. When the menu order is incongruent with the cognitive order, it makes it difficult for the user to locate items. Alphabetic order clearly reduces search time in many lists, but imagine the confusion in searching an alphabetized list of months, days, or numerals:

Select the month in which you were born:		Select the day on which you were born:		Select a numeral:	
1	April	1	Friday	1	Eight
2	August	2	Monday	2	Five
3	December	3	Saturday	3	Four
4	February	4	Sunday	4	Nine
5	January	5	Thursday	5	One
6	July	6	Tuesday	6	Seven
7	June	7	Wednesday	7	Six
8	March			8	Three
9	May			9	Two
10	November			10	Zero
11	October				
12	September				

The effects of menu organization on search time and on learning have been studied by a number of researchers. The results have been mixed because of additional factors, such as the number of items in the list, type of search task, and experience of the subjects.

One clear finding, however, is that alphabetical and categorical ordering are superior to random ordering. What is not clear is the relative advantage of alphabetical vs. categorical ordering. Card (1982) found that for menus of 18 items in a visual search task, there was an advantage of alphabetic ordering over a condition with categorical ordering and a condition with random ordering. On the other hand, for a 16-item list, Liebelt, McDonald, Stone, and Karat (1982) found a slight advantage for categorical organization over alphabetical and random orderings. However, the difference was not statistically reliable.

Often items are displayed according to several ordering schemes at once. Items may be grouped and then alphabetized or ranked in some way within groups. One study illustrates the importance of forming major groupings of items. McDonald, Stone, and Liebelt (1983) formed categorical groups with either similarity, alphabetical, or random ordering within groups. Menus consisted of 64 items arranged in four columns of 16 items. In three conditions, the four lists were categorized by food, animals, minerals, and cities. In Condition CC, the four lists were further ordered by obtaining similarity ratings and ordering the terms using multidimensional scaling and hierarchical clustering techniques.

In Condition CA, the four lists were alphabetized, and in Condition CR the items were random. Two other conditions mixed the categories. Condition A displayed a complete alphabetic ordering of the 64 items and Condition R a random order of all items. A second factor in the experiment was of interest. Half of the subjects were shown the explicit word to search for and the other half were shown a single-line dictionary definition. The task was to locate the item on the display screen and press the key corresponding to the identification letters displayed immediately to its left. The identification letters were randomly assigned to items on each trial to prevent memory association that would circumvent the search process. Subjects were obtained from a temporary employment agency for secretarial help. Response time was measured over a series of five blocks of 64 trials. Figure 6.3 shows the results.

Overall subjects that were given definitions took longer to respond than subjects given the explicit word. Organization of the list had a significant effect on response time. For the explicit word, random ordering was much worse than any other conditions. Subjects were able to perform quickly in all of the categorical conditions and the alphabetized

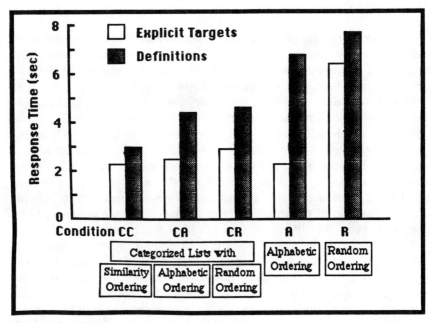

Figure 6.3.   Response time as a function of type of organization for explicit targets and for definitions.

"Searching for items in menus: The effects of organization and type of target," by J.E. McDonald, J.D. Stone, and L.S. Liebolt, 1983. *Proceedings of the Human Factors Society 27th Annual Meeting* (pp. 834–837). Copyright 1983 by The Human Factors Society. Reprinted by permission.

list. It would seem that once the subject identified the category and scanned the column of 16 items, order within the column was not an important factor. On the other hand, for the definitions, the categorical ordering (CC) was slightly superior to the alphabetized or randomized categories. The alphabetic and random lists led to the longest response times, with the alphabetic condition only slightly superior to the random order. This result is important since users may or may not be searching for an exact word match. When they are searching for an item to satisfy a definition (or a command to perform a function), categorical ordering is important.

One would expect that the ordering of the list would become increasingly important as the length of the list gets longer. Perlman (1984) found this to be true. He varied the length of the list to have 5, 10, 15, or 20 items. The items were in one case the numbers 1 to 20 and in another case words beginning with the letters "a" to "t." The lists were either sorted or random. Four groups of eight subjects searched either sorted words, sorted numbers, random words, or random numbers. Each subject searched all different list lengths. The target number or word was shown on the screen and the subject then searched for the item and then pressed the key corresponding to the item. Figure 6.4 shows the results. Response time increased with the length of the list. Response times for sorted items were shorter than for random items and for numbers than words. What is interesting about these results is the

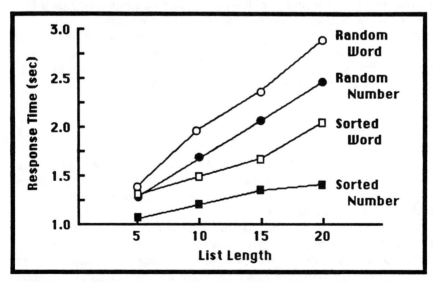

Figure 6.4.   Response time as a function of type of list and list length.

From "Making the right choices with menus," by G. Perlman, 1984, *INTERACT '84* (pp. 317-321). Copyright 1984 by North-Holland. Reprinted by permission.

interaction between the list length and the type of list searched. When lists are sorted, the increase due to list length is less than when lists are random. This suggests that when menus include a lot of items, it is extremely important that the designer consider organization of the list in order to reduce search time.

It is not clear, however, whether alphabetic or semantic organization results in superior performance. Parkinson et al. (1985) found little difference in search time between alphabetic and semantic organization within categories of words when the categories were sufficiently separated by spacing. This is an important finding for designers since alphabetic ordering is easy to achieve while semantic ordering requires extensive pretesting. On the other hand it should be pointed out that if the designer wishes to convey a mental model of the system, semantic ordering may help to achieve this objective. For example, in command specification, Parkinson et al. point out that given the task of executing a set of functions using a menu of commands, naive users would probably learn the system more efficiently if the commands for similar functions were grouped together in the display.

6.1.6 Orientation of the List

Generally, lists of options have been displayed in a vertical list (columns) rather than a horizontal one (rows). The question is whether the vertical or tabular listing is indeed superior to a single horizontal line listing. Single line listing saves space on the screen. In cases where the user input is an associated letter or number, one might expect the tabular arrangement to be superior. In the case of touch screen or a pointing device, it is not clear. In cases where the single line listing is used, items are generally very brief and are often single character options as in the following menu from an electronic bulletin board:

Option (A/T/D/E/T)?

In a study of menu preferences by Norman (1987), computer science majors indicated a preference for single line listings of commands as opposed to a tabular listing. On the other hand, noncomputer science students preferred a tabular listing.

In a study on the organization of items in large menus of 64 items, Parkinson et al. (1985) compared category groupings arranged by column versus row. Menus with categories arranged in columns were searched in approximately 25% less time (one sec faster) than menus with categories arranged in rows. From these results, visual search for targets appears to be substantially facilitated by column presentation. However, it must be noted that this finding is currently limited to large menus and to the particular configuration chosen by Parkinson et al. In their experiment all menus consisted of 64 words listed in four columns of 16. Eight words were chosen from each of eight natural categories and arranged in either columns (two categories per column) or rows (two adjacent rows per category). This arrangement implies that given a target in the menu organized by column, subjects first located the correct category in a 2 x 4 array of categories and then scanned down to find the target within the category to locate the two-digit response code for the item. In the case of menus organized by row, subjects first located the category in a vertical array of eight categories, and then scanned two rows or four items to find the target. It is likely that having categories split on two rows slowed down the search due to the time to jump from line to line as well as from column to column when searching for a word within a category.

This interpretation is further suggested by the results from two alphabetized menus also used in the same study. In one menu, words were alphabetized from top to bottom by column and in the other from left-to-right by row. The difference in search time between these two menus was of approximately the same size as for categorical menus. Furthermore, Parkinson et al. (1985) noted that the row versus column effects may have been confounded by the fact that more space separated words in adjacent columns than in adjacent rows. All this strongly suggests that it was not simply row versus column organization that led to the effect, but that the visual search distance and the number of jumps to reposition each search within categories accounted for the differences.

Although it is not yet clear that row arrangement is itself detrimental, it is clear that large differences in performance can be due to column versus row arrangement of menus. At present the results suggest that designers should attempt to arrange items so as to minimize visual search distance and the need to jump from one location to another when searching within the same category.

The issue of row versus column presentation is important in systems with pull-down menus. Such systems generally display a menu bar which is a horizontal menu listing of vertical pull-down menus. In essence they alternate horizontal and vertical arrays. This idea can be extended as an effective way of handling successive depth of a menu while maintaining context. An example of this is shown in Figure 6.5 for a hierarchical tree of languages having a maximum depth of five. Menu nodes shown in reverse video indicate the selected path.

At present little is known about the use of alternating menus. However, one would expect that with the use of a pointing device such as a mouse, the selection process is much like tracing a route in a maze. As such it will be highly spatial in character and affected by psychomotor processes.

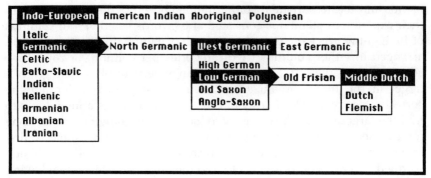

Figure 6.5. An example of alternating horizontal and vertical pull-down menus.

6.1.7 Fixed vs. Variable Format

The literature suggests that the organization of information elements on the screen should be standardized in order to make effective use of spatial context. The user acquires an expectation of where to look to see particular information. When information could appear at different locations, the user must search for it. Teitelbaum and Granda (1983) compared fixed versus variable formatting of the information. When the location of information was inconsistent, the time that it took to answer questions about information on the screen was longer than when the information was in a constant location. Moreover, when information was in a constant location, response times improved with practice indicating that users were acquiring expectations as to where information was located. Response times did not improve when information was presented in random locations.

The importance of consistency in screen and menu design cannot be overemphasized. It is imperative that users develop expectations about the location of information to avoid having to repeatedly search for information. Furthermore, inconsistency probably fosters a level of frustration and confusion in the user that may generalize to the other menu selection processes.

6.2 WRITING THE MENU

Communication is an art. In human/computer interaction, the art is communicating through an interactive media about the control of that media. Fortunately, art is guided by principles. Menus must convey information to the user about (a) the nature of the choice (What is being accomplished in making this choice? What is the purpose of this choice?), and (b) the nature of the alternatives (What will happen if this alternative is selected?).

On the one hand, one would like to convey as much information as possible, explaining all the options in great detail. On the other hand, brevity is important due to screen limitations and the amount of information that the user wants or desires to read. Consequently, there is a tradeoff between thoroughness and brevity, and the tradeoff is to be moderated by the experience of the user. Many systems are developing the concept of dynamic help in which menus are highly descriptive for novice users, but as the user gains experience, the menus become brief mnemonic reminders of the alternatives.

6.2.1 Titling the Frame

Titles of menus should be more than place holders. They should be descriptive of the list of options and the context. The title, "MAIN MENU OPTIONS," conveys little information except that the user is probably at the top of the menu tree.

When a title is superfluous, then it may be omitted. To the extent that the list of options define the context, the title is redundant. This is particularly true for experienced users. Titles merely clutter the screen. It is an empirical question as to whether titles help, and when they have served their usefulness should be dropped. One possibility is to design a system in which the user may hide titles or reveal them as necessary.

The title, however, can be a potent stimulus in defining the context and increasing comprehension of the menu. An experiment by Bransford and Johnson (1972) illustrated this fact. They assessed comprehension and recall of a passage, describing in detail the steps that one must go through in order to accomplish a certain function. In one case, subjects were given the title of the passage, "Washing Clothes," either before or after reading it. In a control condition, no title was given. Subjects given the title before reading the passage reported higher comprehension and recalled about twice as many items from the passage than other subjects. Subjects given the title after reading the passage did no better than the control subjects given no title. In the same way, menu titles have the potential of increasing the comprehensibility of menus and facilitating choice.

We may think of a schema as a conceptual framework that provides "slots" to be filled in with specific information. Menus are schemata of the form: "Of the following options, select one: (a). . .(b). . .(c). . ." Users assimilate the particular options into this framework. Menus are also a part of a larger schema in which they are understood. Without establishing the context of the choice by instantiating a schema, comprehension of the menu frame may be severely limited. Consider, for example, the following menu:

Select function:
Open
Close
Activate top element
Activate bottom element
Clean

The purpose of this choice and the function of the alternatives are not at all apparent. However, if you are told that the schema has to do with the operation of an oven, the menu is comprehensible and easy to remember.

6.2.2 Wording the Alternatives

Alternatives may be single words, brief phrases, or longer descriptions of options. It is generally recommended that when brief phrases are to be used they should be verb phrases that are written in parallel construction (Shneiderman, 1987). For example, rather than phrasing the items as "Print," "Execute a program," and "Disk eject," they should be "Print a file," "Execute a program," and "Eject a disk." In general, it is recommended to not change the construction of a phrase within the same menu frame. In addition, Shneiderman listed the following guidelines:

1.   Use familiar and consistent terminology.
2.   Ensure that items are distinct from one another.
3.   Use consistent and concise phrasing.
4.   Bring the keyword to the left.

An important aspect of wording is not only that it conveys information, but that the alternatives are interpreted as distinctly different. Distinctiveness refers to the semantic aspects of an alternative that enhances its difference from other alternatives in the set. The objective is to word items so as to emphasize differences rather than the commonality of function. Consider, for example, a menu that contains the items: (1) Services for Professionals, (2) Home Services, (3) Business and Financial, and (4) Personal Computing. Items 1 and 2 are not very distinct in that they both emphasize services. Furthermore, the distinction of what is meant by "professional" versus "home" is not clear. Items 1 and 3 lack distinctiveness altogether. Item 1 could be a subset of 3 or vice versa. Items 2 and 4 lack distinctiveness since "home" and "personal" share common aspects. The terms "services" and "computing" are not distinct since any services provided on a time-sharing system must involve computing. Such a menu poses a dilemma for the novice user, who, for example, wants to balance his checkbook. The question is how to design a menu system so as to maximally enhance the distinctiveness of items and minimize their confusability.

In a study by Schwartz and Norman (1986) novice computer users searched either (a) the original menu of a commercial time-sharing system in which items were not worded in a holistic manner, or (b) a modified menu of the system in which items were holistically worded. They hypothesized that the effect of item distinctiveness would vary with the type of search required. In explicit search problems, subjects searched for the exact wording of targets (e.g., "Search for 'Backgammon' "). In information find problems, subjects searched for menu items that provided information about subject matter topics (e.g., "Find information concerning how to balance your checkbook"). These two types of menu problems correspond to the two general uses of menu selection systems. In general, it was found that subjects using the modified menu (a) took less time per problem; (b) found targets in a more direct path; and (c) gave up on fewer problems than the subjects using the original menu. Although information find problems took longer and required a greater number of frames to be traversed than explicit search problems, there was no interaction with distinctiveness. Distinctiveness had a similar effect on search processes for both explicit and information find problems.

Schwartz and Norman (1987) suggest that distinctiveness may be controlled to some extent by the way in which choices are clustered in the menu tree. Items may be shifted from one menu frame to another to enhance the differences among options within a particular frame. When the structure of the menu is fixed, the wording of alternatives may be altered to enhance differences. They suggest the following strategies for improving distinctiveness:

1. Induce holistic, intact, and integral processing of the alternatives. Holistic alternatives are not likely to be decomposed into aspects that may be shared among the items. Options should appear as different as apples and oranges even though they may share many common aspects (e.g., both fruits, both round, both about the same size, etc.).
2. Maximize aspect redundancy and intercorrelations within alternatives and minimize them between alternatives. For example, the

position and color of traffic lights are perfectly correlated and redundant. Consequently, both aspects can be used to discriminate between the alternatives of stopping and going.

3. Present all alternatives simultaneously rather than one by one or page by page. When alternatives are processed sequentially (as in a slow display), a subjective emphasis on the common aspects of the alternatives may occur. Users look for shared aspects that lead from one alternative to another rather than contrasting the aspects when all are seen simultaneously.

4. Explicitly define the universe of options so that each alternative may be understood in this context. If the alternatives are Diet-Rite, Diet Coke, 7-Up, and Fruit Juice, the universe of options is unclear. With one generic drink (Fruit Juice) and three specific drinks, one might overgeneralize to the universe of liquids as the reference, while others might restrict the universe to drinks that refresh. Avoiding this type of ambiguity is important in effective menu design.

5. Ensure that the variability among the alternatives is high in terms of the rationale for the choice. For example, if the universe of choice is among soft drinks and the alternatives are Diet-Rite, Diet Coke, and Diet Pepsi, there is little perceived variability. However, if the universe of choice is limited to dietetic soft drinks, then the perceived variability is high.

6.2.3 Graphic Alternatives

An increasing number of software applications are using graphic symbols called *icons* to represent objects and operations. Graphic symbols have long been popular in cartography. Graphic symbols can be visually more distinct from one another than words, and it is easier to spot a graphic symbol on a map than it is to locate a word. Similarly in human/computer interaction graphic symbols conserve space and yet are more distinct on busy display screens. However, there are a number of questions about the relationship between graphic symbols and the objects and commands that they represent when used in menu selection. Hemenway (1982) distinguished between icons that depict (a) the objects on which the commands operate, (b) the operations or operators themselves, and (c) the operations on the objects. Figure 6.6 gives examples of these three types.

The first panel shows icons that represent objects operated on by some command. Since only the operand is depicted, it is not always clear what the operation is. Often, as in the case of the camera, it is simply an on/off function. In other cases, users must learn that more complex commands are implied. The middle panel shows icons that

Icon	Object Depicted	Description of Command
	TV camera	Turns on the TV camera and snaps its picture onto the display screen (From Superpaint™)
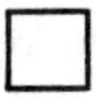	Image area	Removes and inserts image areas (From Markup™)
	Page with left margin	Changes the left margin (From Smalltalk Gallery Editor™)
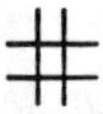	Grid	Changes the grid spacing and alignment (From Markup™)

Icon	Operation Implied	Description of Command
	Translate	Translates lines, curves, and text (From Draw™)
	Delete	Deletes lines, curves, and text (From Draw™)
	Paint	Re-paints lines and curves and re-writes text from (Draw™)
	Cut	Dashes and un-dashes lines and curves (From Draw™)

Icon	Operation Implied	Object(s) Depicted	Description of Command
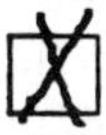	Delete	Image area	Deletes image area (From Superpaint™)
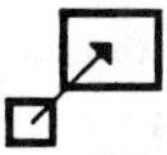	Magnify	Image area	Enlarges image areas (From Superpaint™)
	Magnify	Image area	Enlarges image areas (From Smalltalk Gallary Editor™)
	Fill in	Bounded area and color	Fills in areas with color (From Superpaint™)

Figure 6.6 Icons depicting objects, operations, and combinations of objects and operations.

From "User performance of iconic and command name interfaces," by Y. Rogers, 1987, *Proceedings of the Second International Conference on Human/Computer Interaction* (p. 145). Reprinted by permission.

depict operations. The arrow has the conventional meaning of movement or direction and the X has the meaning of deletion or negation. Both meanings more or less represent the intended command. On the other hand, the operations represented by the paint brush and scissors are implied by what the tools do. Finally, the icons in the last panel combine both objects and operators. The first icon combines the box (image area) and the X (delete) to imply delete image area. The second and third icons show objects before and after the operation. The operation is inferred by the difference between the two. The last icon (fill in) shows a snapshot of the operation in progress. Animation completes the richness of meaning and provides yet a stronger basis for implying the operation by showing the operation in action.

Hemenway (1982) proposed a simple model for the interpretability and effectiveness of icons. When a new icon is encountered its interpretability depends on (a) its comprehension (e.g., the ability to discover what the icon depicts), and (b) its effectiveness as a retrieval cue (e.g., the ability to form a link between what is depicted and the corresponding command). For experienced users, the effectiveness of an icon ability depends on (a) the ability to recognize what the icon depicts, and (b) the ability to retrieve the link between the icon and the command from memory. It is predicted that highly familiar, conventional symbols will be easier to learn and recall than obscure icons that lack distinguishing features. Furthermore, icons that directly depict objects and operations are predicted to be more effective than ones that resort to analogy and convoluted links.

Often the organization and interrelation among commands can be expressed in shared features of the icons. The icon for a tool to generate rectangles and filled rectangles shares the shape but differs in shading. Similarly icons for drawing lines may vary in thickness corresponding to the width of the lines created (see Figure 6.7). Hemenway (1982) suggested that when elements are shared across icons the user has less to learn since familiarity on the shared feature transfers to the new icon. Furthermore, repetition of the elements can make it easier for users to link the elements to aspects of the command and to recognize how icons vary in terms of their features.

An empirical study was conducted by Rogers (1987) to test the prediction that direct linking between icons and commands results in better interpretability of icons. Four types of icon sets for file manipulation, text editing, and printing were designed that were either (a) abstract symbols, (b) concrete analogies, (c) concrete objects, or (d) concrete objects operated on with abstract symbols. Abstract symbols and concrete analogies constitute indirect mapping; whereas, concrete objects provide a direct mapping. For comparison a fifth group was composed

Icon Pair	Distinguishing Feature	Description of Command
 ⬆ (double arrow)	Double	Copies and translates selected lines, curves, and text
⬆ (single arrow)	Single	Translates slected lines, curves, and text (From Draw™)
╋ (thin cross)	Thin	Draws thin vertical and horizontal lines in black or white
✚ (thick cross)	Thick	**Draws thick vertical and horizontal lines in black and white (From Markup™)**
 Ⓘ (boxed I-beam)	Image area	Removes and inserts text and image
I (I-beam)	"T"	Removes and inserts text (From Markup™)

Figure 6.7. Pairs of related icons.

From "User performance of iconic and command name interfaces," by Y. Rogers, 1987, *Proceedings of the Second International Conference on Human/Computer Interaction* (p. 145). Reprinted by permission.

of verbal names consisting of high imagery words. The icon set with the most direct mapping (concrete objects operated on with abstract symbols) resulted in the fewest accesses to the help facility and the least number of errors. However, there was also an interaction between the type of command and the form of representation. File operations, such as "to save," appeared to be easier to use and recall when the commands were verbal. Text editing commands, such as "insert a space," were more discriminable as icons.

These results suggest that designers should not only use icons that have a direct linking, but that they should carefully analyze the nature of the command and its representation. Icons are perhaps best used to represent the operations of graphic tools and objects; whereas, verbal labels are best for formal commands.

A final possibility is to add graphic and verbal labels. It has been speculated that graphic symbols added to menu items could impair the speed and accuracy of performance (Mills, 1981). Studies on categorization provide indirect evidence about how pictures and verbal labels interact. Smith and Magee (1980), for example, found that when subjects were asked to categorize words, the simultaneous presentation of an incongruent picture disrupted processing (e.g., a picture of a car shown with the word *table*). However, when subjects were asked to categorize pictures, the presentation of an incongruent word did not disrupt processing (e.g., the word *car* shown with a picture of a table). Furthermore, it has been shown that the categorization of pictures tends to be faster than of words (Pellegrino, Rosinski, Chiesi, & Siegel, 1977). Such evidence suggests that graphic symbols may facilitate menu selection or at least not degrade performance.

To test the effect of adding graphic symbols, Muter and Mayson (1986) compared three conditions using a videotext database: (a) text-only menus in which verbal items were displayed in a double-spaced linear list, (b) text plus graphic menus in which verbal items were displayed with graphic symbols of the items and distributed in a non-linear fashion on the page, and (c) control menus in which verbal items were distributed in a nonlinear fashion on the page. To enhance the pairing of graphics and labels both were shown in the same color. Subjects were shown menu pages and asked a series of 12 questions (e.g., "Where can you buy a low priced bedroom suite?"; "Where can you locate a handsaw?"). Instructions emphasized both speed and accuracy. It was found that the text plus graphics condition resulted in significantly fewer errors (2.8%) than either the text-only (5.6%) or the control (4.6%) conditions. Overall response times did not differ. Thus, the addition of graphics halved the error rate without significantly increasing the processing time.

On the other hand, a study by Wandmacher and Müller (1987) found no difference in error rate between graphic menus and word menus, but did find a difference in reaction time in both a search-and-select paradigm and a recognition paradigm. On each trial of the search-and-select experiment subjects were given a task description (e.g., "You want to print a document"), and a menu of either word commands or icons was then displayed (see Figure 6.8). Subjects made their selections by entering a number corresponding to the item. The order of the menu items was randomized on each trial so that subjects could not memorize the numbers. On each trial of the recognition experiment only one item was displayed and subjects had to respond by pressing a prelearned number. In both the search-and-select and the recognition paradigm, response time was faster for icons than for words. These authors suggest that the gap between the meaning of an expression and its form is smaller for icons than for word commands. Hutchins, Hollan, and Norman (1986) referred in general, to this gap as the *articulatory distance*. Icons may facilitate menu selection because they provide a more direct

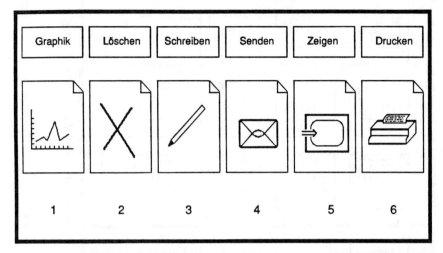

Figure 6.8. Word commands and icons used in the study by Wandmacher and Müller (1987). (English translation of the commands: (I) Graphics, (2) Delete, (3) Edit, (4) Send, (5) Display, and (6) Print.)

access to the meaning of the functions involved. Less time is required to translate an intention into an actual selection.

The use of graphics in menu selection appears to be a promising design feature. However, the effective use of graphic symbols requires thoughtful consideration. Arend, Muthig, and Wandmacher (1987) pointed out that it is not sufficient to just recommend the use of icons. In the same way that Schwartz and Norman (1986) demonstrated that discriminability has an effect on word menus, distinctiveness may have an effect on graphic menus. Arend et al. suggested that the "global superiority" effect in visual perception could affect the degree to which icons facilitate menu selection. The global superiority effect basically is that global features of figures (e.g., shape, color, size) can be selected and responded to considerably faster than local features (e.g., lines and structures within a figure).

Arend et al. contrasted the effects of (a) icon distinctiveness defined in terms of global superiority, and (b) icon representativeness defined in terms of articulatory distance. Distinctive icons were abstract and emphasized one global feature. Representational icons included local features to make the meaning of the icon more apparent. A search-and-select paradigm was used in which subjects were given task descriptions and then had to select the appropriate menu item. Either a word command menu, a distinctive icon menu, or a representational icon menu

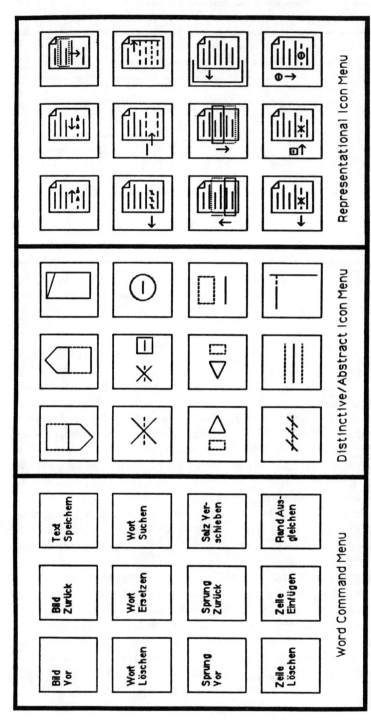

Figure 6.9. Word command menu, distinctive/abstract icon menu, and representional icon menu used by **Arend, Muthig, and Wandmacher (1987).**

From "Evidence for global feature superiority in menu selection by icons," by U. Arend, K.P. Muthig, and J. Wandmacher, 1987, *Behaviour and Information Technology,* 6, 411-426. Copyright 1987 by Taylor & Francis, Ltd. Reprinted by permission.

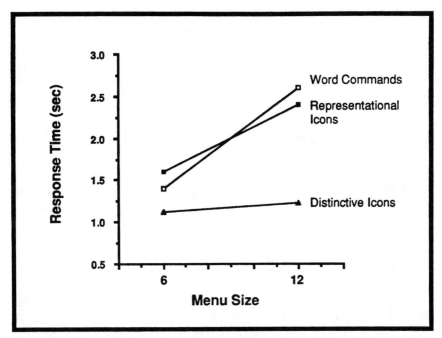

Figure 6.10. Mean response times to word commands, distinctive icons, and representational icons as a function of menu size.

From "Evidence for global feature superiority in menu selection by icons," by U. Arend, K.P. Muthig, and J. Wandmacher, 1987, *Behaviour and Information Technology, 6,* 411-426. Copyright 1987 by Taylor & Francis, Ltd. Reprint by permission.

was presented to different groups of subjects. In addition, menus were constructed of either 6 or 12 items. Subjects made selections by pressing the key corresponding to the position of the menu item on either a 3 x 2 or 3 x 4 key matrix depending upon the menu size condition. Figure 6.9 shows the menu sets used in the 12 item condition.

The results clearly favored the distinctive icon menu over either the word menu or the representational menu. Figure 6.10 shows the mean response time for each menu. Over all conditions, the distinctive icon menu resulted in response times that were nearly twice as fast as word or representational icon menus. Consequently, the type of icon used has a great effect on performance. Distinct, abstract icons which have high global superiority result in the best performance. Representational icons that reduce the articulatory distance, however, do no better than word menus. Apparently, icon distinctiveness is much more important than icon representativeness, at least in this task.

Interestingly, response time increased substantially with menu size for word menus and representational icon menus; however, the increase for the distinctive icon menu was not significant. Distinctive menus seem to be impervious to menu size. Word menus seem to be searched relatively slowly and sequentially. Similarly, representational menus are searched in a slow and sequential manner. In contrast, distinct, abstract icons seems to be searched in a rapid and parallel fashion. The global features of abstract items appear to facilitate parallel visual processing of the items.

These experiments clearly support the positive benefits of graphic menus. But it is clear that icons must be carefully selected. They should depict concrete objects and actions rather than analogies or abstractions. They should be highly discriminable and emphasize global features. Furthermore, icons should be clearly interpretable. Their relationship to commands should be direct and obvious. Finally, one should consider using both icons and verbal labels to retain the advantages of both.

6.3 SELECTION RESPONSE

Once the user has formed an intention and decided upon the desired menu option, the selection must be activated. The *selection response* is the overt act on the part of the user that impacts on the computer. As important as it is, the selection response often seems to be the least of one's concerns in designing a menu selection system. However, it is the focal point of the user's communication with the computer. Clarity, simplicity, speed, and accuracy are essential. For the novice user, instructions must be given. It can be extremely frustrating to the novice user to key in the desired alternative and wait five minutes with no response because the return key had not been pressed. For the experienced user, continual frustration may occur when the user habitually hits the wrong key or overshoots the item with a mouse. Added up over the life of the system, these human/computer errors may reduce the efficiency of the system by 5-25%, depending on the extent of interaction.

Many different types of input devices have been employed in menu systems as noted in Chapter 2. In this section we will be interested not so much in the physical device as in its functionality, location, and state on the display. Whatever the device, some instructions must be given to the user (especially to the novice user) as to how it functions. Furthermore, the response generally is given a visual representation at some location on the screen. Finally, the display conveys the current state of the response. For example, the display may indicate the following states: no selection, tentative selection, or implemented selection.

6.3.1 Response Instructions

Instructions are needed as to how to make the response selection in two cases: (1) the person using the system for the first time; and (2) the person returning to the system who has forgotten how to make a response selection. In the first case, instructions need to explicitly state the sequence of actions, such as "Enter number and press RETURN." Response methods may vary among systems leading to habitual errors. If a user is used to terminating input by pressing the RETURN key, and the system is designed to respond following one key entry, the habitual press of the RETURN key may lead to an error in a subsequent menu. Such a system needs to be able to ignore the RETURN key if pressed within a certain time interval.

On the other hand, if the user is not used to entering a terminating character, he may wait a long time for the system to respond before realizing the problem. One solution to this is to use a time out, so that after a period of time, the system responds to whatever has been input.

6.3.2 Position of Response

With touch screens and pointing devices, the response input is conceptually spatial and congruent with the option; that is, the location of the option is the location of the response. This adds a persuasive sense of compatibility. On the other hand, when the input is via a keyboard or key pad, the spatial position of the response is distal from the option. In the case of special key pads, the entry is conceptually at the key pad. For a standard keyboard input, we generally think of the response as being inserted on the screen. The location of this insertion point generally follows the list of responses. Some systems locate the insertion point following the stem. In a survey of novice and experienced computer users, Norman (1987) found that novices preferred the location following the stem and before the options, and that experienced users preferred the location after the options.

One question is whether a distal insertion point is needed at all. Given keyboard input, it need not be echoed on the screen; but rather cause a highlighting of an alternative. Recent studies comparing *embedded* versus *explicit* menus suggest that when menu items are integrated or embedded in the task or the text being read, users work faster than when items are explicitly listed at a distal point. For example, Powell (1985) compared user search through hierarchical data in order to answer 20 questions in a 15-minute period. Figure 6.11 shows an example

INTRODUCTION: STAMP UNION   PAGE 1 OF 2

    The Adele H. Stamp Union, formerly known as the Student Union, is the
cultural and social center for the University. The Union provides a variety
of services to the faculty, staff, and students. A plethora of **restaurants**
are available providing a wide choice of atmosphere and a variety of menus.
The Union is also a center for **entertainment**. Several **shops** and many
special services are available, too. **Union programs** include concerts,
exhibitions, and craft classes. The Union is open all week from 7 A.M. to
1 A.M. Monday through Friday, and until 2 A.M. on weekends.

[Select option then press RETURN]

NEXT PAGE   END

Embedded Menu

INTRODUCTION: STAMP UNION

Would you like to read more about

    1. RESTAURANTS
    2. ENTERTAINMENT
    3. SHOPS
    4. SPECIAL SERVICES
    5. UNION PROGRAMS
    6. Return to first page of STAMP UNION

Please enter one number and press RETURN:

Enter Q to quit the session

Explicit Menu

Figure 6.11. Top panel shows an embedded menu in which the alternatives
are shown in boldface type in the text. The bottom panel shows the explicit
menu for the same items.

of one of the frames of the embedded menu. Significantly more questions were answered correctly with the embedded menus than with the
explicit menus. Furthermore, subjects preferred using the embedded
menus over the explicit menus. Koved and Shneiderman (1986) found
similar results for information search in online maintenance manuals.

6.3.3 Response Compatibility

An important factor in the theory of cognitive control is the concept of *stimulus-response compatibility,* or as referred to in the human factors literature, *control-display compatibility.* The idea is that aspects of the stimulus should be congruent with aspects of the response. Congruency may be defined along a number of dimensions. Spatial congruency refers to a match between the relative location of the stimulus and the relative location of the response. For example, if the alternatives are arrayed left to right on the screen, responses are congruent if they are arrayed left to right on the keyboard. Spatial congruency is often violated by systems using the keyboard. For example, function keys will be listed along the bottom of the screen in order from 1 to 10. But they appear as two columns on the left of the keyboard. The result is that the user must go through an extra cognitive process in order to translate screen location to keyboard location.

A second type of congruency has to do with letter and number pairing. Table 6.1 illustrates the types of congruency and incongruity that can result.

It is appealing to use single letter responses because it allows up to 26 response alternatives. The first column in Table 6.1 is ideal but rarely does it work out so nicely. In most real-world menus, it is most likely that a number of incompatible pairs will occur. The next two columns show worst cases. In the first case, the design choice was to list the options in alphabetical order, while their associated letter responses are random. In the second case, the choice was to list the responses in alphabetical order, while the associated options are in random order. Fortunately, designers do not generally have to deal with these worst cases, although they illustrate the problem. Unfortunately, they must wrestle with the mixed case illustrated in the last column of Table 6.1.

Table 6.1. Examples of Congruent and Incongruent Option–Response Pairs.

	Incongruent (Worse Case)		
Congruent	**Ordered Options**	**Ordered Responses**	**Mixed**
A-Assemble	E-Assemble	A-File	A-Assemble
B-Buffer	F-Buffer	B-Compile	B-Assign
C-Compile	A-Compile	C-Assemble	C-Buffer
D-Debug	B-Debug	D-Edit	D-Compile
E-Edit	G-Edit	E-Buffer	E-Edit
F-File	C-File	F-Graph	F-Graph
G-Graph	H-Graph	G-Halt	G-Halt
H-Halt	D-Halt	H-Debug	H-Read

Option-Response compatibility has two directions. One is a forward compatibility from the option to the response (e.g., if the option is "Assemble," the response must be "A"), and the other is a backward compatibility from the response to the option (e.g., if the response is "A," the option must be "Assemble"). Forward compatibility is broken down when there is uncertainty as to what the response is given the option. Although the menu requires that there be a unique response for each option, that unique coding may not be apparent to the user. Backward compatibility is broken down when there is uncertainty as to what the option is given the response. This occurs when several options begin with the same letter.

The effect of incompatibility was observed in an experiment by Perlman (1984). Time to press the correct selection response was compared in four menus which varied compatibility with letter responses and number responses: (a) a compatible letter menu in which letter responses were the same as the first letter of each menu item (as in the first column of Table 6.1); (b) an incompatible letter menu in which the letters "a" through "z" were randomly assigned as the responses; (c) a compatible number menu in which the numbers 1 through 8 were assigned as

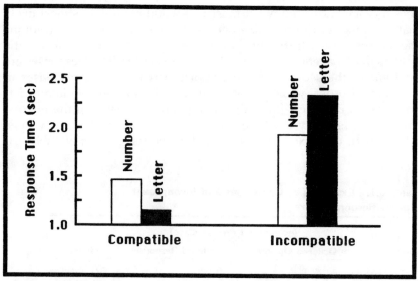

Figure 6.12. Response selection time as a function of the response-option compatibility.

the selection responses; and (d) an incompatible number menu in which numbers were randomly assigned to menu items. Items were always listed in the same alphabetical order.

Figure 6.12 shows the results. Compatible letter responses led to the fastest responses. Subjects were able to circumvent the need to locate the option and then press the response. Compatible number responses were superior to incompatible numbers and incompatible letters were slowest. This suggests that if compatible letter responses can be generated they are preferred. Since this is usually not the case, compatible number responses are the next best design choice.

6.3.4 Response Verification and Feedback

The menu display is generally used to indicate the current state of response selection. Three states exist.

Waiting for response. In this state the user has not yet selected an option. The system may explicitly prompt the user by providing an insertion point for the response and direct the user to the keyboard or pointing device.

Tentative response selected but not implemented. In this state the user has input a selection but has not yet been verified that it is the selection to be implemented. This state is crucial in systems where selections have consequential effects and where response error is a possibility. It allows the user to correct a response before it is implemented. Response error may occur due to pressing the wrong key or missing the target using a pointing device. The disadvantage is that the user has an extra response to make in order to implement the selection. In many cases this is merely pressing the RETURN or SEND key. In other cases, with simultaneous menus, the implement response may activate a whole set of tentative selections.

Response selected and implemented. In this state the user has made a response to implement the selection. The system may provide feedback to the user that the desired selection has been made. If the effect of the selection is not immediately apparent or delayed in some way, the system should provide feedback to the users confirming the selection and informing them of its progress.

6.4 SUMMARY

Each menu frame in a system conveys information and provides a forum for user control. The graphic format of the frame affects attention, interpretation, context, and search time. Well-designed menus help to focus attention on the relevant dimensions of choice; they help to interpret the function of alternatives and the reason for the choice; they help to establish the context for the choice; and they help to facilitate visual search for items in the menu list.

The wording of the items is crucial. To the degree that the items convey unambiguous and highly discriminable options, users will be able to avoid wrong selections and reduce the time that it takes to traverse menu structures. It is noted that guidelines need to be developed to assist designers in writing and evaluating the wording of alternatives. As noted in the subsequent chapter on prototyping, evaluation of the system should be at the individual word level rather than at the global performance level.

The selection response and instructions on how to respond vary greatly among systems. The lack of consistency among systems can result in problems as users go from one system to another. To the extent that any system differs from the expectations of the user, explicit instructions are required. It is noted that the position of response insertion on the display should be consistent with the user's mental model of the system. Responses should be compatible with the alternatives. Finally, the system should give the user an opportunity to verify the selection and change it if necessary before commitment, and should provide acknowledgment that the selected alternative was properly accessed.

The amount of menu detail and response instructions needed by the user will vary with training and experience as discussed in the next chapter. In principle, however, the variables pertaining to format and phrasing will remain important at all levels of experience.

7

Performance, Acquisition, and Training Methods

Performance is an idea easily grasped by users and managers. One can have a clear sense of work being accomplished and tasks being completed. But often performance is difficult to measure objectively. Furthermore, since performance tends to improve over time, one cannot merely assess a system on the basis of first time exposure. Instead performance must be measured at different stages of adoption of the system by the users.

The improvement of user performance is of great concern to all. With respect to users, one may ask, "How much do users improve with practice? What are the benefits of different training programs?" With respect to the machine, software and hardware developers are interested in the improvement of system performance. Ultimately it must be remembered that performance is a function of both the user's ability and the system's capability. It is the synergistic combination of the two that determines overall performance.

This chapter first considers overall performance as the function of user ability and system power. Measures of human performance, system performance, and overall performance will be discussed. Changes in user performance on menu selection systems over time and implications of the learning profile are discussed. Finally, studies that have compared different training methods using documentation and online help are reviewed.

7.1 PERFORMANCE

Performance is considered the bottom-line measure of a system. For the computer itself, performance may be defined in terms of technical specifications, such as system response time and rate of transmission of menu frames. However, when it comes to human performance, it is not always clear what is meant. Performance may be defined along different factors and at different levels of analysis. Table 1.1 in Chapter 1 lists several factors pertaining to system productivity and to human performance. System productivity refers to the overall performance due to the individual performance of the user and the machine.

7.1.1 Measures of User Performance

User performance on a menu system may be assessed from a micro- to a macro-level. In terms of speed, one may look at (a) the time that it takes for the user to look at a menu frame and make the choice, (b) the time to locate a target in a menu tree, up to (c) the total time to complete a whole task using a menu selection system. Accuracy must also be considered. One may look at (a) the probability that a single menu choice is correct, (b) the total probability that the user locates the desired target in the menu tree, up to (c) the probability that the task is correctly completed. The level analysis depends on the researcher's focus on component processes involved in the task.

Performance may also be divided along the factors of quantity and quality. It must be remembered that performance on the menu is, in general, not the end in itself. Rather the menu selection system is in support of some other task, such as word processing, file management, telecommunications, and so on. Ultimately, the issue of performance must relate to productivity in the task domain, rather than merely speed and accuracy in menu selection. It is assumed that improved performance on menu selection will facilitate that task; however, it is quite possible that it may do so in a way that cannot be directly assessed through menu performance measures. For example, the menu may convey an effective model of task structure that may slow menu performance but improve quality of work in the task domain. This possibility is discussed in Chapter 8.

7.1.2 Overall Performance = User Proficiency × System Power

Overall performance of a system is assumed to be a function of the level of proficiency of the users and the power of the system. However, it has not been clear just what the function was for combining the two factors. Some have emphasized the power of the computer to solve problems and the limitations imposed by unskilled users. For example, Licklider (1960) discussed the idea of a "man-machine symbiosis" and identified obstacles to this symbiotic relationship, such as the inability of the user to formulate questions and use the command language. Others have proposed a more synergistic relationship in which overall performance is greater than the sum of the parts contributed by the human and by the computer. It is assumed that there exists some unique combination of the two so that the power of the system and the performance of the user are enhanced by each other. For example, Dehning, Essig, and Maass (1981) distinguished "objective operating complexity," which is the actual complexity of a system, from "subjective operating complexity," which is the user's perception of the operating complexity that must be overcome. In their view, "an optimal man-computer interface design can be regarded as an optimization problem between a maximal flexibility of use and a minimal operating complexity" (p. 6). If system power is synonymous with objective operating complexity, and user proficiency is inversely related to subjective operating complexity, then for any level of user proficiency there should be an optimal level of system power.

Quite a different idea is expressed by Nelson (1970) in discussing the factors of manpower output and equipment output. On the basis of the idea of marginal productivity, he assumed a substitution function between manpower output and equipment output. For a constant level of productivity, the slope of the function is the substitution ratio between the two factors. If user proficiency is directly related to manpower output, and equipment output is a direct function of system power, then performance should be equal to the product of system power and user proficiency.

In order to compare such ideas, Norman and Singh (1989) formulated five alternative models of overall performance as a function of user proficiency and system power. These are shown in Figure 7.1 for four levels of user proficiency and four levels of system power.

Matching Model. It may be assumed that a user of low proficiency will perform best with a simple tool and a user of high proficiency will perform optimally with a more powerful tool that matches his or her ability. Thus, optimal performance is expected when there is a perceived match between user proficiency and system power as suggested by Dehning et al. (1981). The first panel of Figure 7.1 shows the predicted pattern for this model when each level of user proficiency matches the corresponding level of system power. Each line peaks at the point of match.

Averaging Model. A symbiotic relationship may be assumed in which expected performance is the average of user proficiency and system power. In this model, there is no interactive effect between the levels of user proficiency and system power. The two work together but one does not enhance or limit the effect of the other on performance. The averaging model is compensatory in that a deficit in one factor can be made up for by a credit in the other factor. For example, a proficient user may compensate for limited system power by using the system more effectively. On the other side, a powerful system may compensate for low

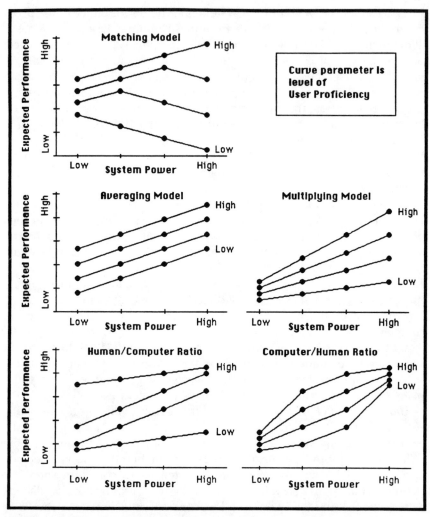

Figure 7.1. Five models of overall performance as a function of levels of user proficiency (lines) and system power.

user proficiency with online help and menu selection. The second panel in Figure 7.1 shows the pattern of expected performance for the averaging formulation. Parallel lines are expected since the effect of each factor is the same for all levels of the other factor.

Multiplying Model. A synergistic formulation may assume that combined performance is equal to the product of the levels of user proficiency and system power. In this case, the effect of system power is enhanced by increased user proficiency. The proficient user is able to gain higher performance with powerful systems. On the other hand, increased system power is of little effect when the user is of low proficiency. The multiplying model is characterized by a diverging fan of lines as shown in the third panel of Figure 7.1.

Human/Computer Ratio Model. Another interesting possibility is a ratio model in which expected performance is determined by the ratio of user proficiency over the total effort expended. The result is that for a user of either very low or very high proficiency, system power has only a small positive effect. In the intermediate range, however, system power has a substantial effect. The idea is that for a user of low proficiency, increases in system power will have little or no impact. At the other extreme, highly proficient users are already performing at such a high level that increased system power again shows only a small effect. This sort of pattern might occur with an expert knowledge system. An expert in the knowledge domain using the system will perform nearly as well with or without increases in system power. It is in the middle range that a user will benefit from the computer. The computer in this model is an aid. The first step is to gain enough proficiency to use the computer, the second step is to gain proficiency in the knowledge domain so that the person can perform without the help of the computer.

Computer/Human Ratio Model. As a complement to the last model, performance may be determined by the ratio of computer power over total effort. For a system of very low power or of very high power, user proficiency has only a small effect. In the intermediate range of system power, user proficiency has a substantial effect. A computer of very low power will result in low performance for all users. Low computer power limits performance. At the other extreme, for a system of very high power, user proficiency will not matter. The machine is not limited by the low proficiency of the user. Systems using natural language comprehension, menu selection, and artificial intelligence techniques may provide examples of this model.

Although actual performance data is difficult to get and validate, expectations about performance can be assessed from users. In order to compare the models, Norman and Singh (1989) presented scenarios representing the 16 combinations shown in the panels of Figure 7.1 to students and managers. Ratings of expected performance followed the multiplying model. It is possible that in specific applications the function may be expected to be different; however, the multiplying model appears to be quite general and can be taken as a good first approximation. The implications are that users of lower proficiency are expected to nullify increases in system power; systems of low power are expected to nullify increases in user proficiency; but a synergistic combination is expected so that increase in either factor enhances the other. Both user proficiency and system power are extremely important. The remainder of this chapter will discuss increases in user proficiency.

7.2 ACQUISITION AND LEARNING

A common misconception is that the user does not need to learn anything when using a menu selection system. The implications of this are that (a) one should not expect improvement with practice; (b) prior experience and familiarity with other systems is of little effect; and (c) training and documentation is not necessary. Although these may hold in some isolated cases, for the most part users engage in substantial learning when using menu systems.

A number of studies have documented the fact that performance changes with practice using a menu selection system. Having established that users learn something, a number of questions become important. At what rate do they improve and to what level of performance? In some systems the change from novice to highly experienced is substantial. For example, as users gain experience with complex systems such as CAD/CAM systems, they will begin to access high frequency menu functions rapidly. In other sorts of systems, there may be little improvement with experience, either because performance is already at a peak or because the system is so vast that the user can remember little about the menu structure that would improve performance. For example, in large information retrieval systems, experienced users may not be able to traverse the tree much faster than novices, particularly when the speed of transmission is slow. However, the experienced user may be able to take advantage of shortcuts and plan more effective search strategies.

Designers of systems must take into consideration the characteristics of the users. For infrequent users, the system should be designed for best early performance. The rate of improvement and asymptotic performance are not important because users are not expected to get to that level. Improvements in performance must be designed into the system itself rather than expected of the user.

For frequent users the system should be designed for best asymptotic performance. Although early performance will suffer, the user will pass that stage with experience into a high level of efficiency. Consequently, user proficiency grows into the system and is expected to combine with system capability in a multiplicative fashion. Menus must allow fast and versatile interaction as well as efficient shortcuts to frequently accessed items.

7.2.1 Components Acquired by Practice

One of the first questions to ask is what is acquired when performance improves with practice. It was suggested in Chapter 4 that menu performance is a function of a number of component tasks. Improvement is due to the mastery of these component tasks. Performance on a component may itself improve with practice or it may be eliminated by a short-circuiting process. Figure 7.2 lists some of the components discussed in Chapter 4 and proposes ways in which they may be facilitated or eliminated.

Association of Functional Requirement with Menu Object. Several studies compared the results of menu performance when users were searching for *explicit* versus *definitional* or *implicit* targets. The difference is that for an *explicit* target the user is shown the exact, verbatim menu item that he or she is to find. For a *definitional* target the user is given a functional requirement in terms of a definition or a situation that is to be satisfied by the selection of some item. The second case seems to be more applicable to everyday use of menu systems. Users may acquire an association between definitions and menu items. For example, the user may be asked to find "a red fruit" for which apple is the correct target. With practice the user acquires the knowledge that "a red fruit" always refers to an apple. Or in a more realistic vein, the user acquires the relational knowledge between a set of desired functions and a set of menu items.

Location of Menu Item within a Frame. Users acquire search procedures for scanning menu frames. When the organization of items is known, users may develop efficient methods for search. Studies referred to in Chapter 6 dealt with the organization of menus and demonstrated the powerful effect of organization. Furthermore, the exact location of an object within a menu frame may be learned by users with repeated exposure to the menu frame. If the location of an object in a frame is remembered, users will be able to fix their gaze on the item faster.

Location of Menu Item in the Structure. When the menu system has a complex structure, users must acquire some knowledge about the organization of frames and develop strategies for effective search. However, with repeated access of the same items, users will begin to remember the exact path to the items. Rote memory of the path eliminates the need for a search strategy.

Association of Menu Item and Response Code. Once an item is located in the frame, the user must then enter the response code in many systems. In many systems the user must simply enter the code listed

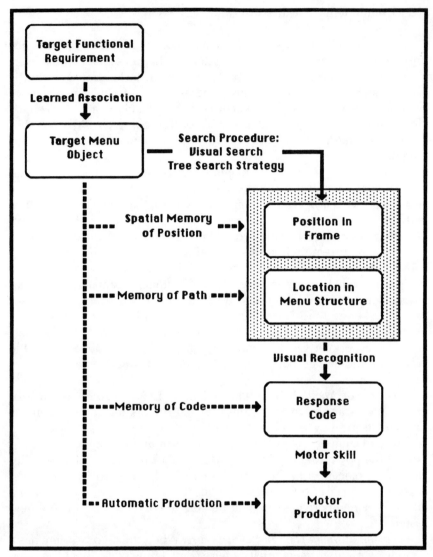

Figure 7.2. Hypothetical components acquired with practice. Solid lines indicate primary associations and dashed lines indicate automatized short cuts.

next to the menu item. However, as users begin to associate menu items with their response codes, they may recall and enter the response without having to locate the item within the frame.

Motor Production of Response Code. Motor skill is required for entering the response code, whether typing, using cursor keys, or moving a mouse. Users may be expected to become more proficient in entering responses. Furthermore, users may learn the motor sequence and short circuit the translation of the response code into the motor response. The motor response may become so habitual that it is automatic in the same sense that a skilled touch typist does not process individual letters and typewriter keys.

Studies of menu performance with practice shed some light on the relative contributions of these components. Systems differ greatly in the demands and difficulty with each of these components.

7.2.2 Frame Search Time

Do users improve with practice when they are searching for an item in a single menu frame? Parkinson, Sisson, and Snowberry (1985) found that the time to search a menu frame and enter the response did improve with practice. In their experiment subjects were exposed to 128 trials on the same menu frame. On each trial they were shown a target and were required to enter its associated two-digit numeric code. Menus contained 64 items and were organized either categorically or alphabetically. Parkinson et al. report the mean response times for eight blocks of 16 trials. Figure 7.3 shows this learning curve.

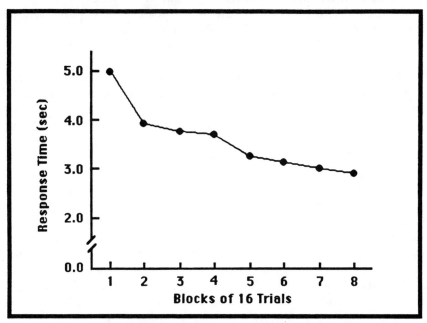

Figure 7.3. **Mean time to select a target item from a menu of 64 alternatives as a function of blocks of 16 trials.**

From "Organization of broad computer menu displays," by S.R. Parkinson, N. Sisson, and K. Snowberry, 1985, *International Journal of Man-Machine Studies, 23,* 689-697. Reprinted by permission.

The greatest improvement was evidenced within the first few blocks. Small but consistent improvements continued out to the eighth block. From these data it is not clear that the subjects reached the asymptote even after 128 trials.

Improvement in response time when searching a single menu could be due to a number of different factors: repeated exposure to the system, repeated exposure to the same menu frame, or repeated trials on the same item. Familiarity with the system, keyboard, display, and so on, and warm-up may account for early reductions in search time. With repeated exposure to the same menu, subjects probably gained a familiarity with the organization of items within the frame. Interestingly, Parkinson et al. noted that improvement across trials did not interact with the type of organization of the menu. Similar improvement was found for both categorical and alphabetical organization of menus. In both cases, familiarity with the organization probably aided search by helping subjects to anticipate the spatial location of an item. Finally, when subjects repeatedly searched for the same target, they may have learned the location of specific items in the menu and/or remembered the numeric code for the item. Unfortunately, it is not clear to what extent these three factors contributed to improved performance across trials. However, the results do suggest that designers should carefully consider the components of the system that are acquired by the user over time in predicting the extend of improvement attainable on the system.

McDonald, Stone, and Liebelt (1983) investigated the effect of target type and organization on response time and errors in 64-item menus across five blocks of 64 trials. Subjects searched for items given either in an explicit target or given a single line definition of the target. Since there is a certain decoupling between definitions and objects, one might suppose that responses given definitions would be longer than for explicit targets. This was the case on the first block of trials. However as shown in Figure 7.4, after practice the difference due to target type disappeared. Apparently, subjects learned the pairing of definitions and objects to a sufficient degree to be as fast as subjects given explicit targets. This finding is encouraging for designers to the extent that they are dealing with a less than explicit environment. Users in general are faced with definitions of items that they wish to select. When those definitional situations are repeated over trials, performance improves to the level of a one-to-one item match. Acquisition of this knowledge appears to occur rather rapidly, in this case after only one exposure to each item.

With practice users may also acquire rules for how items are positioned in the frame despite the fact that actual items may change from

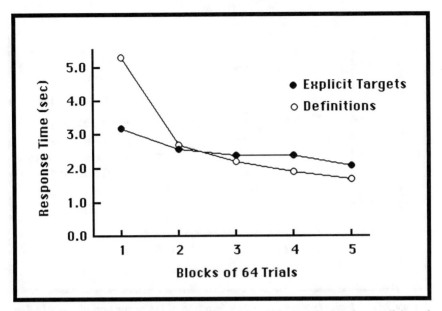

Figure 7.4.   Mean response time as a function of blocks of trials for explicit and definition targets.

From "Searching for items in menus: The effects of organization and type of target," by J.E. McDonald, J.D. Stone, and L.S. Liebolt, 1983, *Proceedings of the Human Factors Society 27th Annual Meeting* (pp. 834-837). Copyright 1983 by The Human Factors Society. Reprinted by permission.

frame to frame in a dynamic system. For example, users may learn that if a particular item does appear, it will be in the same position. To test this, Somberg (1987) compared menus having positional constancy with menus having other rules, such as alphabetic ordering, probability ordering, and random ordering. Menus of 20 items were generated from a pool of 2,000 words. Forty words were chosen as targets. Subjects were tested on six blocks of 82 trials. For positional constancy, 100 words were assigned to each of the 20-list positions and appeared in the same position on each trial (five words per position). For alphabetical ordering, the words were assigned to position according to ascending alphabetic order. For probability ordering, the words were arranged such that the target had highest probability of appearing in the first position (.170), second highest probability of appearing in the second position (.141), and so on down to the smallest probability (.001). Finally, for random ordering, the words were arranged in a different random order on each trial.

Positional consistency resulted in substantial improvement in response time, while the other menu ordering rules resulted in virtually

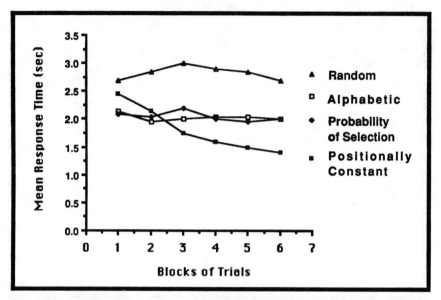

Figure 7.5. Mean response time as a function of list order and blocks of trials.

From "A comparison of rule-based positionally constant arrangements of computer menu items," by B.L. Somberg, 1987, CHI + GI 1987 Conference Proceedings (pp. 255-260). Copyright 1987 by ACM. Reprinted by permission.

no change from the first to the last block of trials (see Figure 7.5). It is clear that item position is learned and used in a relatively short time, even with a fairly large number of target items (40) and a large base of items (2,000).

This result should be of particular interest to designers of dynamic menu systems. Although the occurrence of items in a menu may vary from frame to frame, their positions should remain constant. Consequently, the method of graying out unavailable items in a list would be superior to deleting them and closing up the list. The overriding guideline is to maintain absolute positional constancy, not just relative position.

7.2.3 Menu Tree Search Time

If performance on a single frame improves with practice, we would expect even greater improvement in complex menu trees. As users become more and more familiar with a hierarchical menu system, they should acquire knowledge about the location of items in the tree. Indeed, such improvement has been reported. Seppälä and Salvendy

(1985) looked at improvement from one repetition to another in a study on menu depth. Subjects participated in a simulation task of supervising a flexible manufacturing system. Subjects monitored the functional variables of simulated machines organized in a hierarchical database. Access to a variable, such as a temperature of machine 5, was available through different levels of a hierarchical arrangement of machines within stations within production lines. Subjects were required to check the levels of four variables. Specific variables were selected so that they came from (a) the same machine (Distance 1), (b) different machines within the same station (Distance 2), (c) different machines at different stations within the same production line (Distance 3), or (d) different machines at different stations in different production lines (Distance 4).

Seppälä and Salvendy found a main effect of practice on the performance time. It would appear that subjects were learning to move around through the database with greater speed as they acquired knowledge of how the database was structured. A significant interaction with distance within the hierarchy was also found as shown in Figure 7.6. For longer distances between nodes accessed in the hierarchy, there was a greater reduction in time due to practice than for shorter distances.

Moving through a menu tree requires knowledge not unlike that of a

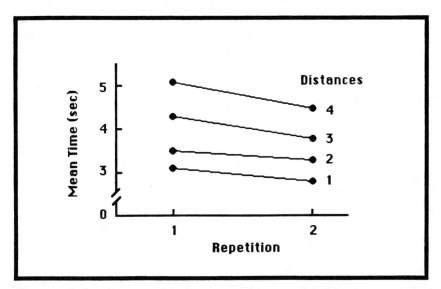

Figure 7.6. Mean time to access nodes of hierarchical database as a function of repetition and distance between nodes accessed.

From "Impact of depth of menu hierarchy on performance effectiveness in a supervisory task: Computerized flexible manufacturing system," by P. Seppälä and G. Salvendy, 1985, *Human Factors*, 27, 713-722. Copyright 1985 by The Human Factors Society. Reprinted by permission.

cognitive map of geographic locations. The ability to move through the menu rapidly and without error will depend on familiarity not only with items but also with paths. It is maintained here that users may (and should) acquire two types of knowledge: rote knowledge of path traversals (*automatic* or procedural knowledge) and conceptual knowledge of tree structure and linkages (*declarative* knowledge). For rapid, repetitive access to menus, such as in the Seppällä and Salvendy study, automaticity will be important. For information retrieval in large databases declarative knowledge about the structure of the tree will be central. Acquisition of procedural knowledge is accomplished by extensive repetition. Acquisition of declarative knowledge is best accomplished by formal training. As seen in the next section, declarative knowledge about the menu system may come from transfer of training.

7.3 TRANSFER OF TRAINING

As users are exposed to more and more systems using menus, what is acquired on one menu system may transfer to another. This is particularly true in "integrated" software packages and environments. Common menus and functions may exist across word processing, file management, and electronic mail systems. Transfer will be positive to the extent that menus are similar in meaning and structure. On the other hand, negative transfer would be expected if menu organization is grossly different and similar menu terms refer to different functions. Positive transfer has been observed in the empirical literature. Negative transfer has been reported in anecdotal accounts.

Dray, Ogden, and Vestewig (1981) found both practice and transfer effects in a study on multiple-item line menus and menus calling submenus. In multiple-item line menus, users had to select a menu line (out of six lines) and then a menu item along that line (three to five per line). Selections were made by using cursor control arrow keys to select the item and the "menu enter key" to effect the choice. In the second condition users selected the menu line which then called a submenu with 3–5 items. The two conditions were counterbalanced so that half of the ten subjects worked on multiple-item line menus first and then switched to menus calling submenus second. The other half received the conditions in reverse order. Users were given 23 practice trials before each condition and then 3 blocks of 46 trials on each menu. Consequently, after receiving practice on one type of menu, users were transferred to a different type of menu. Figure 7.7 shows the mean response times.

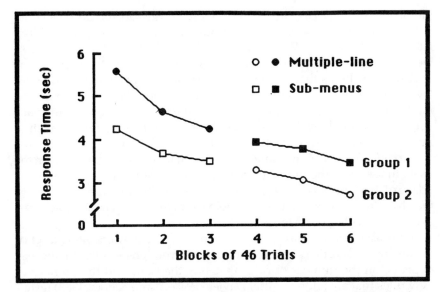

Figure 7.7. Mean time to select a target item from either multiple-line item menus or menus calling submenus across 3 blocks of 46 trials under each of the two conditions.

From "Measuring performance with a menu-selection human-computer interface," by S.M. Dray, W.G. Ogden, and R.E. Vestewig, 1981, *Proceedings of the 25th Annual Meeting of the Human Factors Society* (pp. 746-748). Copyright 1981 by The Human Factors Society. Reprinted by permission.

Substantial practice effects were observed within conditions across blocks for both groups. In the first three blocks response times dropped by about 1 sec. Training in one condition transferred to the other condition resulting in reduced times on blocks 4 through 6. Dray et al. note that neither group nor condition differences were statistically significant. However, the transfer from one condition to the other was significant ($p < .01$). Not only was there acquisition across practice on the same menu, there was also transfer from one condition to another. Subjects may have learned the relative positions of items from one condition to the other.

It is important to be able to characterize what transfers and what does not when users learn new systems or new versions of older systems. Foltz, Davies, Polson, & Kieras (1988) noted three ways in which menu systems may be changed.

Deletions. Frequently used items may be shifted to higher levels of the menu tree thereby deleting intermediating menu levels. For example, in the original Display Writer™ word processor, the options *create* and *revise* a document were nested under the item "Typing Tasks." In a later version (Display Writer III™ on the IBM PC™), *create* and *revise* were moved to the top-level menu, thus deleting part of the menu path.

Additions. Items that are not used very often may be moved to lower levels of the tree. Consequently, additional menu selections must be made in order to access those items. Furthermore, as new features are added, additional levels of the menu hierarchy may be required, thus moving items to lower levels in the tree.

Lexical Changes. Item names may be changed to make it easier for users to associate the function with the name. For example, a command "discard file" may be changed to "delete file." Although the change may benefit new users, it may not help users that have already had prior experience with the system.

If it is assumed that users learn the menu system by encoding a set of production rules, then transfer of learning from one system to another depends on the number of rules that stay the same and the number of new rules that are added. Foltz, Davies, Polson, and Kieras (1988) tested this idea by training subjects on one word processor and then switching them to another. Eight tasks were selected for study that tapped the three types of changes. Foltz et al. developed a predictive model of the time to learn tasks based on the number of new rules required. The results indicated that when tasks required fewer steps (deletions) no new rules needed to be learned. If additional steps were needed to perform a task, the cost of learning was equal to the time required to learn those new rules. However, the model significantly underpredicted the learning time for lexical changes. Subjects did not generalize the rules for a task learned in one system to another, even though they had similar names. Instead, they treated the two tasks as if they were independent and had to learn entirely new tasks.

Prior experience is a powerful factor in the acquisition of performance on menu systems. Systems should attempt to capitalize on what the user already knows. Users are much more likely to adopt a system that is more similar to systems they have used before. Although this may be attributed to brand preference, to a large extent users may be wisely opting for maximal transfer of training. It should be a comfort to designers that additions and deletions to the menu hierarchy are not particularly upsetting in terms of the amount of training needed to master the new system. However, it is most disconcerting that a change in the wording of items that are really the same may totally throw the user. The advise to the designer is to use the right wording in the first version and to stick with it.

7.4 METHODS OF TRAINING

One of the presumed advantages of menu selection systems is that no formal training is necessary before using the system. Although this is true in many systems, in other more complex systems training is required. This is particularly true in hierarchical menu structures in which the clustering of alternatives is not immediately apparent to the user. Training on such systems may be by way of technical documentation of the menu structure, instruction in cookbook routines, and trial-and-error exposure. A casual survey of documentation reveals four major types of training.

Command Sequence Training. Users are typically shown sequences of choices that lead to particular target items. For example, one file management program gives the following sequence for finding restaurants in St. Louis: (1) Choose the Find command from the Organize menu; (2) Click the Clear button; (3) Click in the box next to "city;" (4) Type *St. Louis*; and (5) Click the Find button or press the Enter key.

Such documentation generally lists important software functions and gives "cookbook" procedures for accessing them. Consequently, the menu system may be learned in a piecemeal fashion rather than as an overall structure. Cognitively, one would expect users to encode the menu system as a list of rote associations between targets and menu choices rather than forming a mental map of the menu tree.

Menu Frame Documentation. Users may be shown listings of all the frames appearing in the menu system. Time-sharing systems often provide manuals with such listings. Documentation on personal computer systems often show pictures of pull-down menus, menu boxes, and screen displays of function key options. Such documentation merely reproduces the screens in a printed form and stresses the visual layout of choices at a single level rather than sequences of choices across levels. It allows the user to glance through all the frames and options, but it does not relate one frame to another in the overall menu structure. Cognitively, the user may be expected to encode the system as a set of visual images of frames. Any mental organization of the frames would be the result of inference on the part of the user.

Global Tree Documentation. Users are given a diagram of the menu tree showing all of the menu frames and the links from one to another. A number of systems provide large tree diagrams, but often such documentation takes the form of a functional specification of the system and is buried in an appendix rather than used as a means of training. When it is specifically designed for user training, this type of documentation stresses the hierarchical structure of the menu and the links among the items rather than stressing the tracing of specific paths to accomplish particular functions. When the menu tree is large, it may be subdivided into meaningful subtrees so as not to overwhelm the user. Cognitively, the user is given a visual map of the system. Command sequences for accessing target nodes would be the result of plans formulated by the user by starting at the target node on the map and tracing a route back up the tree to the root or current node.

Trial-and-Error Training. Users are often told to explore the menu system to find out where it goes. The documentation for one such system reads, "The best way to learn this system is to use it!" An advantage of trial-and-error training is that the user gets hands-on experience, develops motor and visual skills at an early stage, and participates in active learning by discovery. On the other hand, such training tends to be unsystematic. The user may end up having never explored large areas of the system. Additionally, the user may become frustrated by having found an important function at one time and later may never find it again. Systems which encourage trial-and-error training tend to be oriented toward discovery and exploration as a central concept of the software. Cognitively, users participate in active learning. Menu organization and command sequences to access targets are the result of discovery and inference on the part of the user. Unfortunately, many users are not as interested in self-discovery and exploration as software designers would hope.

Many systems use a combination of documentation techniques and methods of training in the hope that one or another method will get the point across. However, it is of interest to know which method proves to be the most effective for different types of systems. A series of studies by Billingsley (1982), Schwartz, Norman, and Shneiderman (1985), and by Parton, Huffman, Pridgen, Norman, and Shneiderman (1985) investigated the effect of training methods on performance. The four types of training listed above were chosen as being representative of both formal and informal methods used in the field. The significance of the menus was varied across the studies in order to see if training had different effects at different levels of familiarity.

7.4.1 Training on Content-Free Menus

Schwartz et al. (1985) investigated methods of training on menus that provided no initial clues as to what choice would lead to what target. This was achieved by using meaningless terms as labels for the alternatives. Consequently, the menu was content free. The rationale for using a content-free menu was to be able to observe the effect of training and practice in the absence of prior knowledge about the menu structure. Consequently, users had to acquire the associative links between pointers and objects in the menu tree. The menu tree used in this experiment is shown in Figure 7.8.

Groups of 20 subjects each were assigned to the four training methods (command sequence training, menu frame documentation, global tree documentation, and trial-and-error training). Subjects were allowed

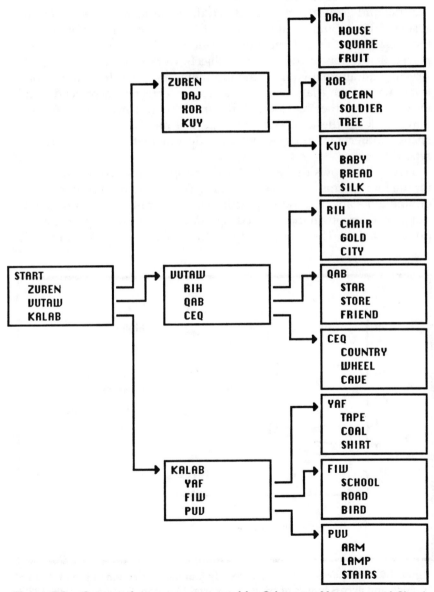

Figure 7.8. Content-free menu tree used by Schwartz, Norman, and Shneiderman (1985).

to study the documentation materials for 5 minutes before being tested on their ability to locate targets. The command sequence training group studied a set of 27 cards containing the choice sequences to all 27 targets (e.g., ZUREN-DAJ-HOUSE). The menu frame group studied a set of 13 index cards containing all 13 menu frames. The global tree group studied a large diagram of the menu tree as show in Figure 7.8. In the case of the trial-and-error group, subjects studied the menu by exploring the system online. Study materials were then removed and subjects were then tested on the 27 targets in a random order. Each target was displayed at the top of the screen. Subjects were to locate the target by selecting an alternative from the top menu and then from the second-level menu. Each trial was scored as either correct or incorrect depending on whether they had located the target. Subjects were not allowed to move back up the tree. Following the test on the 27 targets, subjects spent another 5 minutes studying the documentation. They were then retested.

Figure 7.9 shows the results for the proportion of correct responses for the four groups across the two tests. Trials were blocked into groups of nine to be able to observe practice effects during testing. Overall the number of targets found differed significantly with the type of training documentation. The group studying the global tree outperformed the

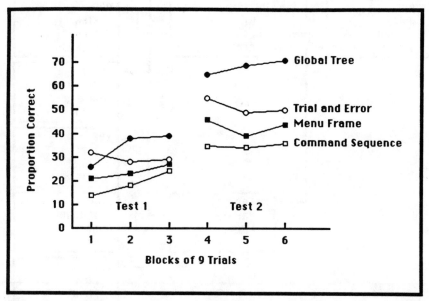

Figure 7.9.   Proportion of items correctly found as a function of the method of training and across blocks of trials (Schwartz, Norman, & Shneiderman, 1985).

other three groups. By the second test, the order of the groups clearly indicated that the global tree documentation was superior. The trial-and-error group was a distant second. Menu frame documentation and command sequence documentation resulted in the fewest number of targets found.

Practice across the three blocks of trials did not result in significant increases in performance. On the other hand, the improvement, due to study between the first and second test, was quite dramatic. Overall, subjects nearly doubled their average number correct from Test 1 to Test 2. This finding underscores the importance of training and especially the benefits of refresher courses after the user has begun to work with the system.

One very important question about training has to do with what it is that the users learn, that is, how do they encode information about the menu system in a way that they can usefully retrieve it in the future. One way of tapping this information is to ask the subjects to recall the terms or to reconstruct the menu tree. Following the second test, subjects in the Schwartz et al. study (1985) were asked to write down all the terms used at the first, second, and third level of the tree. Figure 7.10 shows the proportion recalled at each level. Quite different patterns of recall occurred depending on the method of training. The command sequence group showed approximately equal percent recall across the three levels. Equal attention was paid to each level. On the other hand,

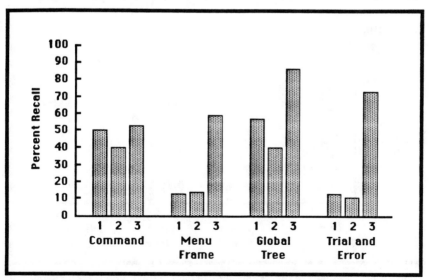

Figure 7.10.   Percent recall of menu terms at levels 1, 2, and 3 for each of the four training conditions (Schwartz, Norman, and Shneiderman, 1985).

the menu frame and trial-and-error groups displayed very poor recall of the terms used at Levels 1 and 2, although they showed good recall at Level 3. Clearly, these subjects attended to the target items but not intermediate terms. Finally, the global tree group displayed the best recall all around. A "level effect" is evident for this group in that recall was best for the bottom of the tree, next best at the top, and worst in the middle. One may object that recall has little to do with performance on menu selection. However, the correlation between number of terms recalled and number of targets found was rather large ($r = .78$), indicating a strong but not necessarily causal relationship between the two.

After recalling the items, subjects in the Schwartz et al. study (1985) were given the list of all terms and a box diagram of the tree, and were asked to write the terms in their correct locations. Figure 7.11 shows the percent of items correctly placed in the tree diagram. All groups placed about 80 to 90 percent correctly at Level 1. The command sequence and menu frame groups did much worse at Levels 2 and 3, showing confusion about the organization of items. The global tree group did the best at Levels 2 and 3, as compared to the other groups. Finally, the trial-and-error group did well at Level 3 but extremely poor at Level 2. It would seem that subjects in this group concentrated on the targets but not the path to the targets. Finally, it is interesting to note that a "level effect" is evident for all groups except for the command group that did so poorly

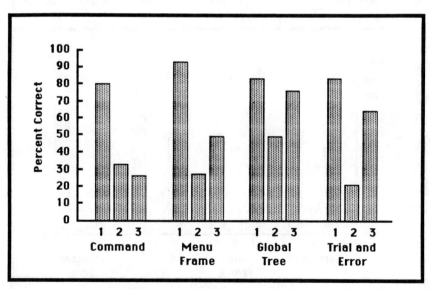

Figure 7.11. Percent of terms correctly placed in the menu three at levels 1, 2, and 3 for the four training conditions (Schwartz, Norman, and Shneiderman, 1985).

at Level 3. The greatest confusion about the structure of a menu occurs at the middle levels of the tree.

The Schwartz et al. study (1985) clearly demonstrated the superiority of global tree documentation and training. One might have supposed that with content-free menus, the subject's only recourse would be to memorize command sequences. This was not the case. Even with a content-free menu, subjects studying the overall organization of the tree were able to locate the most targets. It is possible, however, that the superiority of the global tree training was limited to content-free menus.

7.4.2 Training on Meaningful Menus

Parton, Huffman, Pridgen, Norman, and Shneiderman (1985) conducted a parallel experiment using meaningful terms in the menu system. The menu which they used consisted of a hierarchy of job titles and is shown in Figure 7.12. The training methods used were similar to the Schwartz et al. experiment. Parton et al., however, allowed the users to study information on the menu selection system for 12 minutes rather than 5, and then allowed them to try to find as many targets as possible within a limited period of 10 minutes. The experiment was conducted on an interactive time-sharing system.

The results for the number of targets found, number of selections to reach the target, number of menu items recalled from memory, and ratings of ease of learning are shown in Figure 7.13.

Although the group trained on the global tree found the most targets within the time limit, the difference was not statistically reliable, probably owing to the small number of subjects used (16 per group) and the relatively large variability among subjects. The global tree group also required the fewest selections to reach the target, but again this did not reach significance.

Similar to the Schwartz et al. (1985) study, the global tree group recalled the highest number of menu items and correctly placed them in the tree diagram. A relatively high correlation was found between the recall of items and the number of targets found ($r = 0.77$), indicating that subjects who found more items also tended to recall more items from memory. It would be predicted then that training methods that help the users to recall menu items facilitate performance.

A quite strong finding was that subjects given the global tree gave higher ratings to the ease of learning the system. The validity of the subjective ratings was supported by the fact that subjects who gave higher ratings also tended to find more targets ($r = .46$).

An earlier study by Billingsley (1982) confirms the benefits of studying a map or global tree diagram. Her study compared a control group

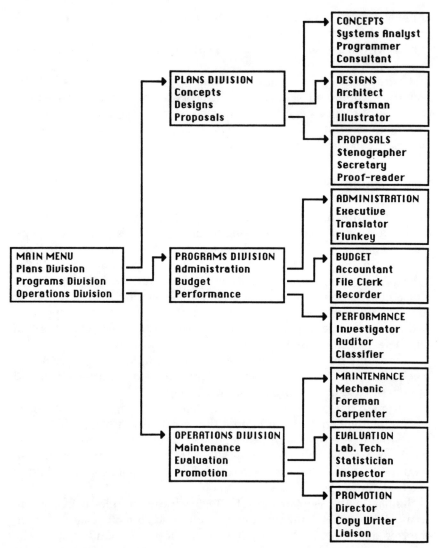

Figure 7.12.   Meaningful menu tree used by Parton, Huffman, Pridgen, Norman, and Shneiderman (1985).

From "Learning a menu selection tree: Training methods compared," by D. Parton, K. Huffman, P. Pridgen, K. Norman, and B. Shneiderman, 1985, *Behavior and Information Technology*, 4, 81-91. Copyright 1985 by Taylor & Frances, Ltd. Reprinted by permission.

using trial-and-error practice, a group studying command sequences, and a group studying a diagram of the structural organization of the menu system. Subjects searched a menu system for names of target animals. Subjects who studied the diagram displayed superior perfor-

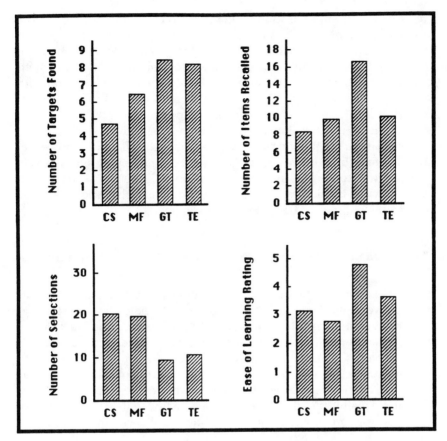

Figure 7.13. Mean number of targets found, number of menu items recalled, number of selections to target, and ease of learning rating for each training condition. **CS** = Command sequence, **MF** = Menu frame, **GT** = Global tree, and **TE** = Trial and error.

From "Learning a menu selection tree: Training methods compared," by D. Parton, K. Huffman, P. Pridgen, K. Norman, and B. Shneiderman, 1985, *Behavior and Information Technology, 4,* 81-91. Copyright 1985 by Taylor & Francis, Ltd. Reprinted by permission.

mance in terms of time per search and number of frames traversed per search. The command sequence group also did better than the trial-and-error group. One additional finding was that subjects studying the global tree showed better retention of menu structure than for the other groups. Following training, subjects searched for nine targets. When they were switched to nine different targets, the map group did just as well as before, but the performance of the trial-and-error and the command sequence groups declined.

The striking conclusion is that documentation that gives the whole tree structure is superior to the other two modes of training tested. This result is perhaps a little stronger for menus of low meaningfulness (Schwartz et al., 1985) than for menus of high meaningfulness (Parton et al., 1985). However, the recommendation to designers of training methods would be to include the global tree in documentation for hierarchical menu systems. Menu diagrams ought to be presented in the training materials for the user rather than in an appendix merely for technical specifications. Just how such diagrams should be laid out is still a matter of speculation. In the studies reviewed here the diagrams proceeded from left to right, whereas in the documentation for many systems, they proceed from top to bottom down the hierarchy. Another issue has to do with how to break large diagrams into manageable sections. How should the submenus be divided and organized?

7.4.3 Methods of Training as a Function of Types of Menu Systems

In practice, documentation and training often combine methods or alternate between methods. It may be that each type of training adds an important component to what is learned by the user. For example, the trail-and-error method allows the user to have hands-on practice with the mechanics of screen display and the selection response. Frame documentation familiarizes the user with the array of frames and alternatives. Command sequence documentation provides explicit pathways to items. Finally, the global tree displays the overall structure. A good training program may well employ a "shot-gun" technique of introducing the user to all methods.

On the other hand, different types of systems and different levels of users may require different types of training. Sometimes it is advantageous to have no documentation and to encourage users merely to try the system. In other cases where heavy memory demands are placed on the user, training should emphasize the learning of terms and pathways. In still other cases, where motor skill is required in selecting responses, training should involve repeated practice. In developing a training method, one needs to assess the critical components to be learned by the user and then identify methods to facilitate the acquisition of those components.

Streitz (1987) suggested that part of the design process is to come up with a way of describing and naming things to convey to users the function and structure of the system in a manner that is cognitively consistent with their existing mental models acquired from experience with other systems. Training often involves the use of a metaphor world. In a way the metaphor helps to create a schema for the user or a global picture of how things operate. Streitz reported on a study by Lieser, Streitz, and Wolters (1987) in which subjects were trained in either the "desk top/office" metaphor or the abstract "computer" metaphor. As a second factor in the experiment, one half of the subjects used menu selection and the other half used control commands. Performance was recorded in terms of time per task. The results indicate that the "desk top/office" metaphor facilitates learning and performance only when it was combined with the menu selection. As shown in Figure 7.14, the group using menu selection in the "desk top/office" metaphor performed tasks nearly 25 percent faster than all other groups. The guideline for design is compatibility. The training method should be compatible with the user's conceptualization of the system and with the mode of interaction between the user and the system.

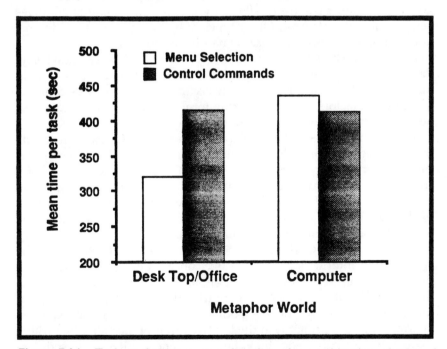

Figure 7.14. Task performance as a function of a combination of type of metaphor and dialogue mode.

7.5 METHODS OF HELP

In more and more instances systems are providing online documentation and training. The advantage to this approach is that users can begin productive work at an early stage and progress until they require help. The disadvantage is the lack of structure and discipline in training. A second problem is that online help may add yet another level of complexity for the user to deal with. The literature on the effect of online help is inclusive due to the type of performance measures used to assess the benefit of help and due to the added time and effort required by users to learn how to use such aids.

Menu selection systems are inherently online help systems. However, the issue is how much help, in terms of additional information, should be given to optimize performance. Help in menu selection is generally provided in one of two ways. The first is to give the user longer definitions or descriptions of the alternatives. The second is to give a look-ahead feature to allow users to see upcoming alternatives before making a selection. Other types of help may provide additional information to reduce memory demands on the user.

Using a deep hierarchical menu ($2 \times 2 \times 2 \times 2 \times 2 \times 2$), Snowberry, Parkinson, and Sisson (1985) provided three different types of help information. They surmised that low accuracy in deep menus could be due to three factors. First, users may forget what they are looking for. Second, users may forget the path they have already taken. Third, users may not remember what the upcoming items are. Consequently, the three types of help provided a display of either (a) the desired target, (b) the list of previous choices, or (c) the list of upcoming items. A control condition was also included which did not receive any additional help information. Two blocks of trials were given so that the effect of help fields could be seen at different levels of practice. Figure 7.15 shows the results for search time and percent error.

Overall, subjects tended to do better with practice. Furthermore the type of help information had an effect on both error rate and search time. The group receiving information about upcoming selections produced significantly fewer errors than the other three groups which did not differ significantly from each other. It was found that the reduction of errors occurred primarily at the top two levels of the menu tree where there may be weak associations between general category descriptors and targets. The group receiving the list of previous selections was significantly slower than the other three groups. The added information presented on the screen may have slowed the subjects down. Although the group receiving upcoming selections did not differ in search time on the first block, on the second block it was the fastest.

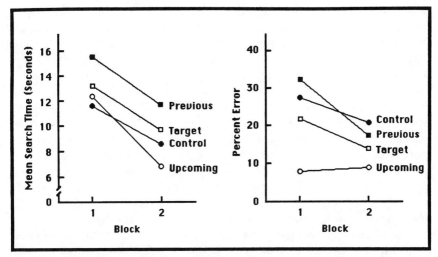

Figure 7.15. Search time (left panel) and percent error (right panel) as a function of type of help information across two blocks of trials.

From "Effects of help fields in navigating through hierarchical menu structures," by K. Snowberry, S. Parkinson, and N. Sisson, 1985, *International Journal of Man-Machine Studies, 22,* 479-491. Reprinted by permission.

In a second experiment, Snowberry et al. (1985) investigated the effect of help fields after increased practice on the menu. After 128 trials on the menu, no significant differences occurred among the groups on error rate. This finding confirms the notion that help fields have decreasing value with increased experience.

Some tentative guidelines may be drawn regarding additional help in menu selection. First, help should be optional. The user should have the option of getting help, but it should not be routinely presented. Excess help information may distract the user. Second, help information should be aimed at critical components in the menu selection process rather than at superficial aspects. Figure 7.2 displays such critical components. Finally, the type of help needed changes with experience. At the early stages of learning, users may need help remembering subsequent choices; at later stages they may desire help in finding shortcuts.

7.6 SUMMARY

Performance is a function of user proficiency and system power. Expectations are that these two factors combine multiplicatively to determine overall performance. Consequently, improvements in one increase the gain in the other. On the one side, system designers are creating more powerful and efficient systems. On the other side, users are trying to come up to speed. Fortunately, when users access a menu selection system on a repeated basis, their performance improves. Studies have shown that both the speed and accuracy of menu search increases with practice. Exactly what users learn is not entirely clear; however, a number of critical components of learning have been identified. Such components are acquired with practice and may transfer from one menu system to another depending on the similarity of the systems. Integrated software takes full advantage of the transfer process, by maintaining common menus across different applications.

Although some menu systems are self-explanatory, most require training and documentation. A number of methods have been developed in order to facilitate the learning process on the part of the user. Four methods have been explored in experimental research training on: (1) command sequences that give the menu selections to find specific targets, (b) menu frames that show the screen displays of menus, (c) a global diagram of the menu system, and (d) trial-and-error practice. While each method has its merits, providing users with a diagram of the overall menu tree proves to be the most effective. Users seem to be able to locate more items with fewer errors after studying a diagram of the global tree. In addition, subjective evaluations favor the use of the diagram.

Online help information has also been provided to facilitate selection performance. The question is how much help should be provided, what type of help, and when. Research indicates that information about upcoming choices is beneficial. On the other hand, information about previous selections made may prove to distract the user. Help systems should probably be optional. The type of helpful information is expected to change with experience. Finally, help should concentrate on information that is critical to performance rather than on superficial aspects.

8
Depth versus Breadth of Hierarchical Menu Trees

Menu selection systems have the power of providing a seemingly unlimited number of choices to the user by generating deeper and more complex menu structures. The power of hierarchical menus is inherent in the exponential growth of the possible number of terminal nodes as a function of level. Menus can access thousands of items. Figure 8.1 gives an example of menu frames to access the hierarchy of living animals. The example shown has eight levels proceeding from subkingdoms down to genera. There are approximately 5,000 genera in this classification. If the menu system continued down to species, it would include approximately one million items. Other menu systems use hierarchical menu structures to access medical and personnel files, demographic data, bibliographic references, encyclopedic information, geographical locations, and so on. Even systems using indices and keywords may use hierarchical menus to a certain extent.

Unfortunately, the added complexity due to the depth of menu is not without cost. Menu designers must carefully weigh the options and consider a number of tradeoffs between factors such as the breadth and depth of the tree. This chapter will review empirical studies on the effect of depth versus breadth of the menu structure on performance in highly predictable and learned menus. At each choice point in such menus the user is highly certain as to the "correct" choice when searching for a target. Performance is primarily a function of the speed with which the user can traverse the menu from the top to the target node. The following chapter will explore search behavior in menus that are not perfectly predictable. The user may have to make educated guesses as to the "correct" choice leading to the target. Performance in such menus is primarily a function of the number of selections and backtracking required to find a target. These studies investigate search patterns and user strategies. Finally, it should be mentioned that the studies reviewed in these two chapters are primarily concerned with the effect of menu structure on performance and not on the relationship between menu content and structure. This important issue will be dealt with in

Animal Kingdom: Subkingdoms:

EOZOA   AGNOTOZOA
PARAZOA   HISTOZOA

Animal Kingdom: Series

ENTEROGOELA   PSEUDOCOELOMATA
ACOELOMATA   COELOMATA

Animal Kingdom: Phylum:

BRYOZOA   ANNELIDA   ECHINODERMATA
PHORONIDA   TARDIGRADA   PTEROBRANCHIA
BRACHIOPODA   PENTASTOMIDA   ENTEROPNEUSTA
MOLLUSCA   ONYCHOPHORA   PLANCTOPHAEROIDE
SIPUNCULOIDEA   ARTHROPODA   TUNICATA
ECHIUROIDEA   CHAETOGNATHA   CEPHALOCHORDATA
MYZOSTOMIDA   POGONOPHORA   VERTEBRATA

Animal Kingdom: Class:

AGNATHA   AMPHIBIA
PLACODERMI   REPTILIA
CHONDRICHTHYES   AVES
OSTEICHTHYES   MAMMALIA

Animal Kingdom: Subclass:

PROTOTHERIA   METATHERIA
ALLOTHERIA   EUTHERIA
PANTOTHERIA

```
Animal Kingdom:  Order:

INSECTIVORA          RODENTIA             DINOCERATA
DERMOPTERA           CETACEA              PYROTHERIA
CHIROPTERA           CARNIVORA            PROBOSCIDEA
PRIMATES             CONDYLARTHRA         EMBRITHOPODA
TILLODONTIA          LITOPTERNA           HYRACOIDEA
TAENIODONTA          NOTOUNGULATA         SIRENIA
EDENTATA             ASTRAPOTHERIA        PERISSODACTYLA
PHOLIDOTA            TUBULICENTATA        ┌─────────────┐
LAGOMORPHA           PANTODONTA           │ ARTIODACTYLA │
                                          └─────────────┘
```

```
Animal Kingdom:  Suborder:

SUIFORMES            TYLOPODA             ┌───────────┐
                                          │ RUMINATIA │
                                          └───────────┘
```

```
Animal Kingdom:  Genus:

TRAGULUS             BOS                  HYEMOSHUS
MOSCHUS              BISON                MAZAMA
DAMA                 HIPPOTRAGUS          ODOCOILEUS
CERVUS               ANTILOPE             SIKA
ALCES                GAZELLA              MUNTIACUS
RANGIFER             RUPICAPRA            ELAPHURUS
OKAPIA               OVIBUS               ANTILOCAPRA
GIRAFFA              CAPRA                ┌─────────────┐
TAUROTRAGUS          OVIS                 │ DAMALISCUS  │
BUBALUS              HYDROPOTES           └─────────────┘
```

Figure 8.1. A path through the hierarchical menu structure of the animal
kingdom. Names in boxes indicate selected classifications defining a path to the
genus Damaliscus. Classification taken from Blackwelder (1963) and Rothschild
(1965).

Chapter 10. Nevertheless, it will be seen that the formal structure of a menu has a substantial effect on performance. The results of these studies will help to tell designers how to structure the tree.

8.1 DEPTH VS. BREADTH TRADEOFF

An extremely important issue in the design of menu systems is the depth vs. breadth tradeoff. For a given number of choices, should they all be presented on one screen or should they be divided among several screens? Figure 8.2 shows an example of two ways of setting up an automatic teller machine. In one case, all of the choices are shown on one screen. In the second case, the alternatives are subdivided so that the customer must make a series of choices. Which organization results in fewer errors, reduced time, and greater customer satisfaction and acceptance?

A number of factors come into play when users are faced with systems that vary in their depth and breadth. With broad menus, visual search time becomes an important factor. Users must scan long lists of alternatives to locate the desired item. In Chapter 6, we looked at how the organization of menu items can greatly improve search time. Broad menus also place an added burden on response selection. If numbers are used, two digits will be required. If letters are used, mnemonic abbreviations are harder to construct and often require more letters. If cursor positioning is used the user must, on the average, move the cursor a greater distance. Furthermore, if a mouse is used the user may have to hit a smaller target. Consequently, both search time and response time are expected to increase with the length of the menu.

On the other hand, with deep menus a greater number of choices are required. Each choice entails visual search, decision, and response selection. Although each choice may require less time per frame, there are more frames to contend with. Furthermore, and perhaps most devastating is the fact that with greater menu depth there is greater uncertainty as to the location of target items. Vaguely worded alternatives and ambiguous terms obscure the defining set of submenus. Consequently, users tend to get lost.

Early design guidelines suggested that the number of alternatives in a frame should be kept to a minimum in adherence to the principle of "frame simplicity" (Robertson, McCracken, & Newell, 1981). In systems such as ZOG and PROMIS (Problem Oriented Medical Information System), each frame presents only a "few sentences of text and no more than half a dozen options" (Robertson et al., 1981, p. 465). Similar guidelines that promoted the "lean, clean, green screen" notion were

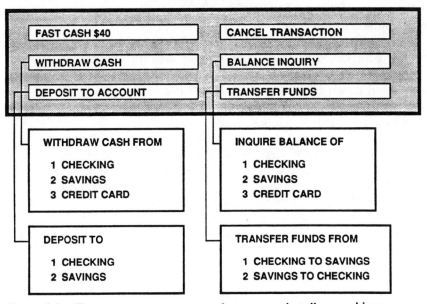

One-Level Menu

FAST CASH $40	CANCEL TRANSACTION
WITHDRAW FROM CHECKING	CHECKING BALANCE
WITHDRAW FROM SAVINGS	SAVINGS BALANCE
WITHDRAW FROM CREDIT CARD	CREDIT CARD BALANCE
DEPOSIT TO CHECKING	TRANSFER FROM SAVINGS TO CHECKING
DEPOSIT TO SAVINGS	TRANSFER FROM CHECKING TO SAVINGS

Two-Level Hierarchical Menu

FAST CASH $40	CANCEL TRANSACTION
WITHDRAW CASH	BALANCE INQUIRY
DEPOSIT TO ACCOUNT	TRANSFER FUNDS

WITHDRAW CASH FROM	INQUIRE BALANCE OF
1 CHECKING	1 CHECKING
2 SAVINGS	2 SAVINGS
3 CREDIT CARD	3 CREDIT CARD

DEPOSIT TO	TRANSFER FUNDS FROM
1 CHECKING	1 CHECKING TO SAVINGS
2 SAVINGS	2 SAVINGS TO CHECKING

Figure 8.2. Two menu arrangements for automatic teller machines.

taken to imply that the number of alternatives per screen should be at a minimum. This meant that designers then had to increase the depth of the tree in order to accommodate more items.

Hardware limitations also served to limit the number of alternatives presented at a time. With slow transmission speeds on time-sharing systems, designers wanted to avoid long lists of alternatives. Moreover, small CRT screens could only display a limited amount of text at one time. Small screens and slow transmission led designers of early systems to opt for menus with no more than eight alternatives at each level. Consequently, designers found it necessary to reduce the breadth of the tree and increase its depth.

On the other hand, there were those who argued that menu depth should be limited. Sensitive to the difficulty of remembering the path and of the increase in time required to make a series of choices, Calhoun (1978) suggested that "no function or piece of data should be more than four switch hits removed from the first menu or display."

The decision to emphasize depth or breadth in menu design has been largely a function of intuitions about the users rather than based on empirical performance results. Shneiderman (1980) pointed out the need for experimental tests on the parameters of menu selection for questions such as: "How many choices are appropriate for a single menu?" and "Does a deep menu lead to loss of orientation?" (p. 241). Clearly, it became necessary to do empirical research to determine what the optimal combination of depth and breath should be.

The tradeoff of depth versus breadth can be reduced to the tradeoff between increased decision time due to breadth versus a decreased number of choices. The total time that it takes for the user to respond to a series of menu choices is given in the following equation:

$$\text{Total Response Time} = \Sigma \{u(n_i) + s(n_i)\}, \tag{8.1}$$

where $u(n_i)$ is the user response time to select from among n items at Level i, and $s(n_i)$ is the computer response time at Level i. In general, the breadth of trees in existing menu systems varies throughout the structure so that the tradeoff between depth and breadth cannot be expressed in a simple way. However, for constant symmetric trees with N terminal nodes, the relationship between depth d and breadth n is given in the equations:

$$N = n^d, \tag{8.2}$$

$$\log N = d \log n, \text{ and} \tag{8.3}$$

$$d = \log N / \log n. \tag{8.4}$$

If $u(n_i)$ could be specified, the optimum tradeoff function could be determined. Two general functions relating response time to menu breadth have been proposed in the literature as a result of theories about the cognitive processes of menu search, choice, and selection. A linear function is the result of a model proposed by Lee and MacGregor (1985) and extended by Paap and Roske-Hofstrand (1986) and by MacGregor, Lee, and Nam (1986). Alternatively, a logarithmic function is the result of models proposed by Landauer and Nachbar (1985) and by Card (1982). It will be seen that these two models result in completely different solutions to the optimal breadth of a menu tree. Although the cognitive processing of menu alternatives is expected to vary with the type of menu, task, and experience, empirical evidence to date supports the logarithmic model. Nevertheless, designers should be especially careful when generalizing theoretical and empirical results to specific applications in the depth versus breadth issue, due to the influence of unexplored factors.

8.2 THE LINEAR MODEL

Response time $u(n_i)$ may simply be a linear function of the number of alternatives n_i. This model may result from a number of simplifying assumptions about the cognitive processes of search, selection time, and computer response time. Lee and MacGregor (1985) discuss a decision model for menu search in videotext databases. They assume that the time that it takes for a user to make a selection will be an additive function of the number of alternatives that the user reads, multiplied by the time that it takes to read an alternative plus the key-press time and computer response time:

$$t(n_i) = E(n) \, t + k + c, \tag{8.5}$$

where $E(n)$ is the expected number of alternatives read, t is the reading time per alternative, k is the key-press time, and c is the computer response time. The value of $E(n)$ depends on whether the user adopts an exhaustive or a self-terminating search strategy. For an exhaustive search, the user reads all of the alternatives in a menu frame before making a choice; consequently, $E(n) = n$. For a self-terminating search, the user stops as soon as an appropriate alternative is encountered. The expected value of the number of alternatives read would then be $E(n) = (n + 1)/2$.

The total response time is then given by multiplying depth and response time per menu frame as given in Equations 8.4 and 8.5:

$$t(N) = \{(\log N) \, / \, (\log n)\} \, (E(n) \, t + k + c). \tag{8.6}$$

Although a direct solution for the optimum values of depth and breadth does not exist, Lee and MacGregor (1985) used numerical methods to find the solution. Figure 8.3 illustrates the relationship between breadth and total response time. As the number of items is increased from 2, the time decreases but then increases again. The optimal number of alternatives is about 4 for slow readers ($t = 1$ sec) and about 7 for fast readers ($t = .25$ sec) when $k = 1$ sec and $c = .5$ sec.

Using numerical methods, the optimum number of menu alternatives per frame was determined for various combinations of the parameters for reading time, key-press time, and computer response time. These are shown in Table 8.1. What is rather astounding about these tables is that within reasonable values for the parameters the optimal number of alternatives per frame is between 4 and 7. However, Lee and Mac-Gregor's (1985) assumptions may be overly restrictive, particularly for organized or highly familiar menus.

Paap and Roske-Hofstrand (1986) have extended the range of search strategies beyond exhaustive and self-terminating menus to include any proportion of items that need to be examined. They suggest that when searching well-practiced menus, or when the alternatives in a menu are organized into categories, the scope of the search may be substantially reduced. For a well-practiced list, users may learn approximately where

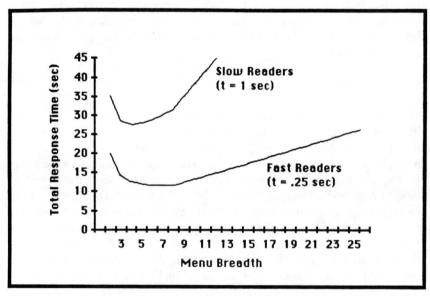

Figure 8.3. Total response time as a function of the number of alternatives per menu frame using exhaustive search ($k = 1$, $c = 50$).

From "Minimizing user search time in menu retrieval system," by E. Lee and J. MacGregor, 1985, *Human Factors*, 27, 157-162. Copyright 1985 by The Human Factors Society. Reprinted by permission.

Table 8.1. Optimum Number of Alternatives per Menu Frame for Exhaustive and Self-Terminating Search Strategies.

Key-Press Time (k)	Reading time (t)	Computer Response Time (c)			
		0.50	0.60	0.90	1.35
Exhaustive Search					
0.50	0.25	6	6	6/7	7
	0.50	4	4	5	5/6
	1.00	4	4	4	4
	2.00	3	3	3	4
1.00	0.25	7	7	7/8	8
	0.50	5	5	5	6
	1.00	4	4	4	5
	2.00	3	3	4	4
Self-Terminating Search					
0.50	0.25	8	8	9	11
	0.50	6	6	6/7	7
	1.00	4	4	5	5/6
	2.00	4	4	4	4
1.00	0.25	10	10	11	12/13
	0.50	7	7	7/8	8
	1.00	5	5	5	6
	2.00	4	4	4	5

From "Minimizing user search time in menu retrieval systems," by E. Lee and J. MacGregor, 1985, *Human Factors, 27,* 157–162. Copyright 1985 by The Human Factors Society. Reprinted by permission.

to look for an item. Consequently, they need to scan only a small portion of the total number of items. To account for this, Paap and Roske-Hofstrand introduce the parameter, $1/f$, to indicate the proportion of items that need to be read before the user terminates the search. The expected number of items read is then:

$$E(n_i) = (n + 1)/f. \tag{8.7}$$

When $f = 2$, the scope is the whole list, when $f = 3$, the scope is reduced to two-thirds of the list, and when $f = 4$, it is reduced to one half. Adding scope to Equation 8.6 results in the following:

$$t(N) = \{(\log N) / (\log n)\} (\{n + 1\}/f) t + k + c). \tag{8.8}$$

The optimal breadth is quite sensitive to $1/f$. For reasonable values of reading time, key-press time, and computer response time, the optimal breadth may increase substantially beyond eight alternatives per frame.

Grouping of items in a menu would also be expected to reduce the scope of search. When items are placed into groups, the visual search process may be in two stages. First the user searches group labels until the desired group is located. Then he or she searches within that group until the desired item is located. The total number of items that need to be read, given a two-stage self-terminating search, would be:

$$E(I_i) = (g + 1)/2 + \{(b/g) + 1\}/2, \tag{8.9}$$

where g is the number of groups. Paap and Roske-Hofstrand introduce a simplifying assumption that the number of groups should be approximately the square root of the number of items. Then the total time to search for an item is given by:

$$t(N) = \{(\log N) / (\log n)\} \, ([(g+1)/2 + \{(b/g)+1\}/2] \, t + k + c). \tag{8.10}$$

When items are organized into groups such as this, the optimal breadth of the menu increases dramatically as shown in Table 8.2.

MacGregor, Lee, and Lam (1986) acknowledge that for command menus which may access fewer than 100 items and which are well-practiced by users, the optimum number of items per frame probably exceeds 8. However, they note that for videotext menus accessing databases in excess of 10,000 documents, it is unlikely that users will learn the location of menu items and restrict the scope of their search. They contend that in such cases, the decision process will be complicated and that users may not only engage in an exhaustive search, but that they may need to read items over again to compare one with the

Table 8.2. Optimum Number of Alternatives per Frame for Grouped Menus Given a Self-Terminating Search Strategy.

Key-Press Time (k)	Reading Time (t)	Computer Response Time (c)			
		0.50	**0.60**	**0.90**	**1.35**
0.50	0.25	38	41	49	63
	0.50	25	26	30	36
	1.00	19	20	22	24
	2.00	16	17	17	18
1.00	0.25	52	55	64	78
	0.50	32	33	37	43
	1.00	22	23	25	27
	2.00	18	18	19	20

From "The optimal number of menu options per panel," by K. R. Paap and R. J. Roske-Hofstrand, 1986, *Human Factors, 28,* 377–385. Copyright 1985 by The Human Factors Society. Reprinted by permission.

other. Such a redundant search may result when the user has read all of the alternatives and several appear to be plausible choices. MacGregor et al. suggest that such redundant search processes may be frequent with broader menus that have more plausible options. Consequently, for videotext menus at least, one should restrict the number of items to about 5.

However, it should be remembered that the linear model may not be at all appropriate. The time that it takes to read an item may not be constant either within menu frames or across menu levels. As the user begins to read items in a frame, he or she may start out slowly and speed up as the context of the choice becomes clearer. Furthermore, the familiarity of alternatives probably varies with the depth of the tree. Top-level menus are seen more frequently and hence will be familiar to the user. Lower menus may only be seen for the first time. Finally, in writing menu items the length of alternatives may vary with the depth of the tree. Superordinate categories typically require longer descriptors. Specific items may require only brief phrases.

The linear model ignores decision time despite the fact that decision time is known to be a function of the number of alternatives. If decision time is a linear function of n_i, then the model still holds. However, the results of choice reaction time studies suggest that decision and key-press time is best described by a log model.

8.3 THE LOG MODEL

Under limited conditions, $u(n_i)$ can be estimated by the Hick-Hyman law for choice reaction time and Fitts' law for movement time. If selection is made by a choice among responses rather than a serial scan-and-match process, the Hick-Hyman law (Hyman, 1953; Welford, 1980) states that

$$dt = c + k\log(n_i),\tag{8.11}$$

where c and k are constants, and n_i is the number of equally likely alternatives at level i of the tree. Fitts' law (Fitts, 1954) specifies the movement time to hit a target of width w from a distance d:

$$mt = c + k\log(d/w).\tag{8.12}$$

These functions were tested in a study by Landauer and Nachbar (1985) who varied the number of alternatives per screen to select either a number or word out of 4,096 possible. Responses were made on a touch screen. The physical width of the alternative was proportional to $1/n$;

and it was assumed that the distance was the same for all alternatives; consequently:

$$mt = c + k\log(n). \tag{8.13}$$

Moreover, it was assumed that the decision time and movement time are additive components in response selection, and that $u(n_i)$ does not depend on depth, consequently:

$$t(n) = dt + mt = c + k\log(n), \tag{8.14}$$

Landauer and Nachbar (1985) varied the breadth of a menu for locating the 4,096 sequential numbers or alphabetized words across 2, 4, 8, and 16 alternatives per level. The exact experimental conditions of the study are important for understanding the results. On each trial, a goal number or word was presented in the middle of a main screen as well as on a second screen to the left. Participants initiated the search by touching anywhere on the main screen. The screen went blank for 1 second. After the delay, an auditory signal occurred and 5 to 33 alternating blue and red horizontal stripes from .5 to 3.5 inches wide appeared on the screen. For integers, ranges were shown by their extreme high and low values on the blue stripes. Participants were to choose the range that contained the goal by touching the stripe between the two values. For words, the procedure was the same except that words replaced numbers in the ranges according to their alphabetical order. Errors were not permitted. Participants had to select the correct bar, at which point a second auditory signal was sounded and the stripe flashed white. Responses were timed from the onset signal to the success signal. After the range was chosen, the main screen went blank for 1 second and another set of ranges was presented and so on until the screen on which sequential integers or words themselves were shown rather than ranges. Goal numbers and words were chosen with the restriction that they never appeared as high- or low-range values. Eight participants served in all conditions in a counterbalanced order. Two sessions in each condition were given on separate days to observe changes with practice.

Figure 8.4 shows the mean response time per selection as a function of the number of alternatives. The lines show the predicted functions based on the Hick-Hyman and Fitts' laws, and the points indicated the observed values. It is clear that the log function fits the data quite well.

Figure 8.4, however, shows only the response time per choice. The total time to locate a target is given by the number of choices multiplied by the time per choice. For a symmetric tree, the number of choices necessary to locate a target is $\log_n N$, where N is the total number of

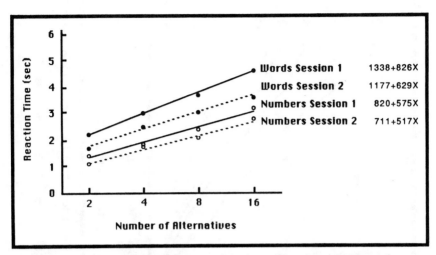

Figure 8.4.   Mean reaction time as a function of number of alternatives per frame. Circles indicate observed points. Lines indicate theoretical values based on Equation 8.6. Best-fitting regression equations are shown to the right of each line, where X is log (base 2) of the number of the alternatives.

terminal items (4,096). The response time per choice is given in Equation 8.5. Multiplying these two results in

$$u(N) = (\log_n N)(c + k\log(n)), \text{ or}$$
$$u(N) = k(\log N) + c(\log_n N). \tag{8.15}$$

The left-hand term does not depend on the tree structure, only on the number of terminal items. The right-hand term gets smaller as n gets larger. The result is that the increased breadth of the tree reduces the overall response time. The constant c, which indicates the time added per choice, determines the magnitude of the effect. When c is large, increased depth becomes more detrimental.

The observed times in the Landauer and Nachbar (1985) study confirmed these predictions. Figure 8.5 shows the cumulative times of numbers and words for each degree of branching. The larger the degree of branching, the faster the total time to locate the target. Two features of this graph are also interesting. First, response times increased slightly with depth. Landauer and Nachbar hypothesized that as the ranges become narrower, the decisions become more difficult. Second, re-

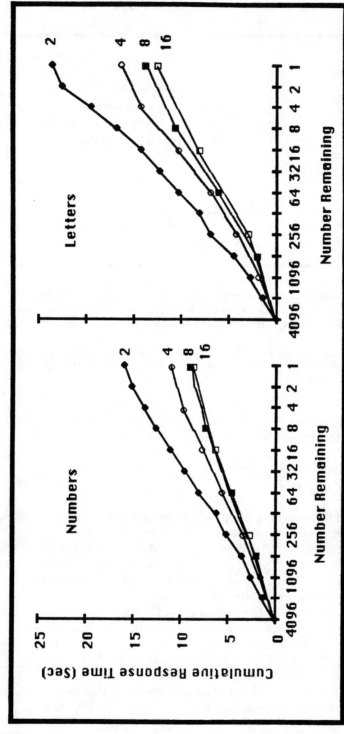

Figure 8.5. Cumulative response time as a function of the number of items remaining for a branching factor of 2, 4, 8, and 16.

From "Selection from alphabetic and numeric menu trees using a touch screen: Breadth, depth, and width," by T.K. Landauer and D.W. Nachbar, 1985, *CHI-85 Proceedings* (pp. 73-78). Copyright 1985 by ACM. Reprinted by permission.

sponse time for the last decision is much faster than for the steps leading up to it. The authors noted that this was probably due to the speed at which an identity match occurs with the goal at the last level over the speed of an order comparison required on earlier screens.

The results of the Landauer and Nachbar study are extremely important. They suggested that for certain menus, breadth should be increased to a practical maximum. However, their results may be confined to the laboratory conditions particular to their studies. Most hierarchical menu systems are not sequential numbers or alphabetized words. Furthermore, most menu alternatives are ill-defined, categorical names rather than ordered ranges. It is quite possible that the logarithmic functions hypothesized for response times do not generalize to other sets of items. Studies using menu selection in hierarchical databases shed light on the generality of the depth versus breadth issue.

Support for a log model also comes from studies on visual search. It is not necessarily the case that users scan the list of alternatives systematically from top to bottom. Instead they may randomly sample items. Card (1982) discussed a visual search model originally developed by Kendall and Wodinsky (1960). If the user is searching for a target item, there is a probability of finding the target on each of a number of saccades. If each saccade requires a fixed amount of time, the total time that it takes to locate the target is a logarithmic function of the number of alternatives.

8.4 TOTAL USER RESPONSE TIME IN HIERARCHICAL DATABASES

Early evidence showing that increased depth of menus was detrimental came from a review of information retrieval studies. Tombaugh and McEwen (1982) concluded that when searching for information, users were very likely to choose menu items that did not lead to the desired information and that they tended to give up without locating the information on a high proportion of searches.

Observations of users working with a large network menu selection system indicated that often users became confused about where they were in the system. Robertson, McCracken, and Newell (1981) described the performance of operators using a menu selection system named ZOG—"Users readily get lost in using ZOG. The user does not know where he is, how to get where he wants to go, or what to do; he feels lost and may take excessively long to respond. This happens in all sorts of nets, especially complex nets or nets without regular structure" (p. 483).

Finally, informal studies on menu-driven teleterminals by Hagelbarger and Thompson (1983) indicated that users took progressively longer to respond as they progressed further down the tree. When users selected a wrong alternative at any point, they became confused, and rather than backing up the tree one level to correct the error, they would return to the main menu.

Allen (1983) investigated the effect of menu depth on response times and error rates at each level of the tree. He found that response times at each level became longer for searches deeper in the tree. Subjects also made more errors with searches deeper into the tree.

In order to understand what was happening in hierarchical menus, a series of controlled laboratory studies investigated the effect of varying depth and breadth while holding the number of terminal nodes constant. Miller (1981) used a constant number of 64 items arranged in symmetric hierarchical menus of 2^6, 4^3, 8^2, and 64^1. The items were nouns and proper nouns in a semantic hierarchy formed by superset-subset associations. Figure 8.6 shows the words arranged in the 2^6 condition, and Figure 8.7 shows the 4^3 condition. Selections were made on a response panel consisting of push buttons adjacent to rectangular viewing holes mounted directly over a CRT display. In the case of the 64^1 menu, buttons were above or below groups of eight words and subjects only indicated which group the word was in.

Subjects studied word hierarchy diagrams prior to being tested so that memory and choice uncertainty would be minimized. Each trial proceeded as follows: (a) a goal word was presented in the middle of the screen for 2 seconds; (b) the screen blanked for 1.5 seconds and then the first set of choices were presented; (c) when the subject responded, the screen was blanked for .5 seconds; and (d) a 4-second rest period occurred between trials. Total response time was recorded as the sum of the response times for each selection. System response time was not counted. Subjects were tested on four blocks of the 64 words. If a subject selected a wrong choice, the word "error" appeared and the trial was repeated at a later point. Subjects were encouraged to work "as quickly as possible without making errors."

The results are shown in Figure 8.8. Total response time was fastest for menus 4^3 and 8^2, and slowest for menus 2^6 and 64^1, as shown by the U-shaped curve in the figure. Subjects using menus 2^6 or 64^1 took approximately twice as much total time to get to the target. On the other hand, as shown in the bottom line, response time per menu choice increased as a function of breadth. Subjects using menus 2^6 and 4^3 took about 1 second to respond; subjects using menu 8^2 took 1.3 seconds; and subjects using menu 64^1 took 5.3 seconds. Consequently, menu 4^3 was faster than 2^6 since response time per choice was about the same, but menu 2^6 required twice as many choices. Broader menus required longer search times. Consequently, menu 64^1 was worse than 8^2 since the

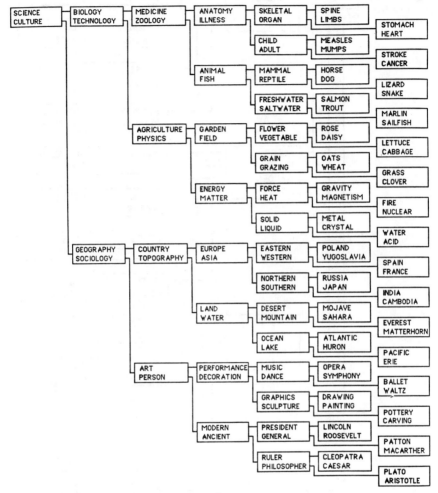

Figure 8.6. Word hierarchy for the 2^6 condition in the study by Miller (1981).

From "The depth/breadth tradeoff in hierarchical computer menus," by D.P. Miller, 1981, *Proceedings of the Human Factors Society 25th Annual Meeting* (pp. 296-300). Copyright 1981 by The Human Factors Society. Reprinted by permission.

response time per choice for 64^1 was much more than twice as long as for menu 8^2.

The percentage of errors also indicated that the 8^2 menu resulted in superior performance, showing less than one percent errors. The most errors occurred with menus 2^6 and 4^3, showing 7.6 and 6.6 percent errors, respectively. The 64^1 menu resulted in 2.9 percent errors.

Miller (1981, p. 300) concluded that "a menu hierarchy of two levels

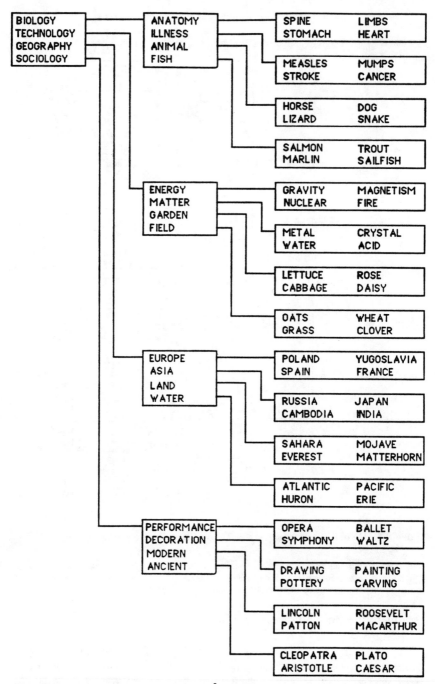

Figure 8.7. Word hierarchy for the 4³ condition in the study by Miller (1981).

From "The depth/breadth tradeoff in hierarchical computer menus," by D.P. Miller, 1981, *Proceedings of the Human Factors Society 25th Annual Meeting* (pp. 296-300). Copyright 1981 by The Human Factors Society. Reprinted by permission.

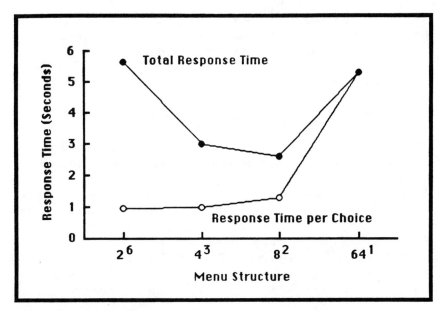

Figure 8.8. Mean total response time and response time per choice as a function of menu structure.

From "The depth/breadth tradeoff in hierarchical computer menus," by D.P. Miller, 1981, *Proceedings of the Human Factors Society 25th Annual Meeting* (pp. 296-300). Copyright 1981 by The Human Factors Society. Reprinted by permission.

was the fastest, produced the fewest errors, showed the least variability, and was the easiest to learn. If for some reason two levels and eight choices per level cannot satisfy system requirements, expansion in breadth is recommended over expansion in depth."

Unfortunately, several shortcomings in the design of Miller's experiment serve to invalidate the results for the 64^1 menu and undermine the generality of the conclusion. It turns out that in all of menus the semantic categories remained intact throughout the hierarchy except for menu 64^1. The 64 items were presented in eight columns of eight items. The eight items were not from the same category but were drawn from four different categories. Consequently, performance was probably impaired due to the lack of categorical organization. Subjects had to search an essentially random ordering of words.

In order to test this possibility, Snowberry, Parkinson, and Sisson (1983) replicated Miller's experiment and included a comparison between a categorical organization versus random display of the 64 items in the broadest menu. The same items were used. In addition, the response requirement was changed so as to be the same across all conditions. Subjects had to enter a two-digit response code to select an item. Response times were measured from the onset of the display to the entry of the first digit so that deep menus would not be penalized by the longer response times due to multiple key entry.

Snowberry et al.'s results for user response times are shown in Figure 8.9. The results replicate Millers findings, with the exception that the categorized display of 64 items is slightly superior to the 8^2 menu. Clearly, a random ordering of words results in search times that degrade performance well below the 8^2 menu. On the other hand, a categorical ordering of the 64 words results in a performance slightly superior to the 8^2 menu. Overall, the results indicate that search time is a decreasing linear function of $\log_2$ number of items up to at least 64. Results for accuracy of choice also support the superiority of broad menus. Snowberry noted that differences in response time and accuracy were not eliminated with practice. Consequently, broad menus can be expected to be superior for experienced users as well as novice users.

A potential problem with both Miller's and Snowberry et al.'s studies is that the difficulty of finding targets may not be equal across different hierarchical structures. Some categorical structures may be more natural

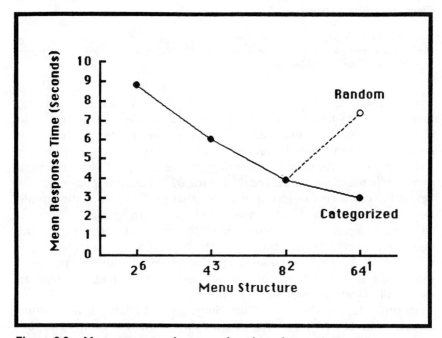

Figure 8.9. Mean response time as a function of menu tree structure.

From "Computer display menus," by K. Snowberry, S. Parkinson, and N. Sisson, 1983, *Ergonomics, 26,* 699-712. Copyright 1983 by Taylor & Francis, Ltd. Reprinted by permission.

and meaningful than others. To recategorize them reduces the semantic associations and increases the uncertainty of choice at the upper levels. Furthermore, certain category names may obscure their members in some menus. The higher error rates for the 2^6 and 4^3 conditions may actually indicate that the menus were not well-matched. Aware of this problem, Snowberry et al. tested an additional group of subjects with specific instructions to avoid errors common in the original test. This group achieved substantially reduced errors with only a slightly slower response time. Half of this group continued for 128 trials and further reduced errors and increased speed. Nevertheless, both speed and accuracy were still below those achieved using broader menus. Although the different menu structures probably differed in terms of the "goodness" of their categorization of words, it would appear that such differences do not undermine the conclusions.

Kiger (1984) extended the research on depth versus breadth by investigating a simulated database of information sources and commercial services on a videotext type system. Sixty-four services were clustered into five different tree structures: 2^6, 4^3, 8^2, 4×16, and 16×4. Figure 8.10 gives an example of the 4^3 menu.

Twenty-two subjects searched for 16 targets in each of the 5 structures. The menu structure was randomly changed very two trials so that subjects would experience all of the structures across different trials.

Both rankings of preference and ratings of ease of use indicated that menus 8^2 and 4^3 were most preferred and menus 16×4 and 2^6 were least preferred. Total user response time was approximately the same for menus 4×16, 16×4, and 8^2, and significantly faster than for menus 4^3 and 2^6. Menu 2^6 was significantly slower than all other structures. Finally, the menu 2^6 resulted in the most errors. Kiger concluded that the 2^6 menu was the slowest, least accurate, hardest to use and least preferred. On the other hand, menu 8^2 appeared superior.

Schultz and Curran (1986) have confirmed the advantage of menu breadth over depth. They compared performance on a one-level, full menu versus a three-level, paged menu of user-familiar functions on a prototype system. Items within menus were either alphabetically arranged or randomly ordered. Even when system response time was subtracted out, search times were 30 percent faster with the full menu (16.4 sec) than with the paged menu (24.0 sec). Randomly ordered paged menus were particularly slow on the first block of trials. With practice, performance on the randomly ordered menus was at least as good as for the alphabetized menus. Schultz and Curran noted that menu structure and ordering are interactively related in early use of the system. The practical conclusion is that the number of pages in a menu system should be minimized and that the items should be arranged in an orderly fashion on the page.

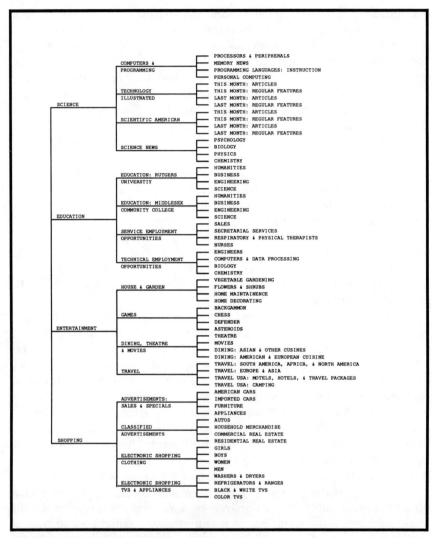

Figure 8.10. **Menu structure of a videotex system for a 4^3 menu structure used in the study by Kiger (1984).**

From "The depth/breadth trade-off in the design of menu-driven user interfaces," by J.I. Kiger, 1984, *International Journal of Man-Machine Studies, 20*, 201-213. Reprinted by permission.

The evidence to this point indicates that where possible, designers should avoid depth and increase the breadth of choice. Certainly a deep binary tree is to be avoided. Menus with eight alternatives are definitely preferable. Furthermore, early thinking that broad menus were to be avoided at all costs has been proven false. Broad menus of 64 items may indeed be superior to two levels of eight alternatives. However, a number of other factors begin to emerge. Some menu structures may convey a better semantic categorization of the items.

8.5 SELECTION TIME AS A FUNCTION OF MENU DEPTH

The time required to select among a set of alternatives depends not only on the number of alternatives, but also on how far the user has traversed down the menu hierarchy. It was noted by Landauer and Nachbar (1985) that selection times increase slightly with depth. In their particular task, this finding was probably due to the increased difficulty in deciding whether or not an item was included in narrower and narrower ranges. Selection time for the last decision at the terminal node, on the other hand, was much faster due to an identity match of the target.

For videotext systems, Kiger reported quite different results. Given a constant number of alternatives, selection time decreased with depth. Figure 8.11 shows selection time per frame as a function of depth for five menu structures. The 2^6, 4^3, and 8^2 structures show a steady decrease from level 1 to the lowest level of the tree. The 16×4 menu also shows a

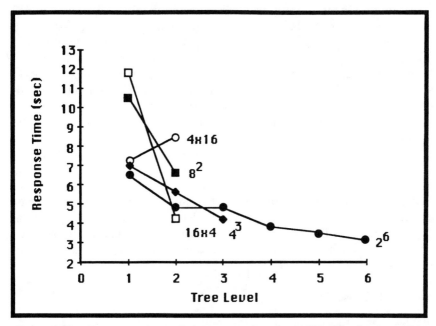

Figure 8.11.   Response time per frame as a function of level in the menu tree.

From "The depth/breadth trade-off in the design of menu-driven user interfaces," by J.I. Kiger, 1984, *International Journal of Man-Machine Studies, 20,* 201-213. Reprinted by permission.

decrease, but this is due in part to the smaller number of alternatives at level 2. The only reversal occurred for the 4×16 menu where a longer selection time at level 2 was probably due to the larger number of alternatives at that level. Kiger noted that the longer selection time at level 1 may be due to the time required for (a) initial orientation to the menu, (b) think time planning a path, and (c) selection among general categories. Fast response times at the terminal menu frames may have been due to target matches.

8.6 FACTORS OF SYSTEM SPEED AND USER RESPONSE TIME

Most of the research on the tradeoff between depth and breadth has investigated time as the primary measure of performance. As noted in Chapter 7, overall performance is a function of system performance and user performance. When the system is very slow, it ultimately determines the overall time. For example, when the transmission speed of the system is 30 cps a typical menu of eight items on the Source™ takes approximately 8 seconds. Consider a 8^3 menu with a total of 512 terminal items. If the user traverses the tree to a depth of three levels and takes only 3 seconds selection time per level, it would require a total of 33 seconds. On the other hand, without a hierarchical menu, if all 512 items were transmitted in one broad menu at 30 cps, it would require 8.5 minutes to display all of the items. Depth leads to a considerable savings!

But what happens when the transmission and display rates are markedly improved? If transmission and display are essentially instantaneous, then it is user performance that determines speed. The total time that it takes to traverse the menu to the desired item is given by the following equation:

$$\text{Total Time} = \Sigma\{ s(n_i) + u(n_i) \}, \tag{8.16}$$

where $s(n_i)$ is the system time for the transmission and display of n items at level i, and $u(n_i)$ is the user time to select a response out of n items at level i. Total time is summed across the number of levels. Total time may also be broken into the components due to the system and the user separately:

$$\text{System Response Time} = \Sigma s(n_i), \tag{8.17}$$

$$\text{User Response Time} = \Sigma u(n_i). \tag{8.18}$$

Sisson, Parkinson, and Snowberry (1986) calculated the communication times for four menu configurations with a constant number of items, but varying in depth for transmission speeds of 10 to 1,920 cps. In addition, Sisson et al. added user times for search and response as empirically determined by Snowberry et al. (1983). The broad menu of all 64 items was superior for transmission speeds of 960 and faster. The 8^2 menu had the best time for speeds from 60 to 480 cps, and the 4^3 menu had the best times for the slowest speeds of 10 to 30 cps. The deepest menu 2^6 was never optimal.

With faster transmission and display rates, it would seem that broader menus become more efficient, that is, if user search and choice times are not inordinately longer with broad menus.

8.7 SUMMARY

Given a set number of terminal nodes in a hierarchical menu, the designer faces the important tradeoff issue of depth versus breadth. Within the constraints of system response and screen display time, size of screen, and meaningful grouping of items, there is a certain amount of leeway as to whether to present long lists of alternatives or subdivide them into shorter groups. Although the literature is somewhat mixed as to the "optimal" number of alternatives per frame, several principles are clear.

For lists of linearly organized arrays, such as numbers, alphabetized lists, letters of the alphabet, and months of the year, one should increase breadth to the maximum practical level. Visual search is optimized in that the intact organization of the list facilitates user response time to the extent that it approximates a logarithmic function.

When there is no inherent linear ordering of alternatives, users may scan items sequentially. When this is the case, user response time may approximate a linear function and the optimal number of alternatives will fall between 3 and 12 depending on various user characteristics and system parameters. However, if multiple levels of the hierarchical menu can be displayed in an organized manner in one frame, response time can be reduced with much broader menus. The overriding principle is to *provide organization*, whether linear or hierarchical, to the user as a vehicle for visually locating target items

It may very well be that the depth versus breadth tradeoff issue is really misplaced, and that the transcending issue is that of effectively revealing menu organization to users, while reducing the number of frames and responses required to locate target items. The issue will be developed further in the next chapter on search behavior in hierarchical menu trees.

9
Search Behavior in Hierarchical Menu Structures

Menu hierarchies are useful in organizing information and reducing the number of alternatives that must be considered at any one time. This advantage is achieved with some cost. As seen in the last chapter, a major cost is the added time it takes to make menu selections at each level. However, a much more significant cost is often accrued by menu depth. Items are buried under successive levels of menus and the user may have to search up and down the tree to locate the desired item. If menu frames give sufficient information regarding the location of the target at each level and users make no mistakes, there would be no problem. Unfortunately, this is not always the case.

The problem is that when items are clustered together in the menu hierarchy, category names must be assigned to those sets of items. In many cases the category names are not adequate descriptors of the subset. Categories such as "Options," "Tools," "Windows," "Functions," fail to guide inexperienced users. Menu frames provide insufficient information when:

1. Items within a cluster can not be adequately characterized by the category name;
2. The user infers that additional items are in a category; or
3. Category names overlap.

Menu items are rarely worded so that users know for certain what selections are required to get to a particular target frame. Items are often vaguely or ambiguously worded so that at first users can at best make only educated guesses about what leads to what. With sufficient use of the system, users learn the idiosyncrasies of the menu and improve their performance. But until that point, users must search as best as they can. This problem is particularly troublesome in vast videotext systems in which one may develop familiarity with only parts of the tree. In such systems the probability of making one or more errors per search is quite high. Whalen and Mason (1981) investigated the problems caused by three types of defects in menu systems: miscategorization of items, ambiguous category labels, and synonymous labels. The most serious defect was found to be miscategorization. Miscategorized items were rarely found by users. While ambiguous and synonymous labels reduce certainty in location, miscategorization produces total uncertainty. If an item is miscategorized, looking for it is like looking for a needle in a haystack.

This chapter investigates the problem of search in hierarchical menus. When searching for an item, users typically follow the most probable path down the hierarchy until either (a) they get to the bottom and the item is either found or not found, or (b) they come to a menu frame that offers little or no possibility of leading to the desired item. The questions are "How do users redirect search when they come to a dead end, what menu structures facilitate search, and how do users differ in strategies and abilities in menu search?"

While performance on well-practiced menus is largely a function of response times along a relatively direct path, performance on unfamiliar and ill-defined menus is largely a function of the number of frames visited during the search. Search behavior may be characterized by the number of off-path choices, the amount of backtracking required, and the frequency of restarting the search. Depending on the menu structure, users may adopt different strategies for backtracking and restarting. Depth and breadth play an important part in search performance in difficult menu hierarchies.

9.1 MENU FOCUSING THROUGH STRUCTURE

From the consumer's perspective there are different advantages to searching for an item at a department store or a shopping bazaar. Aside from selection of goods, the department store provides a focusing structure to direct the consumer to the areas of the store. The bazaar bewilders the naive shopper with a large number of specialty shops along crowded narrow streets. However, once in the right shop, the variety may provide an easy choice of a needed item. Certainly, the relative efficiency of shopping at one or the other will depend on knowing what you are looking for. Moreover, the shopper's search strategy will differ greatly between a department store and a shopping bazaar. Similarly, the efficiency of searching a menu structure may depend on how well the target item is specified and the user's search strategy may vary with the type of menu structure.

It is clear that the depth versus breadth tradeoff has a strong effect on performance. However, it is also likely that other characteristics of the menu structure influence performance when depth is constant. Most real-world menu systems vary in breadth at different levels of the tree. The natural organization of the hierarchy may require groupings that make it top heavy, bottom heavy, or bulging in the middle. In some cases the designer may have sufficient leeway to organize the items in several equally meaningful ways. The question is "What sort of structure best facilitates search?" It may be best to have a broad range of alternatives at the top of the menu and focus in on a small number of choices at the bottom. Or it may be best to have a narrow range at the top and a broad selection at the bottom. McEwen (1981) observed that most navigational errors are made at or near the top of the menu hierarchy. This implies that the greatest effort in menu design should be directed at the top-level menu.

9.1.1 Varying Menu Breadth

Can search in difficult hierarchical menus be facilitated by varying the breadth of the menu at particular points in the tree? Norman and Chin (1988) investigated menu structures having different shape while holding depth constant. Five structures were used (Figure 9.1).

The *constant menu* ($4 \times 4 \times 4 \times 4$) served as a baseline of comparison since it represents the uniform symmetric menu. It has the advantage of providing the user with a fixed number of items at each level. The user knows that there will be four items at each level. Choice uncertainity and decision difficulty are evenly distributed across all levels of the tree.

The *decreasing menu* ($8 \times 8 \times 2 \times 2$) gives a larger number of items at the beginning and narrows the range at the end. Users are initially faced with a broad range of categories leading to a small number of finer distinctions further on. This structure may have the advantage of helping to resolve the general location at the beginning of the search, but it provides little flexibility in search at the bottom.

The *increasing menu* ($2 \times 2 \times 8 \times 8$) gives a small number of choices at the beginning and increases breadth at the end. Users are faced with a small number of general categories leading to a larger number of finer distinctions further on. The increasing menu may have an advantage if the top-level choices are difficult. Furthermore, it provides search latitude at the bottom of the menu.

The *convex menu* ($2 \times 8 \times 8 \times 2$) gives a narrow range at the top, increases in the middle, and then narrows at the bottom. Search latitude is provided at the intermediate levels of the menu. If users redirect search at intermediate levels, this menu has an advantage. On the other hand,

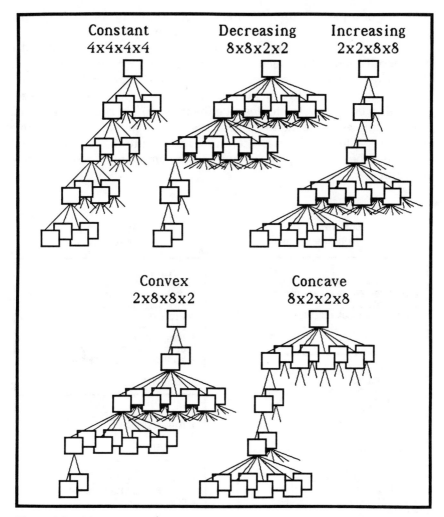

Figure 9.1. **Menu structures having the same number of items and depth but varying the breadth with depth.**

if users tend to get lost in the middle of the tree, this is a distinct disadvantage.

Finally, the *concave menu* ($8 \times 2 \times 2 \times 8$) gives a broad range of choices at the beginning, narrows in the middle, and then broadens at the end. The concave menu has the advantage of search latitude at the beginning and end of a path. If users redirect search locally or at the top of the menu, the concave menu has a distinct advantage.

The five menu structures covered 256 gift items from a popular merchandising catalog. Items were first clustered into groups of 2 or 4. These clusters were successively grouped into clusters of 2, 4, or 8 and so on to generate the five menu structures shown in Figure 9.1. Category labels were generated to describe the items in the cluster. Figure 9.2 gives examples of the menu frames through one path of each of the five structures. Pilot studies were conducted to ensure that clustering and semantic labels were equally meaningful for target items across the five structures.

Constant 4н4н4н4	**Decreasing** 8н8н2н2

CATALOG OF GIFTS 1 ELECTRICAL DEVICES AND EQUIPMENT 2 ACCESSORIES FOR ALL AGE GROUPS 3 HOUSHOLD GIFTS 4 INDOOR/OUTDOOR ACCESSORIES SELECTION: 4
INDOOR/OUTDOOR ACCESSORIES 1 BRASS PIECES 2 OUTDOOR ACCESSORIES 3 BUSINESS/TRAVEL ACCESSORIES 4 COLLECTIBLE ART SELECTION: 2
OUTDOOR ACCESSORIES 1 GENERAL PICNIC ACCESSORIES 2 SPORTS RACKETS 3 SPECIFIC BARBEQUE ACCESSORIES 4 CAR ACCESSORIES SELECTION: 3
SPECIFIC BARBEQUE ACCESSORIES 1 SILVER CHEF GAS GRILL 2 BARBEQUE TOOL SET 3 WEBER CHARCOAL KETTLE 4 READY LIGHT SELECTION: 2

CATALOG OF GIFTS 1 WOMEN'S ACCESSORIES 2 COOKWARE 3 MEN'S ACCESSORIES 4 RECREATION 5 COLLECTIBLES 6 HOME FURNISHING 7 OUTDOOR AND BAR ACCESSORIES 8 TECHNOLOGICAL EQUIPMENT SELECTION: 7
OUTDOOR AND BAR ACCESSORIES 1 BAR ACCESSORIES 2 DECANTERS 3 WINE SETS 4 CRYSTAL GLASSWARE 5 PICNIC ACCESSORIES 6 SPORTS RACKETS 7 SPECIFIC BARBEQUE ACCESSORIES 8 CAR ACCESSORIES SELECTION: 7
SPECIFIC BARBEQUE ACCESSORIES 1 GRILLS 2 GRILL ACCESSORIES SELECTION: 2
GRILL ACCESSORIES 1 BARBEQUE TOOL SET 2 READY LIGHT SELECTION: 1

Increasing
2x2x8x8

Convex
2x8x8x2

```
CATALOG OF GIFTS
1 APPLIANCES AND ACCESSORIES
2 LUXURY ITEMS AND OTHER GIFTS

SELECTION: 1
```

```
APPLIANCES AND ACCESSORIES
1 ELECTRICAL
2 KITCHEN AND BAR ACCESSORIES

SELECTION: 2
```

```
KITCHEN AND BAR ACCESSORIES
1 COOKWARE
2 DINNERWARE AND ACCESSORIES
3 SILVERWARE ACCESSORIES
4 COOKING EQUIPMENT AND CANISTER SETS
5 PICNIC AND COOKOUT ACCESSORIES
6 BAR ACCESSORIES AND DECANTORS
7 WINE SETS AND CRYSTAL GLASSWARE
8 CHAIRS AND SERVING TABLES

SELECTION: 5
```

```
PICNIC AND COOKOUT ACCESSORIES
1 PICNIC BASKET
2 BARBEQUE SET
3 GIANT COOLER
4 CHARCOAL KETTLE
5 SILVER CHEF GAS GRILL
6 BARBEQUE TOOL SET
7 WEBER CHARCOAL KETTLE
8 READY LIGHT

SELECTION: 6
```

```
CATALOG OF GIFTS
1 APPLIANCES AND ACCESSORIES
2 LUXURY ITEMS AND OTHER GIFTS

SELECTION: 1
```

```
APPLIANCES AND ACCESSORIES
1 OPTICAL EQUIPMENT
2 DIGITAL DEVICES
3 RADIOS
4 GAMES AND RECREATION
5 COOKWARE AND EQUIPMENT
6 DINNERWARE AND SILVER ACCESSORIES
7 BARWARE AND GLASSWARE
8 PICNIC ACCESSORIES

SELECTION: 8
```

```
PICNIC ACCESSORIES
1 GRILLS
2 GRILL ACCOMPANIMENTS
3 BARBEQUE GRILLS
4 PICNIC CARRY-ALLS
5 SNACKING TABLES
6 WOODEN TABLES
7 FOLDING CHAIRS
8 STOOLS

SELECTION: 2
```

```
GRILL ACCESSORIES
1 BARBEQUE TOOL SET
2 READY LIGHT

SELECTION: 1
```

Subjects searched the menu for eight "explicit" targets in which the actual gift name was presented and for eight "scenario" targets in which a scenario was given and subjects were asked to find the most appropriate gift for the situation. Figure 9.3 shows typical situations used in the scenario condition. Subjects continued to search until the designated target was located. If subjects selected a gift that was not designated as the target, they were told to continue searching. In the case of scenario targets, they were told that the item they selected was not in stock and that they had to search for another item that would be appropriate.

Subjects had two menu commands to traverse back up the tree: a "previous" command to move up one level at a time, and a "top" command to return to the beginning of the menu hierarchy.

Concave
8ʜ2ʜ2ʜ8

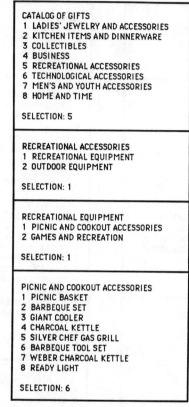

```
CATALOG OF GIFTS
1  LADIES' JEWELRY AND ACCESSORIES
2  KITCHEN ITEMS AND DINNERWARE
3  COLLECTIBLES
4  BUSINESS
5  RECREATIONAL ACCESSORIES
6  TECHNOLOGICAL ACCESSORIES
7  MEN'S AND YOUTH ACCESSORIES
8  HOME AND TIME

SELECTION: 5
```

```
RECREATIONAL ACCESSORIES
1  RECREATIONAL EQUIPMENT
2  OUTDOOR EQUIPMENT

SELECTION: 1
```

```
RECREATIONAL EQUIPMENT
1  PICNIC AND COOKOUT ACCESSORIES
2  GAMES AND RECREATION

SELECTION: 1
```

```
PICNIC AND COOKOUT ACCESSORIES
1  PICNIC BASKET
2  BARBEQUE SET
3  GIANT COOLER
4  CHARCOAL KETTLE
5  SILVER CHEF GAS GRILL
6  BARBEQUE TOOL SET
7  WEBER CHARCOAL KETTLE
8  READY LIGHT

SELECTION: 6
```

Figure 9.2.   Examples of menu frames through five menu structures leading to "barbeque tool set."

From "The effect of tree structure on search in a hierarchical menu selection system," by K.L. Norman and J.P. Chin, 1988, *Behaviour and Information Technology, 7,* 51-65. Copyright 1988 by Taylor & Francis, Ltd. Reprinted by permission.

Overall, scenario targets required twice as much time as explicit targets in all tree structures except the concave tree ($8 \times 2 \times 2 \times 8$) where search times were nearly equal (Figure 9.4). For explicit targets, search times were relatively constant across menu structures and did not vary significantly. However, for scenario targets, search time was fastest for the concave menu ($8 \times 2 \times 2 \times 8$). Search time was nearly twice as long for the convex menu ($2 \times 8 \times 8 \times 2$). Although the decreasing menu ($8 \times 8 \times 2 \times 2$) resulted in faster times than the increasing menu ($2 \times 2 \times 8 \times 8$), the difference was not significant. The constant menu ($4 \times 4 \times 4 \times 4$)

Target: Sterling Silver Candlesticks

YOUR FRIENDS ARE ABOUT TO CELEBRATE THEIR 25TH WEDDING ANNIVERSARY. YOU KNOW THAT THEY ARE VERY ROMANTIC AND LOVE CANDLELIGHT DINNERS. YOU ALSO KNOW THAT ANOTHER FRIEND IS GETTING THEM A BEAUTIFUL SET OF SILVERWARE. YOU WOULD LIKE TO BUY AN APPROPRIATE GIFT.

Target: Worldwide Alarm Watch

YOUR ROOMMATE JUST GOT A NEW JOB AS AN AIRLINE PILOT FLYING THE AIRLINE'S NEW TRANS-ATLANTIC ROUTE TO LONDON. THIS ROOMMATE HAS A TENDENCY TO LOSE TRACK OF TIME AND OVERSLEEP. YOU NEED TO BUY A GIFT FOR A PILOT ALWAYS ON THE GO WITH TIME TABLES TO MEET.

Target: Cordless Electric Razor

YOUR FATHER DOES A GREAT DEAL OF BUSINESS TRAVEL. IT IS IMPORTANT THAT HE APPEAR NEATLY GROOMED FOR ALL OF HIS LATE MEETINGS. HE OFTEN HAS A FIVE O'CLOCK SHADOW, ALTHOUGH HE SHAVES EVERYDAY. YOU WOULD LIKE TO BUY HIM SOMETHING USEFUL FOR HIS BUSINESS TRIPS.

Figure 9.3. Examples of "scenario" targets.

From "The effect of tree structure on search in a hierarchical menu selection system," by K.L. Norman and J.P. Chin, 1988, *Behaviour and Information Technology, 7*, 51-65. Copyright 1988 by Taylor & Francis, Ltd. Reprinted by permission.

appears to fall in the middle with the concave and increasing menus being faster and the convex and decreasing menus being slower.

The minimum number of frames traversed would be four given no wrong selections. Overall, subjects tended to visit an average of eight additional frames per search (Figure 9.4). The pattern of results is highly similar to that for search time. Overall, scenario targets resulted in more frames traversed except for the concave menu ($8 \times 2 \times 2 \times 8$). Groups did not differ significantly for explicit targets. However, for scenario targets there was a significant effect. The concave menu resulted in the fewest frames traversed and the convex in the largest number. The decreasing menu resulted in significantly fewer frames traversed than the increasing menu, and again the constant menu fell in the middle.

The superiority of the concave menu indicates that breadth is advantageous at the top *and* bottom of the menu. The fact that the increasing

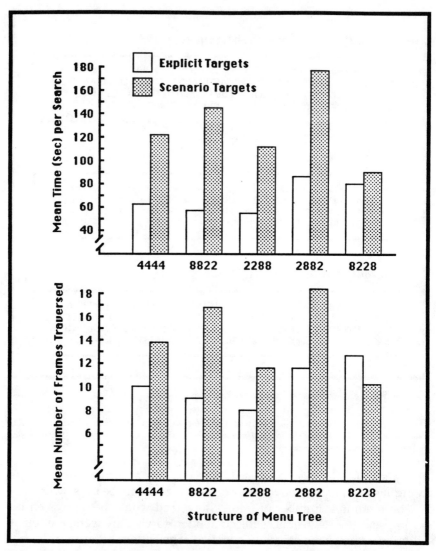

Figure 9.4. Mean time per search and number of frames traversed for each menu structure and type of search.

From "The effect of tree structure on search in a hierarchical menu selection system," by K.L. Norman and J.P. Chin, 1988, *Behaviour and Information Technology*, 7, 51-65. Copyright 1988 by Taylor & Francis, Ltd. Reprinted by permission.

menu was superior to the decreasing menu further indicates that breadth at the bottom is of prime importance. It may be that a wide number of choices *at the top* helps the user to formulate an idea for generating an item that meets the conditions of the scenario and, *at the bottom*, the specific listing of items may help to suggest a solution to the scenario. Furthermore, since users generally get lost in the middle of the tree rather than at the beginning or end, the concave menu reduces the probability of a wrong selection in the middle of the tree.

If users have an explicit target and merely need to locate it in the tree, the shape of the tree does not seem to matter as long as depth is constant. It is only when users are searching for a solution or a likely candidate to meet a set of conditions that breadth at the top and bottom makes a difference. Since this is the case with many database retrieval problems, menus for such systems should opt for a concave structure.

9.1.2 Decision Uncertainty Evidence for Breadth

Menu search is a problem because target items are in a sense, hidden under successive layers of vague clues. Consequently, the user has to spend a lot of time peeking under the shells to find the pea. Large memory demands are placed on the user to remember where things are buried in the menu structure. Breadth, however, allows the system to lay the cards on the table, so to speak.

There is a fundamental difference between choices among subcategories in upper-level menu frames and choices among items in terminal menu frames (Norman & Chin, 1988). The upper-level menus involve uncertainty; whereas, the terminal menu frames provde choice certainty. Menu structures with greater breadth at the bottom reduce the total uncertainty of the menu. In all levels of the menu tree except the bottom, there is a degree of uncertainty as to whether a choice will lead to the target item. As selections are made by the user, the system reveals the next level of items.

Cognitive control in menu search involves the transmission of information from the user to the system and from the system to the user. In hierarchical menu structures, *user choice information* is conveyed to the system each time the user makes a selection. *Menu information* is conveyed to the user each time the system displays a new set of options. User choice information resolves uncertainty as to what the user wants to do while menu information resolves uncertainty on the part of the user as to what an item means and where it leads.

Choice uncertainty depends on the perspective. From the system's perspective, uncertainty as to what the user will select is constant across all structures containing the same number of items. However, from the user's perspective, uncertainty as to what leads to what is reduced by semantic labeling of items. If the labels are perfect (or the user had perfect memory of the menu structure), uncertainty would be zero. At the other extreme, if the category labels conveyed no information, then

Table 9.1. Choice Uncertainty of 5 Menu Structures.

Menu Structure	System Perspective	User Perspective
Constant	2 + 2 + 2 + 2 = 8	2 + 2 + 2 + 0 = 6
Decreasing	3 + 3 + 1 + 1 = 8	3 + 3 + 1 + 0 = 7
Increasing	1 + 1 + 3 + 3 = 8	1 + 1 + 3 + 0 = 5
Convex	1 + 3 + 3 + 1 = 8	1 + 3 + 3 + 0 = 7
Concave	3 + 1 + 1 + 3 = 8	3 + 1 + 1 + 0 = 5

From "The effect of tree structure on search in a hierarchical menu selection system," by K. L. Norman and J. P. Chin, 1988, *Behaviour and Information Technology, 7*, 51–65. Copyright 1988 by Taylor & Francis, Ltd. Reprinted by permission.

there would be maximal uncertainty at all but the terminal level. Of course, actual uncertainity falls somewhere between the two extremes. An analysis of choice uncertainty in the menu structures used by Norman and Chin (1988) using information theory (see Chapter 3) is shown in Table 9.1. It is interesting to note that choice uncertainty from the user perspective accurately predicts search performance (Figure 9.4). The increasing and concave menus were superior to the constant menu which was superior to the decreasing and the convex menus.

This analysis reinforces the rule that breadth is most advantageous at the terminal level of the menu tree where the specific names of the items are listed rather than category labels. The guideline for designers should be to maximize the number of alternatives at the bottom.

9.1.3. Number of Discrete Menu Frames

Menu structure not only affects depth and breadth, but also the total number of menu frames in the system. Table 9.2 lists the menu structures used by various investigators. For example, in Miller's (1981) study the number of frames required varied from 1 to 63. In the study by Norman and Chin (1988), one menu required only 39 frames; whereas, another required 201. If the menu system is stored as discrete frames, a broader menu requires less storage space, particularly when each frame is stored with a title and other overhead and housekeeping information.

From the user's perspective, each frame represents a bundle of information. Frames need to be recognized and scanned. Familiarity with frames, acquired by repeated exposure, aids users in recognizing and selecting items. With a large number of menu frames it is difficult for the user to become familiar with all of them. Part of the advantage of broad menus may be that there are only a small number of menu frames for the user to learn.

Table 9.2. Number of Frames Required for Different Menu Structures.

Menu Structure	Frames at Level						Total
	1	2	3	4	5	6	
Miller (1981); Snowberry et al. (1983); Kiger (1984)							
2^6	1	2	4	8	16	32	63
4^3	1	4	16	—	—	—	21
8^2	1	8	—	—	—	—	9
Snowberry et al. (1983)							
64^1	1	—	—	—	—	—	1
Kiger (1984)							
4×16	1	4	—	—	—	—	5
16×4	1	16	—	—	—	—	17
Norman & Chin (1988)							
$4 \times 4 \times 4 \times 4$	1	4	16	64	—	—	85
$8 \times 8 \times 2 \times 2$	1	8	64	128	—	—	201
$2 \times 2 \times 8 \times 8$	1	2	4	32	—	—	39
$2 \times 8 \times 8 \times 2$	1	2	16	128	—	—	147
$8 \times 2 \times 2 \times 8$	1	8	16	32	—	—	57

The results of the four studies listed in Table 9.2 indicate a strong relationship between the number of frames and performance time. Although the number of frames is confounded with menu depth in all but the Norman and Chin (1988) and Kiger (1984) studies, the results suggest that the number of menu frames serves as a good predictor of performance. Designers should strive to reduce the overall number of frames required in the system. A small number of highly familiar, albeit broad, menu frames may prove to be superior to a large number of infrequently encountered menus.

9.2 PATTERNS OF SEARCH

What do users do when, after a series of selections, they come to the terminal level of the menu hierarchy and do not find the target? They may give up, believing that the desired information or function is not a part of the database or the system. Whalen and Latrémouille (1981) note that searches may be prematurely terminated in poorly designed menu trees if users are not sure that the item exists. On the other hand, if there is reason to believe that the item is somewhere in the tree, users may continue the search in other places.

Search may be redirected in several ways. The user may back up the menu tree one level at a time to a point where another branch downward is selected. On the other hand, the user may simply start over again at the top of the tree. The structure of the tree determines to some extent the most efficient way in which it may be searched. Some parts or levels of the tree may provide better points from which to redirect search. These may be points that offer users the highest probability of finding a successful path or they may be points that are cognitive landmarks.

9.2.1 Reposition to Breadth

One strategy for redirecting search is to move to a level of the menu tree that affords the greatest breadth of choice. The study by Norman and Chin (1988) varied the breadth of the menu tree at different levels. The number of "previous" and "top" commands issued by subjects searching for explicit or scenario targets was recorded. The means are shown in Figure 9.5 for each of the five menu structures searched.

It can be seen that the type of repositioning varied greatly among the types of menu structures. The most "previous" commands were issued in the convex menu ($2 \times 8 \times 8 \times 2$) for both explicit and scenario targets. It would appear that subjects gravitated toward the greatest concentration of breadth in the tree. Interestingly, the fewest "previous" commands were issued in the concave menu ($8 \times 2 \times 2 \times 8$) for scenario targets. Once down at the bottom of the tree, moving to a previous frame provided only a binary choice except at the top of the menu.

The pattern of "top" commands also suggests that subjects repositioned their search at the greatest breadth of the tree. For explicit targets, the greatest number of "top" commands was issued in the concave tree ($8 \times 2 \times 2 \times 8$). For scenario targets, the least number was issued in the increasing tree ($2 \times 2 \times 8 \times 8$) where the top of the menu provided the least breadth.

It would appear that when a particular path has failed, users attempt to reposition the search at a level that affords the greatest opportunity to locate a more likely path. The greater the number of items, the greater the probabilty of making a better selection. Consequently, users gravitate toward greater breadth, whether at the top of the tree or further down, and use the menu commands to reposition search to that point. These results, and those in the previous chapter, suggest that menus should be designed with maximum breadth. However, when menu systems do vary in breadth, they might be designed so that if the user needs to backtrack, one command would automatically reposition search to a higher level giving the greatest breadth of choice. Thus, if a user were at the terminal level of an $8 \times 8 \times 2 \times 2$, the command would reposition search to the second level (equivalent to two "previous" commands).

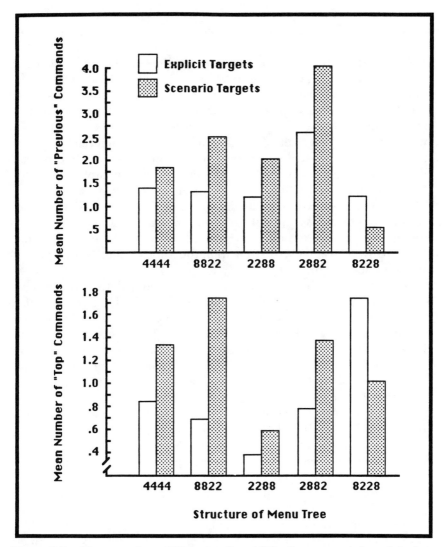

Figure 9.5.   Mean number of "Previous" and "Top" commands issued during search for explicit and scenario targets for each of menu structure.

From "The effect of tree structure on search in a hierarchical menu selection system," by K.L. Norman and J.P. Chin, 1988, *Behaviour and Information Technology*, 7, 51-65. Copyright 1988 by Taylor & Francis, Ltd. Reprinted by permission.

9.2.2 Reposition to High Probability Paths

In general, users backtrack to the point where they suspect that they took a wrong turn. Most likely this is a point at which there was uncertainty in choice. Thus, if a user was fairly sure about a choice, that frame would not be a good point to reposition search. But if the choice was a toss-up, then the frame would be a good candidate for repositioning.

Rather than using actual menus in which the perceived confidence of choice would vary from user to user, Norman and Butler (1989b) generated menus which listed the initial probabilities that targets would be found by selecting each item. Probability distributions were varied to favor different levels. Subjects were asked to search for a file in a hierarchical filing system. A mental model of hierarchical filing was given. Files were described as being located in folders of file cabinets. Subjects were told that they could only go by the probabilities for determining where the file might be. Searches began by selecting the cabinet, then a drawer, and finally a folder. Once the folder was selected, the subject was told if it contained the desired file or not. If it did not, the subject was to continue to search. At any level the subject could decide to switch cabinets, doors within the same cabinet, or files within the same door (Figure 9.6).

Patterns of search indicated that subjects tended to perform local searches at the bottom of the hierarchy. Specifically, once within a drawer, they would check all of its folders in descending order of their probabilities. When folders were exhausted, they tended to reposition the search at either the top level (cabinet) or middle level (drawer). The level selected depended on the location of the next highest probability. For example, subjects would move to set {.6, .3, .1} and select the .3 alternative before moving to set {.6, .2, .2} and selecting either .2 alternative. Thus, subjects followed a conditional probability model in which they selected paths based on updated probabilities.

An additional finding was that although searches tended to be systematic at first, subjects tended to repeat paths and forget where they had looked before. When targets were at low probability branches, searches took much longer than a systematic algorithm either using the given probabilities or random probabilities. For example, in the case of the $3 \times 3 \times 3$ menu, the expected number of frames visited would be 13.5 (27/2). The average number of frames visited by subjects was much greater.

Obviously, designers seek to avoid uncertainty in real menus. Unfortunately, few menus are perfect and many are fraught with uncertainty at numerous points. Since users seek to reposition search at points of uncertainty, it may be useful to provide a "bread crumb" capability to the menu. When users come to a point in the menu where uncertainity is high, they may issue a "bread crumb" command to mark that frame. If they further traverse the menu and do not find the target, they can activate the "bread crumb" command to bring them back to the frame in question.

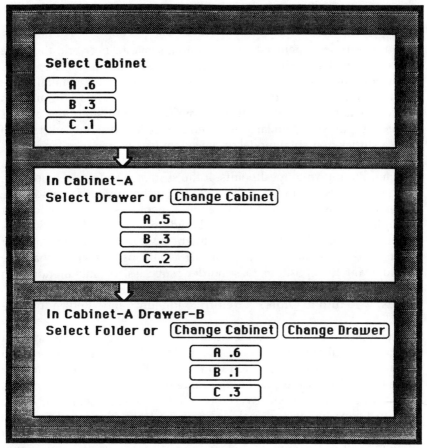

Figure 9.6. Menu frames for probability alternatives. (Norman & Butler, 1989b.)

In cases where search is particularly difficult, the user may be aided by efficient search algorithms supplied by the computer based on subjective probabilities supplied by the user. Rather than making an overt selection, the user would input a probability distribution for the alternatives in each frame traversed. The menu system would then make selections automatically based on these probabilities, updating them when paths are exhausted, or allowing the user to update them based on new information. Whenever new frames are encountered, the system would solicit subjective probabilities from the user. Although time-consuming, the advantage of systematic search might outweigh the burden of inputting probabilities on the part of the user.

9.2.3 Reposition to Cognitive Landmarks

When menus are organized according to a semantic network, there are generally pivotal landmarks at which fundamental turns are taken. When we give directions to geographical locations, we generally use landmarks. If one gets lost, one can return to the landmark in order to redirect search. Major intersections, highways, and shopping centers serve this purpose. Similarly, in menu selection systems, users who have a sufficient mental model of the sytem use its cognitive landmarks to find their way around. When they get lost or fail to find a target item, they tend to return to focal points of the system. Landmarks tend to be frequently accessed nodes in the system. Furthermore, they tend to be transition points from one type of environment or state to another. For example, if the menu of the animal kingdom shown in Figure 8.1 was continued down to the species, one might want to reposition to another genus, order, phylum, or kingdom. It would be less likely that one would want to reposition to suborder, subclass, or subkingdom. To facilitate this, the system could include the alternatives "Return to Genus," "Return to Order," "Return to Phylum" and "Return to Kingdom."

The top or root node of a hierarchical menu system is by its nature a landmark. Similarly, the "Home Card" in stackware applications is a landmark. Consequently, when users get lost in the system, they are more likely to reposition to the root node or home card. Unfortunately, this can be very unproductive when a local search is required. If one were in a department store looking for an electronic blender and came to a table of electric can openers, he or she would not reposition the search by going out of the store and starting over again. Instead, one would back up to the level of electric kitchen appliances and scan the selections from there. Unfortunately, too often users reposition in computer menu systems by returning to the top for lack of better cognitive landmarks (Norman & Chin, 1988; Norman, 1988).

Many complex office automation systems, electronic mail systems, and the like contain a number of focal points toward which users gravitate. A few highly familiar, distinctive screens serve as landmarks to start and end local search processes. Systems which present more global views of the environment make use of such landmarks. For example, in the Rooms environment such landmarks are displayed graphically. The more salient such landmarks can be made, the better they will serve as focal points in search processes. Repositioning to such points rather than all the way back to a root node should greatly improve search performance.

9.3 INDIVIDUAL DIFFERENCES IN SEARCH BEHAVIOR

Tremendous variability exits in performance, style of search, cognitivie ability, knowledge, and prior experience among users. This is particularly true in the area of search behavior. The average time it takes to find items in hierarcical databases by different users can vary by an order of magnitude. Researchers are interested in both characterizing this variability (e.g., in what ways and to what extent do users vary?) and determining its sources (e.g., what person variables affect search performance?).

9.3.1. Characterizing Differences

Individual differences can be conceptually divided into *inherent differences* in perceptual ability, memory capacity, and cognitive processing, and *acquired differences* in specific knowlege of the subject matter domain and general knowledge of problem-solving strategies. In terms of characterizing individual differences among computer users, inherent differences affect users' ability to scan choices, perceive patterns, remember items and paths, and plan paths. Acquired differences affect performance in that users learn information and strategies over experience that facilitates performance. Research on the development of expertise helps to characterize the differences between novices and experts.

Forward Search versus Backward Search. Larkin (1980) found that novices and experts search for solutions to geometry proofs and physics problems in quite different ways. Experts tend to reason from the givens to the goal in a forward search. Novices, on the other hand, reason from the goal to the givens in a backward search. Larkin speculated that the direction of search is the result of the subjects' record of past experience. In the past, particular configurations of information resulted in patterns of successful inference. These patterns may have originally been discovered in backward search, but once discovered, subjects begin to transform them to forward production rules.

Although Larkin's studies were on geometry and physics problems, the idea clearly generalizes to search in difficult hierarchical menu structures. In general, hierarchical menu structures promote forward search; however, when novice users are more familiar with the target item than they are with the forward path, backward search may be used. If novices are searching for an explicit target item, they may initially try to think backwards up the tree, "What do I select to get X? If Y leads to X, what do I select to get Y?" In general, this line of reasoning is time-consuming and fraught with problems. However, with experience, the user may acquire forward production rules that start at the top of menu hierarchy. Search and the reasoning processes that support it are then performed in the same direction as the intended hierarchical structure of the menu.

Recognition of Recurring Patterns. Studies show that experts tend to perceive recurring patterns much more than novices. Experts are more likely to see clusters of items, to chunk things into larger perceptual units, and to pick up on the overall organization of things. Experience results in a large repertoire of patterns that can be applied to current problems.

Simon and Gilmartin (1973) estimate that chess masters have acquired something on the order of 50,000 different chess patterns. These patterns are quickly recognized during play, and this accounts for the superior memory performance of experts over novices when asked to reconstruct board positions. Similarly for computer programming, experts show better memory. It is argued that the development of programming expertise depends on the acquisition of a large number of patterns or templates (Soloway, 1980). Programmers associate these templates with the goal of the program. Given a goal, they can generate the appropriate templates; and given a novel program, they infer its function from the templates that it contains.

In menu search, expert users, no doubt, perceive recurring patterns of menu structure, common menus, types of menu screens, and paths through menu structures. Experts are able to recognize the intent of menus, identify potential paths for search, and search chunks of menu structures rather than individual items. Extensive familiarity with computer menus allows experts to direct search more efficiently by eliminating large sections of the menu hierarchy and inferring possible locations from past experience. Well-designed interfaces promote rapid expertise by enhancing the commonality of menu patterns and screens across the whole interface.

Planning. People differ greatly in the degree to which they plan before they act. Planners work out solutions and contingency plans in great detail before they attempt implementation. Others jump immediately into action letting trial and error guide them. In a way, menu selection appeals to the trial-and-error method. However, trial and error as a method of search becomes impractical (a) when the menu system is very extensive, and (b) when computer response time is very slow. In these cases, prior planning is imperative. By formulating a plan, the user accomplishes much of the search mentally rather then overtly. The plan may eliminate unfruitful branches, determine the most direct path to the target, and incorporate backup search procedures if the item is not found on the first try.

Planning ability depends greatly on the user's knowledge of the system and on the user's cognitive ability to transform, manipulate, and process the mental elements that represent the system. Planning requires a certain degree of expertise in the system structure and a tendency to think out a course of action in-depth rather than pursue a breadth of immediately available alternatives.

9.3.2 Predictors of Search Performance

Direction of search, recognition of patterns, and degree of planning behavior help to characterize differences between expert and novice users in terms of the acquired knowledge. The next question is whether there are inherent differences among users that predict search performance in complex hierarchical menus.

Vicente, Hayes, and Williges (1987) conducted an extensive study on individual differences in the ability to find information in a hierarchical arrangement of files. A large number of candidate factors was investigated which are listed in Table 9.3. The six spatial abilities were assessed using the Kit of Factor-Referenced Cognitive Tests (Ekstrom, French, & Harmon, 1976). Reading rate, vocabulary, and comprehension were assessed using the Nelson-Denny Reading Test (1973). The demographic variables were assessed by simply asking the subjects. Abstractness was assessed by the Abstract Orientation Scale (O'Connor, 1972), and field dependency was assessed using the Embedded Figures Test (1971). Anxiety was assessed using the State-Trait Anxiety Inventory (1983). Finally, the information processing rate was assessed by giving a choice

Table 9.3.   Candidate Person Variables Investigated by Vicente, Hayes, and Williges (1987).

Spatial	Demographic
Flexibility of closure	Sex
Perceptual speed	Computer experience
Spatial orientation	Computer courses
Spatial scanning	
Spatial visualization	**Cognitive Style**
Visual memory	Abstractness
	Field dependency
Verbal	
Vocabulary	**Other**
Reading rate	Anxiety
Comprehension	Information-processing rate

From "Assaying and isolating individual differences in searching a hierarchical file system," by K. J. Vicente, B. C. Hayes, and R. C. Williges, 1987, *Human Factors, 29,* 349–359. Copyright 1987 by The Human Factors Society. Reprinted by permission.

reaction time test among two, four, or eight alternatives and calculating the slope of the Hick's Law function for one, two, and three bits of uncertainty (Wickens, 1984).

Six person variables correlated significantly with the performance variables of time, total number of commands, and/or number of different commands (see Table 9.4). The variable of time seemed to be the most diagnostic performance variable. A regression analysis indicated that the best prediction equation for time included only the variables of vocabulary and spatial visualization. Other variables did not contribute substantially once these were taken into account. For example, computer experience had a correlation of $-.34$ ($p = .06$) with time; however, when spatial visualization was partialled out, computer experience had a negligible correlation with time. Either those with computer experience gained a higher spatial visualization, or those with higher spatial visualization gained more computer experience. All that can be concluded is that there appears to be a relationship between the two variables and that spatial visualization was a better predictor.

The difference in performance between subjects with low and high spatial visualization ability was quite dramatic. Spatial visualization accounted for approximately 25 percent of all individual differences. Furthermore, the magnitude of the difference is shown in Figure 9.7. A median split of the subjects into low and high groups of equal size reveals that low-visualization subjects took nearly twice as long as high-visualization subjects.

Vicente et al. attempted to isolate the components of the search process that seemed to account for the difference in times to locate information. They found that of 12 menu commands available, subjects

Table 9.4.   Correlations Between Person Variables and Performance Variables Investigated by Vicente, Hayes, and Williges (1987).

	Time	Number of Total Commands	Number of Different Commands
Vocabulary	$-.41^*$	$-.42^*$	$-.34$
Comprehension	$-.37^*$	$-.35$	$-.26$
Spatial scanning (1)	$-.38^*$	$-.34$	$-.33$
Flexibility of closure	$-.41^*$	$-.30$	$-.25$
Spatial visualization (1)	$-.47^{**}$	$-.42^*$	$-.44^*$
Spatial visualization (2)	$-.57^{***}$	$-.46^*$	$-.46^*$

$^*p < .05$
$^{**}p < .01$
$^{***}p < .001$

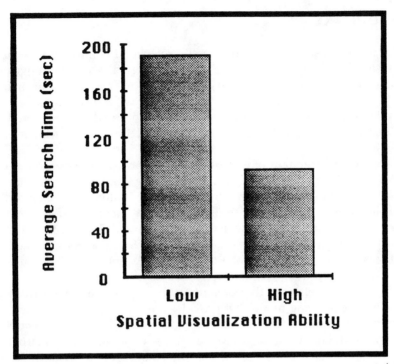

Figure 9.7. Average time per trial for low- and high-spatial visualization groups.

From "Assaying and isolating individual differences in searching a hierarchical file system," by K.J. Vicente, B.C. Hayes, and R.C. Williges, 1987, *Human Factors*, 29, 349-359. Copyright 1987 by The Human Factors Society. Reprinted by permission.

with low spatial ability tended to use three of them significantly more than subjects with high spatial ability. One command was a procedure to move up one level of the hierarchy (ZOOM OUT). Subjects with low spatial ability tended to go to incorrect files and then had to back up the hierarchy. In addition, these subjects used two commands for searching through the files (SCROLL UP and SCROLL DOWN) significantly more often than subjects with high spatial ability. Vicente et al. concluded that subjects with low spatial ability tended to get lost more often, both searching for the right file and searching for the right information in a file. Subjects with low spatial ability may have had a harder time visualizing paths between files and visualizing the location of information within files. Consequently, rather than manipulating the structures mentally in order to plan and test paths, they did so directly resulting in longer search times and a greater number of commands issued.

9.4 SUMMARY

With the increasing complexity of menu selection in information retrieval systems and in command and control systems, it can no longer be assumed that menu selection will guide the user along an error-free path. Consequently, when the first try doesn't work, users must rely on strategies for redirecting search. The concern of the designer should be to identify ways that the system can help to redirect and facilitate that search.

A major determinant of effective search is breadth of selection at the bottom of the menu hierarchy. The resulting guideline is that menu structures should be designed so that they are bottom heavy. Once the user has traversed down to the bottom of the menu, a wide range of alternatives should be selectable. Users tend to redirect search to a level that provides the greatest breadth of choice. Since search is generally redirected after a failure at the bottom of the tree, it makes sense to provide breadth at the same level.

A secondary effect is that breadth at the top of the menu facilitates search. The opening menu that provides a wide range of alternatives is superior to a limited, focused menu. Since search is often redirected to the top of the menu, it makes sense to provide a number of alternative search routes at this point. On the other hand, menu breadth in the middle levels of the structure seems to hinder search. It is here that search may need to be focused so as to reduce the probability of path errors.

Menu structure determines the number of discrete frames in the system. It is suggested that menus that minimize the total number of menu frames may facilitate search in that the user has fewer frames to search and may have a greater likelihood of remembering the critical menu frames that lead to the target item.

Users vary greatly in their ability to locate information in hierarchical menu structures. As users gain experience with a system their search behavior improves. Expertise is characterized by (a) a foward search from the given situation to the target item, rather than a backward search from the target back up the hierarchy, (b) the ability to recognize recurring patterns in menu structures, and (c) the ability to plan out a search path. Finally, the best predictors of search performance are (a) spatial visualization ability, and (b) vocabulary and comprehension abilities.

10
Rapid Access Menus

It seems natural that highly practiced actions should require the least time and effort to perform. Rapid action is due in part to the learning of automatic behavior on the part of the user, but it is also due to the fact that people arrange objects in their environment for fast and easy access. When an electrician or a carpenter begins a task, he or she makes sure that the needed tools and parts are within easy reach. Less frequently used items are left in the truck or back at the shop. In the same way, frequently chosen menu items should be easily and rapidly accessible to the user. Less frequently used functions may be buried under layers of menus. There are many situations in which items are selected so frequently or in rapid repetition that designers are challenged to minimize selection time and effort. The question is "How?"

Previous chapters have dealt with the overall efficiency of menu structure and access. These chapters and the research they have reported have assumed a more or less uniform use of menu options. In reality, access of menu options is extremely uneven. Some options are accessed with high frequency at the rate of hundreds of times per session. Style and editing functions in a word processor, shapes, lines, and patterns in a graphics package, and rows, columns, and functions in a spread sheet program are selected with great frequency. Other items, however, are accessed only rarely though they may nevertheless be vital to the operation. For example, options to open or close a file may only be used once per session but are absolutely necessary. The differences in frequency of use can be very drastic. Figure 10.1 shows the frequency of use of 49 options in the pull-down menu bar of MacWrite™ accessed by one user.

Laverson (1985) introduced the notion of a "menu utilization profile" to characterize the uneven access of items in a hierarchical menu system. He hypothesized that the efficiency of different rapid access methods would depend on the utilization profile. His ideas need to be extended, however, since the differential access of items varies as a function of two important factors. The frequency of use may be either *task specific*, in that the particular task performed determines the frequency of use, or *user specific*, in that the type of user determines the frequency of use. As an example of *task specific* utilization profiles, the frequency of use of menu

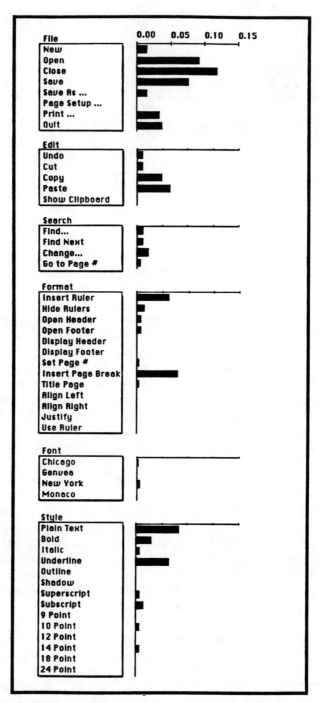

Figure 10.1. Menu utilization profile of a pull-down menu in MacWrite™ showing the frequency of use of each item based on one user.

items in a word processor varies substantially between the task of composing a paper and editing a paper. As an example of *user specific* utilization profiles, the frequency of complex, technical items may be higher for experienced users and simple, direct items for inexperienced users of a graphic program.

Two basic methods of rapid access have been explored. One is to arrange items in the menu frame and/or hierarchy to minimize the distance from the initial menu state to the location of high frequency targets. The second is to provide various forms of menu "bypass," "jump-ahead," or direct commands that reduce the distance by defining shortcuts through the menu space. In this chapter, studies will be reviewed that bear on the efficacy and importance of such approaches.

10.1 LOCATION IN THE MENU

Although it may seem obvious that highly used options should be the most readily accessible items, many systems bury these items in the middle or at the bottom of menu lists and hierarchies. Such designs may be driven in part by the fallacy that menu selection makes everything uniformly rapid and easy. The idea is that since menus are inherently easy to use, all items must be easy to access. While this may be the perception of novice users and some designers, experienced users all too quickly detect the bottlenecks and frustratingly slow access to frequently required items.

10.1.1 Pull-down Menus

This is particularly true of pull-down menus. All items appear to be easily and rapidly available. Consequently, the order of items in pull-down menus is rarely designed around frequency of use.

Empirical results, however, indicate that access time depends on the location of items in the pull-down menu. In one experiment, 24 items were presented in four different menu configurations varying in the number and length of the pull-down menus (Norman, 1989). The conditions were as follows: 3×8, 4×6, 6×4, and 8×3, where the first number in each product is the number of pull-down lists and the second number is the length of each list. In addition, prior knowledge of target location was varied by using three different types of menus (see Figure 10.2). For array menus, items were simply 24 letter-number combinations. The letter indicated which pull-down list to access and the number indicated the target item in that list. Array menus provided the user with complete

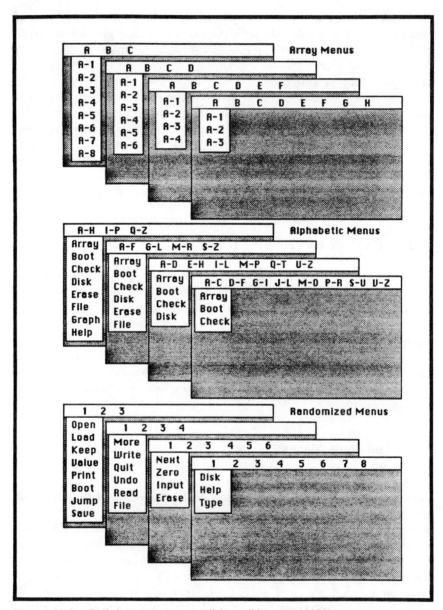

Figure 10.2.　Pull-down menus conditions (Norman, 1989).

prior knowledge as to the location of target items before menus were pulled down. For alphabetized menus, items were 24 common words each beginning with a different letter of the alphabet. Pull-down lists indicated a letter range and items in each list were in alphabetical order.

Although the menus provided a degree of prior knowledge as to location, it was somewhat more difficult and incomplete in comparison to the array menus. Finally, for randomized menus, the items were the same 24 words, but on each trial the words were cast in a different random order across all of the lists. The random menus provided no prior information to the user as to location. In effect this condition simulated the novice user on all trials having no experience.

Subjects were randomly assigned to one type of menu item and were tested on each of the four menu configurations in a counterbalanced order. Sixteen subjects participated in each of the three menu conditions. For each configuration, subjects were given a set of practice trials and then tested on two replications of each of the 24 target items in a randomized block order. On each trial the target item was displayed in a small window just to the left of the center on a Macintosh™ screen. Subjects used a mouse to pull down and select the target item from the menu bar at the top of the screen. Times were recorded from the onset of the target to the selection response. If the subject selected an item that was not the target, it was recorded, a tone was sounded, and the target item was recycled in the pool of targets to be presented.

Response times were fairly fast for the array menus, averaging about 2.6 sec, and varied significantly with target location (see Figure 10.3). Access times were fastest for the first positions in each pull-down and increased linearly with position down the list. Response times, however, did not vary with the position of the pull-down, but only with the position of items in the list. Linear regression equations of access time as a function of list position indicated that the time increment per item in the pull-down menu was 104 ms for the 3×8 condition, 147 for the 4×6 condition, 251 for the 6×4 condition, and 228 for the 8×3 condition. Consequently, although the lists were shorter in the 6×4 and 8×3 conditions, the pull-down time per item position was significantly longer than in the 3×8 and 4×6 conditions. Access times to the pull-down lists (as indicated by the intercept of the regression lines) were fairly similar across conditions, and there was no significant difference in overall response time among the four conditions. It would appear that for highly predictable menus, the tradeoff between list position and pull-down time cancels out when items are accessed with equal frequency. However, if the designer knows that some items will be more frequently accessed than others, they should be placed in a broad menu at the top positions of the pull-downs to minimize access time.

Response times for the alphabetized menus were somewhat longer, averaging about 3.2 sec (see Figure 10.4). For these menus, the first and last positions in each list tended to show the fastest access times. The limits of the alphabetic ranges probably served as markers that aided

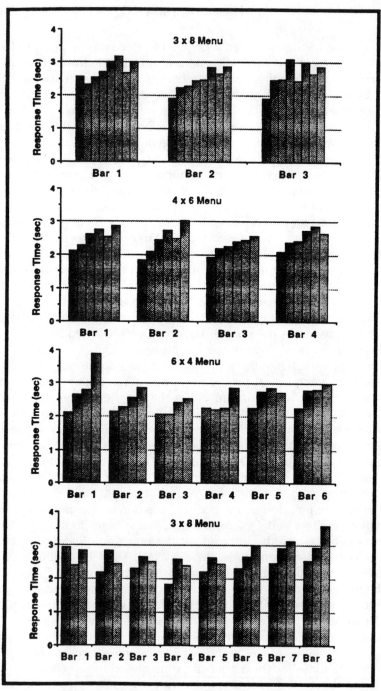

Figure 10.3. Mean response times for pull-down array menus in conditions 3×8, 4×6, 6×4, and 8×3 (Norman, 1989).

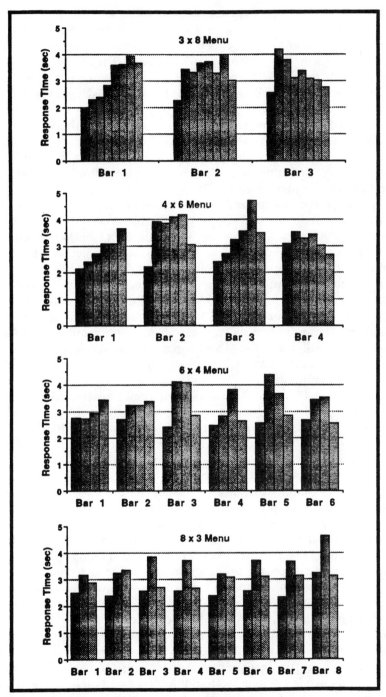

Figure 10.4. Mean response times for pull-down alphabetic menus in conditions 3×8, 4×6, 6×4, and 8×3 (Norman, 1989).

location for these items. This effect occurred both within a pull-down list and across lists for the 3×8 and 4×6 conditions. The access times for the first and last pull-down were skewed so that time increased with list position for the first pull-down (A-H), but decreased with list position for the last pull-down (Q-Z), with the exception of the first position (Q). Overall access time decreased significantly as the breadth increased and the lists were shorter. The reason for this also lies in the fact that broader menu bars display more alphabetic markers that aid in locating items. Consequently, for alphabetic search, designers should increase the number of pull-down lists.

Finally, for the randomized menus, response times were much longer, averaging about 4.7 (see Figure 10.5). Subjects seemed to search this list in a linear order, viewing the first pull-down from top to bottom, then the second pull-down, and so on until the target was found. A multiple regression analysis of pull-down position and list position for each condition indicated that the time increment for processing each pull-down was 935 ms for the 3×8 condition, 479 ms for the 4×6 condition, 582 ms for the 6×4 condition, and 346 ms for the 8×3 condition. These differences were due to the time required to visually search each pull-down list. The longer the list, the longer it took to search. The increment for list position within a pull-down was 207 ms for the 3×8 condition, 249 ms for the 4×6 condition, 307 ms for the 6×4 condition, and 154 ms for the 8×3 condition. These increments were due to both search time and cursor positioning time, and revealed the magnitude of added time to locate items buried in a pull-down. Finally, overall response time was somewhat faster for the 3×8 and 4×6 conditions. Apparently search within a few long pull-downs was faster than within a number of short pull-downs.

While only minor differences on the order of .5 sec were found in overall performance due to menu structure, major differences on the order of 2 sec were found due to position in the menu. Consequently, the recommendation is to locate frequently needed items in positions that show the fastest access times. The efficacy of menu location, however, also depends on the user's prior knowledge as to the location of the item. Novice users spend most of their time searching for the location of an item (as simulated by the random menu). Frequently needed items should, consequently, be placed in the pull-down locations searched first (in this case the top left-most pull-down). Experienced users spend most of their time in cursor movement (as simulated by the array menu). Consequently, it doesn't matter in which pull-down a frequently needed item is located, but it is important that it is in a top position.

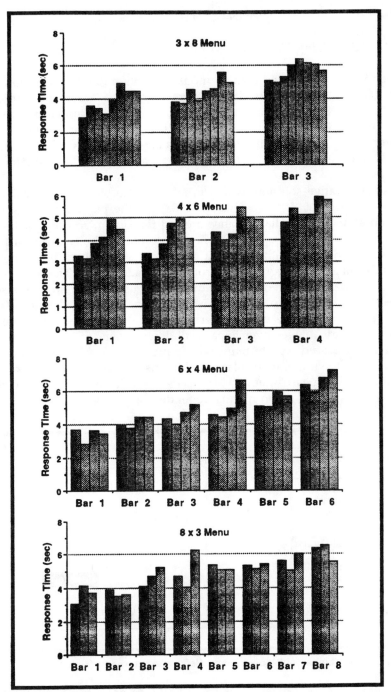

Figure 10.5. Mean response times for pull-down random menus in conditions
3 × 8, 4 × 6, 6 × 4, and 8 × 3 (Norman, 1989).

10.1.2 Minimizing Distance/Maximizing Size

When items are selected using a mouse, selection time is a function of the distance of the cursor to the target and the size of the target, according to Fitts' law (see Chapter 8). Consequently, rapid access may be achieved by making items closer to the initial cursor position and larger in physical size. Pull-down menus have the disadvantage in that the larger the target, the greater the distance to all but the first item in the list.

An innovative solution to this problem is the pie menu (Callahan, Hopkins, Weiser, & Shneiderman, 1988). In the pie menu items are placed at an equal radial distance around the circumference of a circle (see Figure 10.6). The starting or home position of the cursor is at the middle of the circle rather than at the top of a pull-down list. Consequently, all items are equidistant from the home position. The selectable area is a pie-shaped wedge beginning at the center of the circle. Consequently, the distance to the target is very short. Items may be increased in size by making the circle larger. Thus, pie menus seem to have a number of advantages over linear pull-down menus.

In a recent study, performance using pie menus was compared with linear pull-down menus (Callahan, Hopkins, Weiser, & Shneiderman, 1988). Three types of items were used to see if performance on pie menus versus pull-down menus depended on the organization of the

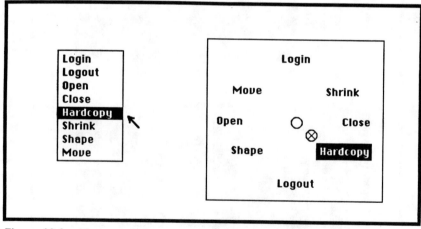

Figure 10.6. Linear pull-down menu (left) and pie menu (right).

From "An empirical comparison of pie vs. linear menus," by J. Callahan, D. Hopkins, M. Weiser, and B. Shneiderman, 1988, *CHI '88 Conference Proceedings on Human Factors in Computing Systems* (pp. 95–100). Copyright 1988 by ACM. Reprinted by permission.

items. It was thought that pie menus would be particularly good for items that could be organized around a circle, such as compass locations (e.g., North, NE, East, SE, South, SW, West, and NW). Pull-down menus may be more appropriate for linear organizations of items (e.g., First, Second, Third, Fourth, Fifth, Sixth, Seventh, and Eighth). Finally, unclassified groupings of items were used (e.g., Center, Bold, Italic, Font, Move, Copy, Find, and Undo) with no prediction as to which would be more appropriate. Five menus were generated for each type of organization and were displayed twice in both the pie and pull-down formats. A completely within-subject design was used in which subjects selected items in all of the menu types and formats in a randomized order of presentation. Subjects had little or no prior experience using the mouse. On each trial, a target item was displayed at the top of the screen. Item selection involved three stages. The user invoked the menu by pressing the mouse button (invocation), held the mouse button down and moved to an item which was then highlighted (browsing), and released the mouse button to confirm the selection (confirmation). Selection times were measured from the point when the mouse button was pressed to when it was released.

Overall response times were significantly faster for pie menus (2.26 sec) than for pull-down menus (2.64 sec), a performance advantage of about 15 percent. Although response times for the unclassified items were longer than for the compass and linear types, there was no interaction between menu format and organization of items. Pie menus were uniformly superior across all types of items. Furthermore, fewer selection errors were made using the pie menu; however, the difference was not statistically significant.

A closer analysis of results indicates that the advantage of pie over pull-down menus was due to the items in the lower half of the list. Response times for items 1 through 4 in the list were approximately the same for pie and pull-down menus. However, for items 5 through 8, response times for the pie menu were considerably faster than for the pull-down menu (see Figure 10.7). Response times increased linearly for pull-down menus from the first to the last item. For pie menus, response times were faster for the top and bottom points on the circle. Response times appeared to increase clockwise around the circle from the top position, but decreased sharply at the bottom position where they again increased clockwise around the circle until the top was reached.

Although the items are all equidistant from the home position in pie menus, response times are not uniform. Visual search time probably accounts for this effect. Items in the top and bottom positions of the compass are mostly quickly located. Search then proceeds in a linear manner around the compass.

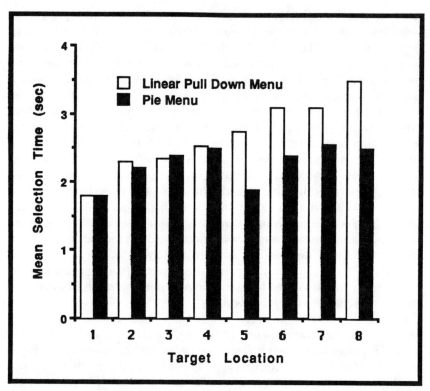

Figure 10.7. Mean selection time for linear pull-down and pie menus as a function of target location. (After Callahan, Hopkins, Weiser & Shneiderman, 1988.)

From "An empirical comparison of pie vs. linear menus," by J. Callahan, D. Hopkins, M. Weiser, and B. Shneiderman, 1988, *CHI '88 Conference Proceedings on Human Factors in Computing Systems* (pp. 95–100). Copyright 1988 by ACM. Reprinted by permission.

Pie menus offer a promising alternative to linear pull-down menus. However, it is not yet clear when and how they should be used. Clearly they are limited in the number of items that can be displayed around the circle and require substantially more space on the screen. It is clear that cursor movement time is reduced, but it is not clear what happens with visual search around a circle. Further research is needed to partial out visual search time from movement time in such studies. In addition, it is not clear how experience affects selection time with pie menus. In the study by Callahan et al. (1988), subjects were only exposed to the same menu twice. Consequently, subjects had little prior knowledge as to the location of target items. The real advantage of pie menus may be for high predictable or well-learned menus where visual search time is at a minimum.

10.1.3 Position in the Hierarchy

Hierarchical menus pose a greater problem for rapid access. Each level down the hierarchy requires time and effort. If frequently needed items are buried several levels down, the user must enter a series of menu selections each time the item is required. Many systems place all target items at the same level in the hierarchy for the sake of consistency. Unfortunately, this places all items at the same level of effort.

A better approach may be to move frequently used items up the hierarchy and infrequently used items further down. Figure 10.8 shows a system in which primary functions are accessible at the top level of the menu, secondary functions at the next level, and tertiary functions are buried at the bottom. An enhanced telephone provides a good example of such a system. Options to answer the phone, dial emergency numbers, and disconnect are primary functions that are available at the touch of one button. Options to enter telephone numbers into memory, set

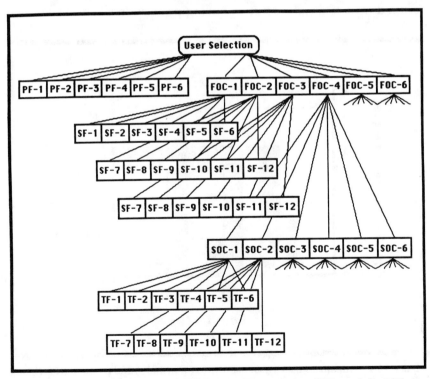

Figure 10.8.   Hierarchical clustering of functions. Primary Functions (PF) are at the top level. Secondary Functions (SF) are at the second level clustered under First-Order Categories (FOC), and Tertiary Functions are at the third level clustered under Second-Order Categories (SOC).

time and date, and set mode to pulse or touch tone are secondary or tertiary functions that might require several levels of menu selection.

Response times for functions at successive levels can be estimated using the log model discussed in Chapter 7. Figure 10.9 (gray bars) shows an idealized graph of response times for the menu in Figure 10.8. It can be seen that primary functions are accessed faster than secondary functions and secondary functions are accessed faster than tertiary functions. The combination of primary functions and first-order categories at the first level increases user response time due to the larger number of items. This problem may be ameliorated, however, by the way in which the menu is laid out. For example, one may place primary items in a separate window or on a separate keypad. If they are cognitively distinct, the number of primary items n_{pf} and the number of first-order categories n_{foc} will not summate to a breadth of $n_{pf} + n_{foc}$.

Ultimately, one must consider the average access time over all menu items. If all items are accessed equally often, the expected access time is just over 7 seconds. However, when the menu utilization profile is factored in, a clear advantage in having primary functions at that first

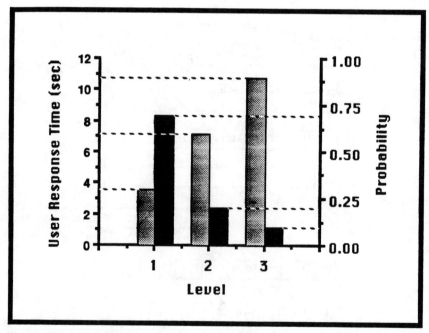

Figure 10.9. Idealized user response times (gray bars) and probabilities (black bars) for Primary Functions and First-Order Categories (Level 1), Secondary Functions and Second-Order Categories (Level 2), and Tertiary Functions (Level 3) as shown in Figure 10.8.

level should emerge. Figure 10.9 (black bars) shows the case where primary functions are accessed with .7 probability, secondary functions with .2 probability, and tertiary functions with .1 probability. The expected access time for this utilization profile is only 5 sec. Thus, expected access time (5 sec) is more than halved over a menu in which all items are at the third level (10.8 sec).

An additional advantage of varying position in the menu hierarchy is that one can intentionally hide specialized functions and make them more difficult to access. The idea is to place items that change important system parameters or could have major negative consequences at the bottom of the hierarchy. Setting the date and time, configuring the printer, specifying terminal emulation parameters, and reformatting the disk are examples of items that might be hidden at lower levels of a menu hierarchy.

A number of researchers have proposed the idea of adaptive menus that seek to match the menu utilization profile over frequency of use (e.g., Berke & Vidal, 1987). For pull-down menus, the system could reposition items in lists to reduce the distance that the cursor must traverse to select high-frequency items. In hierarchical menus, high-frequency items could percolate up the tree to reduce the length of the path. Although adaptive approaches to rapid access appear promising at first glance, they may carry a fatal flaw. While the system "learns" and adapts the menu to usage patterns, the user is kept guessing as to the location of an item. High-speed automaticity on the part of the user may be frustrated by a seemingly inconsistent system. A second problem is that the menu utilization profile may not be just user specific. It may vary drastically depending on the task. As soon as the system has adapted to the user browsing through messages in an automatic message handler, the user may shift tasks and start composing messages. To accommodate such abrupt changes in the menu utilization profile the system must have a more sophisticated model of user behavior. Finally, there is yet no empirical research supporting the idea of self-adapting menus and their superiority over user-controlled rapid access methods.

10.2 ACCELERATING THROUGH THE SYSTEM

Rapid access may be accomplished by location, but often it is judicious to arrange the menu in a semantic, logical, or even alphabetic order without regard to the frequency of use, and then provide a jump-ahead or direct access facility to a subset of high-frequency items. This approach is particularly valuable when the menu utilization profile is task or user specific. When the designer cannot accommodate all profiles by menu location, users can accommodate themselves by learning jump-ahead commands. Direct access menus allow the user to select frequently used items by a single command and bypass intermediate layers of menu selections. Direct access is memory mediated in the sense that the distance from the initial state to the target is short circuited via a memory path rather than a menu path. For example, access to an item in a videotext service that is three or four levels down may be achieved by typing its command name (e.g., Stocks, WPost, or Games). Furthermore, direct access may allow the user to completely bypass the menu hierarchy. The user may enter a direct command at any point in the menu to access any other function.

In the case of cursor-based and/or mouse-based selection systems, the user enters a command mode typically by the selection of a special function key. A command line prompt is displayed and the user types the desired command. Consequently, this form of direct access switches the user out of menu selection and into a simple command language as a mode of interaction. The empirical issues regarding command entry have been covered in other texts and will not be repeated here. However, the interaction between commands and menu selection is of great interest and is the subject of the following sections.

10.2.1 Alternate Command Keys

The most abbreviated menu bypass commands are single-key (e.g., program function keys) or dual-key commands (e.g., *Alt*-keys or *Control* keys). Access to menu functions may be facilitated by providing command key selection in predominantly mouse-based menu systems. Often the reason for providing keyboard selection is to eliminate the time that it takes for the hand to travel from the keyboard to the analog input device (homing time). When a user is entering text on the keyboard and must repeatedly make menu selections to change style, the use of command keys can drastically reduce task time.

There are two basic problems with alternative command keys: learning and relearning. The user must learn the alternate command keys to make the menu selection. Learning is typically facilitated by (a) listing key equivalents in the menu display, and (b) by using keys that are associated with the menu alternative, such as the first letter of the menu alternative. While incidental learning of the key equivalents is probably minor, the menu itself provides an online help system for the user to find key equivalents when needed. Alternative command keys pose a design problem when a number of them are needed and when several menu names begin with the same letter.

However, some simple rules can be used to generate keybindings. Walker and Olson (1988) describe three rules that result in easy learning and resistance to forgetting:

1. Different function keys should be used for the highest level of command structure. For example, the *Esc* key might be used for all system-related commands, the *Alt* key for all deletions commands, and the *Control* key for all other types of actions.
2. Provide a one-to-one mapping between a key press and an appropriate action or object. For example, if there is only one save command (e.g., Save File), it might be accessed with *Esc S*. Additional keys might be needed for specific different directions or actions and different objects. For example, *Alt FW* might mean *delete forward a word*, and *Alt BC* mean *delete back a character*.
3. The order of keybindings should follow the English pattern of Verb-Adjective/Adverb-Object. For example, *Alt BW* might mean *delete back a word*.

Walker and Olson found that by using these rules they could create a set of keybindings that were easier to learn and more resistant to forgetting than those provided by a standard word processor. Furthermore, they noted that the rules led to keybindings that were more extensible than rules proposed by others (Green & Payne, 1984). This is extremely important as the complexity and functionality of software increases.

As users transfer among a number of different applications, they often encounter the problem that key equivalents do not transfer. *Control-U* in one application may perform an undo function, and in another *Control-U* may set the text input to superscript. As noted in Chapter 7, transfer of learning may be impaired when lexical changes (renaming items) are made from one application to another.

To the extent that designers can adopt standard key equivalents across applications for high-frequency items, there should be a positive transfer of performance. Unfortunately, this is a near impossible design objective, primarily because of the variability in user-specific and task-specific menu utilization profiles. For one user/task the key equivalents are fine, but for another the most frequently used menu items have no key equivalents. The only solution may be to allow users to define their own key equivalents in addition to, or as an alternative to, those provided by the application. At present there is no major research on the issue of user-defined key equivalents.

10.2.2 Direct Access vs. Type Ahead

When rapid access is required for all terminal items, or at least a number larger than the number of command keys available, access may be provided by entering a command string. At least two types of command strings can be used. One method is to provide a mnemonic name for the menu item for direct access. In essence, this implements a vast, but unlisted set of options at each choice point. The user must remember the full name in order to jump to that item.

An alternative to command entry is the type-ahead method in which the user enters a number of sequential choices at one time. All of the choices are processed at one time so that intervening menus are by-passed. Users may enter as many levels as they can recall. If the user enters the entire path, the system implements that function. If the user enters only a partial path, the system implements selections up to that point and displays the next menu in the series. While the direct-access method of jump-ahead is essentially all-or-nothing, the type-ahead method allows partial jump-ahead.

The direct-access and type-ahead methods were evaluated to determine which (a) takes the least number of trials to learn, (b) produces the lowest error rates, and (c) receives the greater approval by users (Laverson, Norman, & Shneiderman, 1987). Thirty-two subjects searched for targets in a hierarchical database of college course information clustered by academic division, department, and level (see Figure 10.10). In the direct-access condition, subjects learned to find targets using five-letter names (e.g., HUCMO for human and community resources, MAPST for mathematical and physical sciences; see Figure 10.11). In the type-ahead condition, subjects learned to find targets using a series of five letters normally selected along the path to access the target. Subjects participated in both conditions in a counterbalanced order.

The results indicated that the direct-access method (a) required significantly fewer trials to learn than the type-ahead method, (b) resulted in significantly lower error rates, and (c) significantly reduced response time. Furthermore, subjective evaluations indicated that subjects preferred the direct-access method over the type-ahead method. Subjects indicated that direct-access commands were easier to learn, easier to recall, easier to use, and resulted in greater overall satisfaction. Most subjects reported that they used rote memory for learning and recalling jump-ahead commands. However, if subjects attempted to derive the commands in the type-ahead method, they had to recall the items chosen in the correct order. If subjects attempted to derive the commands in the direct-access method, they had to figure out the nomenclature of names.

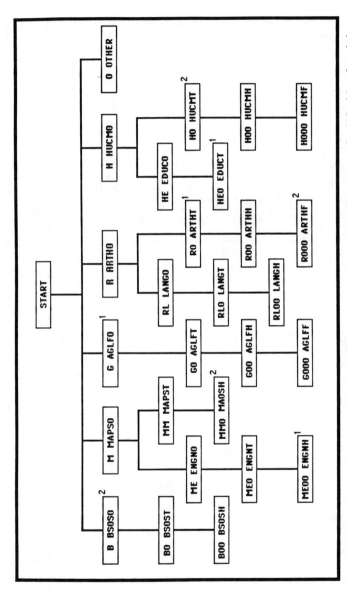

Figure 10.10. Hierarchical database of college course information. Letters on the left side of each box represent the type-ahead command to jump to that node. Letters on the right side of each box represent the direct-access command to jump to that node. If a course of study is selected, two additional frames are presented, one for the course of study and the second for the course description. (See Figure 10.11 for example.)

From '"An evaluation of jump-ahead techniques in menu selection," by A. Laverson, K.L. Norman, and B. Shneiderman, 1987, *Behaviour and Information Technology, 6,* 97–108. Copyright 1987 by Taylor & Francis, Ltd. Reprinted by permission.

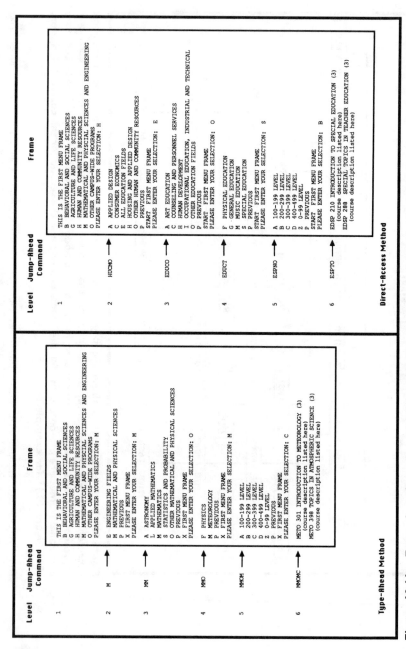

Figure 10.11. Examples of menu paths using the Type-Ahead and Direct Access methods of jump ahead.

From "'An evaluation of jump-ahead techniques in menu selection," by A. Laverson, K.L. Norman, and B. Shneiderman, 1987, *Behaviour and Information Technology, 6*, 97–108. Copyright 1987 by Taylor & Francis, Ltd. Reprinted by permission.

Although the study by Laverson et al. favored the direct-access method, it is not clear whether the advantage of direct access over type ahead was due to the jump-ahead method or due to differences in the meaningfulness of the two sets of commands. Meaningfulness is a very potent factor in the ability to commit information to memory. A study by Jofre and Pino (1987) illustrates this point. They implemented a menu tree in which the concatenation of selection codes produced a pronounceable strings of letters. They noted that in the Spanish language pronounceable strings could be easily constructed by alternating consonants and vowels. Subjects that used the pronounceable codes performed significantly better than subjects that used randomly generated codes. Although Jofre and Pino did not compare the type-ahead method with the direct-access method, it is clear that meaningfulness, or a strong correlate of meaningfulness (i.e., pronounceability), is an important factor in developing menu bypass commands. It would appear that whichever method can be implemented with greater meaningfulness of the commands should be implemented. In general, direct access allows the designer to generate commands with the highest meaningfulness.

10.3 SPEED-ACCURACY TRADEOFF IN RAPID MENU SELECTION

When users are forced to speed up on a task there is generally an increase in errors. This is known as the speed-accuracy tradeoff. In menu selection this tradeoff is evidenced by wrong selections. Selection errors are generally of two types: discrimination errors and movement errors. Discrimination errors occur when the user selects an item that is similar in physical or semantic features to the target, for example, selecting "Save" rather than "Save As." Movement errors occur when the user attempts to select the correct item, but misses it and selects another. Movement errors generally result in the selection of an item that is one off from the target, for example, one above or below in a pull-down list or an item keyed next to the correct key on a keyboard (e.g., "v" or "n" rather than "b"). On pull-down menus, the proportion of errors in timed tasks is on the order of 2–4 percent with about 80 percent being one-off errors (Norman, 1989).

Time pressure may be forced on users by the environment or by the system itself. In many cases, the user must complete a menu search before a deadline. In other cases the system may institute a time out if the user has not responded within a set period of time. When the menus are long, the user may be hurried scanning the list and making a selection. With short menus, scanning time is reduced, but the user has to make more selections and potentially more errors. It should be no surprise that empirical results indicate a significant advantage for broad menus. Wallace (1988) investigated menu search under time pressure in hierarchical menus of 256 items varying the breadth and depth in three structures: 2^8, 4^4, and 16^2. While there was no significant difference in the number of searches that timed out using the three menu structures, the narrow/deep structure (2^8) resulted in 174 percent more errors than the broad/shallow structure (16^2). Clearly, broad/shallow menus are required when users are under time pressure.

10.4 SUMMARY

When users access menus hundreds of times per hour over extended periods of work, they become highly proficient and demand rapid access to frequently used functions. The way in which a menu is organized can go a long way toward decreasing access time. For pull-down menus, frequently accessed items should be placed in the top positions in pull-down lists. In other mouse-based systems, innovative menu design, such as pie menus, can reduce access time by minimizing cursor movement and maximizing the size of the selectable area. The location of pop-up menus and the use of other selection topologies, such as grids, may also reduce response time.

Access time may also be reduced by minimizing switching from one mode of input to another. Many mouse-based applications provide alternate command keys to eliminate homing time. In hierarchical menus, access time may be reduced by placing frequently used items at higher levels in the menu tree and burying infrequently used items at the bottom. Unfortunately, there is often a conflict between frequency placement and logical placement. Logically, a menu item may belong in a group of items four levels down the hierarchy, but its frequency of use may suggest that it should be placed at the top of the tree.

A solution to this problem is to provide rapid access via a jump-ahead method. Jump-ahead may be provided by either a type-ahead in which the user enters a series of menu selections all at once, or a direct-access method in which the user enters a frame name. Research favors the method that can provide the most meaningful string of characters. In general, design favors the use of meaningful frame names for direct access.

Despite the emphasis on rapid access, selection errors in well-practiced menus tend to be rare. Generally they are one-off errors in which the user inadvertently selects an item next to the target item. It is only with extreme time constraints that errors appear with any great frequency.

III
IMPLEMENTATION AND EVALUATION OF MENU SYSTEMS

It is easy to write menus. Perhaps this is the reason why many programmers use them extensively. However, it is no easy task to write good menus. The previous chapters provide a wealth of information about good and bad menu design. Although it may be too early to set forth documented principles of design and tried-and-true guidelines, the designer at least has a lot to work with. Designers can start from the theory of cognitive control, work through the empirical results on design features, and implement a system to the best of their ability.

The last section of this book considers the problem of implementation. It is not enough to just provide theories and guidelines. If it were, one could merely read a book on the technique and theory of art and paint a masterpiece. The problem of implementation is that one must integrate and execute a number of principles simultaneously and harmoniously. Designing a menu system is often like putting together a jigsaw puzzle. Each part must fit, or at least not conflict, with others. Furthermore, the designer must consider a number of tradeoffs. Applying one guideline often violates another guideline due to the limits of the machine or the abilities of the user. The menu must somehow strike a balance between conflicting forces.

Chapter 11 summarizes a number of guidelines about when menus are the appropriate form of interaction as opposed to command line and form-fill modes. In addition, it deals with issues about where and how menus should be implemented. Menus may be explicit: "Select one of the following:", or implicit: "Coffee, tea, or milk?" They may be integrated and embedded in the task as tools, or separated in pop-up windows or pull-down menus. The main thrust of this chapter is to ask, "What is appropriate? What works? What fits with the flow of the program and task?"

A major consideration in implementation is how to organize information or sets of functions. Chapter 12 discusses the issue of organization of menus and menu hierarchies based on semantic information and user input. It is pointed out that the structure that designers impose on the system may not match that of users. The difference may be as fundamental as whether one takes a top-down perspective of the system or a bottom-up one. It should be remembered that it is the user that traverses the menu over and over again and it should be designed from that perspective. Efficiency of menu traversal should be from the user's point of view and not from formal top-down specifications of system requirements.

Prototyping and usability testing has become a standard component in the evolution of design. Chapter 13 discusses menu prototyping and the methodology of prototyping systems. A number of user interface management systems allow rapid prototyping. Few possess the capabilities of experimental control and data collection. Without such capabilities these programs serve only as demonstrations rather than empirical tests. User evaluation is of primary importance in prototyping. Consequently, Chapter 13 presents work on subjective evaluations of interactive systems as well as on menu systems in particular.

The final chapter in this book looks forward to a continuing development of the human/computer interface. It is expected that menu selection is here to stay, but that it will dramatically change in complexity and richness in the coming years as technology provides bigger, faster, higher resolution interface devices. Chapter 14 presents some ideas about the future directions of menu selection in the context of the theory of cognitive control.

11
Clustering of Menus

It has been asserted in previous chapters that menu structure and organization have a great impact on performance. It has also been asserted that menu organization should in some way convey a meaningful mental model of the system. The question then is how to generate good menus. Good menu organization can dramatically facilitate the search process by taking advantage of the user's knowledge about relationships among items. The menu may be organized by similarity, by hierarchical relationships, by categorization, and by clustering of items. In Chapter 8 it was concluded that organization is one of the primary factors driving the depth versus breadth tradeoff and that menu organization is important both within and between menu frames.

In this chapter methods of organizing menus will be discussed. Several issues arise regarding the source of organizing information. The first question pertains to whether organizing information is inherent in the menu items or is imposed by the task. In the first case, the database of items itself contains some sort of clustering information that can be used to organize the menu. In this case, the object is to discover the inherent organization *from within*. In a sense, the menu items are self-organizing. Alternatively, procedural knowledge may be inferred from tasks being performed that impose an organization and sequencing of functions. In this case, the object is to discover structure in the task that imposes organization *from without*. Menu items are organized by task needs.

The second question is whether the organizing information should come from system designers or system users. In the first case, designers organize menus and cluster items according to their knowledge of the system. Designers are experts on how the system works and are most knowledgeable about its functionality. Database experts organize the items into clusters and categories according to their extensive knowledge about how the database is constructed. For example, databases for medical information, periodicals, and encyclopedic information are organized by those who have a vast knowledge of the subject matter domain. If experts were the only users of such systems, there would be little question as to who should organize the menu. Experts would cluster items and create structures that reflected their best knowledge of the system or database. Unfortunately, this is no small task in itself.

However, systems are, in general, not only used by subject matter experts, but also by day-to-day users of varying levels of familiarity with the system. The user's conception of how a menu is organized or should be organized to perform a certain task may be quite different from the designer's. Similarly for databases, the user's conception of how information should be organized may be quite different from the scientific or technical organization of the information. Designers of easy-to-use systems for consumer products realize that the layout of controls should conform to user expectation rather than internal machine efficiency. Consequently, it is imperative to elicit user expectations and conceptions about how things work as basic input into the design of menus. One way to tap the information about how to organize a menu is to look at the access of items in a current system. Frequency of access and the order in which items are selected provide hard data that can be used to organize a menu system.

11.1 KNOWLEDGE REPRESENTATION

What kind of knowledge is used to organize the menu? Cognitive psychologists make a distinction between procedural knowledge and declarative knowledge (Anderson, 1980). Declarative knowledge essentially consists of known facts about the world. For example, knowing that "run" is the first item on the menu is a fact. Declarative knowledge tends to be static and can easily be expressed verbally. Procedure knowledge, on the other hand, consists of the production rules about how to perform a task. Production rules consist of a condition and an action. When the condition is met, the action is performed. For example, knowing how to start the program by selecting "run" is procedural knowledge. The condition is wanting to start the program; the action is selecting "run." Because procedural knowledge is more action oriented, it is more difficult to express verbally.

Menu systems are composed of both declarative and procedural knowledge. The categorical structure of the system generally reflects declarative knowledge. The hierarchical structure of the categories, such as the animal kingdom shown in Figure 8.1, is factual information. The properties of the objects dictate their location in the menu structure. Consequently, menus of objects rely heavily on declarative knowledge.

Action-oriented menus rely on procedural information. An item is an appropriate action given a particular condition. The user, for example, may select "stop" if the program is running. The conditional nature of items is conveyed in the hierarchical ordering of the paths in a network menu. Consequently, menus composed of functions and procedures contain information about the ordering of actions and rely heavily on procedural knowledge.

Both declarative and procedural knowledge may be represented in different types of data structures. Figure 11.1 shows four types of data structures investigated by Durding, Becker, and Gould (1977). Sets of items tend to be organized in terms of hierarchies, networks, lists, or tables. The hierarchical structure of a book, for example, is represented in the table of contents, the network of communication between friends may be represented in a graph, and so on. The inherent organization within a set of terms should be apparent to the user and should be structured in the appropriate way. It is hypothesized that the greater the congruency between the inherent organization of the data and its representation by the computer, the easier it will be for the user to comprehend and use the information.

A series of experiments by Durding et al. (1977) showed that when subjects were given the terms shown in Figure 11.1, they systematically organized them on the basis of the semantic relationships inherent in them. The utility of these structures was demonstrated in a second experiment. It was shown that given skeleton structures of the appropriate type, subjects could efficiently fit items into the structure. Finally, they showed that subjects had difficulty in preserving relations when they had to organize the items into inappropriate structures. The lesson to be learned is straight forward. The inherent structure of the items conveyed by their semantic relations should be conveyed by their organization on the screen.

Consequently, it is important to capture the inherent organization in the items displayed. From a design perspective, the question then is how to capture the appropriate knowledge to organize the menu. The next section discusses procedures for eliciting such information for hierarchical structures.

11.2 HIERARCHICAL CLUSTERING METHODS

Imagine that a person has an unorganized set of menu items. How can they be organized? One easy method is that of clustering. Clustering may proceed in either a top-down or bottom-up manner. The approaches are illustrated in Figure 11.2. In the top-down approach the designer thinks of first-order categories. Then each category is further divided into subordinate categories, and so on until the actual menu items are categorized. In the bottom-up approach, the designer thinks of all of the menu items first. Similar items are clustered together in groups. Then groups of items are further clustered into larger groups, and so on until all groups are combined.

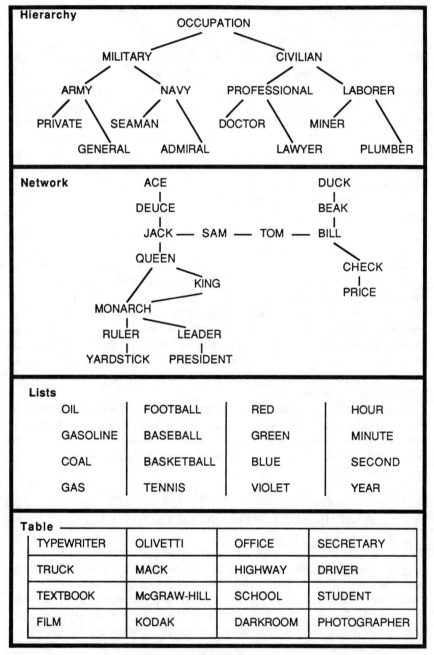

Figure 11.1. Examples of data structures that are inherent in the set of items.

From "Data organization," by B.M. Durding, C.A. Becker, and J.D. Gould, 1977, *Human Factors, 19,* 1-14. Copyright 1977 by The Human Factors Society. Reprinted by permission.

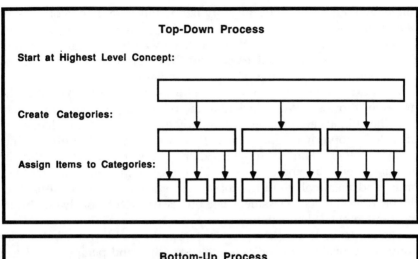

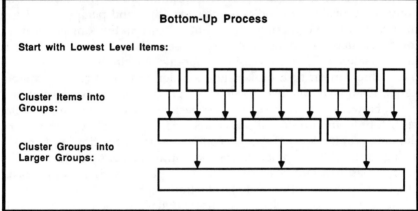

Figure II.2. **Top-down and bottom-up approaches to creating menu hierarchies.**

The top-down approach is conceptually driven in that the person has a set of concepts in mind that serve to generate categories. Lindsey and Norman (1977) noted that top-down processing of information helps to structure expectations about incoming data. Top-down processing emphasizes the differences between pieces of information. Items are discriminated from one another along categorical boundaries and conceptual dimensions. On the other hand, bottom-up processing is thought of as data-driven in that inspection of the items results in grouping and clustering. Bottom-up processing emphasizes the similarities among items. Items are grouped into larger and larger categories depending on common aspects.

The children's book, *Benny's Animals and How He Put Them Together* by Selsam (1966), illustrates top-down and bottom-up processing when thinking about animals. In the story Benny took a large pile of pictures of animals and grouped them in a bottom-up process. Benny put birds, butterflies, and bats in one pile because they all had wings. In another pile he put worms and snakes because they were long and thin. Obviously, Benny was focusing on surface similarities.

The next day Benny's father took him to see Professor Wood at the museum. Professor Wood looked at the piles and proceeded to explain how the animals are grouped by underlying structure not by looks. He provided a top-down conceptualization by saying that the first distinction is whether an animal has a backbone. After this was done, the pile of animals with backbones was divided into fish, amphibians, reptiles, birds, and mammals; and the top-down process continued until all of the pictures had been classified. The professor was obviously emphasizing fundamental distinctions.

The tendency to consider a system from the top-down or bottom-up approach probably depends on one's expertise and perspective. From the perspective of computer programming, current thinking advocates a top-down stepwise refinement of processes. The main program loop is first considered. Then processing is subdivided into higher level modules, which are in turn broken into smaller and more refined components. High-level distinctions help the programmer structure the program. However, from the user's perspective of working on a particular task, top-down conceptualization may not be productive. The user's thinking is at the level of specific commands and operations rather than at higher level conceptual processes. Although Benny's clustering of animals has no scientific merit, it may be superior for many search tasks (e.g., find pictures of animals to illustrate flight).

The greater the knowledge of surface detail and the range of specific items, the more likely it is that a person organizes the system by bottom-up clustering. The greater the knowledge of a system-wide perspective, the more likely it is that a person organizes the system by top-down categorization. But it has been noted that users of most menu systems are forced to consider the system from a top-down manner, due to the hierarchical organization of menus (Somberg, Boggs, & Picardi, 1982). High-level categories are presented to the user over and over on every traversal down the menu tree. Low-level items are generally hidden and the user may never be aware of their vast number.

The question is whether menus should be generated using a top-down approach or a bottom-up approach. Chin (1986, 1987) directly compared the top-down and bottom-up clustering procedures. Twenty-five commands for an automatic teller machine were listed on cards. Some cards contained a brief description of the command. Subjects sorted the cards in either a top-down or bottom-up task. In the top-down group, subjects inspected all of the cards one at a time. They were then asked to construct hierarchical trees by first dividing the deck of cards into meaningful groups. Next they were asked to name each group and list them in a meaningful, logical order. These groups were then further subdivided and the newly created groups were labeled and listed in a meaningful, logical order. This process was continued until the terminal nodes were reached.

In the bottom-up group, subjects inspected all of the cards spread out on a table. They were then told to form a large number of small groups of commands. Next they were asked to name each group and to list the commands within each group in a logical order. Clusters were then aggregated into larger groups. The larger groups were assigned names and the subordinate groups were listed in a meaningful order. This continued until all groups were joined at a root node.

It was predicted that the bottom-up sorting task would emphasize similarities among commands and result in larger terminal clusters than the top-down task. As expected the bottom-up task resulted in an average of 3.74 items at the terminal group which was significantly greater than the average of 2.35 for the top-down task. It was also predicted that the top-down task would result in greater menu depth. This was also confirmed. Consequently, the top-down and bottom-up methods tap different aspects of menu organization which result in different hierarchical structures.

Clustering data were aggregated across subjects using a hierarchical cluster analysis to create a menu tree based on the groups. Figure 11.3 shows the dendrogram resulting from the top-down sorting task and Figure 11.4 for the bottom-up task. The bottom-up sorting reveals a major division between object-oriented commands (e.g., "$60 Cash", $80 Save") and action-oriented commands (e.g., "Checking to Savings", "Deposit to Savings"). The top-down sort reveals greater breadth at the top with five groups, cash withdrawal, save amount, payments, checking and savings account functions, and process commands.

Each dendrogram shows the hierarchical structure as well as the degree to which items are closely joined. Groupings are tighter to the extent that they occur closer to the left, and looser to the extent that they are delayed and occur more to the right. Consequently, the items "$60 Save" and "$80 Save" are tightly clustered as compared to the commands "Checking to Savings" and "Savings to Checking." Inspection of the two dendrograms reveals some interesting differences. First, top-down clustering results in looser groups than bottom-up clustering. Again, in top-down clustering it is hypothesized that subjects look for dissimilarities; whereas, in bottom-up clustering they attend to similarities. Second, the top-down task resulted in more terminal nodes (17)

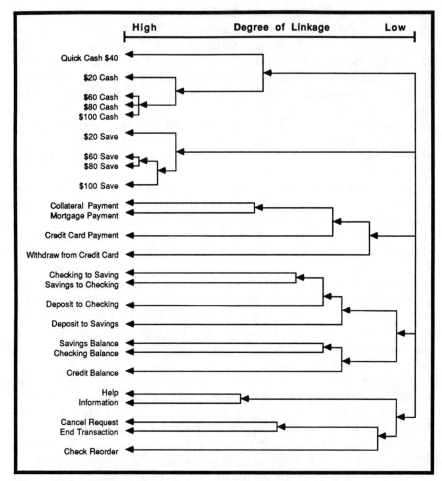

Figure 11.3. Dendrogram using average linkage between clusters in a top-down sorting of ATM commands (Chin, 1986).

than the bottom-up (13). Bottom-up sorting yields a smaller number of terminal nodes containing a larger number of items than top-down sorting.

The conclusion suggested here is that both the bottom-up and top-down sorting tasks should be used. Each captures an important aspect of the menu structure that can be effectively combined to generate the menu. Bottom-up sorting results in a tighter structure with greater breadth at the bottom of the tree, while top-down sorting results in greater breadth at the top of the tree. By integrating the results from the two types of sorts, as well as by rating data on frequency and order, Chin generated a menu with two levels as shown in Figure 11.5.

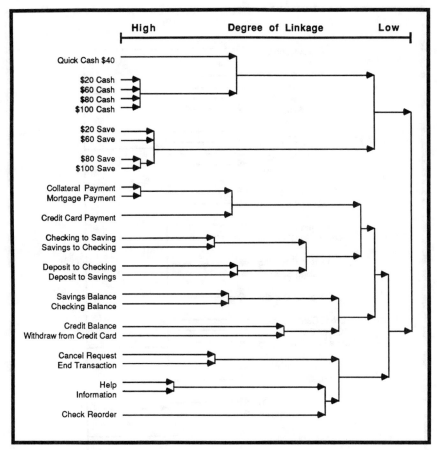

Figure 11.4. Dendrogram using average linkage between clusters in a bottom-up sorting of ATM commands (Chin, 1986).

Although clustering procedures have been experimentally tested in only small menu systems, in principle it can easily accommodate larger numbers of items. One of the virtues of clustering is that the clustering task itself can be partitioned into smaller tasks for different teams to work on. Clustering methods form the basis of top-down design of large systems and the categorization of large knowledge databases.

11.3 SEMANTIC SPACE

A second approach to menu organization is to lay out items in physical space. Menu items are essentially placed at coordinates in space whose dimensions represent psychological factors. The coordinates may be

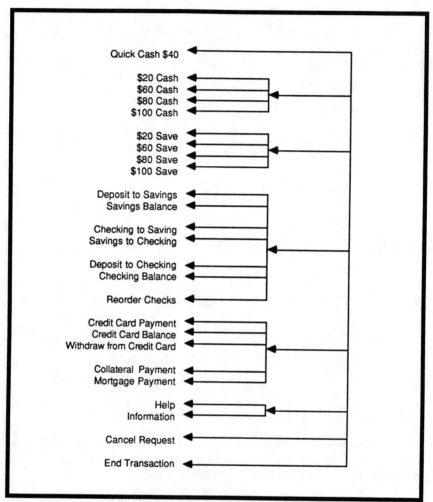

Figure 11.5.   Ideal two-level menu for ATM commands (Chin, 1986).

found directly by asking subjects to place the items in a physical space or indirectly from a multidimensional scaling of similarity measures. The dimensions of the space are assumed to have semantic meaning and serve as an organizing principle for users. Furthermore, the spatial representation may in some way capture the user's cognitive structure of the task or knowledge base.

The general methodology for determining an organization is first to obtain subjective estimates of the relatedness of all pairs of items. Measures of relatedness are then treated as distances in an n-dimensional space. Second, the obtained distance matrix is analyzed using a multidimensional scaling technique. Finally, the resulting multidimensional representation is translated into a physical layout or structure of the menu items.

McDonald, Stone, Liebolt, and Karat (1982) used a multidimensional scaling of items to design menus for a text editor. Users experienced with text editing made similarity ratings of editing functions. Menus were then designed so that similar items were closer together in lists. Performance of novice users was tested on the semantically organized menus and for comparison purposes on random menus. Although novices made fewer errors on the semantically organized menus than on the randomized menus, the difference was small. It could be that cognitive structures of the experienced users were not of great use to the novice users who may have organized the functions differently.

Menus may be laid out according to different semantic spaces based on the type of psychological distance among items. For example, items may be related because they are similar in type or because they frequently occur together. The utility of a particular menu layout depends on the task to be performed. Tasks may require users to pick groups of similar items (e.g., documents on the related topics, inventory items in the same department) or complementary items (e.g., paint brush tool and a particular color, font and point size). In an experiment by McDonald, Dayton, and McDonald (1986), subjects rated pairs of food items on the basis of similarity ("How similar are these foods?") and on the basis of co-occurrence ("How well do these two foods go together?"). The ratings were analyzed using nonmetric multidimensional scaling. The menu items were placed at the resulting coordinates with boxes placed around them to serve as selectable areas on a touch screen. The space between the items was then reduced while preserving the ordinal relations among the items within and between clusters. Although the items were clustered, they did not use the keyboard area efficiently. Layouts were scattered and irregular in comparison to the standard tight rectangular arrangement of keyboards.

Nevertheless, the results confirmed the utility of the menu organization. Subjects using the frequency layout and the similarity layout were able to perform selection tasks faster than subjects using menus that they had personally arranged. Furthermore, subjects using the frequency layout performed better filling orders with complementary items (e.g., Hamburger, French Fries, and Coke). Subjects using the similarity layout tended to perform better filling orders with similar items (e.g., Coke, Root Beer, and Iced Tea); however, this difference was not significant.

In a similar experiment, McDonald, Molander, and Noel (1988) replicated these finding using rectangular menu layouts. A simulated annealing analysis was used on the previous similarity and frequency ratings to lay out the 24 food items into a 4 × 6 rectangular array (see Figure 11.6). In addition, color codes were assigned to five similarity and frequency clusters. Four menu layouts resulted: (a) frequency layout with redundant color coding of complementary clusters, (b) frequency layout with color coding of similarity clusters, (c) similarity layout with redundant color coding of similarity clusters, and (d) similarity layout with color coding of complementary clusters.

The results confirmed the previous findings that performance is facilitated when subjects used menus whose semantic space supported the particular task required. Subjects using the similarity layout filled orders for similar items faster than for complementary items, and subjects using the frequency or co-occurrence layout filled orders for complementary items faster than for similar items. On the other hand, color coding did not facilitate performance. It is likely in the present case that color reduced the readability of the items and obscured the effect. The authors suggested that redundant color coding may be beneficial particularly for the frequency layout by helping to clarify complex organizations of items. But there is no indication that double semantic coding (e.g., physical layout based on frequency of co-occurrence and color coding based on similarity) facilitated performance in selecting multiple items.

These results strongly suggest that when designers organize menus they need to take into consideration the type of tasks performed by the users. It is likely that in real-world applications menu layouts based on frequency of co-occurrence are, in general, superior to layouts based on similarity. Although users may naturally cluster items based on similarity, menu selections in most systems are highly contingent upon other items selected. This raises some question about the appropriateness of user-derived semantic structures. Ratings of item relatedness by the users may result in structures that are in some sense meaningful, but not appropriate to the task at hand. Empirically derived measures of frequency of co-occurrence performing a given task may be more appropriate and are discussed in a later section.

Spatial structure may also be used to generate a hierarchical ordering of items. An experiment on problem solving by Carroll, Thomas, Miller, and Friedman (1980) illustrates this approach. The experiment required subjects to place 12 library procedures in a two-dimensional matrix, while at the same time satisfying 24 functional design requirements. The library procedures were hypothetical and listed only by letter rather than explicitly (e.g., cataloging a book, shelving a book). Functional requirements had to do with a facilitation of one procedure by another (e.g., cataloging a book facilitates shelving a book), the priority of procedures (e.g., signing a book out has higher priority than tidying up

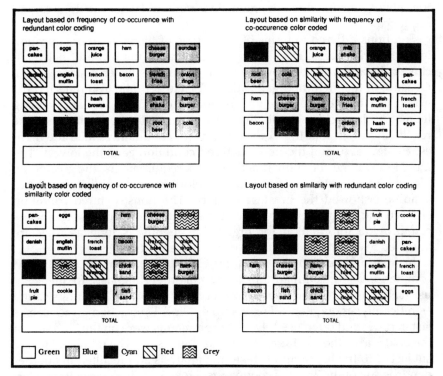

Figure 11.6. Four layouts and color codings of menus based on frequency of co-occurence and similarity of items.

From "Color-coding categories in menus," by J.E. McDonald, M.E. Molander, and R.W. Noel, 1988, *CHI '88 Conference Proceedings* (pp. 101-106). Copyright 1988 by ACM. Reprinted by permission.

the reading room), and use of resources (e.g., storing and retrieving use the same people). One dimension of the matrix represented priority (from high to low) and the other time (from earlier to later). Carroll et al. varied the amount of prior information available to the subjects in four different conditions. In the *simultaneous condition*, subjects received all 24 functional requirements on one page and placed the 12 tasks in the matrix. In the *explicit structures condition*, subjects were given a hierarchical description of the relationships among three procedure sets; then they were shown 4 functional requirements and placed the 12 tasks; they were shown another 4 and placed the 12 tasks a second time; and so on until all 24 requirements had been shown and the subjects had placed the 12 tasks 6 times. In the implicit structures condition, subjects were given the same functional requirements, but without the hierarchical description. Finally, in a nonstructured condition, subjects received the sets of functional requirements in a random fashion with no logical sequence.

Solutions differed in terms of the degree of hierarchical organization in the matrix. Carrol et al. used a cluster ratio (the mean of between-cluster distances divided by the mean of within-cluster distances) as a measure of hierarchical organization. The cluster ratio also reflected the extent to which clusters are well-defined with a high similarity among items within a cluster, and high dissimilarity between clusters. The results indicated that the explicit structures condition yielded the highest cluster ratio, and the nonstructured condition gave the lowest. The more knowledge about the functional task requirements, the greater the hierarchical structure. Over the six solutions, the explicit structures condition showed the greatest stability. The nonstructured condition showed the greatest changes. Results such as these suggest that users can provide information for organizing menus as long as they are knowledgeable about the functional requirements.

In a second part of the study by Chin (1986), subjects rated ATM commands on three dimensions: temporal order (first-last), frequency of use (seldom-often), and in/out box metaphor (in-out). The ratings varied significantly among items. For example, "End Transaction" was seen as last in order and often used. Deposit commands were on the "in" side of the box, and withdraw functions on the "out" side. The rating data were subjected to the hierarchical clustering analysis and resulted in another dendrogram of the 25 ATM commands. However, the logic of its clustering was not readily apparent.

A subsequent study by Chin and Norman (1988) specifically investigated the elicitation of both declarative and procedural knowledge in structuring menus for ATM commands and enhanced function telephones. Declarative knowledge was elicited by having subjects place items on a large 14×10 grid. Items were clustered on the basis of their proximity to one another. Procedural knowledge was elicited by having subjects draw directional lines connecting commands. Procedural knowledge was added to the structure by weighting distances in the multidimensional solution. While structures resulting in declarative knowledge were logical, procedural knowledge seemed to add very little additional information.

Semantic clustering methods have often proved to be more work than they are worth. They are generally limited to small sets of items; and the number of pairwise ratings required in even moderate sets of items can be prohibitive. The dimensional solution is too often without clear meaning or practical use. And the resulting hierarchical menu tree may be a hodgepodge of noise. One of the main problems is the reliance on the user to provide structure. When the user is highly knowledgeable about the items, it may be possible to extract a coherent organization of items. However, this occurs in only selected and usually trivial cases, such as with food items. Less familiar items, such as the functions of a word processor or options in a communication program, may be rated by highly experienced users. However, the resulting semantic space may have little utility to other users, let alone novices. To make matters even worse, the menu items that compose real-world systems are generally unknown or unfamiliar to potential users prior to acceptance of the system. Menu items are often a product of system architecture rather than having a life of their own. Consequently, users can only rarely contribute in any meaningful way to the initial organization of the system. Organization of menu items must rely on the semantic knowledge of the designer who is hopefully an expert in the task domain. On the other hand, when menus are composed of well-understood concepts, such as the tools in a graphics program (e.g., paint brush, pencil, text, etc.), user knowledge may add to menu organization. When possible, semantic scaling should be used by designers as an exploratory tool for deriving cognitive structures to aid in the design of menus.

11.4 EXPERT VS. NOVICE USERS

There are many situations in which knowledge about how items should be organized exists prior to system design and is inherent in the database. In this case experts in the subject matter domain can be used to generate the structure. On the other hand, there are cases where the knowledge does not exist prior to design. In essence, the structure is a result of the design and there are no experts except the system analyst. Prior to the first design of electronic spreadsheets, graphics packages, and disk operating systems, no potential users had a good conception of what the menu items were, let alone how they should be organized. Knowledge about the system must be learned from the system itself. Consequently, it is important that users experienced with the operations of the system be used to organize the menu structure.

The difference between the knowledge of the expert and the novice is illustrated in a study by Snyder, Happ, Malcus, Paap, and Lewis (1985). They used a clustering task to structure a menu. Nine experts and 10 novices looked at 43 MS-DOS commands printed on cards with a brief definition and example. Subjects were asked to combine them into any number of groups of any size. After this sorting, subjects were asked to label the groups. If a group could not be labeled, a letter was assigned as the label for the group. Subjects then subdivided the groups into smaller groups if they wished. This method may be considered a hybrid of the top-down and bottom-up processes in that the subjects started with the total set to form groups in a bottom-up manner, but once these groups were composed, they were subdivided in a top-down manner. Additional relational information was collected by having subjects make pairwise similarity ratings between the groups. An analysis of the data was conducted to generate a two-level menu system. It was designed such that all commands could be reached by starting from one of several dominating nodes at the top, and by traversing one link. The networks generated by novices included 71 links and 11 dominating nodes. The networks of experts were composed of 75 links and 10 dominating nodes. But the striking difference between the novices and experts was that only 28 links and one dominating node were the same between the two networks. In effect, experts had maintained 28 links that the novices created, broke 43 old links, and added 47 new ones. These findings suggest that a fundamental restructuring of the internal mental model of how systems are organized occurs with experience.

11.5 FREQUENCY OF USE

Many users are not concerned with the overall clustering of items or the semantic space. Rather, they are only interested in following a relatively small number of paths through the menu structure. Such paths are solutions to user requests, such as "Show me how to print this document? Show me how to change the clock?" When the user is performing such tasks via menu traversal, the structure of the menu should minimize the number of selections required to go from one function or object to another, as discussed in Chapter 10. In hierarchical menus, this is accomplished by placing frequently selected items at the top of a hierarchy, and by placing infrequently selected items at more remote locations at the bottom of the menu.

11.5.1 Command Frequency

When hierarchical menus are constructed for ordered directories there is no semantic structure on which to base the hierarchy. In such cases, one may dynamically generate the menu according to the frequency of access in order to minimize the expected number of nodes traversed. Often the display has a fixed menu size of M items. The question is how to divide up the list for optimal performance. Witten, Cleary, and Greenberg (1984) presented top-down menu-splitting algorithms. The best of their algorithms splits a list of ordered items in M parts which have approximately equal total probabilities. The first split is made as close as possible to 1/M of the total probability. The second split is made as close as possible to 1/(M-1) of the remaining probability after the first split, and so on. Parng and Goodman (1987) extended this work and compared a bottom-up algorithm and a two-way algorithm. The bottom-up algorithm creates a subtree that yields a minimum sum of M adjacent access probabilities. The two-way algorithm combines the top-down and bottom-up approaches by alternating between the top-down menu-splitting procedure and the bottom-up subtree building whenever it is appropriate. The top-down algorithm was designed to balance the probabilities in the trees. The bottom-up algorithm was designed to generate full menu trees in which all of the menus are of maximum size. Parng and Goodman found that the two-way algorithm was somewhat superior to the top-down. The bottom-up algorithm was the worst in terms of the average number of selections to reach a target item.

Menu structure based solely on frequency is not likely to capture or convey either declarative or procedural knowledge. The only advantage is efficiency in errorless menu traversal. Unfortunately, since the menus may contain little in the way of semantic structure, it is likely that users will easily get lost.

11.5.2 Command Transitions

In network menus where the user may be cycling back and forth between items, the distance between adjacent items should be as short as possible. For example, in a word processor, the path between the options to cut and to paste should be as short as possible. Typically, however, the user must select the text, go to a list of editing options, and select the option to cut. Then the user must back out of the menu to select an insertion point, and then go back to the list of editing options and select the paste option. When hierarchical structures are used in networks they often require the user to go down the tree to an item, climb back out, and then go back down to select the item in the same region of the tree. Although command keys can be used to overcome this sort of problem, a less memory demanding approach would be to temporarily elevate the most likely items to the top, or to allow the user to reenter the tree at the same point where it was left. The last menu frame becomes the default starting frame.

The design problem is to identify typical paths through the menu. A task analysis can help, as discussed in Chapter 3. The task analysis, however, is generated by knowledgeable users and relies on their ability to anticipate the types of tasks performed. This approach represents rational design. Unfortunately, rational design often misses reality. The designers simply may not foresee an important task that users frequently perform. However, empirical methods can be used to identify such tasks and their paths through the menu. Given an existing menu and sufficient data, one may identify frequently traversed paths. Price (1982) gave a good example of how path data may be used in the evolution of a system. She described a CAD system using a very broad command menu that included 276 items. In the original system, 120 selections were displayed in the top and right margins of screens. Several "levels" of the menu were displayed and user could move from one to another. Price collected data over approximately 200 hours of interaction and recorded over 22,500 commands. A data log file contained a complete record of commands. Data were summarized in tables listing the frequency of occurrence of commands following other commands. In essence, these tables constituted a large command transition table listing the number of times one command followed another command.

The initial tables revealed patterns for the most frequent commands that were more or less context independent (e.g., commands to refresh the screen and to expand, contract, or shift the current view). Due to the pervasive nature of these commands, the frequency tables were recomputed with these commands ignored. The new tables indicated that for many commands it was possible to identify only a small group of commands that were likely to follow. Price noted, for example, that the "GET" command occurred 2,238 and was followed by 43 different commands. However, the 12 most frequent commands following "GET" occurred 95 percent of the time. Overall, an average of only 7 commands accounted for 95 percent of the commands to follow.

These results were used to design a new system with three primary menus: a constant menu, a dynamic menu, and a menu of menus. The constant menu contained the most frequent context independent commands, as well as the help command. The constant menu contained a total of 11 commands. Dynamic menus were constructed on the basis of the command transition frequencies. Of the 276 commands, 88 resulted in a change of the dynamic menu. There were 31 such dynamic menus containing from 2 to 22 commands. In addition, there were 14 commands that were followed by one of a small predictable group of commands or the same command. These 14 commands temporarily added 1 to 3 items to the current dynamic menu. Finally, the menu of menus was used to access any command that did not appear on either the constant menu or the dynamic menu. It consisted of a hierarchical menu of 24 command categories containing from 3 to 26 commands per category. Once a command was selected from the menu of menus, the dynamic menu displayed the list of commands most likely to follow the selected command. Selection of commands from the constant menu left the dynamic menu unchanged.

The new menu was tested in a simulation using the original data log file. The design indicated that only 11 percent of the menu selections would require the use of the menu of menus; 37 percent of the commands could be selected from the current dynamic menu, 50 percent of the commands could be selected from the constant menu, and the remaining 2 percent of commands were user-defined macros. The average dynamic menu contained 13 commands, the constant menu 11 commands, and one command to bring up the menu of menus. Thus, a total of 25 commands were displayed on average.

The generation of menus from command transitions captures the procedural knowledge of the system. Although a command language may allow the user to follow any command with any other command, the procedural knowledge about the system dictates what sequence is actually appropriate. It is suggested that menus should convey procedural knowledge about the system in the way that they are displayed. Hierarchical menus do this automatically. In broad pull-down menus, however, procedural information is often missing and the user does not know in what order selections must be made in order to perform a task. Well-designed menus convey procedure as well as breadth of choice.

11.6 SUMMARY

Menus are inherently data structures that contain knowledge about the domain of items. Menu design rests heavily on the elicitation of that knowledge from users and its incorporation in the organization of menus. Three approaches to menu organization were presented. The clustering approach is a relatively simple procedure for generating hierarchical structures. The top-down variant of clustering starts with the total set, and successively subdivides items according to some organizing principles. The bottom-up variant starts with forming a number of clusters of items and then forming clusters of clusterings.

The second approach is to extract a semantic space from user assessments of similarity or relatedness among items. This approach has been used for hierarchical structures, but it is probably best suited for organizing items within single menu frames. The third approach is to use observed frequency and sequence information to structure the menu in terms of efficiency. This approach may be devoid of semantic knowledge about the menu since it is based only on frequency of use.

All three approaches have considerable merit in eliciting relational information from the users that can be used to organize menus. Each method captures a different aspect of organizing knowledge and must be used appropriately in the design of real systems. Whatever the organizing principle, it must fit the task to be performed by the user.

It is clear that the quality of organization depends on the amount of knowledge of the individuals organizing the menu. It is important that designers solicit input from knowledgeable users rather than just any users, and remember that menu organization should be congruent with the way in which users think about the system.

The organization and layout of menus are extremely important in design. They determine not only the superficial "look and feel" of the system, but its very essence. Menu organization contains the declarative and procedural knowledge that drives the system. Consequently, the challenge is to generate and organize the system according to principles of efficient menu design, and at the same time project a knowledge structure that in some meaningful way guides the user through the system.

12
Prototyping and Evaluation of Menu Selection Systems

After following all of the guidelines, incorporating a cognitive theory of control, and involving the users in the clustering of menus, the designer still has to see if it flies. It is too easy to miss the obvious, forget the fundamentals, and overlook the inconsistencies. Published guidelines and research results take us a long way toward good design. However, they can never close the gap between generalization and application. Isa, Ogden, and Korenshteink, (1986 p. 69) noted, "The only way that an interface can be evaluated is through user testing of that particular implementation." One must prototype the system and evaluate the result. Prototyping is cost effective to the extent that it is rapid, easy, and provides informative results. Prototypes vary from simple paper mockups or story boarding to full-blown implementations. The fidelity of the prototype to the final system is of great concern. The type of computer screen and keyboard layout may be critical, while system timing may not be. Prototyping provides the opportunity to discover flaws while it is still possible to change the design. Issues and examples of prototyping menu selection systems will be presented in this chapter.

Prototyping must be supported by a careful analysis of the results. Analyses should be based on the measures presented in Table 1.1 Performance measures are important and have been emphasized in previous chapters. User evaluations are of particular importance in prototyping and will be stressed in this chapter. Evaluations of a system vary from open-ended questions and informal comments to standardized questionnaires and performance measures. This chapter will consider issues in user evaluation and present several approaches.

12.1 PROTOTYPING SYSTEMS

Prototyping is not a new idea, and its place in the life cycle of a system is extremely important. But for prototyping to be useful in the development of a computer system, it must be relatively fast and easy to implement and change. Menu selection systems are particularly good candidates for prototyping since it should be easy to change them without greatly affecting the rest of the software. For that matter, when complete fidelity is not required, it is often possible to prototype only the menus without any further program functionality. This is particularly the case with videotext, bibliographic, database, and help systems.

Prototyping a menu selection requires an initial idea of three major aspects of the system: (a) the menu structure (composed of the selectable items and clustering), (b) screen layout (composed of graphics and text supporting the menu items), and (c) screen-to-screen transitions (composed of input and output dynamics). The menu structure can be prototyped as a database of items and often drawn as a network or hierarchical graph. Alternative structures can be compared in terms of depth and breadth and expected access times for items of different frequency. Screen layout can be drawn either on paper or on the screen itself. Alternative layouts can be compared side by side. The entire set of screens completes the static prototype of the system. However, screen-to-screen transitions which require user input must be prototyped in a dynamic emulating environment. Figure 12.1 outlines the three levels of prototyping associated with the three aspects of menu selection systems: structure, layout, and dynamics.

Prototyping should be done at the structural and layout level, using the tools of graphs and storyboarding. However, it is essential in the final analysis to prototype the dynamic system at least at a superficial level. Dynamic prototyping can be done in the native programming language of the destination system. However, it is generally better to use a rapid prototyping system or a system that supports user interface management. Prototyping efforts suffer when menus are written into the program code rather than in a separate driver with an easily modifiable file of menus. Without a separation of the menu driver from the rest of the program code, programs have to be revised and recompiled for each change in the menu. The advantage of current user interface management systems is that they allow the designer to modify menus and menu organization at the same time without necessarily changing the functionality of the program. Changes to screens, additions of items, and links can be made more or less on-the-fly.

For menu prototyping to be cost effective, the system must allow fast and easy implementation and revision. It should provide an authoring system that allows the designer to generate the structure, screen layout, and dynamics in a quick and simple format.

Dynamic prototyping can be done on a fully functional system using a user interface management system (UIMS), or on just the "front end" of the system using a menu driver or a UIMS that presents the menus to

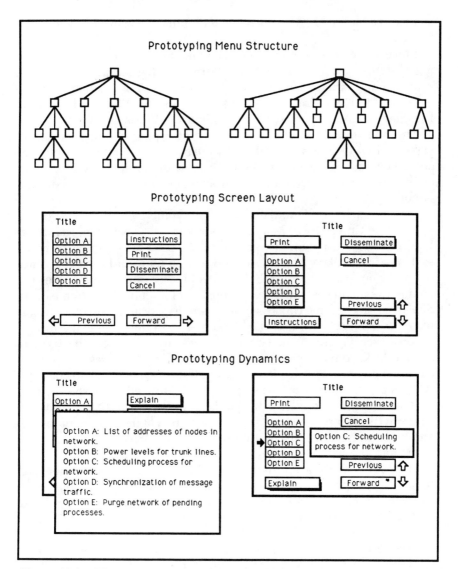

Figure 12.1. Three levels of prototype comparision.

the user but may not necessarily access actual functions that have been selected.

One of the earliest experimental systems capable of prototyping menus at the dynamic level was ZOG, first begun in 1972 (Akscyn & McCracken, 1984). The ZOG system and its predecessor, KMS, use the basic constructs of frames and links. Frames are screen-sized workspaces (see Figure 12.2). Links relate individual items in a frame to other frames.

In recent years user interface management systems (UIMS), windowing systems, and specialized menu drivers have facilitated the rapid prototyping of menu selection systems. Examples of commercial packages include HyperCard™, X-Windows™, and NeWS™, and a host of hypermedia and hypertext systems (Smith & Weiss, 1988).

The one thing that most dynamic prototyping systems lack is an experimental testing and evaluation environment. Systems should be able to emulate real-world tasks and record performance. Without this ability prototypes provide no measurable or quantifiable means of evaluation.

One system, the Menu Selection Prototyping System (MSPS) developed at the University of Maryland (Norman, 1984; Norman, Mantel, & Wallace, 1988), is a menu driver that can be used to (a) prototype menu systems, (b) emulate task environments, and (c) record the behavior of the users and the system. MSPS works by accessing a source file containing the menu system. The file consists of a set of menu frames with directives. Each frame consists of a screen display and a set of allowable response options with associated pointers to other frames or to procedures (see Figure 12.3). Certain frames in the file can be used to present tasks to the user. The tasks generally involve accessing particular target items or series of items. Other frames can be used to check for successful completion of tasks and to provide feedback. The file also contains a set of timer values to simulate system response time (interval between the user response and the presentation of the next menu frame) and time out intervals (maximum time between presentation of a menu frame and the user response).

The MSPS writes a journal file in which it records each frame presented, the response option selected, and the user response time (interval between presentation of the frame and the user response). These data allow analyses on

- user response time per screen or item
- user response time to perform overall tasks
- selection errors per screen or item
- selection errors in performing a task
- frequency of access to menu items
- patterns and co-occurrences of menu selections.

These data can be analyzed to determine problem areas in the menu system: (a) items which may be misinterpreted, (b) high frequency items that should be made more accessible, and (c) the need for reorganizing or reclustering items. MSPS has been used in various versions since 1983

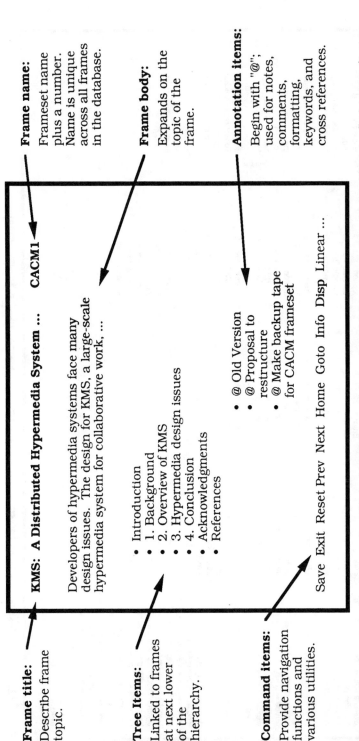

Frame name:
Frameset name plus a number. Name is unique across all frames in the database.

Frame body:
Expands on the topic of the frame.

Annotation items:
Begin with "@"; used for notes, comments, formatting, keywords, and cross references.

Frame title:
Describe frame topic.

Tree Items:
Linked to frames at next lower of the hierarchy.

Command items:
Provide navigation functions and various utilities.

CACM1

KMS: A Distributed Hypermedia System ...

Developers of hypermedia systems face many design issues. The design for KMS, a large-scale hypermedia system for collaborative work, ...

- Introduction
- 1. Background
- 2. Overview of KMS
- 3. Hypermedia design issues
- 4. Conclusion
- Acknowledgments
- References

- @ Old Version
- @ Proposal to restructure
- @ Make backup tape for CACM frameset

Save Exit Reset Prev Next Home Goto Info Disp Linear ...

Figure 12.2. An example of menu frames in MSPS for presenting instructions, prompting the subject to find target items, generating a hierarchical menu structure, and presenting feedback to the subject.

Experiment Control	Test Items	Hierarchical Menu	Terminal Items	Feedback
.frame = randomize_1 .option execute = scramble * > prompt_A * > prompt_B NEXT . randomize_2	.frame = prompt_A Find TERMINAL A .option execute = prompt_target * > root * > term_A	.frame = root Top level menu Enter 1 or 2 .option 1 > frame_AB 2 > frame_CD	.frame = term_A TERMINAL A .option execute = target r > right_text w > wrong_text	.frame = right_text You have found the correct terminal. .option execute = next_target * > end_text
.frame = randomize_2 scramble = TRUE repeat_count = 4 queue = TRUE .option execute = scramble * > prompt_C * > prompt_D END > start_text	.frame = prompt_B Find TERMINAL B .option execute = prompt_target * > root * > term_B	.frame = frame_AB Second level menu Enter a or b .option a > term_A b > term_B	.frame = term_B TERMINAL B .option execute = target r > right_text w > wrong_text	.frame = wrong_text You not have found the correct terminal. .option execute = next_target * > end_text
.frame = start_text You will be prompted to search for targets in a hierarchical menu. If you fail to find a target, you will be prompted again. If you miss again, it will be queued to the end of the list of targets and you will be prompted to search for the next target in the list. After you have completed searching for the last target, the queued targets will be presented again. Press any key to begin. .option execute = next_target * > end_text	.frame = prompt_C Find TERMINAL C .option execute = prompt_target * > root * > term_C	.frame = frame_CD Second level menu Enter c or d .option c > term_C d > term_D	.frame = term_C TERMINAL C .option execute = target r > right_text w > wrong_text	.frame = end_text To exit press any key. .option * > quit
	.frame = prompt_D Find TERMINAL D .option execute = prompt_target * > root * > term_D		.frame = term_D TERMINAL D .option execute = target r > right_text w > wrong_text	.frame = quit .option execute = quit_menu * > quit

Figure 12.3. A typical frame in the KMS menu system (Akscyn, McCracken, & Yoder, 1988).

in a number of laboratory studies as the experimental workbench for menu research.

Finally, it should be added that usability testing of prototypes should also be supported by video, verbal protocols, and subjective evaluation. Video taping captures user access to auxiliary material (manuals, forms, notes, etc.), vacillation between alternatives, and signs of confusion and/or frustration that cannot be captured using software. Verbal protocols capture the step-by-step thought processes involved in performing a task. They may reveal the need for additional menu items, paths, and user guidance. User evaluation and reaction to the prototype are important and are addressed in the next section.

12.2 GUIDELINES FOR MENU DESIGN

At some point it is necessary to bridge the gap between the theory and research of menu selection on the one hand, and the direct application of results to real problems on the other. The translation of theory and results into guidelines and standards is necessary so that software designers have a target to aim for. Standards and guidelines documents provide a concise summary that aid in the development of human/computer interfaces. Several standards and guidelines documents have been produced in the area of human/computer interaction (e.g., Smith & Mosier, 1986; MIL-STD-1472C, 1981). These documents have helped to avoid catastrophic problems as well as minor frustrations that users have with the interface and at the same time facilitate performance.

There are, however, a number of dangers in setting forth such documents. The specification of guidelines and standards are always suspect due to the problems of generalizability and applicability discussed in Chapter 5.

First, it is possible that a standard or guideline has resulted from theory or research results that do not generalize beyond the specific assumptions of the theory or the conditions of the study. Such a standard or guideline may be irrelevant or simply wrong. Additional research is required to clear up such problems.

Second, standards and guidelines may be incorrectly interpreted and/or incorrectly applied by designers. It is too easy to read a standard or guideline at only the superficial level without having a deeper understanding of its intent, implications, and limitations. Without such understanding, standards and guidelines may be applied in a way never intended by their originator. The application of a guideline is often an issue of interpretation, and the conformance to a standard is often an issue of degree. Consequently, the blind application of guidelines can be a major problem.

Third, standards and guidelines documents generally do not address the problem of importance or tradeoffs of design options. Some standards and guidelines are essential; others are of minor importance. While all of the standards and guidelines may promote principles of good design, some will have little impact on performance and user evaluation of the system. Consequently, designers need to prioritize standards and guidelines. Furthermore, a number of standards and guidelines interact. The application of one may limit the application of another. Designers need to be aware of such tradeoffs and must be able to strike the right balance between them.

Fourth, the application of guidelines and the conformance to standards are often a matter of opinion or expert evaluation. Some guidelines are objective in the sense that it is clear whether a system meets the guidelines or not (e.g., "Items in a list should be left-justified.") Other guidelines define metrics that can be objectively empirically assessed and either set criteria to be passed or optimized (e.g., such as by measuring performance). Others are judgment calls and depend on the subjective metrics of an evaluator (e.g., "Items should be given meaningful labels").

Finally, standards and guidelines may overly restrict the design space, preclude innovative solutions to problems, and lead a premature standardization on less than optimal designs. The problem is that theory, research, and technology are still moving targets. Standards and guidelines cannot be considered as final documents, only as current iterations.

With these problems accepted as caveats and disclaimers, Appendix A is offered as a checklist for menu design. The checklist is presented as a series of questions that should help designers make sure that they have addressed as many aspects of menu design as possible. The items were intentionally written in a general form without specifying a specific design option, but rather encouraging consideration of design issues. Each item has a cross reference to a section in the text to allow the reader to gain a deeper understanding of the issue. When reviewing a system, designers should go through the list and check off whether or not each item has been met satisfactorily.

12.3 USER EVALUATION

Evaluation of a prototype cannot rest totally on designers and experts. It is important to solicit input from the user community itself. Experts cannot always be trusted to represent the best interest of the users. A study by Lee, Whalen, McEwen, and Latremouille (1984) confirms this admonition. They had experts design the top index page for an electronic shopping and information retrieval system. A second group of experts ranked the menus produced by the first group for ease of use. Virtually no correlation was found between the rankings of the experts ($r = .08$). However, when a group of representative users ranked the menus there was high agreement among them as to which menus would be easier to use ($r = .49$). Furthermore, performance measures were highly correlated with user predictions ($r = .72$). Users were the best judges of menu design and best predictors of future performance.

Certainly it behooves the designer to consider seriously evaluation of systems by users. The question is "How?" It is an easy thing to make up a few questions and solicit ratings from users. It is not so easy to validate the subjective measures and interpret the results relative to known user populations. Although a number of questionnaires have been developed to measure subjective satisfaction with computer systems, few have focused on the user interface. Those that have been developed have been highly specific to particular systems, limited in their application across different systems and users, and limited to one shot experiments rather than refined over a number of applications. Reviews of these questionnaires have been critical and have cited the problems of (a) lack of validity (Gallagher, 1974), (b) low reliability (Larcker & Lessig, 1980; Ives, Olson, & Baroudi, 1983), (c) insufficient sample sizes, and (d) nonrepresentative populations (Bailey & Pearson, 1983).

12.3.1 Standardized User Evaluation of Interactive Systems

What has been needed has been a generic questionnaire, developed and applied over a number of applications, standardized on a wide variety of users, with proven reliability and validity. Shneiderman (1987) originally proposed a "generic user evaluation questionnaire for interactive systems" with the idea that interactive systems share a set aspects that can be assessed relative to one another. Furthermore, each aspect can be broken down into more and more specific aspects.

This questionnaire, now called the Questionnaire for User Interaction Satisfaction (QUIS) has been repeatedly used, refined, and validated over a number of studies (Chin, Diehl, & Norman, 1988; Chin, Norman, & Shneiderman, 1987). The current version of the QUIS measures six aspects of the user's overall reaction to the system and 21 system attributes (see Figure 12.4). The system attributes are clustered into four major categories: the screen, terminology and system information, learning, and system capabilities. In addition, the QUIS includes indicator variables supporting the 21 system attributes. The QUIS is hier-

QUIS—Questionnaire for User Interaction Satisfaction

Please circle the numbers which most appropriately reflect your impressions about using this computer system. Not Applicable = NA.

Overall reactions to the system:

terrible   wonderful
1 2 3 4 5 6 7 8 9   NA
frustrating   satisfying
1 2 3 4 5 6 7 8 9   NA
dull   stimulating
1 2 3 4 5 6 7 8 9   NA
difficult   easy
1 2 3 4 5 6 7 8 9   NA
inadequate power   adequate power
1 2 3 4 5 6 7 8 9   NA
rigid   flexible
1 2 3 4 5 6 7 8 9   NA

PART A: SCREEN

1. Characters on the computer screen

    hard to read   easy to read
    1 2 3 4 5 6 7 8 9   NA

    1.1 Image of characters

    fuzzy   sharp
    1 2 3 4 5 6 7 8 9   NA

    1.2 Character shapes (fonts)

    barely legible   very legible
    1 2 3 4 5 6 7 8 9   NA

2. Highlighting on the screen makes task easier

    not at all   very much
    1 2 3 4 5 6 7 8 9   NA

    2.1 Use of reverse video

    unhelpful   helpful
    1 2 3 4 5 6 7 8 9   NA

    2.2 Use of blinking

    unhelpful   helpful
    1 2 3 4 5 6 7 8 9   NA

3. Screen layouts make tasks easier

    never   always
    1 2 3 4 5 6 7 8 9   NA

    3.1 Amount of information that can be displayed on screen

    inadequate   adequate
    1 2 3 4 5 6 7 8 9   NA

    3.2 Arrangement of information on screen

    illogical   logical
    1 2 3 4 5 6 7 8 9   NA

4. Sequence of screens

    confusing   clear
    1 2 3 4 5 6 7 8 9   NA

    4.1 Next screen in a sequence

    unpredictable   predictable
    1 2 3 4 5 6 7 8 9   NA

    4.2 Going back to the previous screen

    impossible   easy
    1 2 3 4 5 6 7 8 9   NA

    4.3 Beginning, middle, and end of tasks

    confusing   clearly marked
    1 2 3 4 5 6 7 8 9   NA

PART B: TERMINOLOGY AND SYSTEM INFORMATION

5. Use of terms throughout system

    inconsistent   consistent
    1 2 3 4 5 6 7 8 9   NA

    5.1 Task terms

    inconsistent   consistent
    1 2 3 4 5 6 7 8 9   NA

QUIS—Questionnaire for User Interaction Satisfaction (cont.)

5.2 Computer terms	inconsistent _____ consistent 1 2 3 4 5 6 7 8 9	NA
6. Terminology relates to the work you are doing	unrelated _____ related 1 2 3 4 5 6 7 8 9	NA
6.1 Computer terminology is used	too frequently _____ appropriately 1 2 3 4 5 6 7 8 9	NA
6.2 Terms on the screen	ambiguous _____ precise 1 2 3 4 5 6 7 8 9	NA
7. Messages which appear on screen	inconsistent _____ consistent 1 2 3 4 5 6 7 8 9	NA
7.1 Position of instructions on the screen	inconsistent _____ consistent 1 2 3 4 5 6 7 8 9	NA
8. Messages to the user	confusing _____ clear 1 2 3 4 5 6 7 8 9	NA
8.1 Instructions for commands or choices	confusing _____ clear 1 2 3 4 5 6 7 8 9	NA
8.2 Instructions for correcting errors	confusing _____ clear 1 2 3 4 5 6 7 8 9	NA
9. Computer keeps you informed about what it is doing	never _____ always 1 2 3 4 5 6 7 8 9	NA
9.1 Performing an operation leads to a predictable result	never _____ always 1 2 3 4 5 6 7 8 9	NA
9.2 User can control amount of feedback	never _____ always 1 2 3 4 5 6 7 8 9	NA
10. Error messages	unhelpful _____ helpful 1 2 3 4 5 6 7 8 9	NA
10.1 Error messages clarify the problem	never _____ always 1 2 3 4 5 6 7 8 9	NA
10.2 Phrasing of error messages	unpleasant _____ pleasant 1 2 3 4 5 6 7 8 9	NA

PART C: LEARNING

11. Learning to operate the system	difficult _____ easy 1 2 3 4 5 6 7 8 9	NA
11.1 Getting started	difficult _____ easy 1 2 3 4 5 6 7 8 9	NA
11.2 Learning advanced features	difficult _____ easy 1 2 3 4 5 6 7 8 9	NA
11.3 Time to learn to use the system	slow _____ fast 1 2 3 4 5 6 7 8 9	NA
12. Exploration of features by trial and error	discouraged _____ encouraged 1 2 3 4 5 6 7 8 9	NA
12.1 Exploration of features	risky _____ safe 1 2 3 4 5 6 7 8 9	NA
12.2 Discovering new features	difficult _____ easy 1 2 3 4 5 6 7 8 9	NA
13. Remembering names and use of commands	difficult _____ easy 1 2 3 4 5 6 7 8 9	NA
13.1 Remembering specific rules about entering commands	difficult _____ easy 1 2 3 4 5 6 7 8 9	NA

QUIS—Questionnaire for User Interaction Satisfaction (*cont.*)

14. Tasks can be performed in a straightforward manner	never 1 2 3 4 5 6 7 8 9 always NA
14.1 Number of steps per task	too many 1 2 3 4 5 6 7 8 9 just right NA
14.2 Steps to complete a task follow a logical sequence	rarely 1 2 3 4 5 6 7 8 9 always NA
14.3 Completion of sequence of steps	unclear 1 2 3 4 5 6 7 8 9 clear NA
15. Help messages on the screen	confusing 1 2 3 4 5 6 7 8 9 clear NA
15.1 Accessing help messages	difficult 1 2 3 4 5 6 7 8 9 easy NA
15.2 Content of help messages	confusing 1 2 3 4 5 6 7 8 9 clear NA
15.3 Amount of help	inadequate 1 2 3 4 5 6 7 8 9 adequate NA
16. Supplemental reference materials	confusing 1 2 3 4 5 6 7 8 9 clear NA
16.1 Tutorials for beginners	confusing 1 2 3 4 5 6 7 8 9 clear NA
16.2 Reference manuals	confusing 1 2 3 4 5 6 7 8 9 clear NA

PART D: SYSTEM CAPABILITIES

17. System speed	too slow 1 2 3 4 5 6 7 8 9 fast enough NA
17.1 Response time for most operations	too slow 1 2 3 4 5 6 7 8 9 fast enough NA
17.2 Rate information is displayed	too slow 1 2 3 4 5 6 7 8 9 fast enough NA
18. Reliability of the system	unreliable 1 2 3 4 5 6 7 8 9 reliable NA
18.1 Operations are	undependable 1 2 3 4 5 6 7 8 9 dependable NA
18.2 System failures occur	frequently 1 2 3 4 5 6 7 8 9 seldom NA
18.3 System warns the user about potential problems	never 1 2 3 4 5 6 7 8 9 always NA
19. System tends to be	noisy 1 2 3 4 5 6 7 8 9 quiet NA
19.1 Mechanical devices, such as fans, disks, and printers	noisy 1 2 3 4 5 6 7 8 9 quiet NA
19.2 Computer tones, beeps, clicks, etc.	annoying 1 2 3 4 5 6 7 8 9 pleasant NA
20. Correcting your mistakes	difficult 1 2 3 4 5 6 7 8 9 easy NA
20.1 Correcting typos or mistakes	complex 1 2 3 4 5 6 7 8 9 simple NA
20.2 Ability to undo operations	inadequate 1 2 3 4 5 6 7 8 9 adequate NA

QUIS—Questionnaire for User Interaction Satisfaction (*cont.*)

21. The needs of both experienced and inexperienced users are taken into consideration	never 1 2 3 4 5 6 7 8 9	always NA
21.1 Novices can accomplish tasks knowing only a few commands	with difficulty 1 2 3 4 5 6 7 8 9	easily NA
21.2 Experts can use features/ shortcuts	with difficulty 1 2 3 4 5 6 7 8 9	easily NA

Figure 12.4. The QUIS Version 5.0-Questionnaire for User Interaction Satisfaction. (Copyright © 1988 Human/Computer Interaction Laboratory, University of Maryland.)

archically organized so that the ratings of the indicator variables impact upward on the system attributes, which in turn impact the overall user reactions (see Figure 12.5). This approach to psychological scaling is rather novel since it involves a hierarchical model rather than merely a set of independent scales. The hierarchical structure reflects the model of both the inherent structure of the system and the way in which users organize their attitudes about the system. Consequently, items in the QUIS have been organized according to a hierarchical format.

Several versions of the QUIS have been developed. The long version is shown in Figure 12.4. A short version has been used extensively that omits the indicator variables and greatly reduces the number of items to be rated. Both paper and pencil and online versions exist.

The generality of the QUIS was developed by having different user populations evaluate different systems using the questionnaire. Additional sections have always been added to the QUIS to characterize the user and the software being evaluation. Users included (a) undergraduate students, (b) computer professionals, (c) computer hobbyists, and (d) novice users. Systems have included (a) programming environments, (b) bibliographic retrieval systems, (c) disk operating systems, and (d) word processors. Furthermore, the conditions under which the questionnaire was administered have varied considerably. Conditions have included (a) strictly controlled laboratory studies in which subjects were exposed to systems for a short time, (b) less rigorous studies in which subjects used systems on a more or less casual basis, and (c) field studies in which conditions and demands varied widely. Over repeated applications, items and scales were revised and reworded to produce a more robust version.

The reliability of the QUIS was established by measuring the intercorrelation among items. Cronbach's alpha, which quantitatively measures reliability on a 0 to 1 scale, was consistently in the .89 to .94 range over a

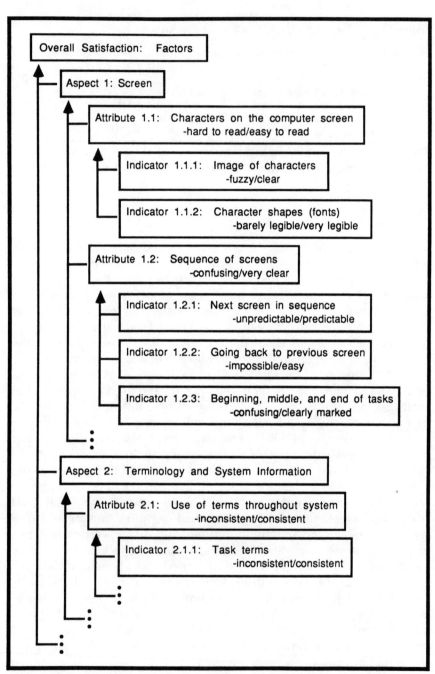

Figure I2.5. Hierarchical interrelationship of the ratings in the QUIS.

series of studies. Thus, the overall reliability of the QUIS is quite high.

The validity of the QUIS was measured in two ways. Internal validity was established by substantiating the hypothesized hierarchical organization of the QUIS. Ratings on indicator items were correlated with higher level system attributes, and system attributes were correlated with overall ratings of satisfaction. Data over several studies both supported the hierarchical structure as a whole and helped to eliminate inconsistent items.

External validity was established by using the QUIS to compare different systems. For example, in one study (Chin, Diehl, & Norman, 1988) users were asked to rate one system that they liked and one that they disliked. All of the overall reactions to the system differed greatly between the liked and disliked systems, except for the difficult versus easy rating. It is probable that the difficulty in using a system depends more on the functionality of the program rather than on the satisfaction with it. System attributes having to do with learning (operating, exploring, and performing tasks in a straightforward manner) and system capabilities (speed, reliability, correcting mistakes, and considering experience of users) also differed between liked and disliked systems. In another part of that study a comparison was made between a command-line system (MS-DOS™) and menu-driven applications (e.g., Word-Star™, Lotus™, DBase™, etc.). Again, all of the overall reactions to the system differed greatly between the two types of systems, except for the difficult versus easy rating. The menu-driven applications were rated much more favorably. Furthermore, 18 or the 21 system attributes were rated more favorably for the menu systems. These results lend strong support to the external validity of the QUIS.

Finally, the diagnostic power of the QUIS to detect problem areas has been confirmed by a usability study of a menu system for home control (Wallace, Norman, & Plaisant, 1988). The system was not compared to an alternative so no differences could be obtained. However, items scoring exceptionally high or low, relative to the mean of all the responses, helped to reveal the strengths and weaknesses of the system. The QUIS indicated that like many commercial systems, home control by menu selection was perceived as wonderful and satisfying, but rigid with inadequate power. In addition, particular items indicated that additional system feedback and user guidance was needed.

The QUIS has proven to be useful as a generic instrument for assessing interactive systems. As such it taps a number of system attributes related to menu selection. The system attributes of particular relevance to menus system are

• Screen layouts (Attribute 3)
• Sequence screens (Attribute 4)

- Use of terms throughout system (Attribute 5)
- Messages which appear on screen (Attribute 7)
- Tasks can be performed in a straightforward manner (Attribute 14).

However, there are additional attributes specific to menu selection that need to be assessed. These are addressed in the next session.

12.3.2 Evaluation of Menu Selection

Few studies have specifically investigated ratings of menu selection systems or attributes that specifically pertain to menu selection. Recently, Norman (1988) described five basic factors along which menu systems can vary. These factors attempt to capture the basic dimensions of menu systems that users are sensitive to and are described to users as follows.

Display and Response Time. Systems vary in terms of how long it takes for the menu to be displayed on the screen and how long it takes for the system to respond once an item has been selected. A *very poor system* keeps the user waiting; whereas, a *very good system* displays the menu quickly and implements the selection quickly.

Path Efficiency. Systems vary in terms of the efficiency of the path to the goal. *Very poor systems* appear to lead one along an endless garden path; whereas, a *very good system* quickly homes in on the goal and does not ask for redundant or irrelevant input.

Clarity of Menus. Systems vary in terms of the clarity versus vagueness of the choice and the particular alternatives. In a very *poor system* it may not be clear what sort of choice is being made and what the options denote. This may be because of the brevity of the menu or poor wording. In a *very good system*, the user knows the implications of each choice and he or she knows what each option does.

Sense of Direction Toward Goal. Systems vary in terms of the sense of movement in the direction of the goal. In a *very poor system* users may get lost in the maze and not know whether they are getting closer or further from the goal. In a *very good system*, users have a sense of control and accomplishment as they progress.

Recovery from Errors. Systems vary in terms of their capability for allowing the user to recover from errors easily and quickly. A *very poor system* is "unforgiving." If a wrong choice is made it takes considerable time and effort to restart to the point of error. In a *very good system*, the user can quickly undo the error and start where the error had occurred.

Users are asked to rate how good or poor the system is on each of the five factors. Each rating is made on a line mark scale as shown in Figure 12.6. Users are instructed to make their mark toward the left end of the

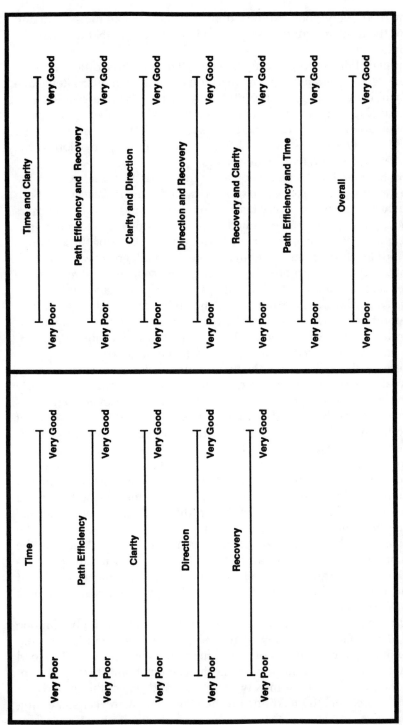

Figure 12.6. Rating scales used for five factors of menu selection systems (Norman, 1988).

line marked "very poor" to the extent that they dislike the system and toward the right and marked "very good" to the extent that they like the system.

Norman (1988) reports rating data on 229 users. Three different menu systems were evaluated: (1) a hierarchical organization of 256 items in a merchandising catalog, (2) a prototype of a popular time-sharing system, and (3) an online card catalog. In addition, a number of computer science students rated various menu systems that they were familiar with. Figure 12.7 shows the profiles for these four groups by plotting the mean ratings on the five menu factors.

Both the merchandising catalog and time-sharing system received the highest ratings for *display and response time* and *recovery from errors*. Both of the these systems had very fast response times and allowed the users to back up the tree or move immediately to the top with one command. *Path efficiency* was rated lower on both systems. Both of these menus were four levels deep, and user made frequent path errors when searching for targets. Furthermore, the wording of these menus left much to be desired as indicated by the low ratings on *clarity of menus* and *sense of direction toward goal*. The group rating the online card catalog gave much a lower rating for *response and display time* and *recovery from errors*. Finally, the group rating a variety of familiar systems showed a similar pattern, except that *response and display time* was much superior.

These results indicate that the menu rating scales are able to diagnose the weaknesses and strengths of systems. Users seemed particularly positive about fast response times and the ability to recover from errors in some systems. None of the systems fared particularly well in terms of path efficiency, clarity of menus, or sense of direction toward the goal.

Users were also asked to rate the menu systems on five combinations of two factors at a time, as well as to rate the systems overall as shown in Figure 12.6. These ratings were needed to test the internal reliability of the ratings and also to assess the relative importance of the five menu factors. It was expected that a rating on the combination of *display and response time* and *clarity of menus* would depend on the ratings of the single factors, and that the ratings of the combinations would lean in the direction of the most important factor of the two. A factor analysis was conducted to determine how the menu factors and combinations loaded on the extracted factors. Table 12.1 shows the factor loadings for a varimax solution.

It can be seen that each of the five menu factors loads highly on one factor. These factors basically correspond to the five menu factors that were initially rated. Ratings of the combinations of factors tend to load highly on the two factors composing the combination. This result supports the idea that the ratings were reliable and reflect the underlying factors. Moreover, the loadings on the combinations reveal something

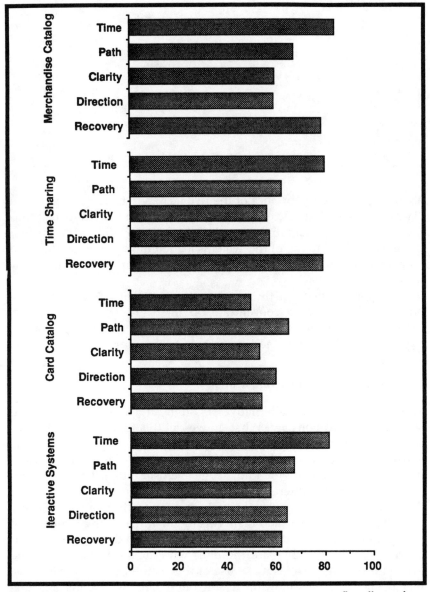

Figure 12.7. User ratings of four different menu systems on five dimensions (Norman, 1988).

Table 12.1.   Factor Analysis of Five Factors Using the Varimax Procedure.

Rating Scale	Factor 1	Factor 2	Factor 3	Factor 4	Factor 5
Time	.93				
Path Efficiency	.27	.83	.37		
Clarity			.90		
Direction			.43	.84	
Recovery	.24				.88
T X C	.55		.72		
P X R		.54	.30		.68
C X D			.78	.40	
D X R		.26	.46	.38	.65
R X C	.26		.74		.46
P X T	.70	.38	.36	.22	
Overall	.31	.34	.66	.30	.24

about the relative importance of the five factors to the users. Whenever clarity was one of the factors in the combination, it tended to load most highly, indicating that ratings were most affected by this factor. Furthermore, the overall rating of the systems loaded most highly on the factor corresponding to clarity. Clarity was the most important factor to the users.

As a general finding, these results suggest that menu prototyping and evaluation should concentrate on the wording of menus. Each menu and each menu alternative should be evaluated and changed based on its clarity and meaningfulness to the user.

12.3.3 Menu-by-Menu Evaluations

The wording of menu alternatives is often an agonizing chore to designers. The questions are: What do we call this function? What do we call this group of functions? Language is limited; terms are ambiguous; and consistency an unachievable ideal. Much of the problem is that naming is best done by the knowledgeable user rather than the omniscient designer. It is interesting that in the Genesis account of creation, Adam (the user) was given the task of naming the animals (Genesis 2:19-20). Whatever he called them became their name. In a similar way, it might be suggested that users have an input to the names of menu alternatives because they are the ones who must call them by name. While no current systems make use of this feature, some user interface management systems allow the user to build their own menus or change the wording of existing menus. These features, however, are generally not for the novice user and require considerable knowledge of the system.

A more practical approach would be to start with an initial set of names for menu alternatives and let the users rate the suitability, clarity, and meaningfulness of the names, and then enter suggested names or changes in wording. Thus, the users would have an editorial role in producing the menu system. Ratings can be used to evaluate a number of aspects of menu frames as well as the traversal of those frames. Listed below are four different types of ratings that can be used in a menu-by-menu evaluation. Each type of rating is illustrated in Figure 12.8.

Ratings of Individual Terms. Given a particular menu, users can be asked to rate the meaningfulness, explicitness, and familiarity of parts of the menu. For example, they could be asked to rate the meaningfulness of the choice: "Select the type of registration:" and their familiarity with the items: "passive", "passive-fixed", "dynamic." The ratings will be a function of both the subject matter knowledge of the user as well as the clarity and specificity of the passages. One would expect large differences between experienced and novice users; however, well-written menus may help to attenuate differences by educating novice users as to the meaning of the alternatives.

Ratings of Prior Probabilities. Given a target function or object to be located in the menu structure, users can be asked, "What is the probability that you will find the target given that you select Alternative *i*?" These ratings assess the subjective probability that a particular path leads to the goal. To the extent that the probability is high on the correct alternative, the menu conveys the proper expectations to the user of where paths lead.

Norman and Chin (1988) used these sorts of ratings in a pilot study to test the comparability of different menus used in their experiment on the effect of menu structure. Subjects were shown a target item and the first frame in the menu tree. They rated the probability that each alternative would lead to the target with the restriction that the probabilities sum to one. The subject was informed of the correct choice, moved to the next menu along the path, and asked to rate the probabilities for alternatives at the next level. This continued until the target was one of the menu items. These data helped to diagnose poorly worded menu frames and particularly hard to find targets.

Ratings of Screen Layout. Users can be asked to rate the way in which menus are displayed on the screen. These ratings should include (a) how well organized the items are, (b) how meaningful and useful the organization is to the user, (c) how easy it is to locate desired items on the screen, and (d) how confusing or cluttered the screen appears. Screen layout is a highly subjective issue and should follow the principles of artistic design as well as. Additional ratings might include artistic aspects such as (a) line, (b) form, (c) value, (d) space, (e) texture, and (f) color (Simmons & Winer, 1977).

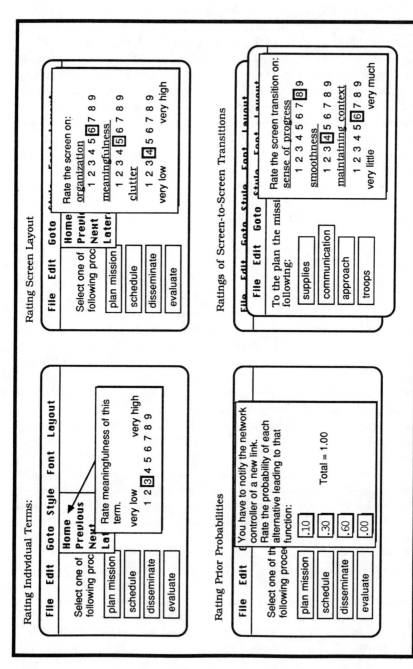

Figure 12.8. Four types of menu-by-menu ratings.

Ratings of the Screen-to-Screen Transitions. The way in which a system moves from screen to screen can create either an impression of discontinuity or of graceful progress. Discontinuity can occur when transitions are abrupt either visually or in terms of context. Some screen transitions seem to inch along by conveying too small a sense of change. Such an impression can frustrate the user. Other transitions may seem to move to a new galaxy in that they move too far with no sense of context or continuity. Users can rate screen-to-screen in terms of (a) step size, (b) sense of progress, (c) smoothness, and (d) maintenance of a sense of context.

To rate all of the above aspects of all screens on even a small system might be excessive. Fortunately, most real-world systems use only a limited number of screen layouts and types of transitions. Meaningfulness of terms and probability ratings, however, may pose a problem if the menu includes a large number of items and is hierarchical. One possibility would be to rate only a sampling of the total number. Alternatively, users could be given the capability of annotating items or features of menus that were particularly problematic. Nevertheless, menu-by-menu ratings should prove extremely useful in evaluating prototypes of menu selection systems and should be a standard part of usability testing.

12.4 SUMMARY

Prototyping is an essential element in design and evaluation. Prototyping of menu selection systems should allow for quick and easily modifiable mockups. More and more software tools and user interface management systems make it possible to alter the human/computer interface more or less independently from the application program underneath. However, few systems support an experimental workbench for prototype evaluation by generating tasks and monitoring user performance. MSPS, however, is one system that does and has been successfully used in a number of studies.

Prototyping must be supported by user evaluation. While user satisfaction has been acknowledged as important, empirically tested instruments to assess user evaluation have been lacking. The QUIS was developed and tested over a number of studies to fill that need. The QUIS provides both ratings of overall satisfaction and ratings of specific system attributes that help to diagnose the strengths and weaknesses of the system. Other scales have been developed to assess factors more directly related to menu selection. These reveal that the most important factor of design from the user's standpoint is clarity of the menu items.

Finally, menu systems should be subjected to menu-by-menu evaluations by users. Embedded rating scales provide a tool for user feedback.

Prototyping and evaluation are essential in the design of menu selection. To many, the design of a menu selection system seems to be a trivial process of merely specifying the items and writing menu frames. Prototyping and user evaluation may seem superfluous. On the contrary, menu design is neither trivial nor obvious. Designers can only make informed guesses. The initial design must be prototyped and iterated several times in response to user evaluation.

13
The Future of Menu Selection

Some have suggested that menus are merely an interim solution to the problem of human/computer interaction. Menus are regarded as only a stage in the metamorphosis of novice users into expert users. Or perhaps they are a way station on the road between command language and direct manipulation of the "soft machine," a malleable interface that takes on the shape and characteristics of the device that it emulates.

Some may feel that research should wait until the interface settles down. Findings today may not be relevant tomorrow. However, it is argued that although the implementation of the human/computer interface may change dramatically in the future, the theory and principles of cognitive control grounded in the user will not. While the technology driving the computer display and input devices undergoes evolution, the psychological processes driving user behavior are fixed. Although users vary among themselves in learning new ways of doing things and adapting to the interface over time, humans basically come in only one configuration with no revisions.

Furthermore, the concept of menu selection and the underlying cognitive processing are not likely to be supplanted by a new technology, but rather further entrenched in new designs. Whatever metaphor one projects, whether the restaurant menu, the desktop, soft machines, or beyond, all involve the organization and activation of objects and require the fundamental processes of attention, comprehension, selection, choice, traversal of functions, and search on the part of the user to establish cognitive control over the interface.

Rather than diminish, it is expected that the impact of menu design will increase in the next generation of systems. Furthermore, the need for well-designed menus will increase as more of our work becomes computer mediated and as more of our files become computer accessible. The complexity of the computer environment will approach, if not surpass, that of the physical environment in which we operate. Advanced menu selection, navigation, and direct manipulation are required for the user to operate with control in such an environment.

In this chapter a number of new directions in menu selection will be explored. Projecting the future development of a technology is not without its embarrassing pitfalls. Nevertheless, it is worth taking the shot. It is expected that menu systems will move far beyond the current generation as high-performance workstations become the norm. Innovations in menu selection design will continue to reshape the human/computer interface. A number of new types of menus will be discussed. It is expected that menu systems will provide a number of new capabilities to the user in an effort to enhance their power and adaptability. Systems will continue to grapple with the problem of when to use menu selection as the mode of interaction, but it is expected that systems will provide a better integration among alternative modes of interaction. Finally, one must think about the future of research on menu selection. A number of fundamental research issues are yet outstanding that need to be addressed in the coming years.

13.1 MENU GENERATIONS

To project the future it is instructive to plot the past. Menu selection has come through several generations up to this point in time. Surveying number of systems, one can date the software by the stereotypic way in which menus are implemented. Listed below are three generations of menus. As is the case with most technologies, a later generation rarely supplants a former generation, but rather it coexists for an extended period of time. Furthermore, one cannot conclude that later generations are necessarily better than former generations. Older tools may get the job done just as effectively as new ones.

First Generation. Menus are characterized as lists of options. They have been displayed one by one on slow terminals, or rapidly on fast workstations and personal computers. Selection is generally by a keyboard response, such as a letter or number or function key. The first generation is typified by video text services, electronic bulletin boards, and programs designed for novices.

Second Generation. Menus are characterized by pull-down and pop-up lists. Selection is generally made by cursor keys, a mouse, or by touch screen. The second generation is typified by applications such as WordPerfect and Lotus 1-2-3. The second generation sought greater speed and ease of access, thus securing a greater market among experienced users.

Third Generation. Menus are characterized by selecting and moving icons representing objects or tools. Selection is made by clicking, double clicking, and dragging objects using a mouse or some other pointing device. The third generation is typified by the desktop metaphor and direct manipulation.

Several trends are discernible in the progression from one generation to the next. The first trend has been increased speed and flexibility.

Faster user response time, alternative selection methods, and increased number of items were the driving force in leading to the second generation. The second trend has been the addition of graphics and metaphor to the selection process. The third generation was motivated by an analysis of the user tasks and the need for a usable mental model to support the task.

Looking to the forth generation, there are three formidable problems that must be overcome. First, it must provide fast access to extremely large numbers of items. Second, it must allow complex formulations of processes and commands. Third, it must provide new methods for user customization. The next section explores some of the innovations that hope to make this possible.

13.2 INNOVATIONS IN MENU LOOK AND FEEL

Menu interfaces convey a sense of look and feel. Users immediately see what they look like and quickly gain a feeling for how they work. But it is more than a superficial issue. The "look" of menu displays must convey choice information in a concise, information rich form that allows the user to efficiently scan and select items with a minimum number of errors. The "feel" of a menu must allow the user access to large numbers of objects with minimal movement and effort on the part of the user.

A number of innovations are being explored which increase the field of view of menu options and extend the power of selection of the user. These innovations are exciting, but it will remain to be seen which approaches accomplish that goal in a way that is compatible with good principles of cognitive control.

13.2.1 Nonlinear/Spatial Menus

Conventional menus list items in a linear array. A list has the characteristics of having a beginning, an end, and hopefully a meaningful ordering among the items. The beginning and end items are special and serve as anchors. Other items have president/successor relationships that help the user to locate items and structure the list. Many sets take advantage of linear order, but many other cases suggest nonlinear layouts of items that convey different relationships among items.

Rectangular layouts convey multiple dimensions and classes of related items. In addition to the row and column location (a linear ordering), rectangular menus convey similarity and neighbor relations (nonlinear diagonal orderings). For example, the periodic table of elements (see Figure 13.1) arranges items in rows according to their period (number of shells of electrons) and according to their atomic number (number of protons). Vertical columns of elements are related groups of elements that have similar properties.

Other sets of items are best represented with a cyclical order, for example, hours on a clock face or months of the year. Such orders convey cyclical orders in which, for example, January comes both before and after December. Circular menus can convey other relationships too. The color wheel conveys complementary relationships between colors. The circle of fifths conveys multiple sequences of wholetone and semitone scales. Figure 13.1 displays examples of such nonlinear/spatial layouts of menus.

In other cases, items have a traditional or standard graphic layout that is familiar to the user. Graphic menus faithfully represent these layouts on the screen. Figure 13.3 illustrates the layout of the states and zip codes. Other examples abound in cartography, schematics, illustrations, and diagrams that can be used to organize menu items in a way that uses and strengthens the user's prior visual organization of information.

Nonlinear/spatial menus have two advantages. Visual recognition and spatial memory are powerful and efficient means that users have for locating items on the screen. The graphic representation conveys a context for choice and structure for visual search.

A second advantage is that nonlinear/spatial menus may be arranged to facilitate selection time. Research on pie menus demonstrates the reduction in selection time that can be achieved by reducing the mouse or cursor movement distance from home to the desired item (Callahan,

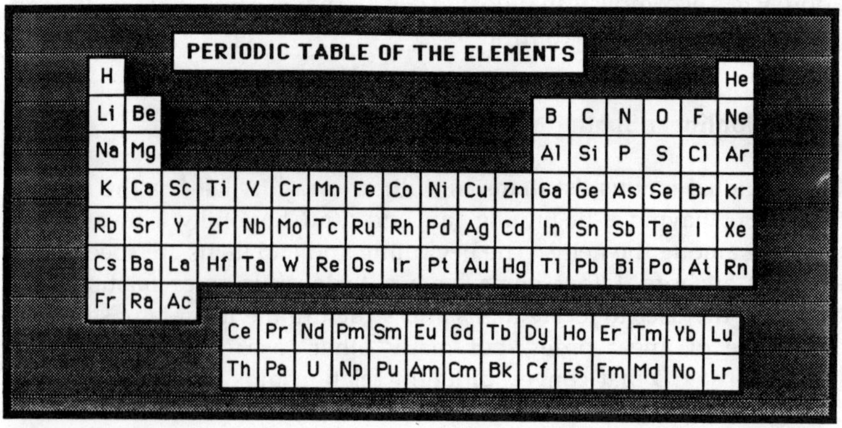

Figure 13.1. An example of a nonlinear menu layout: The periodic table of elements.

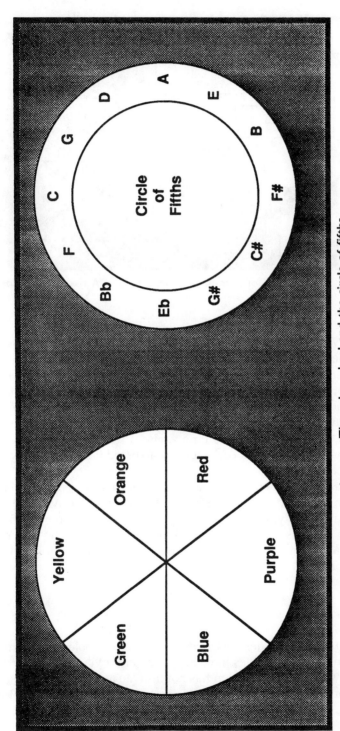

Figure 13.2. Examples of nonlinear menu layouts: The color wheel and the circle of fifths.

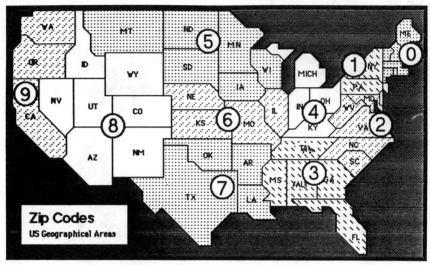

Figure 13.3.   An example of a nonlinear menu layout: A map of Zip Codes.

Hopkins, Weiser, & Shneiderman, 1988). In this case the starting point for the mouse is in the middle of the circle. Slight movement in any direction serves to highlight an item for selection. Rectangular and other spatial layouts may also have an advantage in that they allow for diagonal movement in which the user can only move across or down at a time. Finally, nonlinear/spatial menus may be able to make the most efficient use of space. Response time is also a function of the physical size of the target. Important or frequently accessed items can be given a larger selection area.

Nonlinear/spatial menus are beginning to have a great impact in human/computer interaction as graphic interfaces become available. Despite their availability, a potential designer should show some restraint in their use. It is easy to overdo a good thing and confuse the user with unfamiliar and complex graphics. There must be a balance of simplicity and functionality.

13.2.2 Analog Menus

Input of numerical values has been a constant problem in human/computer interaction. Values have had to be input via the keyboard or numeric keypad. Menu selection has not been an acceptable mode since the selection of digits on the screen is no better than key input. However, with pointing devices, such as the mouse or touchscreen, analog menus allow the user to input apparent continuous values. This innovation has two forms. One is accomplished by moving the cursor and clicking on a scale. The other is done by using the mouse to click on and drag a marker along a scale. Generally feedback is given to the user. The feedback may be a numeric display or a spatially translated effect, such as seeing a geometric form rotate or a manuscript scroll to a relative position. One of the obvious difficulties with analog menus is granularity. One solution has been to shift from macromovement to micromovement of the mouse using a gear shift key to change the ratio of translation.

Analog menus are rapidly being incorporated in the next generation of menu design and are replacing other modes of input. It is expected that they will fulfill an important role in increasing the cognitive control of users over the interface.

13.2.3 Power Pointing

Current selection devices provide only a limited channel for selection. The keyboard is limited by the number of keys. Cursor/arrow keys are limited by the number of key presses required. The mouse and other input devices are more powerful and versatile for selection by pointing since they provide a direct spatial mapping of x-y hand movement to the selection of items laid out on a two-dimensional screen. However, the movement capabilities of the user are not limited to two degrees of freedom. Maximally, the user has six degrees of freedom in which to move a pointing device: the three-dimensional x, y, and z coordinates, and the axises of pitch, roll and yaw rotation. Hand controllers and data gloves have the capability for sensing the full compliment of movement.

To a large extent this movement can be mapped to the screen using three-dimensional representation in space. One mouse dimension may be used to zoom through layers and the other two to scan across. The axises of rotation may be used to rotate objects on the screen. Selectable items may be graphically displayed on the surface of three-dimensional objects (e.g., rotating a lunar globe to select landing sites).

Added degrees of freedom may also allow the user to input gestures. Gestures are stereotyped movements that have specific meaning. For example, a squiggle or twist over an item on the screen may be used to delete the item, a "Q"-shaped movement may be used to quit an application, or a twist in one direction or another may align an item in different directions. Exploration of these features may add tremendous power to many applications that support high-resolution graphics.

13.2.4 Apparent Menus

Menu systems that involve control of processes and functions generally have a build-in interdependency among items. For example, Function C cannot be selected until either Function A or B have been selected. Hierarchical menus build this interdependency into the structure and present items only when they are appropriate for selection. The inherent interdependency of items, however, is buried in the hierarchy of menus and is not always apparent to the user. Menus which display all functions at the same time use some mechanism, such as graying out items to indicate that they are not active given the current state. Unfortunately, the interdependency that activates or deactivates them is generally not apparent to the user. The user is left to hunt forever , it would seem, to find the right combination to activate a desired item.

A major innovation is needed in making the inherent interdependency among items apparent to the user. Norman and Butler (1989a) addressed several approaches. One possibility would be to have the user select deactivated items in order to access context-dependent help information about that item. Such information might inform the user as to what is necessary to activate the item. For example, selecting the function "Align Objects" would inform the user that two or move objects must first be selected in order to perform the function. This approach may be sufficient for simple interdependencies, but not for complex network relationships.

A second approach would be to graphically display relationships using a schematic diagram. Figure 13.4 shows a hierarchy of functions and how a static diagram (second panel) might convey some of the relationships. Unfortunately, this diagram is complex and insufficient.

A third approach is a combination of the first two. The user would select a deactivated item which would then display a trace back through the items in the network showing possible paths to achieve that function (see the third panel of Figure 13.4). If the user wants to perform several functions in a series, the desired functions could be selected and the system would trace a route through a necessary series of functions to perform the desired subset of functions.

The point is to find ways of using the dynamics and graphics of the interface to reveal the structure inherent in the system to the user. This is a challenge to designers; however, it is essential if the menu interface is to provide true transparency and ease of use.

13.2.5 Simultaneous/Linked Menus

Conventional menus generally incorporate only one menu hierarchy. However, it happens that often one needs to traverse the same menu

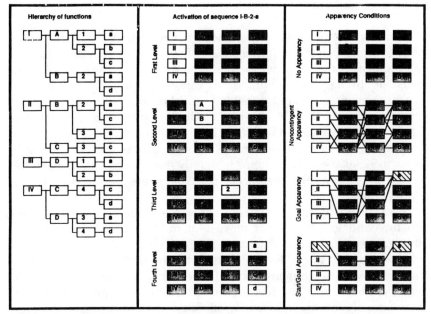

Figure 13.4. Making hierarchical menu relationships apparent to the user. Left panel shows hierarchical menu structure required to access functions a, b, c, and d. Middle panel gives an example of activating the sequence I-B-2-a. Right panel shows four levels of apparency by displaying paths between functions. (From Norman & Butler, 1989a).

tree in two or more independent passes, or one needs to traverse two or more different menus in linked passes. The first case is desirable if one needs to compare or to link different nodes of the same menu tree. For example, if one wants to compare different citations in a bibliographic database or to create cross references. One innovation would be to open multiple windows to a menu system and to provide tools to perform, link, copy, or compare functions between them.

The second case is desirable if traversing one menu is related to traversing another menu. Traversing a menu-driven help system provides information to the user about traversing a menu-control system. In control systems, operations in one menu system may conditionalize a second menu system. Furthermore, menu systems may be embedded in other menu systems. This sort of complexity will be required if menu systems are to perform complex jobs in command formulation and programming.

Finally, menu systems may be used to alter or adapt other menus. User-adaptable menus are an important innovation, as seen in a following section, but to implement adaptability, additional menus may be required to operate on top of the menu being adapted.

13.2.6 Vast and Fast Menus

Research on menu depth and breadth suggests that broad organized menus result in faster performance and fewer errors than deep menus. The problem is that in order to access databases with large numbers of items, depth has been required. Advances in large, high-resolution screens, however, make it possible to display menus that have 50–200 items per screen. The MacIntosh™ Finder program, for example, can display over 50 folders in its hierarchical file system. Pull-down menus can display 150 or more options. Numbers such as these can provide access to 125,000–8,000,000 items with only three menu selections. If the screens are graphically organized, selection times per screen may be relatively fast.

The difficulty in achieving vast and fast menus is in generating menu structure and graphic layout of vast menu frames that conveys the inherent structure of the database. This can be an extremely laborious task, particularly at the lower levels of the hierarchy. Furthermore, it may be in vain since many menu frames may be only rarely visited. Some systems may overcome this problem by providing a self-organizing algorithm. Others may allow the user to organize and even to prune menu frames based on need. Innovations are clearly needed to help the user organize the growing mass of documents and tools in the electronic media.

13.2.7 User-Constructed/User-Adaptable Menus

Storage and retrieval of information are often handled via user-constructed menus. Users may create folders, and by using direct manipulation or conventional menus, store files in the folder. Such hierarchical filing systems are essentially menu-driven, but are constructed by the user.

Similarly, users may organize tools or functions for access via menus. And to an increasing extent software designers are giving users the ability to customize or build their own menu structures. On the one side, this ability allows users to create efficient systems tailored to their needs. On the other side, it places a burden on the user to become the designer. The tradeoff is an important one and users must gauge the extent to which they want to invest their own time constructing or adapting a menu system versus using a fixed off-the-shelf system. To make matters worse, user design may result in a morass of redundancy, over-complexity, and sheer idiosyncrasy. Users may not be good designers. They will require considerable guidance to avoid irrational design.

The challenge is to design a user-designable system that avoids the pitfalls of bad design. Such a system must impose the principles of good design in the same way that a syntax-directed editor imposes correct statement construction on programmers. For example, a menu-builder may assess the discriminability of item labels, the organization of items in the frame, and the structure of the network, and alert the user/ designer when problems occur.

User adaptable menus provide five primary tools for redesign as listed below:

1. *Rename.* Users should be able to change the name or other designating information of menu items so as to add to its meaningfulness.
2. *Delete.* Users should be able to delete items. Deletion may be of terminal items or whole branches in a hierarchy. Pruning the menu system of unused items can greatly simplify the interaction.
3. *New Node.* Users should be able to create new menu items or frames that will serve as new groupings of items.
4. *Copy.* Users should be able to create copies of items. Copies may be of terminal items or whole branches in a hierarchy. Copies can be placed anywhere in the menu system to provide multiple access to frequently needed items at different locations in the system.
5. *Link.* Users should be able to create links from any item in the menu system to any other item. Links provide new pathways that can be used to create fast access to frequently used items or to link related items.

Construction of customized menus can also be accomplished by the tools listed above. The difference is that the user would begin with a library of items that could be assembled into a custom menu. The tool kit would first have to provide users with access to the library of items. Second, it must provide tools for organizing, editing, and assembling menus. Figure 13.5 shows a schematic of such a process. The left side of the figure shows the library access of objects available to the user. Tasks will not be performed using the library menu structure. It is only used when the user is selecting a menu or an item for inclusion in the user-designed menu system. Once the menu or item is located via navigation through the library, it is picked and marked for inclusion in the new menu. On the right side of the figure, the user builds a menu structure for a particular task. The user locates the desired point in the new system and puts the selected menu or item at that point. Other editing features are needed to create new menu frames (nodes), new links between items, and clusters of items. Working menus are pieced together and customized from stock software.

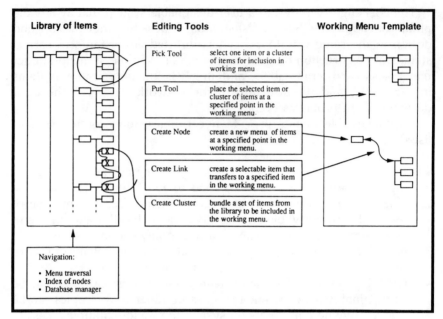

Figure 13.5. Editing of a stock menu system (library of items) to create a working menu using menu editing tools.

User-constructed and user-adaptable menus allow users complete freedom to do what they want. But freedom can be time-consuming and full of pitfalls. User-constructed and user-adaptable menus require a great amount of time, effort, and knowledge on the part of users. It may unreasonable to expect users to bear such a great burden of design. Ultimately, it will again be the designer and the human/computer interaction specialist who will be the ones to use the menu tool kit.

13.3 LIMITS TO MENUS

The number and variety of interaction styles available to the designer for human/computer interaction are steadily increasing. Command languages have long dominated human/computer interaction and have provided a powerful but error-prone environment to users willing to spend the time to learn the syntax and semantics of the language. Form fill as an interaction style has been implemented for low-level data entry tasks. Although it minimizes learning time, it lacks power and, in most cases, flexibility. Menu selection has an advantage over command language in that it greatly reduces the amount of syntactic and semantic knowledge required on the part of the user. It has an advantage over form fill when data entry is limited to a relatively small set of values. However, menu selection can't do it all. There are times when command language is clearly required and times when keyboard and form fill are more efficient.

The question is, "What is the optimal interaction style?" The answer depends on the type of user, the degree of cognitive control required, the point in the dialogue, and the type of task being performed. Time critical situations may call for a high degree of user-directed control. Passive learning situations may call for a low degree of user-directed control and active learning situations may require a constant shifting of control between the user and the system. As experience, mental workload, stress, and time pressures change one expects corresponding changes in the way the user interacts with the system. Consequently, interaction is not static. There are ever changing demands on the user and the system.

If interaction is not static, then it stands to reason that the mode and form of that interaction should not be fixed. The interface should be constructed so as to facilitate the changing needs of the user and the task. The appropriateness of menus as the mode of interaction will vary.

13.3.1 Early in the Learning Process

It is often argued that menus are most appropriate for novice users, but that experienced users prefer command languages. Certainly, menus are an aid to the novice in that they do not need to recall commands. However, it must be remembered that users do not remain novices for long and there may be a point at which the user may wish to switch to command input. The question is whether users starting with a menu selection system are hampered later on in learning a command language. If there is negative transfer from menus to command language, it would suggest that users should not start with menu selection. On the other hand, there may be a graceful transition from one mode to the other.

Streitz (1987) provided empirical evidence that menus do provide positive transfer to command language learning. In an experiment, one group gained experience using a menu selection system for editing text. A second group gained experience using a command language with a help window for editing text. Two additional groups were given no prior experience. All four groups then participated in the learning phase in which texts were edited using the command language only, with menus, or the help window as a help device. Learning curves were assessed for a limited set of commands, and subjects were tested on their knowledge over all of the commands available. No difference was found in the slope of the acquisition curves for the two groups with prior experience on menus versus commands. However, the menu group fared better in their overall kowledge of the functionality of the system. Subjects in the command language condition learned only a limited number of task-specific functions. It would appear that menu selection promoted a greater breadth of system knowledge.

Menus are not only appropriate for novice users who are expected to remain novices, they are also appropriate for novice users who are expected to become experienced users. This suggests a radical rethinking of many user training programs. Rather than starting training on the command language, users may begin working productively using menus. This allows them to actively gain an understanding of the functionality of the system through its use. Commands may be introduced at later stages as users master the concepts. This approach encourages active exploration on the part of the user and may promote a deeper understanding of system functionality and a broader range of use.

13.3.2 At Transition Points

Human/computer interaction is often characterized by intense periods of focused interaction (e.g., designing in a graphics application or entering data in a text editor) and transitions from one task to another (e.g., terminating one application and moving to another). Transition points involve important decisions and actions (e.g., what to name a file, what to do next, where to locate the next file). Such points are characterized by changes in the type and degree of cognitive control.

Exiting and entering applications require considerable structured control. The initiation and shut down of a system may be a demanding task involving check lists and sequencing of events. Menus are likely to aid in structuring the task and providing user guidance.

13.3.3 At Different Mental Workloads

Menu selection is often viewed as a more casual, relaxed mode of interaction; whereas, command language is a formal, fast-paced mode used under stress. When all the alarms are going off, users may not be in the appropriate mental state to wait for a menu display, scan the options, and make selections. Instead they want to blurt out commands as fast as possible to control the situation. Menus that are several layers deep are a particular problem. Broad menus may display the needed items, but under stress the perceptual scanning and selection process may be impaired. Menus may accommodate stress by providing large, dominant alternatives that can serve as panic buttons, or they can allow the user to input direct commands.

Mental workload, stress, and other situational factors vary greatly during interactive sessions using a computer. How should mode vary during such changes? A study by Eberleh, Streitz, and Korfmoacher, (1987) and reported by Streitz (1987) investigated the use of direct manipulation versus command modes under different levels of mental workload. The task was to work with a graphics program. Sixty subjects learning both a complex but fast method of interaction using a command mode, and a simple but slow method using direct manipulation. After all of the subjects met the learning requirement, one group of 15 subjects had to use only the command code, another group of 15 had to use direct manipulation, and a third group of 30 subjects had the choice of either method. The situation was varied in the same way for all three groups. They were subjected to a time pressure condition, an office noise condition, and a neutral control condition. Mental workload was measured using a dual task paradigm in which the user performed a primary task, but had to respond to a secondary task when it was presented. Reaction time to the secondary task and the number of omissions measured the mental workload on the primary task (Wickens, 1984). It was found that mental workload was not closely tied to any one mode, but depended on the compatibility of the interaction mode and the situation. Overall, there were more omissions with command language than with direct manipulation; however, under time pressure, command language led to fewer omissions than direct manipulation. It would appear that when working quickly under time pressure, command language requires less mental effort than direct manipulation. Results from the third group indicated that under time pressure subjects chose to use the command mode (68%) significantly more often than direct manipulation (32%). The implication is that under time pressure, menu selection may not be as appropriate as command codes. This result must be taken with caution, however, as much depends on the way in which direct manipulation is implemented.

Perhaps the best solution, in terms of cognitive control, is to provide users with both modes of interaction and let them decide which is appropriate. A further analysis of the third group indicated that 60 percent of the subjects switched between the command and direct manipulation modes, depending on the situation, while 20 percent used the command mode and 20 percent primarily used direct manipulation.

13.3.4 Flexibility

It may be that one cannot direct design toward the "best" mode of interaction. Instead, the interface might allow users to individually arrange their interaction style, sequence of subtasks, and screen layouts so to best suit their needs and preferences. Ulich (1987) extended the "principle of differential work design" applied in organizational psychology to human/computer interaction. The point was that different people may for different reasons prefer different tasks or work structures. The "principle of differential work design" was that there should be an optimal development of personality in interaction with the work activity in the context of individual differences. Consequently, he suggested that dialogue sequences in software should leave various modes of procedure open. The program sequence should have as few preset stages as possible, allowing users to work in a way best suited for them.

Menu systems have varied tremendously in terms of how much flexibility has been afforded to the user. At one extreme menus may present a rigid, fixed flow of interaction. All work proceeds in a predetermined sequence of menus and the user cannot vary that order. In some cases, such structure may be required by the logic of the task. In others it may be capricious, based on an arbitrary selection by the designer of one of many possible ways of doing the task. Moreover, the interaction may be unforgiving, in that if one component is incorrect, it is difficult if not impossible, for the user to correct the error.

At the other extreme, menus may provide extreme flexibility. Pulldown event-driven menus may allow the user to perform a set of prcedures in any order. Errors may be corrected at any point by retracing back to the point of error. Menus themselves may be open to modification and restructuring by the user. Such a system allows users to set up the organization and sequence of menus according to their preferences and work styles.

A study by Aschwanden and Zimmermann (1984) cited by Ulich (1987) supported the contention that such flexibility is desirable. Two groups of 15 female subjects were compared using two different types of dialogue to perform the task of handling a customer order. One type was highly rigid and the other highly flexible. The flexible dialogue allowed the user to control screen layout, choice of procedures, and modify keyboard functionality. No significant difference was found in the time to perform the task; however, the rigid dialogue resulted in a greater number of gross errors than the flexible dialogue. Furthermore, it was found that (a) users did in fact make use of the greater flexibility afforded them by the dialogue; (b) the increased use of the flexibility did not result in decreased performance or additional strain; and perhaps most importantly, (c) the individualized work procedures stimulated the user to become innovative, in that they offered numerous suggestions for improvement of the system.

13.4 RESEARCH ON MENUS

It is obvious that interest in menu selection has generated a considerable amount of research. The content and direction of this research reveals the major issues and emphases. Although some lines of research have dealt with fundamental questions, much of the research has had a tendency to dwell on detail. Detail is important since seemingly minor design issues can have large effects on performance and subjective impressions. There is no end to the number of additional design details that need to be studied. Moreover, whole new cases of details will need to be addressed as new innovations in menu design are explored.

The results of these studies can be divided into two classes: enduring results and technology-dependent results. The former are more or less independent of technological advances. They deal with the general principles that are cut across all designs (e.g., complexity, functionality) or they involve psychological processes in the user that will always be the human part of the interface (e.g., mental models, visual scanning).

On the other hand, technology-dependent results will be obsolete when the technology changes. This is not to say that this type of research lacks importance, only that its value is time-dependent. Such results often help to drive technological improvement. For example, the work on screen readability of older VDUs has helped to motivate the development of high-resolution workstations.

It is anticipated that great changes are in the wings for menu selection. Research is needed more than ever to support this development.

What is particularly exciting is that research on human/computer interaction contributes to the development of cognitive psychology in an unprecedented way. The human/computer interface taxes all of the cognitive aspects of the human and requires a greater understanding of human processing capacities than ever before. Research in this area will consequently be doubly fruitful, adding both to the technology and to the basic understanding of human cognitive processing. Menu selection, in particular, will contribute to theories of attention, problem solving, decision making, memory, and intelligence.

13.5 SUMMARY

Menus have come a long way. But there is still a long way to go before menu selection, as a mode of interaction, reaches its maximum potential. The thrust of current and foreseen innovation is to provide a control surface to the user that (a) is spatially organized, (b) accommodates selection in both discrete and continuous sets, (c) conveys visually apparent relationships, (d) provides maximum degrees of freedom in selection, (e) is vast and fast, (f) allows complex forms, and (g) is user adaptable.

Advancements in these areas has already placed menu selection as a prime candidate for control of the human/computer interface. Furthermore, trends in the development of different modes of interaction suggest that menu selection is headed in the right direction. The development of command language as a mode of interaction came first from within the computer community and has only recently been extended to the user in the marketplace by simplification, training, and sometimes use of natural language. It has moved from a versatile and powerful mode to limited application. In contrast, menu selection was developed first for the novice user and later extended to the more experienced and demanding computer literate community. Its versatility and power are constantly being enhanced.

Moreover, interfaces have in the past been characterized as being of one mode or another. Currently, applications find it necessary to shift modes as needed. The intelligent construction of the human/computer interface makes the best use of each mode as tasks shift between sequencing and control on the part of the user to computer-directed request for data input. Menu selection is perhaps the most versatile of modes for this purpose, accommodating novice to experience users, running at low to high workloads, and providing transitions between tasks and environments. Consequently, designers are using menu selection as the principle base of operations; and only when needed do they digress to other modes.

In conclusion, it must be realized that the human/computer interface is a rapidly changing surface. It is not clear what it will ultimately be. But it is becoming clear that it is extremely important. Indeed, the balance of power of the computer rests at the human/computer interface. In the years to come, research and development of the interface will be a major thrust in bringing about the next wave in a computer revolution of society. Menu selection is on the crest of that wave.

REFERENCES

Aksycn, R.M., & McCracken, D.L. (1984, March). *The ZOG approach to database management* (CMU-CS-84-128). Pittsburgh, PA: Department of Computer Science, Carnegie-Mellon University.

Allen, R.B. (1983). Cognitive factors in the use of menus and trees: An experiment. *IEEE Journal on Selected Areas in Communication, 1,* 333–336.

Anderson, J.R. (1980). *Cognitive psychology and its implications.* San Francisco: W.H. Freeman.

Anderson, N.H. (1981). *Foundations of information integration theory.* New York: Academic Press.

Anderson, N.S. (1988, August). *Two spheres of ambiguity in human computer interaction.* Invited Address, Division 21 (Applied Experimental and Engineering Psychology), Atlanta, GA.

Anderson, N.S., & Olson, J.R. (Eds.). (1985). *Methods for designing software to fit human needs and capabilities.* Washington, DC: National Academy Press.

Arend, U., Muthig, K.P., & Wandmacher, J. (1987). Evidence for global feature superiority in menu selection by icons. *Behaviour and Information Technology, 6,* 411–426.

Arthur, J.D. (1986). A descriptive/prescriptive model for menu-based interaction. *International Journal of Man-Machine Studies, 25,* 19–32.

Aschwanden, C., & Zimmerman, M. (1984). *Flexibilität in der Arbeit am Bildschirm.* Diploma thesis, University and ETH Zurich.

Bailey, J.E., & Pearson, S.W. (1983). Development of a tool for measuring and analyzing computer user satisfaction. *Management Science, 29,* 530–545.

Barnard, P., Hammond, N., Maclean, A., & Morton, J. (1982). Learning and remembering interactive commands. *CHI '82 Proceedings* (pp. 2–7). New York: Association for Computing Machinery.

Barnard, P.J., Hammond, N. V., Morton, J., Long, B.J., & Clark, I.A. (1981). Consistency and compatibility in human-computer dialogue. *International Journal of Man-Machine Studies, 15,* 87–134.

Bartlett, F.C. (1932). *Remembering: A study in experimental and social psychology.* New York & London: Cambridge University Press.

Beach, L.R., & Mitchell, T.R., (1987). A contingency model for the selection of decision strategies. *Academy of Management Review, 3,* 439–449.

Berke, P., & Vidal, J.J. (1987). Menus: A real-time adaptive interface. *Proceedings of the Second International Conference on Human/Computer Interaction,* p. 138. Honolulu, HI.

Billingsley, P.A., (1982, October). Navigation through hierarchical menu structures: Does it help to have a map? *Proceedings of the 26th Annual Meeting of the Human Factors Society* (pp. 103–107). Santa Monica, CA: Human Factors Society.

Blackwelder, R.E. (1963). *Classification of the animal kingdom.* Carbondale, IL: Southern Illinois Press.

Bransford, J.D., & Johnson, M.K. (1972). Contextual prerequisites for understanding: Some investigations of comprehension and recall. *Journal of Verbal Learning and Verbal Behavior, 61,* 717–726.

Calhoun, G.L. (1978). Control logic design criteria for multifunction switching devices. *Proceedings of the 22nd Annual Meeting of the Human Factors Society,* pp. 383–387.

Callahan, J., Hopkins, D., Weiser, M., & Shneiderman, B. (1988). An empirical comparison of pie vs. linear menus. *CHI '88 Conference Proceedings on Human Factors in Computing Systems* (pp. 95–100). New York: Association for Computing Machinery.

Canter, D., Rivers, R., & Storrs, G. (1985). Characterizing user navigation through complex data structures. *Behaviour and Information Technology, 4,* 93–102.

Card, S.K. (1982). User perceptual mechanisms in the search of computer command menus. In *Proceedings of Human Factors in Computer Systems* (pp. 190–196). New York: Association for Computing Machinery.

Card, S., Moran, T. P., & Newell, A. (1983). *The psychology of human-computer interaction.* Hillsdale, NJ: Erlbaum.

Carroll, J.M., & Mack, R.L. (1985). Metaphor, computing systems, and active learning. *International Journal of Man-Machine Studies, 22,* 39–57.

Carroll, J.M., Thomas, J. C., Miller, L.A., & Friedman, H.P. (1980). Aspects of solution structure in design problem solving. *American Journal of Psychology, 93,* 269–284.

Chin, J.P. (1986). *Mental models: Hierarchical categorization of computer menu functions derived from top-down/bottom-up processing.* Masters thesis, University of Maryland, College Park, MD.

Chin, J.P. (1987). Top-down and bottom-up menu design. *Proceedings of the Second International Conference on Human/Computer Interaction,* p. 144. Honolulu, HI.

Chin, J.P., Diehle, V.A., & Norman, K.L. (1988). Development of an instrument measuring user satisfaction of the human-computer interface. *CHI '88 Conference Proceedings: Human Factors in Computing Systems* (pp. 213–218). New York: Association for Computing Machinery.

Chin, J.P., & Norman, K.L. (1988, June). *Declarative and procedural knowldege in menu systems: Diagraming cognitive maps of phone and ATM commands* (CAR-TR-366 and CS-TR-2053). College Park, MD: Center for Automation Research, University of Maryland.

Chin, J.P., & Norman, K.L., & Scheiderman, B. (1987, July). *Subjective user evaluation of CF Pascal programming tools* (CAR-TR-304 and CS-TR-1880). College Park, MD: Center for Automation Research, University of Maryland.

Cohen, J. (1977). *Statistical power analysis for the behavioural sciences* (Rev. ed.). New York: Academic Press.

Cropper, A. G., & Evans, S.J.W. (1968). Ergonomics and computer display design. *The Computer Bulletin, 20,* 369–384.

Danchak, M.M. (1967). CRT displays in power plants. *Instrumentation Technology, 23,* 29–36.

Dehning, W., Essig, H., & Maass, S. (1981). *The adaptation of virtual man-computer interfaces to user requirements in dialogs.* Berlin: Springer-Verlag.

Dray, S.M, Ogden, W.G., & Vesterwig, R.E. (1981, October). Measuring performance with a menu-selection human-computer interface. *Proceedings of the 25th Annual Meeting of the Human Factors Society* (pp. 746–748). Santa Monica, CA: Human Factors Society.

Durding, B.M., Becker, C.A., & Gould, J. D. (1977). Data organization. *Human Factors, 19,* 1–14.

Eberleh, E., Streitz, N.A., & Korfmacher, W. (1987). Denken oder Handeln: Zur Wirkung von Dialogkomplexität und Handlungsspielraum auf die mentale Belastung. In W. Schönpflug & M. Wittstock (Eds.), *Software-Ergonome '87.* Stuttgart: Teubner.

Ekstrom, R. B., French, J.W., & Harmon, H.H. (1976). *Manual for kit of factor-referenced cognitive tests.* Princeton, NJ: Educational Testing Service.

Embedded Figures Test. (1971). Palo Alto, CA: Consulting Psychologists Press.

Engel, S.E., & Granada, R.E. (1975, December). *Guidelines for man/display interfaces* (Tech. Rep. TR 00.2720). Poughkeepsie, NY: IBM.

Fitts, P.M. (1954). The information capacity of the human motor system in controlling the amplitude of movement. *Journal of Experimental Psychology, 47,* 381–391.

Fitts, P.M., & Seeger, C.M. (1953). S-R compatibility: Spatial characteristics of stimulus and response codes. *Journal of Experimental Psychology, 46,* 199–210.

Fitts, P.M, & Switzer, G. (1962). Cognitive aspects of information processing: I. The familiarity of S-R sets and subsets. *Journal of Experimental Psychology, 63,* 321–329.

Foley, J.D., Wallace, V.L., & Chan, P. (1984, November). The human factors of computer graphics interaction techniques. *IEEE CG&A,* pp. 13–48.

Foltz, P.W., Davies, S.E., Polson, P.G., & Kieras, D.E. (1988). Transfer between menu systems. *CHI '88 Conference Proceedings Human Factors in Computing Systems.* (pp. 107–112) New York: Association for Computing Machinery.

Galitz, W.O. (1981). *Handbook of screen format design.* Wellesley, MA: Q.E.D. Information Sciences.

Gallagher, C.A. (1974). Perceptions of the value of a managment information system. *Academy of Management Journal, 17,* 46–55.

Gray, J. (1986). The role of menu titles as a navigational aid in hierarchical menus. *SIGCHI Bulletin, 17,* 33–40.

Green, D.M., & Swets, J. A. (1966). *Signal detection theory and psychophysics.* New York: Wiley.

Green, T.R.G., & Payne, S.J. (1984). Organization and learn ability of computer languages. *International Journal of Man-Machine Studies, 21,* 7–18.

Hagelbarger, D., & Thompson, R. (1983). Experiments in teleterminal design. *IEEE Spectrum, 20,* 40–45.

Hays, W.L. (1981). *Statistics*. New York: Holt, Rinehart & Winston.

Hedges, L.V. (1985). *Statistical methods for meta-analysis*. Orlando, FL: Academic Press.

Hemenway, K. (1982). Psychological issues in the use of icons in command menus. *Proceedings of CHI '82* (pp. 20–23). New York: Association for Computing Machinery.

Hick, W.E. (1952). On the rate of gain of information. *Quarterly Journal of Experimental Psychology, 4*, 11–26.

Hogarth, R.M. (1975). Decision time as a function of task complexity. In D. Wendt & C. Vlek (Eds.), *Utility, probability, and human decision making* (pp. 321–338). Dordrecht, Holland: Reidel.

Hold, H.O., & Stevenson, F.L. (1974). Human performance considerations in complex systems. *Science, 195*, 1205–1209.

Hunt, E. (1978). The mechanisms of verbal ability. *Psychological Review, 85*, 109–130.

Hunter, J.E. (1982). *Meta-analysis*. Beverly Hills, CA: Sage.

Hutchins, E.L., Hollan, J.D., & Norman, D.A. (1986). Direct manipulation interfaces. In D. A. Norman & S.W. Draper (Eds.), *User centered system design* (pp. 87–124). Hillsdale, NJ: Erlbaum.

Hyman, R. (1953). Stimulus information as a determinant of reaction time. *Journal of Experimental Psychology, 45*, 188–196.

Isa, B.S., Odgen, W.C., Wolfe, S.J., & Korenshteink, R. (1986). Navigation issues related to menu-based software products. *SIGCHI Bulletin, 18*, 68–69.

Ives, B., Olson, M.H., & Baroudi, J.J. (1983). The measurement of user information satisfaction. *Communications of the ACM, 26*, 785–793.

Jensen, R., & Tonis, C. (1979). *Software engineering*. Englewood Cliffs, NJ: Prentice-Hall.

Jofre, M.E., & Pino, J.A. (1987). Choosing codes to improve menu interfaces of software systems. *Proceedings of the Second International Conference on Human/Computer Interaction*, p. 143. Honolulu, HI.

Keeney, R.L., & Raffia, H. (1976). *Decisions with multiple objectives: Preferences and value tradeoffs*. New York: John Wiley & Sons.

Kendall, E. S., & Wodinsky, J. (1960). *Journal of the Optical Society of America, 50*, 562–568.

Kiger, J.I. (1984). The depth/breadth trade-off in the design of menu-driven user interfaces. *International Journal of Man-Machine Studies, 20*, 201–213.

Kinney, G.C., Marsetta, M., & Showman, D.J. (1966). *Studies in display symbol legibility, part XXI. The legibility of alphanumeric symbols for digitized television* (ESD-TR-66-177). Bedford, MA: The Mitre Corporation.

Kirk, R.E. (1982). *Experimental design: Procedures for the behavioural sciences* (2nd ed.). Belmont, CA: Brooks/Cole.

Koved, L., & Shneiderman, B. (1986). Embedded menus: Selecting items in context. *Communications of the ACM, 29*, 312–318.

Landauer, T.K., & Nachbar, D.W. (1985). Selection from alphabetic and numeric menu trees using a touch screen: Breadth, depth, and width. *CHI-85 Proceedings* (pp. 73–78). New York: Association for Computing Machinery.

Larcker, D.F., & Lessig, V.P. (1980). Perceived usefulness of information: Ap-sychometric examination. *Decision Science, 11*, 121–134.

Larkin, J. H. (1980). Teaching problem solving in physics: The psychological laboratory and the practical classroom. In D.T. Tuma & F. Reif (Eds.), *Problem solving and education: Issues in teaching and research.* Hillsdale, NJ: Erlbaum.

Laverson, A. (1985). *Menu selection system jump-ahead techniques: An evaluation of type-ahead vs. direct-access methodologies.* Master's thesis, University of Maryland, College Park, MD.

Laverson, A., Norman, K.L., & Shneiderman, B. (1987). An evaluation of jump-ahead techniques in menu selection. *Behaviour and Information Technology, 6*, 97–108.

Ledgard, H., Singer, A., & Whiteside, J. (1981). *Directions in human factors for interactive systems.* New York: Springer-Verlag.

Lee, E., & MacGregor, J. (1985). Minimizing user search time in menu retrieval systems. *Human Factors, 27*, 157–162.

Lee, E.S., Whalen, T., McEwen, S., & Latremouille, S. (1984). Optimizing the design of menu pages for information retrieval. *Ergonomics, 27*, 1051–1069.

Licklider, J.C.R. (1960). Man-computer symbiosis. *IRE Transactions on Human Factors in Electronics, HFE-1*, 4–11.

Liebelt, L.S., McDonald, J.E., Stone, J.D., & Karat, J. (1982). The effects of organization on learning menu access. *Proceedings of the Human Factors Society—26th Annual Meeting* (pp. 546–550). Santa Monica, CA: Human Factors Society.

Lieser, A., Streitz, N.A., & Wolters, T. (1987). *Einfluß unterschiedlicher Metaphern-welten und Dialogformen auf das Erlernen interaktiver Systeme.* Report of the Institute of Psychology, Technical University Aachen, West Germany.

Lindsey, P.H., & Norman, D. A. (1977). *Human information processing.* New York: Academic Press.

Luce, R.D. (1959). *Individual choice behavior.* New York: Wiley.

McCracken, D., & Akscyn, R.M. (1984). Experience with ZOG human-computer interface system. *International Journal on Man-Machine Studies, 21*, 293–310.

MacGregor, J., Lee, E., & Lam N. (1986). Optimizing the stucture of database menu indexes: A decision model of menu search. *Human Factors, 28*, 387–399.

McDonald, J.E., Dayton, T., & McDonald, D.R. (1986). *Adapting menu layout to tasks* (MCCS-86-78). Las Cruces, NM: Memoranda in Computer and Cognitive Science, Computing Research Laboratory, New Mexico State University.

McDonald, J.E., Molander, M.E., & Noel, R.W. (1988). Color coding categories in menus. *CHI '88 Conference Proceedings: Human Factors in Computing Systems* (pp. 101–106). New York: Association for Computing Machinery.

McDonald, J.E., Stone, J.D., & Liebolt, L.S. (1983). Searching for items in menus: The effects of organization and type of target. *Proceedings of the Human Factors Society—27th Annual Meeing* (pp. 834–837). Santa Monica, CA: Human Factors Society.

McDonald, J.E., Stone, J.D., Liebolt, L. S., & Karat, J. (1982). Evaluating a method for structuring the user-system interface. *Proceedings of the Human*

Factors Society—26th Meeting (pp. 551–555). Santa Monica, CA: Human Factors Society.

McEwen, S.A. (1981). An investigation of user search performance on a Telidon information retrieval system. In *The design of videotex tree indexes* (pp. 35–64). Ottawa, Ontario: Behavioural Research and Evaluation, Department of Communications, Government of Canada.

MIL-STD-1472C. (1981). *Human engineering design criteria for military systems, equipment and facilities.* Washington, DC: Department of Defense.

Miller, D.P. (1981). The depth/breadth tradeoff in hierarchical computer menus. *Proceedings of the Human Factors Society—25th Annual Meeting* (pp. 296–300). Santa Monica, CA: Human Factors Society.

Miller, G.A., Galanter, E., & Pribram, K.H. (1960). *Plans and the structure of behavior.* New York: Holt, Rineholt, & Winston.

Mills, M.I. (1981). A study of the human response to pictorial representation on Telidon. In D. Phillips (Ed.), *Telidon behavioural research III.* Ottawa, Ontario: Department of Communications.

Mitchell, C.M. (1983). Design strategies for computer-based information displays in real-time control systems. *Human Factors, 25,* 353–369.

Montgomery, H., & Svenson, O. (1976). On decision rules and information processing strategies for choices among multiattribute alternatives. *Scandinavian Journal of Psychology, 17,* 283–291.

Muter, P., & Mayson, D. (1986). The role of graphics in item selection from menus. *Behaviour and Information Technology, 5,* 89–95.

Neisser, U. (1963). Decision-time without reaction-time: Experiments in visual scanning. *American Journal of Psychology, 76,* 376–385.

Neisser, U. (1976). *Cognition and reality: Principles and implications of cognitive psychology.* San Francisco: W.H. Freeman.

Nelson-Denny Reading Test, Form C. (1973). Boston: Houghton Mifflin.

Nelson, E.A. (1970). Some recent contributions to computer programming management. In G. F. Weinwurm (Ed.), *On the management of computer programming* (pp 159–184). New York: Auerbach.

Newell, A., & Simon, H. (1972). *Human problem solving.* Englewood Cliffs, NJ: Prentice-Hall.

Nilsson, N.J. (1971). *Problem solving methods in artificial intelligence.* New York: McGraw-Hill.

Norman, D.A., & Draper, S.W. (Eds). (1986). *User centered system design.* Hillsdale, NJ: Erlbaum.

Norman, K.L. (1981). Judgment and decision models with the Christian presuppositional system. *Journal of Psychology and Theology, 9,* 144–158.

Norman, K.L. (1983) Development of direct-search strategies in hill-climbing problems. *Bulletin of the Psychonomic Society, 21,* 469–472.

Norman, K.L. (1984). *MSPS: A menu selection prototyping system.* Unpublished document, University of Maryland, College Park, MD.

Norman, K.L. (1986) *The problem of defining user friendliness* (Working Paper). College Park, MD: Automation Psychology Lab, University of Maryland.

Norman, K.L. (1987, April). *Conflicts in design preference for menu selection: Programmer vs. novice computer users.* Paper presented at CHI + GI 1987 Human Factors in Computing Systems and Graphics Interface, Toronto, Canada.

Norman, K.L. (1988). *Five basic aspects of menu selection: An empirical measure* (Working Paper). College Park, MD: Automation Psychology Lab, University of Maryland.

Norman, K.L. (1989, November). *User response time for pulldown menus as a function of knowledge of location and structure of menu.* Paper presented at the Psychonomic Society, Atlanta, GA.

Norman, K.L., & Anderson, N.S. (1981). *Psychological factors in computer assisted instruction: Development of a computer interaction satisfaction scale* (CLC No. 20). College Park, MD: Center for Language and Cognition, University of Maryland.

Norman, K.L., Anderson, N.S., Schwartz, J.P., Singer, M.J., Shneiderman, B., Bartol, K., & Weiser, M. (1980). *Computer aided decision making and problem solving: A program of research* (CLC No. 19). College Park, MD: Center for Language and Cognition, University of Maryland.

Norman, K.L., & Butler, S. (1989a, November). *Apparency: Guiding sequential decision making by revealing inherent contingencies.* Paper presented at the Society for Judgement and Decision Making, Atlanta, GA.

Norman, K.L., & Butler, S. (1989b). *Search by uncertainty: Menu selection by target probability* (CAR-TR-432 and CS-TR-2230). College Park, MD: Center for Automation Research and the Department of Computer Science, University of Maryland.

Norman, K.L., & Chin, J.P. (1988). The effect of tree structure on search in a hierarchical menu selection system. *Behaviour and Information Technology, 7,* 51–65.

Norman, K.L., & Chin, J.P. (1989). The menu metaphor: Food for thought. *Behavior and Information Technology, 8,* 125–134.

Norman, K.L., Mantel, W., & Wallace, D.F. (1988). *User's guide to the menu selection prototyping system* (CAR-TR-393 and CS-TR-2114). College Park, MD: Center for Automation Research and the Department of Computer Science, University of Maryland.

Norman, K.L., & Singh, R. (1989). Expected performance at the human/computer interface as a function of user proficiency and system power. *Journal of Behavioral Decision Making, 2,* 179–195.

Norman, K.L., Weldon, L.J., & Shneiderman, B. (1986). Cognitive layouts of windows and multiple screens for user interfaces. *International Journal of Man-Machine Studies, 25,* 229–248.

O'Connor, J. (1972). Developmental changes in abstractness and moral reasoning. *Dissertation Abstracts International, 32,* 4109a.

Paap, K.R., & Roske-Hofstrand, R.J. (1986). The optimal number of menu options per panel. *Human Factors, 28,* 377–385.

Parkinson, S.R., Sisson, N., & Snowberry, K. (1985). Organization of broad computer menu displays. *International Journal of Man-Machine Studies, 23,* 689–697.

Parng, A.K., & Goodman, D.R. (1987). Menu construction algorithms. *Interface '87: Human Implications of Product Design, Proceedings of the 5th Symposium on Human Factors and Industrial Design in Consumer Products* (pp 363–371). Rochester, New York, May 13-15. Santa Monica, CA: Human Factors Society, Consumer Products Technical Group.

Parton, D., Huffman, K., Pridgen, P., Norman, K., & Shneiderman, B. (1985). Learning a menu selection tree: Training methods compared. *Behaviour and Information Technology, 4,* 81–91.

Pellegrino, J.W., Rosinski, R.R., Chiesi, H.L., & Siegel, A. (1977) Picture-word differences in decision latency: An analysis of single and dual memory models. *Memory and Cognition, 5,* 383–396.

Perlman, G. (1984). Making the right choices with menus. In B. Shackel (Ed.), *INTERACT '84. Proceedings of the First International Conference on Human-Computer Interaction* (pp. 317–321). Amsterdam: North-Holland.

Peterson, D.E. (1979, February). Screen design guidelines. *Small Systems World,* pp. 19–21, 34–37.

Poulton, E.C., & Brown, C.H. (1968). Rate of comprehension of an existing teleprinter output and of possible alternatives. *Journal of Applied Psychology, 52,* 16–21.

Powell, D. (1985). *Experimental evaluation of two menu designs for information retrieval.* Unpublished research.

Price, L.A. (1982, June). Design of command menus for CAD systems. *ACM IEEE Nineteenth Design Automation Conference Proceedings,* pp 453–459.

Ramsey, H.R., & Atwood, M.E. (1979, September). *Human factors in computer systems: A review of the literature* (Tech. Rep. SAI-79-111-DEN). Englewood, CO: Science Applications, Inc.

Raymond, D.R. (1986, November). *A survey of research in computer-based menus* (CS-86-61). Ontario, Canada: Data Structuring Group, University of Waterloo.

Robertson, G., McCraken, D., & Newell, A. (1981). The ZOG approach to man-machine communication. *The International Journal of Man-Machine Studies, 14,* 461–488.

Rogers, Y. (1987). User performance of iconic and command name interfaces. *Proceedings of the Second International Conference on Human/Computer Interaction,* p 145. Honolulu, HI.

Rosch, E., & Lloyd, B.B. (Ed.). (1978). *Cognition and categorization.* Hillsdale, NJ: Erlbaum.

Rothschild, N.M.V. (1965). *A classification of living animals* (2nd ed.) London: Longman.

Rumelhart, D.E., & Norman, D.A. (1978). Accretion, tuning, and restructuring: Three modes of learning. In R.L. Cotton & J.W. Katsky (Eds.), *Semantic factors in cognition.* Hillsdale, NJ: Erlbaum.

Running Shoes. (1986, October). *Consumer Reports,* pp. 650–655.

Shank, R.C., & Abelson, R.P. (1977). *Scripts, plans, goals and understanding.* Hillsdale, NJ: Erlbaum.

Schneider, W., & Shiffrin, R.M. (1977). Controlled and automatic human information processing: I. Detection, search, and attention. *Psychological Review, 84,* 1–66.

Schultz, E.E., Jr., & Curran, P.S. (1986). Menu structure and ordering of menu selections: Independent or interactive effects? *SIGCHI Bulletin, 18,* 69–71.

Schwartz, J.P., & Norman, K.L. (1986). The importance of item distinctivness on performance using a menu selection system. *Behaviour and Information Technology, 5,* 173-182.

Schwartz, J.P., & Norman, K.L., & Shneiderman, B. (1985). *Performance on content-free menus as function of study method* (CAR-TR-110 and CS-TR-1477). College Park, MD: Center for Automation Research and the Department of Computer Science, University of Maryland.

Selsam, M.E. (1966). *Benny's animals and how he put them together*. New York: Harper & Row.

Seppälä, P., & Salvendy, G. (1985). Impact of depth of menu hierarchy on performance effectiveness in a supervisory task: Computerized flexible manufacturing system. *Human Factors, 27*, 713–722.

Shiffrin, R.M., & Schneider, W. (1977). Controlled and automatic human information processing: II. Perceptual learning, automatic attending, and a general theory. *Psychological Review, 84*, 127–190.

Shneiderman, B. (1980). *Software psychology: Human factors in computer and information systems*. Cambridge, MA: Winthrop.

Shneiderman, B. (1987). *Designing the user interface: Strategies for effective human computer interaction*. Reading, MA: Addison-Wesley.

Shneiderman, B., & Kearsley, G. (1989). *Hypertext hands-on!* Reading, MA: Addison-Wesley.

Shurtleff, D.A. (1980). *How to make displays legible*. La Mirada, CA: Human Interface Design.

Simmons, S., III., & Winer, M.S.A. (1977). *Drawing: The creative process*. Englewood Cliffs, NJ: Prentice-Hall.

Simon, H. (1969). The architecture of complexity. In H.A. Simon (Ed.), *The sciences of the artificial*. Cambridge, MA: MIT Press.

Simon, H. (1976). *Administrative behavior: A study of decision-making processes in administrative organization* (3rd ed.). New York: Free Press.

Simon, H.A., & Gilmartin, K.A. (1973). A simulation of memory for chess positions. *Cognitive Psychology, 5*, 29–46.

Sisson, N., Parkinson, S., & Snowberry, K. (1986). Considerations of menu structure and communication rate for the design of computer menu displays. *International Journal of Man-Machine Studies, 25*, 479–489.

Smith, M.C., & Magee, L.E. (1980). Tracing the time course of picture-word processing. *Journal of Experimental Psychology: General, 4*, 373–392.

Smith, S.L., & Mosier, J.N. (1986). *Guidelines for designing user interface software* (ESD-TR-86-287). Hanscom Air Force Base, MA: Electronic System Division, AFSC, United States Air Force.

Smith, E.E., Shoben, E.J., & Rips, L.J. (1974). Structure and process in semantic memory: A feature model of semantic decisions. *Psychological Review, 81*, 214–241.

Smith, J.B., & Weiss, S.F. (1988). An overview of hypertext. *Communications of the ACM, 31*, 816–819.

Snowberry, K., Parkinson, S., & Sisson, N. (1983). Computer display menus. *Ergonomics, 26*, 699–712.

Snowberry, K., Parkinson, S., & Sisson, N. (1985). Effects of help fields on navigating through hierarchical menu structures. *International Journal of Man-Machine Studies, 22*, 479–491.

Snyder, K.M., Happ, A.J., Malcus, L., Paap, K.R., & Lewis, J.R. (1985). Using cognitive models to create menus. *Proceedings of the Human Factors Society—*

29th Annual Meeting (pp. 655–658). Santa Monica, CA: Human Factors Society.

Soloway, E. (1980). *From problems to programs via plans: The context and structure of knowledge for introductory LISP programming* (COINS Tech. Rep. 80–19). Amherst, MA: University of Massachusetts at Amherst.

Somberg, B.L. (1987). A comparison of rule-based positionally constant arrangements of computer menu items. *CHI + GI 1987 Conference Proceedings: Human Factors in Computing Systems and Graphics Interface* (pp 255–260). New York: Association for Computing Machinery.

Somberg, B.L., Boggs, G.J., & Picardi, M.C. (1982, October 25–29). *Search and decision processes in human interaction with menu-driven systems.* Paper presented at the Seattle, Washington, Human Factors Society 26th Annual Meeting.

State-Trait Anxiety Inventory, Form Y. (1983). Palo Alto, CA: Consulting Psychologists Press.

Sterling, T.D. (1974). Guidelines for humanizing computerized information systems: A report from Stanley House. *Communications of the ACM, 17,* 609–613.

Sternberg, R.J. (1977). *Intelligence, information processing, and analogical reasoning.* Hillsdale, NJ: Erlbaum.

Streitz, N.A. (1987). Cognitive compatibility as a central issue in human-computer interaction: Theoretical framework and empirical findings. In G. Salvendy (Ed.), *Cognitive engineering in the design of human-computer interaction and expert systems* (pp 75–82). Amsterdam: Elsevier Science Publishers.

Teitelbaum, R.C., & Granada, R.E. (1983). The effects of positional constancy on searching menus for information. *CHI '83 Proceedings* (pp 150–153). New York: Association for Computing Machinery.

Tesler, L. (1981, August). The Smalltalk environment. *BYTE,* pp. 90–147.

Tombaugh, J.W., & McEwen, S.A. (1982). Comparison of two information retrieval methods on Videotext: Tree-structure versus alphabetical directory. *Communications of the ACM,* pp. 106–110. *(Proceedings of a Conference on Human Factors in Computer Systems,* pp. 106–110, Gaithersburg, MD.)

Tullis, T.S. (1981). An evaluation of alphanumeric, graphic, and color information displays. *Human Factors, 23,* 541–50.

Tullis, T.S. (1983). The formating of alphanumeric displays: A review and analysis. *Human Factors, 25,* 657–682.

Tversky, A. (1972). Elimination by aspects: A theory of choice. *Psychological Review, 79,* 281–299.

Ulich, E. (1987). Individual differences in human-computer interaction: Concepts and research findings. In G. Salvendy (Ed.), *Cognitive engineering in the design of human-computer interaction* (pp. 29–36). Amsterdam: Elsevier Science Publishers.

Vicente, K.J., Hayes, B.C., & Williges, R.C. (1987). Assaying and isolating individual differences in searching a hierarchical file system. *Human Factors, 29,* 349–359.

Walker, N., & Olson, J.R. (1988). Designing keybindings to be easy to learn and resistant to forgetting even when the set of commands is large. *CHI '88*

Conference Proceedings on Human Factors in Computing Systems (pp. 201–206). New York: Association for Computing Machinery.

Wallace, D.F. (1988). *Forced pacing and environment driven time pressure effects on menu selection systems.* Master's thesis. University of Maryland, College Park, MD.

Wallace, D.F., Norman K.L., & Plaisant, C. (1988). *The American voice and robotics guardian system: A case study in user interface usability evaluation* (CAR-TR-392 and CS-TR-2112). College Park, MD: Center for Automation Research, University of Maryland.

Wandmacher, J., & Müller, U. (1987). On the usability of verbal and iconic command representations. *Zeitschrift für Psychologie.*

Webster's New Universal Dictionary of the English Language. (1976). New York: Webster's International Press.

Welford, A.T. (1980). Reaction time: Basic concepts. In A.T. Welford (Ed.), *Reaction time* (pp. 73–128). New York: Academic Press.

Whalen, T., & Latrémouille, S. (1981). The effectiveness of a tree-structured index when the existence of information is uncertain. In *The design of videotext tree indexes* (pp. 3–14). Ottawa, Ontario: Behavioural Research and Evaluation, Department of Communications, Government of Canada.

Whalen, T., & Mason, C. (1981). The use of a tree-structured index which contains three types of design defacts. In *The design of videotex tree indexes* (pp. 15–34). Ottawa, Ontario: Behavioural Research and Evaluation, Department of Communications, Government of Canada.

Wickelgren, W.A. (1974). *How to solve problems: Elements of a theory of problem solving.* San Francisco: W.H. Freeman.

Wickens, C.D. (1984). *Engineering psychology and human performance.* Columbus, OH: Merrill.

Winer, B.J. (1971). *Statistical principles in experimental design.* New York: McGraw-Hill.

Witten, I.W., Cleary, J.G., & Greenberg, S. (1984). On frequency-based menu-splitting algorithms. *International Journal of Man-Machine Studies, 21,* 135–148.

Appendix
Checklist for Menu Design with Cross-References to Sections in the Text

Menu Structure:

- Does the menu structure match the task to be performed by the user? (2.l, 11.5.2)
- Does the apparent system complexity/functionality match the user/ task need? (3.3)
- Does the system state transition diagram optimize the user subtask transition matrix? (3.3)
- Does the system inform the user as to whether selections merely move from node to node in a menu structure, request the display of information, or have the effect of executing procedures or entering data or changing parameters? (3.4)
- Does the system take advantage of menu selection as a metaphor? (4.3.1)
- Does the structure of the menu adequately embody the procedural and declarative knowledge of the database? (11.1)
- If the menu structure represents the organization of a database, is it organized according to an appropriate data structure (e.g., hierarchy, network, list, table)? (11.1)
- If a clustering method was used to generate the structure of the menu, did it extract groupings form a top-down or bottom-up approach that adequately matches the way in which the user searches the database? (11.2)

Application Menus:

- For command menus, does the order of selecting commands, operands, and options match the cognitive processing of the user? (3.5)
- For command menus, does the system adequately handle the changing availability of commands, depending on the state of the system? (3.5)

- Has the menu structure been designed to minimize menu traversal by taking into consideration command transitions required by the task? (11.5.2)
- For decision menus, are the contingencies of the decision tree properly represented in the menu hierarchy? (3.6.1)
- For decision menus, are all of the revelant factors involved in the decision accounted for? (3.6.2)
- For decision menus, is the rule for combining attributes appropriate for the user? (3.6.2)
- For information menus, is the menu structure appropriate for the way in which users desire to search the database and for their familiarity with the database? (3.7)
- For category menus, does the men structure contain the appropriate scope and refinement for proper classification of instances? (3.8)
- For category menus, does the order of defining attributes agree with either order of importance to the user, or a prescribed or a natural order? (3.8)

Sequencing of Menus:

- Does the processing of a single menu frame follow the expected sequence of actions? (2.1.1)
- If sequential linear menus are used, do they match the user's expectations of sequence, or do they provide sufficient flexibility in changing the sequence? (2.1.2)
- If simultaneous menus are used, is it necessary for the user to see and select from several menus at once, and are the items organized in a way that facilitates section? (2.1.3)
- If connected graph menus are used, do they convey a sense of control over the flow of actions, and do the paths match the flow of control required by the task? (2.1.5)
- If event-trapping menus are used, do they provide the necessary background control over system, state, options, and parameters required by the foreground task? (2.1.6)
- If pull-down menus are used, do they position high-frequency items in locations that minimize user selection time? (10.1.1)

Hierarchical Menus:

- If hierarchical menus are used, do they convey a sense of stepwise refinement and take advantage of the ideas of branching and funneling? (2.1.4)

- If hierarchical menus are used and transmission time is not a problem, do they adequately take advantage of breadth to minimize total user response time and navigational errors? (8.4)
- If hierarchical menus and transmission time is slow, does the menu structure minimize total system time plus user response time? (8.6)
- If hierarchical menus are used, is a wide breadth of choice given at the top of the structure to help minimize early navigational errors? (9.1.1)
- If hierarchical menus are used, is a narrower breadth of choice given in the middle to help focus and reduce immediate navigational error? (9.1.1)
- If hierarchical menus are used, is a wide breadth of choice given at the bottom of the structure to help reduce choice uncertainty revealing long lists of final options? (9.1.2)
- If hierarchical menus are used, is the structure designed so as to reduce the total number of menu frames? (9.1.3)
- If hierarchial menus are used, are high-frequency and highly critical items located near the top of the menu structure? (10.1.3, 11.5.1)

Menu Information:

- Does the menu layout convey an appropriate metaphor that facilitates user understanding of the system? (4.3.3)
- Is the amount of information/explanation in the menu frame appropriate for scan/reading time required? (6.1.1)
- Is the amount of information/explanation in the menu frame appropriate for the level of experience/knowledge of the user? (6.1.1)
- If a menu requires several screens, has the information been appropriately divided among the multiple screens? (6.1.1)
- Do menus create a meaningful linkage from one menu frame to the next? (2.2.1)
- Do menu frames provide adequate context information about what led up to the current frame, the reason for the current selection, and the nature of the selection? (2.2.1, 6.1.4)
- Does the menu frame provide a meaningful label that identifies the rationale for the selection? (2.2.2, 6.2.1)

Item Information:

- Do the labels of the menu items provide meaningful, unambiguous information about the items? (2.2.3)

- If the labels are brief phrases, have they been written as verb phrases in parallel construction? (6.2.2)
- Do the labels use familiar and consistent terminology? (6.2.2)
- Are the labels distinct from one another? (6.2.2)
- Do important keywords stand out? (6.2.2)
- If graphic images are used to represent items, are they highly distinctive and recognizable? (6.2.3)
- If graphic images are used to represent items, is there a direct linking between the item and its representation? (6.2.3)
- Does the label assist in the association of functional requirement and the menu item? (7.2.1)

Selection Response Information and Location:

- Does the menu frame provide necessary information about how the selection is entered? (2.2.4, 6.3.1)
- When there is an insertion point on the screen for the selection response, is it located in a position expected/preferred by the users? (6.3.2)
- When items are selected from within a body of text, are the item and selection point embedded in the text rather than distal from the item? (6.3.2)

Information Format:

- Does the format of the menu convey the layout expected by the user? (2.2.5)
- Are the parts of the menu organized in a meaningful way? (2.2.5)
- Does the screen layout focus attention on the appropriate menu? (6.1.2)
- Does menu layout make effective use of perceptual grouping to organize items? (6.1.3)
- Is the format of information constant from menu to menu? (6.1.7)
- Does the layout of the menu promote learning of the location of an item within the frame? (7.2.1)

Selection Method:

- Is the mode of response to a menu consistent across menus? (2.3)
- Does it provide for verification prior to implementation? (2.3, 6.3.4)

- Is the mapping from menu item to selection response compatible? (2.3, 6.3.3)
- Does the spatial layout of items on the screen agree with the arrangement of keys on the keyboard? (6.3.3)
- If the response mode requires a standard keyboard, are users familiar with the layout of the keys? (2.3.1)
- If special function keys are used, are they meaningfully labeled? (2.3.2, 6.3.3)
- If special function keys are used, are they meaningfully arranged on the keypad? (2.3.2, 6.3.3, 11.33)
- If virtual keypads are used on the screen, do they obstruct work? (2.3.3)
- If virtual keypads are used on the screen, do they provide adequate feedback that an item is being pointed at? (2.3.3, 6.3.4)
- If response selection is accomplished by pointing, are selectable fields large and easy to hit? (10.1.2)
- If response selection is accomplished by pointing, are selectable fields arranged in such a way as to minimize selection errors? (10.3)
- Does the response mode minimize user selection time and frequency of selection errors? (4.1.3)
- Does the system provide sufficient feedback to help the user evaluate the success of a selection, or determine whether an error has been made? (4.1.4)
- Does the system promote learning of the association between the menu item and the response code? (7.2.1)
- Does the system promote learning of the motor selection response? (7.2.1)

Learning and Transfer:

- Does the system promote learning of the location of items in the menu structure? (7.2.1)
- Does system design capitalize on prior learning and experience of the intended users? (7.3)
- Does the system avoid lexical changes (relabeling) from prior learning and experience with prior versions of the system? (7.2.1)
- Is the system designed to facilitate transfer of learning from one area (e.g., application) to another? (7.2.1)
- Does the system provide training or assistance that allows the user to study the global organization or map of the menu structure? (7.4)
- Does the system provide training or assistance that makes effective use of appropriate metaphors? (7.4.3)
- Does the system avoid giving the user help information that appears excessive, superfluous, or distracting? (7.5)

Search Facilities:

- Does the menu system allow for a variety of user search styles? (4.2.2)
- If hierarchical menus are used, does the system provide options to redirect search to the beginning of the menu (top) and one level up (previous)? (9.2.1)
- If hierarchical menus are used, does the system provide cognitive landmarks that can be used in redirecting search? (9.2.3)
- Does the system provide a menu bypass facility to facilitate speed of performance? (10.2)
- If the system provides alternate command keys, have they been assigned to facilitate learning and not conflict with assignments by other software used? (10.2.1)
- If a system provides direct access to menu frames, does it use meaningful labels for the menu frames? (10.2.2)

Menu Item Organization:

- Does the layout of the menu facilitate visual scanning by the user? (4.1.1)
- Do the set size and composition of menu items facilitate the user choice process? (4.1.2)
- Do the number of items per frame and the number of levels optimize choice time? (4.1.3)
- Has random or arbitrary ordering of menu items been avoided? (6.1.5)
- Are lists of menu items presented in a logical order to facilitate search? (6.1.5)
- Are lists ordered in such a way as to reveal structure and relationships among items? (6.1.5)
- Do the order menu items agree with the user's expected ordering of items? (6.1.5)
- Does the layout of menu items adequately convey and take advantage of the semantic space of the items? (11.3)

Author Index

Subject Index